RED HARBOR

EMIL AND KATHLEEN SICK SERIES
IN WESTERN HISTORY AND BIOGRAPHY

RED HARBOR

RADICAL WORKERS AND COMMUNITY STRUGGLE IN THE PACIFIC NORTHWEST

AARON GOINGS

University of Washington Press *Seattle*
in Association with the Center for the Study of the Pacific Northwest

Red Harbor was made possible in part by a grant from the Emil and Kathleen Sick Fund of the University of Washington's Department of History.

Design by Mindy Basinger Hill / Composed in Minion Pro

29 28 27 26 25 5 4 3 2 1

Printed and bound in the United States of America

CENTER FOR THE STUDY OF THE PACIFIC NORTHWEST
sites.uw.edu/cspn/

UNIVERSITY OF WASHINGTON PRESS
uwapress.uw.edu

Cataloging information is available from the Library of Congress

LIBRARY OF CONGRESS CONTROL NUMBER 2024056905
ISBN 9780295754000 (hardcover)
ISBN 9780295754017 (ebook)

♾ This paper meets the requirements of ANSI/NISO Z39.48-1992 (Permanence of Paper).

TO MY PARENTS, CHRISTINE AND MICHAEL GOINGS

CONTENTS

ABBREVIATIONS

AFL	American Federation of Labor
CIO	Congress of Industrial Organizations
CP	Communist Party
FOW	Federation of Woodworkers
FSF	Finnish Socialist Federation
GHCC	Grays Harbor Commercial Company
GHCLC	Grays Harbor Central Labor Council
ILWU	International Longshoremen's and Warehouse Union
IUSWSWW	International Union of Shingle Weavers, Sawmill Workers and Woodsmen
IUT	International Union of Timberworkers
IUTW	International Union of Timber Workers
IWW	Industrial Workers of the World
ISWUA	International Shingle Weavers' Union of America
IWA	International Woodworkers of America
KKK	Ku Klux Klan
LSMWU	Loggers and Saw Mill Workers' Union
LWIU	Lumber Workers' Industrial Union
NLRA	National Labor Relations Act
NLRB	National Labor Relations Board
NLWU	National Lumber Workers' Union
SPA	Socialist Party of America
STWU	Sawmill and Timber Workers' Union
TUEL	Trade Union Educational League
TUUL	Trade Union Unity League
UBCJA	United Brotherhood of Carpenters and Joiners of America
WSFL	Washington State Federation of Labor

RED HARBOR

INTRODUCTION

In the spring of 2016 I made one of my regular trips to Grays Harbor. Driving into Aberdeen, Washington, along US Highway 12, I gazed north to the base of the bluff standing high above the Chehalis River where signs had long welcomed people to the region's largest city. As with countless other cities, markers greet visitors to Aberdeen, announce local events, and list the signs' sponsors, mostly fraternal clubs and businesses. For years the most provocative sign read "Come As You Are," the slogan drawn from one of the top songs of the 1990s and a major hit for Aberdeen's most famous native sons, the band Nirvana. For a region so marked by exclusion—deportation of labor radicals and ethnic minorities, the presence of vigilantes drawn from the Ku Klux Klan and businessmen's organizations, the promotion of renowned exclusionists like Congressman Albert Johnson, and violent treatment of unionists—the "Come As You Are" sign had always seemed a strange mix of ironic and inappropriate. Most likely it was chosen by those ignorant of the region's past, perhaps even picked by the newest members of the local chamber of commerce, successors of the organization at the center of violent exclusion a century earlier.

On this trip, however, something had changed. Just behind the Nirvana sign was one reading "Lumber Capital of the World." While the new sign's slogan lacked the celebrity appeal of the earlier one, it did have a realistic connection to the past. Aberdeen, or more precisely the Grays Harbor region, had for much of the early twentieth century stood as the leading lumber producer and largest lumber port in the world.[1]

For more than a century, the riverside lands adjacent to these signs had been occupied by large enterprises: lumber and shingle mills, docks, and canneries. Tens of thousands of men and women had worked in these operations, their labor providing the region with its most valuable resource and their lively working-class traditions making Grays Harbor a notable getaway for anyone looking to experience working-class culture at its rough, gritty best. In many ways, Grays Harbor was also the "Lumber [Workers'] Capital of the World," as thousands of militantly class-conscious laborers called the region home during the first four decades of the twentieth century. Although situated only a short distance apart, the signs spoke from two sides of a region's history. "The Lumber Capital" harkened back to the pre-1980s when wages were high, unemployment was often low, and much of the region's workforce belonged to labor unions. "Come As You Are" fit nicely to welcome folks to a region hard hit by waves of deindustrialization in the late twentieth century, as tourists drove through the once-thriving industrial center on their way to vacation amid the glorious evergreen trees or drizzly ever-gray beaches of the Olympic Peninsula.

Large numbers of lumber operations shut down during the late 1970s and '80s. Capital mobility, speedups, and stretch-outs enhanced by new technologies had cost thousands of workers their jobs in lumber—long the region's economic engine. The decline of logging, sawmills, and pulp and paper manufacturing was a traumatic blow to the region's working families as phrases like "the smell of paper mills is the smell of money" faded from memory. The grim reality of a century-long lumber and wood-products boom in its final death throes was apparent. "Official" unemployment lingered at about 15 percent in this once-great industrial area. Those who could find work labored in the area's low-paying service industries or at a "good" union job overseeing other working people in jails and prisons. Where mighty lumber and shingle mills had stood, there were now box stores, strip malls, empty lots, and mothballed factories.

The unions formed in the first four decades of the twentieth century, which had provided the region's workers with political education and modes of resistance, were beaten into submission or decline. Workers were less organized and unprepared to respond to neoliberalism of the 1970s and beyond, when mechanization, decreased natural resources, and bipartisan governmental hostility to unions ravaged organized labor and plunged the harbor into what, thus far, looks like a permanent depression.

Historians often mourn the lack of historical memory in the United States; more than one has suggested USA stands for "United States of Amnesia." But the process of recovering Grays Harbor's history, particularly that of its working class, is an especially tall task, so effectively has the region been marginalized, buried, and condescended to by those with power. The area's labor-history sites have been destroyed, mostly unmarked and unmourned. Even the massive Aberdeen armory building—home to the Aberdeen Historical Museum—burned to the ground in June 2018, taking with it priceless sources that included thousands of records from the formation of the International Woodworkers of America—and its Grays Harbor roots.[2] But the task of this book is not to wallow in the present, but to tell the history of a rich past when workers united to shape their workplace, neighborhoods, and wider communities.

The harbor's impressive working-class history deserves to be returned to the center of the region's memory. As such, the focus of this book is on the relationships of class as viewed not in the early twenty-first century but in the first four decades of the twentieth. It examines class, conflict, and class consciousness—and is in agreement with historian Bryan Palmer's statement "Class . . . is inseparable from class struggle," and thus I view class as an active social force, with workers and employers struggling in plain sight and behind closed doors to advance their interests.[3] Set in Grays Harbor, one of the great early twentieth-century lumber centers whose history is punctuated by labor conflicts, this book focuses specifically on the lives and struggles of workers and employers in the lumber industry, the largest and most important industry in the Pacific Northwest. On Grays Harbor, class consciousness was displayed in an array of social activities, as workers created insurgent, expansive institutions to express their interests, placed petitions before city councils, or scrawled cartoons mocking oafish bosses. It too was visible in workers' culture: hall celebrations, Labor Day and strike parades, socialist newspapers, and free-speech demonstrations. Moreover, I do not view class struggle as some exceptional occurrence, located only in the rare moments of mass insurgency. Instead, class is an everyday lived experience, embodied certainly in the strikes and demonstrations of radicals, but no less clearly in the daily struggles of workers, whether by expressing them eloquently in angry editorials written to labor newspapers or by simply quitting their job and "moving on."[4] Thousands of working-class militants and radicals understood full well that theirs was neither a cooperative nor an equal relationship with the boss, a fact underscored by articulate statements and direct actions alike. Though a life of brutal conditions, long hours of labor, bouts of poverty, and an early death were the fruits of capitalism for working people in the lumber empire, theirs was a world not just of despair, but also of possibilities.

During the late nineteenth and early twentieth centuries, two generations after settlers and state agents expropriated Indigenous lands to build a thriving industrial empire along Washington's Pacific Coast, a militant struggle between organized employers and workers visibly took center stage. Thus, in September 1919, employers and workers met in an explosive public conflict that illustrated the bitter divisions at the heart of lumber and labor. That month, members of the radical industrial union known as Industrial Workers of the World (IWW or Wobblies) held one of their regular meetings in Aberdeen's cavernous Finnish Socialist hall. For the previous two years, labor radicals across the Pacific Northwest had experienced crushing attacks by vigilantes, employers' groups, police, and even the US military. As in so many centers of radicalism, Grays Harbor's working class responded to that repression in part by organizing underground, preserving their movement for friendlier times. Recognizing that most authorities and vigilantes were ignorant of the Finnish language and reticent to upset the region's largest immigrant group on the harbor, the Wobblies cloaked their movement within that of the Socialist Red Finns, hosting cultural events alongside this group or using their hall.

At that September 1919 meeting, a group of "Holigans [*sic*]" and "gangsters," drawn mostly from the American Legion, planned to attend the meeting "to arise up en-masse and clean up with saps." Fortunately, the Aberdeen Wobblies avoided the fate that befell their fellow workers in Centralia two months later in the infamous Armistice Day Tragedy, largely because of the advanced warning given the workers and the show of strength they mobilized among the region's workers. After advertising the meeting "solely by word of mouth," Wobblies waited until "the gang" of Legion men arrived in the hall, "puffed out their chests and swaggered thru the door," before "a continual stream of loggers and Finnish Fellow Workers" joined them. The "husky, grim faced workers banked the gang on all sides," filling "the remaining seats and overflowed in the aisles, in the gallery and out on the street." Realizing a trap had been set, the thugs' "former boisterous manner, evolved into a respectful silence," a silence that remained until an IWW speaker heaped scorn upon the Legion men as "stool pigeons" and "lick-spittles." After some tense moments, the American Legion's leader left the hall. From the street, he let out a whistle, and answering his call, the Legionnaires "edged through the crowd of grinning workers, not unlike cowed dogs, with eyes on the floor and shamefaced."[5]

The Wobblies recorded this incident, but they left little evidence of precisely who attended the meeting. Still, it's likely that the crowd included Jennie Sipo, a Finnish-born worker and one of the most prominent radicals in Grays Harbor history. Sipo was nearly always present—and often up front—in those years of conflict between labor and capital. The IWW had more progressive ideas about gender inclusion than most of the era's unions. Still, within the movement, she performed tasks commonly coded as "women's work," including those often assigned to women's auxiliaries—serving food, making handicrafts, and fund-raising. Finnish IWW women formed sewing clubs to make goods to sell for Wobbly defense and literature fund-raisers.[6] Sipo took part in this type of female-coded activism, earning recognition for her fine crafting when she produced a pillow that local Wobblies auctioned off at a fund-raiser to assist their imprisoned fellow workers. But her work as a radical unionist provides useful reminders of the wisdom of Wobbly Elizabeth Gurley Flynn's words: "The IWW has been accused of putting the women in the front; the truth is: the IWW does not keep them at the back—and they go to the front."[7] In fact, Sipo, like many Finnish American women of her era, pushed her way to the radical movement's forefront, challenging stereotypes about "proper place" in the labor movement.

Arriving from Finland in the early 1910s as Jennie Heikkila, she moved to the great western mining labor capital of Butte, Montana, where she married John Sipo. John died of influenza in 1919, shortly after their (and their son Oras's) arrival on Grays Harbor. To make ends meet, Sipo worked as a waitress, a common job for Northwest women who worked in both restaurants and logging camps. As women entered these masculine workspaces, they became radical hotbeds as IWW women unionized and struck in the 1910s and 1920s. There she became organizer for the Foodstuffs Workers Industrial Union, Local 460, the second IWW local organized by Grays Harbor women.[8] Long active in raising money for political prisoners, after 1922 Sipo had firsthand understanding of the need for prison relief since authorities jailed her on criminal syndicalism charges. In a nod to Elizabeth Gurley Flynn, widely known as the "Rebel Girl," Sipo earned the title "a real rebel girl" for her activism on the IWW's jail committee and her refusal to accept the early release offered female prisoners.[9] A year later, in May 1923, she again strode to the front when she joined her soon-to-be husband, Wobbly longshoreman Robert Benson, in prominent spots at the front of a mass parade through downtown Aberdeen that culminated in a funeral for IWW member William McKay, who had been shot down earlier that week.[10] Thereafter, the Sipo-Benson family remained active in the Wobbly movement; Robert served as an important member of the Pacific Coast maritime union drive in the 1930s.

If the Finn hall scene—blue-collar workers in a physical standoff with vigilantes—resembles popular conceptions about the Wobblies, then Sipo and her family's involvement with the IWW might bring surprise. But in Grays Harbor, the Wobblies, one of the most radical organizations in US history, crafted a community-based form of unionism, one responsive to the needs of the local population that was supported by long-term Grays Harborites. This conception of the Wobblies contradicts most scholarship on the union in the West, which has portrayed IWWs as single young migratory men who traveled between towns stirring up discontent.[11] In Grays Harbor, a different IWW existed, drawing support from men, women, children, and families. With support from a cross section of the community, the IWW remained a significant part of the labor movement into the 1930s. These findings parallel historian Elizabeth Jameson's study of the Western Federation of Miners in Cripple Creek,

Colorado, in which she argues that settled workers had a greater stake in bringing about social change at the local level than did itinerant radicals, the group most commonly associated with radicalism in the American West.[12] However, *Red Harbor* extends Jameson's argument to the IWW, a revolutionary industrial union that has, at least in western contexts, been portrayed as unusual and unpopular—a small group favored by social outcasts who lacked connections to kin and community and who withered under repression of the postwar years. In fact, the Grays Harbor IWW was largely a family-based movement, and the Wobblies' families, like their communities, provided support for the movement.

GRAYS HARBOR, LAND, LUMBER, AND LABOR

Grays Harbor lies at the southwest corner of Washington's Olympic Peninsula. If the peninsula is the thumb on the mitten of Washington State, then Grays Harbor is the knuckle. It forms a relatively coherent geographic area, bordered to the north by the Olympic Mountains and Quinault Indian Reservation, west by the Pacific Ocean, south by the Willapa Hills and Willapa Harbor, and east by the Black Hills and Capital Forest. Viewed from the sky, the harbor towns of Aberdeen, Hoquiam, and Cosmopolis appear like urban islands set among an ocean of forests—in the center of one of the planet's greatest stretches of green.

Many of the leading figures in this book perceived these forests as inexhaustible. Rather, the lumbermen who owned those lands treated them as inexhaustible. An 1890 *Seattle Post-Intelligencer* writer expressed amazement by the area's timberlands—seeing in them an endless supply of commodities: "There are tributary to Grays Harbor 1,700,000 acres of land densely covered with forests of red and white fir, spruce and cedar, estimated to contain from 20,000 to 100,000 feet per acre, making a total of about 90,000,000,000 feet of lumber."[13]

In the lumber towns of Aberdeen, Hoquiam, and Cosmopolis, as well as the dense Olympic Peninsula forests that surrounded them, industry developed at a breakneck pace. Its trees, which had grown sky-high for centuries, were gobbled up by an industrial machine of axes and saws, human sweat and blood. Workers and mills transformed the forests into billions of board feet of lumber and billions of shingles, while the harbor's maritime workers transported more lumber than any other early twentieth-century port. Tens of thousands of men spent at least some time laboring in Grays Harbor's lumber industry during the first four decades of the twentieth century, performing the work necessary to cut the trees and manufacture the lumber and shingles—turning forests into vital cogs necessary to operate national and international commerce: wooden ships, rails, mining timbers, businesses, and homes. By 1905, Grays Harbor had established itself as the world's largest lumber port, a title it held for much of the first three decades of the twentieth century.

Throughout the early twentieth century, Aberdeen and Hoquiam ranked among Washington's largest cities, in 1920 home to populations of 15,337 and 10,058, respectively. In 1912, eighteen large sawmills lined the region's major rivers; thousands labored in the harbor's logging camps and lumber mills.[14] Maritime and rail workers connected the harbor's mills with markets by land and by sea. Ships carrying billions of board feet traversed the harbor transporting critical building materials to markets including Mexico, Hawaii, China, and beyond. In 1978, looking back at a century of industrial-scale lumbering on Grays Harbor, a US Forest Service report summarized the scope and scale of the harbor's industrial might: "In the first 50 years, Grays Harbor shipped over 30 billion board feet of lumber around the world." The report continued, "In the six years from 1924–29, annual lumber output by the Harbor's 12,000 lumberjacks was 1,352,000,000 board feet and in the twin peak years of 1925 and 26, some 1,600 ships hauled off the bulk of a cut totaling 3,120,958,591 board feet."[15]

Relationships of class—a world of work, drudgery, injuries, and an early death for one class, and profits and prestige for the other—helped inspire the area's workers to build militant labor institutions that could challenge elites, in hopes of reshaping workplace and social conditions. Indeed, thousands of working-class militants and radicals understood full well that theirs was neither a cooperative nor equal relationship with the bosses, a fact underscored by articulate statements and direct actions alike. Though a life of brutal working conditions, long hours of labor, bouts of poverty, and an early death were the fruits of capitalism, theirs was a world not just of despair, but also of possibilities.

Part of the wider Northwest "empire of timber," Grays Harbor was not some backwater merely following wider trends on Puget Sound and in Oregon's Willamette Valley. Instead, several of the Northwest's significant "lumber wars" began on the harbor; many of the activists and institutions dedicated to forming "one union in wood" had Grays Harbor roots.[16] This was especially true of the labor movement during the "Radical Thirties," which in part emerged out of Grays Harbor, where radicalism dropped some of its deepest anchors. During the Great Lumber Strike of 1935, Grays Harbor workers established the Northwest Joint Strike Committee, the militant arm of the lumber workers' movement that refused conciliation with the region's employers and wrested control of the strike from moderate leaders. That same year, harbor workers founded and published the *Timber Worker*, which grew into the official newspaper of the Federation of Woodworkers—the Pacific Coast's largest union—and later the International Woodworkers of America.

Red Harbor places the relationships between workers, employers, and their communities at its center. By focusing on four decades of working-class, social, and business history in Grays Harbor, this book advances four main lines of analysis. The first and most fundamental goal is to analyze forty years of working-class activism and class confrontations in Grays Harbor. To paraphrase the historian Robin D. G. Kelley, Grays Harbor was, like Birmingham, Alabama, in the South or Coeur d'Alene, Idaho, and Cripple Creek, Colorado, a "cauldron of class conflict" threatening to explode at any point during the first four decades of the twentieth century.[17] To get at the substance of these conflicts, this book explores the sharp divisions between workers and employers, the class-based organizing by each group, and the multitude of conflicts they waged. Workers organized to bring local changes such as increased wages or safer working conditions. Additionally, the community itself became contested terrain, as workers and employers both staked their claim to public and private spaces such as city streets, neighborhoods, buildings, and elected offices.

Class was not some alien concept thrust upon workers by Marxist ideologues or social scientists. Instead, in both everyday speech and official documents, Grays Harbor workers described social relations in terms of class, using terms like "worker" and "laborer" to self-describe and "boss" for employers.[18] Many Grays Harbor workers believed that employers acted in lockstep in pursuit of their class interests. It's in this spirit that this book's second objective is to analyze the organized activities of employers, antilabor state officials and journalists, and strikebreakers and spies. As was common across the United States, Grays Harbor employers relied extensively on vigilantism to fight labor and the left: beatings, kidnappings, expulsions, and murders—or at least the threat of murder. Supplementing their attacks, employers and friendly journalists used racist and nativist language against immigrants and workers of color, seeking to keep the working *class* divided into smaller *groups*. *Red Harbor* goes into depth to analyze the formation, actions of, and continuities between violent right-wing organizations: the citizens' committees that terrorized unionists and leftists during the early 1910s; the American Legion, a right-wing veterans' club; and the Ku Klux Klan, the largest and most notorious American vigilante movement. Acting upon their concepts of "community" and "citizenship," terms that excluded radicals and "new" immigrant strikers, employers and their allies used these clubs to provide extralegal regulation of local behavior.[19]

Antilabor vigilantism was one of many tactics that employers used to suppress workers' movements. This book challenges earlier scholarship that argues Pacific Northwest lumber manufacturers and boss loggers were guided by principles of individualism or preferred independent action over the class-based activism so common to employers in other industries. Rather than clinging to individualism, when it came to dealing with workers, unions, government, and the media, Grays Harbor lumbermen acted like elites in other regions and industries. For example, during his European tour to "collect evidence" as part of his racial classification system, the patrician author Kenneth L. Roberts described English workers as grotesque creatures: "runty, stunted, malformed, buck-toothed, obviously mal-nourished, diseased, and generally wretched specimens."[20] Indeed, the great historian Eric Hobsbawm was not exaggerating when he wrote that the world's middle and ruling classes viewed the emergence of an industrial working class with horror—seeing the proletariat as barbarians, fundamentally different from and inferior to the "better" classes.[21] Employers' views of themselves as superior to members of the working class were alive and well among Grays Harbor lumbermen such as George Emerson, who in 1894 responded to strike threats by promising to shut his mill down, thereby "letting the poor devils starve to a sense of their position."[22]

This book challenges the mythical conception of the individualistic lumberman by showing the process by which employers forged powerful class-based movements. Lumbermen were by far the Northwest's most powerful group. The early chapters of this book explore how employers organized to make best use of that power, and the ultimately failed efforts by trade unions to present a long-term challenge to capital—particularly the militant, unified employers' movement that emerged after 1905. As unionists learned in the face of growing employer power, any hope of challenging such a powerful class required significant organizing by workers. It's with that understanding that I pursue the book's third main objective: to analyze the leading part played by radicals in building the Northwest's labor movement.

Building common cause among the thousands of diverse lumber workers was a decades-long project—and the seeds of earlier struggles helped grow the ultimately successful industrial union movement of the thirties and beyond. At the core of these movements were radical workers, those who, in historian Rosemary Feurer's words, sought "to link union and community concerns to a far-reaching critique of corporate power and capitalism animating the organizing, collective bargaining, and broad based planning visions."[23] This was certainly the case in Grays Harbor and the wider Pacific Northwest, where lumber workers showed an enduring affinity for radical politics. When Northwest lumber workers unionized, radicals led the way into organizations with anticapitalist politics. Shop-floor militants joined left-wing immigrants, socialists, syndicalists, and communists to spread lumber unionism from a small group of unionists unrepresentative of the region's working class into a powerful engine for challenging a group known widely as "the lumber trust." Whether the socialist shingle weavers and timber workers, the revolutionary industrial unionists of the 1910s and 1920s, or the communist-influenced industrial unions of the 1930s, it was radicals who formed and organized the pre–World War II lumber unions. While it's clear that not all—or even most—loggers and mill workers held anticapitalist views, when they did strike and unionize, it was not the conservative trade unionists that they joined, but instead left-led industrial unions that fought for both daily life improvements and to challenge capitalism.

The two most successful radical union movements in Northwest lumber were the IWW and Communists. But their successes hinged not only on their radical politics or even the commitment of the radicals who led successive movements but instead on the links they forged between unions and the wider community. The fourth goal of this book, then, is to show how unionists connected their workplace-based movements to their communities.

The importance of community-based unionism in strengthening and sustaining the labor movement was clearest in the cases of the IWW and the Communist-influenced industrial union movement of the early and mid-1930s. Key to this lasting strength of the harbor's leftist movements was the large and remarkably organized Finnish population. Finns were the most numerous, militant, and radical section of the Grays Harbor working class; they shared the latter two characteristics with Finns across North America who organized, hosted, funded, and sustained radical movements for more than two decades. The "hosted" portion of their history is especially significant. *Red Harbor* thus highlights the significance of Finnish halls, the most important physical structures to local radicals—and home to many of the harbor's radical social and cultural activities from 1903 to at least 1940.[24] It was within Grays Harbor's Finn halls that radicals produced song, dance, poetry, journalism, literature, and unique forms of hall radicalism—among Grays Harbor's socialists, Wobblies, communists, and militant industrial unionists.

The IWW was founded in June 1905 by a diverse group of militant trade unionists, socialists, and anarchists as both an industrial union and a revolutionary organization. The IWW hoped to organize all workers, regardless of race, sex, or skill, into one big union. In the militant anticapitalist view of the Wobblies, employers and wage laborers had an inherently oppositional relationship, as laid out in the preamble to their constitution:

> The working class and the employing class have nothing in common. There can be no peace so long as hunger and want are found among millions of working people and the few, who make up the employing class, have all the good things of life. Between these two classes a struggle must go on until the workers of the world organize as a class, take possession of the earth and machinery of production, and abolish the wage system.[25]

The Wobblies were the embodiment of American syndicalism, fighting to overthrow both the capitalist system and the state, and refusing to follow a political party or a centralized union bureaucracy.[26] The Wobblies also practiced an inclusive style of unionism different from the narrow craft unionism of most contemporaries. The IWW's membership was as diverse as the North American working class itself: African American longshoremen in Philadelphia, Pennsylvania, and lumber workers in the Deep South; native-born white miners in the West; and immigrant workers in eastern urban areas. On the Pacific Coast, the Wobblies' calls for solidarity among all workers, regardless of race, flew in the face of decades of discrimination and violence against Asian Americans.[27] Whereas bosses paid Asians less than white counterparts, and trade unionists and many socialists condemned the employment of Asian laborers, the Wobblies saw eastern and southern Asian laborers as exploited workers—and thus potential additions to the labor movement.

The Northwest's largest group of Wobblies came from the region's Finnish communities. Historian Joseph Robert Conlin's assertion that there were "many IWWs" is a useful reminder that most Wobblies functioned at the local level—the town, mill, or camp where they lived and worked—and thus treating the IWW as a centralized institution is problematic.[28] Studies divorced from the local contexts where activists operated tell us little about the rank and file, especially about these radical workers' lives stretched out over several years.

The dismissal of the IWW's long-term significance and community rootedness is partly due to historians' reliance on English-language sources, as scholars have generalized about a movement with "the World" in its name by using only English sources.[29] In the words of the path-breaking *Wobblies of the World*, this narrow reliance on English-language sources has been a hallmark of IWW scholarship, which "neglect(s) the rich archive of non-English-language sources."[30] From the 1910s until the 1930s (and beyond), Northwest IWW writings appeared in Finnish, reflecting the fact that thousands of Wobblies spoke and wrote in Finnish and many of their activities occurred within Finn halls. The neglect of Finnish Wobblies stands as a major problem considering the large trove of Finnish-language sources on the IWW and that Finns represented the largest ethnic group within the Wobbly movement. Weaving in Finnish-language materials has allowed me to include the perspectives of radicals previously ignored in Pacific Northwest history and to tell a different narrative about lumber and labor.

Their deep roots were a major reason why the local IWW persevered for so long amid some of the most vicious repression in US history. However, in large part because of repression, the IWW ultimately failed to organize a permanent one big union in lumber.[31] Thus, much as this study begins years before the formation of the IWW, it also extends into the mid-1930s, culminating in the 1935 lumber strike. The final chapters deal with relations between the IWW, members of the communist movement, and the workers who waged the Great Strike of 1935—a vast and diverse workforce that ultimately founded the West's largest industrial union, the Federation of Woodworkers (FOW) and in 1937 the Congress of Labor Organizations' (CIO) base of Northwest operations, the International Woodworkers of America (IWA). The transition from revolutionary syndicalism to communism at the head of the left-wing workers' movement occurred later in Grays Harbor than in many other places, but the reasons for the shift were largely the same. Radical workers across the globe gained inspiration from the Russian Revolution. Many shared the experience of Big Bill Haywood who, according to fellow Wobbly Ralph Chaplin, stated, "The Russian revolution is the greatest event in our lives. . . . It represents all that we have been dreaming of and fighting for all our lives."[32]

Across the country and in Grays Harbor, Finnish radicals brought a large body of first- and second-generation immigrants into the Communist Party (CP). They joined itinerant Communist organizers in aiding Grays Harbor shingle and lumber strikers during the late 1920s and early 1930s, providing the type of material and tactical assistance that in years prior would have come from the Wobblies. By the early 1930s, Communists in several parts of the country gained credibility for fighting to organize the nation's most oppressed workers, including southern textile mill laborers and Appalachian mine workers.[33] Much like the IWW in previous decades, Communists showed creativity in their community organizing, leading anti-eviction campaigns and forcing politicians to provide relief to workers hard hit by the Great Depression. Like all previous labor activists, they ran up against employers, the state, and media, who saw every red flag as a Soviet threat. Collectively, Communist activism built a deep allegiance among some Grays Harbor workers to the international communist movement, and to the local CP organizers who dedicated their lives to improving the lives of local workers.

As the final chapters show, the movement was the product of both outsider CP officials and the actions of Grays Harbor residents who, responding to their daily, lived experiences in a capitalist society, participated in Communist organizations with practically no outside assistance. The CP's history on Grays Harbor largely supports the conclusions made by radical social historians, who argued that Party activists based their program around local conditions directed toward improving the material existences of working people, rather than being a vanguard for the Soviets. By the early 1930s the harbor had become a focus for members of the CP, in part because of the area's traditions of militancy and radicalism. Party sources reveal CP branches in Aberdeen, Hoquiam, and Montesano and Communist auxiliaries based in the shop floor and community, as the division between workplace and community became increasingly clouded. Like the Wobblies before them, Communists led strikes in the isolated logging camps, in urban lumber mills, and at the shingle mills scattered across the coast.

This book reaches the shelves in the 2020s, an era featuring an increasingly prominent and militant labor movement, and growing public acceptance that class and class conflict are central features of the American experience. This transformation has been led by workers themselves who have unionized and struck in industries and regions once thought to be impenetrable by the labor movement, and workers across industries demanding respect, reasonable hours, living wages, and a say in the workplace. Employers have not sat idly by to see workers gain power or inject democracy to their workplaces. Instead, from manufacturing firms with a union past like Boeing to companies like Walmart, Amazon, and Starbucks that have always crushed unions in their nascent stages, we see a militant employers' movement with allies among lawmakers, courts, and police. Much like lumber workers discovered a century ago, corporate giants of today will do most everything in their power to keep workers divided, unorganized, and powerless. Notable journalists and public intellectuals have thrust discussions of class into the popular consciousness, while even corporate media like the *New York Times* and the *Washington Post*, the latter owned by one of the era's most notorious union-busters, Amazon's founder, have begun covering some issues with an eye toward fairly representing workers and unions. *Red Harbor* thus hits at an appropriate moment as the workers themselves are recognizing common interests, forming new organizations and new media that represent their interests, and initiating militant, creative union campaigns. In this book, I endeavor to create a faithful representation of radical workers and class conflict in the lumber empire; like that past, this book centers working people and their efforts to create a more just society.

1

LUMBER EMPIRE

MAKING INDUSTRIAL GRAYS HARBOR

Shortly after the turn of the twentieth century, J. G. Brown made the first of his many trips into Grays Harbor. Hired on in Cosmopolis, Brown worked three months at the Grays Harbor Commercial Company, a sprawling operation employing hundreds of workers in its mills and camps. Brown's route was one of the most common ways into Grays Harbor, taken by thousands of men each year. Hired at employment agencies in Portland, Oregon, or one of the Puget Sound metropoles, workers bought jobs and traveled by rail to the harbor. In Cosmopolis, virtually no workers found prosperity and few found conditions tolerable. Like countless others, Brown's stay at the Commercial Company was short. But the company made quite an impression. He labored there for three months, experiences that led him to ask rhetorically, "Is this hell? No, it is worse."[1] We know of Brown's experiences because once he left the Commercial Company's employ, he moved to Hoquiam, where he climbed the Pacific Northwest's labor bureaucracy and wrote for labor and left publications. In 1903, he ran unsuccessfully as a socialist for the mayor of Hoquiam.[2] A few years later, Brown had risen to a peak of the American labor-left. In 1907, he became president of the International Shingle Weavers' Union of America, the lone American Federation of Labor (AFL) union based in Washington State. He later headed the thousands-strong International Union of Timber Workers. He led that union in 1914 when he testified about life, labor, and union-busting in the lumber industry before the US Commission on Industrial Relations.[3]

Not long after leaving Cosmopolis, Brown went to work at the Hoquiam Lumber and Shingle Company, one of the world's largest shingle manufacturers. The company's owners, Joseph and Robert Lytle, came to the harbor, like Brown, because of the booming industry. Unlike Brown, the Lytles boasted considerable capital from earlier enterprises that enabled them to purchase industrial equipment and swaths of forestlands in Grays Harbor and to hire workers to construct their operation on the Hoquiam River. Built in 1902, the Hoquiam Lumber and Shingle Company was among the most prolific shingle-producing mills in the world, declared by Brown to be "probably the greatest shingle producing plant in the state."[4] By 1905 the mill was one of the world's leading shingle producers. Two years later, the mill employed 325 men, turned out 200,000 board feet of lumber on the ten-hour day shift and 125,000 on the night shift. Workers at the shingle mill cut 650,000 shingles per day.[5]

Brown and the Lytles came to the harbor to make money in the area's lumber industry—and their positions as militant socialist worker and equally militant anti-union bosses placed them on opposing sides of a decades-long labor conflict in the Pacific Northwest's largest and most profitable industry. By the start of the new century, the lumber boom had transformed Grays Harbor into a center of the lumber empire. Arriving in the first years of the twentieth century, Brown came to an area experiencing rapid industrial and population growth. Had he arrived a generation earlier, the sights and sounds would have seemed little familiar: the deforested hillsides would have been covered in Douglas fir, western red cedar, and Sitka spruce; the screeching saws he encountered would not have yet started spinning; and the raucous scenes of a Wild West port town would have been mostly silent. Brown's and the Lytles' personal experiences, and the men's relationship with one another, provide a useful window into life, labor, and class conflicts in the heart of what historian Erik Loomis calls the "empire of timber."[6] In the early twentieth century, lumber ranked as one of the largest sources of industrial employment in the United States, with between 500,000 and 600,000 working in the lumber industry and more than 750,000 laboring in the broader wood-products industries. During the period, more than 100,000 men worked in Pacific Northwest logging camps and sawmills.[7] Lumber was one of the key ingredients in the making of industrial America; as the twentieth century dawned, Grays Harbor was one of the industry's kings.

The area that became Grays Harbor has been occupied since time immemorial by Indigenous Americans. Drawn from diverse groups, principally the Quinault, Humptulips, Wynoochee, and Upper and Lower Chehalis peoples, the region's original inhabitants tended the forests and used wood for housing, transportation, art, and more. A full account of the original inhabitants of this area is beyond the scope of this book, but a brief look at the region's Indigenous history and ongoing practices of settler-colonialism provide vital context for the harbor's twentieth-century history. For centuries before Robert Gray "discovered" in 1792 the harbor that bears his name today, people lived with their backs to the peninsula's dense rain forests, looking to the bountiful sea and rivers for food. The forests, commodified and industrialized by Euro Americans, had for centuries been nurtured and crafted into tools and art by Native Northwesterners. For example, Quinault peoples cut down trees—carefully selecting individual cedars—and crafted the fallen trees into canoes, paddles, plank houses, and a variety of tools and other goods.[8]

Euro-American settlers, who began arriving on the harbor at midcentury, marveled at the vast forests of the Olympic Peninsula and wider Northwest Coast. European and American colonizers saw the trees as potential sources of wealth, commodities to be exploited. James Swan, a prominent chronicler of the nineteenth-century Northwest Coast, used the word "inexhaustible" for the expansive forests that fueled Washington's industry: "The staple of the land must continue to be the one which Nature herself has planted, in the inexhaustible forests of fir, of spruce, and of cedar."[9] Few nineteenth-century settlers expressed the importance of resource extraction and commodification of the Northwest environment as clearly as railroad magnate James J. Hill, who observed that the Northwest "has within itself an abundance of wealth, in the water, in the fields, in the mines, and her forests." The railroad tycoon concluded, "Permanent and great prosperity will come through the development of these resources."[10]

Euro-Americans removed most Indigenous people from the areas prized by the interlopers. Disease caused much of the devastation to coastal Native peoples during the eighteenth and nineteenth centuries. What disease could not accomplish came through direct violence: warfare, murders, kidnappings and expulsions, and treaties signed and enforced by the federal government. In 1855, after months of intimidation and prodding led by Washington Territorial governor and Indian agent Isaac Stevens, several coastal tribes signed treaties, including the Quinault Treaty that created the Quinault Indian Reservation located in northwest Grays Harbor. To further the region's settlement, the federal government joined private boosters in offering "inducements for immigration." These early American settlers capitalized on the Oregon Donation Land Act, which allowed white men and married women to claim 320 acres of free land beginning in 1850—notably, years before the United States had reached treaties with Washington's many tribes. Only a few Donation settlers acquired land on Grays Harbor, but the act spurred the way to future legislation—notably the 1862 Homestead Act that opened the floodgates to settlement. Regional newspapers encouraged settlers to move to the far Northwest. One such 1863 article, "Inducements for Immigration," in the *Washington Standard* of Olympia told of practically empty lands fit for the taking: "The whole Chehalis valley is almost entirely unoccupied, and offers greater inducements for settlement than any part of the Pacific coast."[11]

Violence or the threat of violence accompanied all early Euro-American efforts to claim and settle Indigenous lands on the Olympic Peninsula. The first recorded contact between Europeans and the Quinault peoples concluded in the mid-1770s when an armed crew of Spanish sailors laid claim to Quinault lands and murdered six or seven of the area's Native inhabitants.[12] Quinault historians suggest that early white settlers mostly behaved honorably and "accepted the Indians' presence without question," in contrast to the avaricious lumbermen and land speculators who arranged to exploit the Quinault's timberlands.[13] But Indigenous inhabitants of the harbor certainly knew of the "frontier justice" meted out by the territorial government and vigilantes during the early territorial period. Settlers pledged violence if they felt threatened—promises reinforced by armed settlements and a military garrison. White settlers were well armed, both for hunting and for intimidating the region's Indigenous inhabitants. In 1865, Grays Harbor settler John Dickson stabbed to death Tenamas, a local chief, during a dispute in Dickson's home.[14]

To bolster the settlers' presence and apparently in response to settlers feeling "apprehension of attack from the neighboring Indians," the US Army established a military garrison called Fort Chehalis.[15] Built in late 1859 and occupied in January 1860, the garrison housed more than sixty troops.[16] Headed by Captain Maurice Maloney, an Irish immigrant whose earlier military career saw him fight in wars against Native Americans in the American South and Northwest, the garrison provided an armed presence to warn against potential rebellions.[17] Violence accompanied every step of settlement as new American arrivals understood that the lands and resources were "theirs," and they had the military and US courts to protect them. According to early Hoquiam settler James A. Karr, when a local settler "courageous as he was outspoken" felt vulnerable, he responded by threatening mass murder: 'If you Indians don't quit your d——n foolishness, there is five hundred soldiers at Olympia just waiting to come down here and kill every d——n one of you.'"[18] Only a handful of territorial Grays Harbor disputes ended in death, but the threat lay just below the surface as white settlers looked to clear out the Indigenous population for industrial and agricultural development.

Indigenous people have never disappeared from the harbor or the surrounding Pacific Northwest and, through resistance and accommodation, set some of the boundaries for the development of the timber economy. Moreover, Native shaping of the region did not end in some undefined past. Quinault, Chehalis, and other local Natives did much of the early work to establish the Northwest's lumber industry—as loggers, longshoremen, and sawmill laborers.[19] At Port Gamble's Puget Mill Company, the territory's most productive early mill, the area's original inhabitants (S'Klallam) performed much of the work. Mill manager Josiah Keller made clear the company's reliance on Indigenous workers in 1855 when he commented, "We now just about make the mill go with what native help we get."[20]

Farther to the southwest, during the late nineteenth and early twentieth centuries, Native peoples helped establish the Grays Harbor lumber industry. Native workers labored in logging camps, sawmills, and shingle mills and along the shore, moving wood products to market. Discussing the early industrialization of Grays Harbor, historian Alexandra Harmon notes that "Indians were among the men who felled trees for the mills."[21] An official history of the Schafer Brothers Logging Company partly credited Indigenous men such as Billy Quiack, Amos Commenout, and Hyasman for initiating the company's lumbering efforts in the 1890s.[22]

Grays Harbor was one of the last areas of the Pacific Coast's forested lands to experience industrialization. Until the start of the twentieth century, the harbor lagged well behind the Puget Sound region in population and industrial production. In 1860, fewer than 300 settlers lived in Chehalis (now Grays Harbor) County.[23] Thirty years later, while Seattle, Portland, and Tacoma had blossomed into important western cities, Grays Harbor's towns remained little more than villages. Only 9,000 people resided in the county in 1893.[24]

By the time of the Civil War, lumber had emerged as the Pacific Northwest's dominant industry. During the 1850s and 1860s, the territory's lumbermen, usually backed by California capital, built mills along the shores of Puget Sound. But the territory's industrialization and settlement proceeded slowly.[25] In 1869, there were forty-six sawmills in the territory; most of the region's mills lay in the Puget Sound region. Lumbermen established notable mills, including those at Port Gamble and Port Ludlow—both owned by California capitalists. As historian Kornel Chang observes, Washington was little more than an outpost at the far stretches of the American empire: "The region's identity became associated with that of a colonial hinterland, a place known to extract and furnish raw materials for more advanced economies on the East Coast and across the Pacific, an empire of extraction."[26]

White settlers arrived by water and overland into other (future) prominent Washington cities, including Tacoma, Seattle, and Olympia, before 1880. Often through the labors of Indigenous residents—and always on Indigenous lands—settlers built towns and operated logging camps, sawmills, shingle mills, canneries, and smaller industries. By 1880, Seattle's population already topped 3,500. Still, the lumber boom lay in the future as population and production came after the 1883 completion of the Northern Pacific Railway, which linked Puget Sound to the Midwest and beyond. In the two decades after 1889, the state's lumber output nearly quadrupled, reaching almost four billion board feet in 1909. In the spring months of 1900, nearly six thousand loggers worked in Washington's timber camps.[27]

On the harbor, white settlement and industrial growth lagged behind Puget Sound, only slowly transforming the more western stretches of coastal Washington into cities—or even towns. Those who made the trek into the West's rainiest lands couldn't help but notice the region's extensive resources. The harbor boasted navigable rivers useful for transporting timber between camp and mill. As early as 1882, one commentator remarked, "All along the Chehalis River and the various streams tributary to it grow the most magnificent forests of fir and cedar."[28] The late arrival of the transcontinental railroad slowed all of Washington's industrial growth, but given Grays Harbor's location—on the coast rather than on Puget Sound—it faced further obstacles. Its cities did not connect to the major Northwest rail lines until the 1890s. Moreover, Puget Sound lumbermen cooperated to slow industrial development on Grays Harbor—fearing the competition from mills and docks closer to markets in California and beyond.[29]

Industrial enterprises arrived slowly on Washington's coast. In 1880, a small mill began cutting in Cosmopolis, but early mills "were only preliminaries to the initiation of full-scale lumbering."[30] In 1894, five years after Washington achieved statehood and as the Puget Sound mills churned out lumber, *The Oregonian's Handbook of the Pacific Northwest* took note of the ongoing importance of agriculture to Grays Harbor's future: "The country back of the harbor is not only rich in the resources of available timber alone, but it also contains thousands of acres of the finest agricultural land in the Northwest, which, when fully settled, will support a large and prosperous population."[31] The days of booming lumber lay in the future.

THE INDUSTRIAL HARBOR TOWNS

Large-scale industrialization and urbanization came late to Grays Harbor. Often hailed as the "father of Aberdeen," Samuel Benn provided much of the early leadership in transforming this forested land into an industrial behemoth. In 1865, he traded his farmlands in eastern Chehalis County to his father-in-law for six hundred acres of land along the Wishkah and Chehalis Rivers—the area that became Aberdeen. Benn and other settlers saw the region as ripe for profit and he actively promoted the region's potential. In his memoir, Samuel Benn recalled that he "lived upon my ranch at Melburn [*sic*] for nine years and having become acquainted with the country and believing that some day there would be a great city on Grays Harbor and conceiving the idea that the place for that city was where the Wishkah river empties into the Chehalis, I located where the city of Aberdeen now lies."[32] Benn deserves credit for his foresight and promotion skills. In the words of longtime Grays Harbor journalist Ed Van Syckle, in the 1880s the future mill town had "hardly forty buildings in sight, including makeshift barns, chicken coops, privies, woodsheds, and Sam Benn's salt house; no streets, no sidewalks, and over all a pervading odor of tidal mud and slash fires."[33]

In the 1880s, Benn's promotion helped convince lumbermen to move their Midwest operations to the Pacific Coast. Lumberman A. J. West was the first to be enticed by the promise of purchasing an Aberdeen sawmill site. In 1884, West's family moved to Grays Harbor; he located his mill on the Wishkah River where it meets the Chehalis.[34] By 1890, workers at West's operation produced thirteen million board feet annually.[35] In 1885, Michigan lumberman John M. Weatherwax joined West in establishing Aberdeen as a lumber manufacturing hub. Rather than rely on materials being available in the isolated outpost on Washington's coast, the family and laborers transported machinery by rail and ship to Grays Harbor before assembling the operation and cutting lumber for Pacific shipments. In 1886, a year after Weatherwax's arrival on the harbor, locals shipped the first load of lumber from its docks.[36]

From its inception, Aberdeen's lumbermen played a major role in running the city.[37] These men formed the Aberdeen Board of Trade in 1889, which in the words of one writer "advertised their great pride in the growing metropolis."[38] The board publicized opportunities for settlers and investment, adopting slogans such as "the Duluth of Washington" and "the San Francisco of the Northwest" to lure prospects into the damp, gray, forested lands.[39] The city's industrial growth was dramatic. From 1889 when Aberdeen had four sawmills, the city's industry expanded to

The North Western Lumber Company sawmill seen from Beacon Hill in Hoquiam. Polson Museum, Hoquiam, Washington.

more than a dozen large lumber operations by 1906. The 175 laborers employed at Weatherwax's Aberdeen Lumber and Shingle Company produced 125,000 board feet of lumber and 300,000 shingles per ten-hour shift.[40]

Hoquiam's path toward industrial prominence paralleled Aberdeen's, its "twin city." In 1880, George H. Emerson, an agent for lumberman A. M. Simpson of San Francisco, traveled to Grays Harbor where he purchased three hundred acres in what is today Hoquiam. By 1882, his company completed construction of the North Western Lumber Company mill, Hoquiam's first large sawmill. By 1897 it turned out about 100,000 board feet per day; after years of operating under Simpson's control, the company was purchased by Emerson in 1901.[41]

On June 4, 1889, prominent Hoquiam residents established Hoquiam's first government. Early boosters united to form the city government, to publicize its potential to attract workers for the mills and woods, and to convince officials of the Northern Pacific Railway to extend their lines into Hoquiam. Along with Otis Moore, editor of the *Washingtonian*, these Hoquiam "city fathers" conducted several trips to metropolitan areas in hopes of inducing the type of land speculation and rising land prices that would result from news of the imminent arrival of a rail line into Hoquiam.[42] Their efforts yielded great results. In 1889 alone, the population of Hoquiam rose from 400 to 1,500.[43] In 1890, building in the city tripled and property values advanced by more than 1,000 percent. That same year, on May 21, 1890, Hoquiam officials incorporated the city. In 1927, an official with the Hoquiam Chamber of Commerce summarized the relationship between capital and the establishment of Hoquiam as a city, writing, "The development of Hoquiam has been possible thru [*sic*] the energy and foresight of its industrial leaders. The site of the city was chosen for its locations as a point of least resistance in the receiving of logs and the shipping of lumber. The industries flourished and the town had to grow."[44]

Pacific Northwest industrialists shipped lumber east via rail and both west and south using a fleet of sail and steam vessels. Thousands of seamen worked aboard schooners that carried Northwest lumber. The lumber trade occupied most of the Northwest's maritime shipping in the late nineteenth and early twentieth centuries.[45] Sailors, mostly northern European immigrants, carried lumber to US and international ports, where dock workers unloaded it. Historian Bruce Nelson explained the place of the Northwest's lumber schooners, writing that "more than half of the Pacific Coast seamen were employed in the steam schooner trade whose source was the lumber trade of northern California, Oregon, and Washington."[46] These men traveled the world over by ship, visiting port cities in far-flung parts of the globe, connecting with workers along the way. By the first decade of the twentieth century, more than one hundred sailors, longshoremen, and other maritime workers called Grays Harbor home—dozens of migratory seamen stayed in the cities' boardinghouses and riverside shacks and aboard ships as they awaited the next job. William Gohl, a longtime migratory sailor and union leader, described life aboard ship: "Forty per cent of all vessels have no messrooms and the crews are compelled to eat their meals on the deckload. The forecastles, where the sailors live, are generally three-corners holes and all hands can not always get out of their bunks and dress at the same time."[47] Major waterborne shipments began in 1882 when the North Western Lumber Company in Hoquiam shipped out 700,000 board feet of lumber. From 1882 to 1895, the harbor's ten mills shipped more than 673 million board feet. This astounding feat, achieved over a decade and a half, would pale in comparison to future shipments as the harbor's workers produced billions of board feet in the decades to come.[48]

Workers transported most of the harbor's lumber output by water, but lumbermen knew they needed rail to fully develop the harbor and exploit its resources. In the 1880s and 1890s, cities in Washington fought bitterly for the extension of rail lines into their settlements. The railroad promised both a quick way to transport workers and supplies into the growing settlements and a way to connect the rich Grays Harbor forest products with the markets to the east.[49] In 1892, Northern Pacific rail workers connected Grays Harbor to Puget Sound when the 100-mile railroad reached Ocosta, its ocean terminus. The line led to a brief boom for the ocean city, as hundreds settled at the seaside town. By 1894, though, Ocosta was an afterthought as landowners and industrialists turned their attention to the Chehalis, Wishkah, and Hoquiam Rivers—the harbor towns.[50] Still, Aberdeen and Hoquiam failed to convince officials from Northern Pacific to extend the line into Aberdeen. In 1894, after refusing the Northern Pacific's exorbitant price of $35,000 to extend the line into their city, some "public spirited" Aberdeen residents pledged to do the work themselves—or, rather, to use their wealth to pay workers to do the work. Three wealthy Aberdonians, including lumberman John M. Weatherwax, purchased five thousand pieces of salvaged rail. Joining Weatherwax were lumber mill owners A. J. West and Henry Wilson, who donated railroad ties to the project, while town founder and major landowner Samuel Benn offered land parcels to potential laborers in exchange for ten days' work or a twenty-dollar donation to the project.[51] On June 1, 1895, having completed the rail connection, Aberdonians turned the track over to the Northern Pacific.[52] The great promise represented by a rail line to the east, a seaport to the west, and located "in the middle of the greatest forest of big timber on the face of the earth" brought new and hitherto undreamed-of development to Aberdeen.[53]

Lumberman George Emerson showed the importance of rail to his operation in his 1902 manager's report for Hoquiam's North Western Lumber Company: "Of this Twenty-three million feet has gone East by Rail; Four and one-half million Coastwise by vessel; One and one-half million local; Four and one-half million into boxes; Balance is still on hand. The rail demand has been good and prices better than ever before."[54]

The press boosted Grays Harbor—much as it did areas across the West. Long before the area reached prominence after 1900, newspapers promoted the harbor as "the Richest in the Great Northwest," boasting "Unlimited Resources." According to an 1884 article in the *Grays Harbor News*, the area was "a grand country—beautiful in its scenery, delicious in its climate, immense in its productiveness, and a good country to make money in."[55]

But the overwhelming impression one gets from studying the era's reporting is that Grays Harbor's "best men" were in charge and that they were guiding the area's economy and politics in a righteous direction. Built upon dominant American themes of capitalism, whiteness, respectable masculinity, and unfettered growth, the local newspapers helped to lay ideological foundations of the area. They cast managerial elites as benevolent fathers who acted in the best interest of the community, overseeing its development for the common good. The *Aberdeen Daily Bulletin* praised lumberman A. J. West for "his usual public-spiritedness" in offering "at least $1,000 worth of the bonds" to help construct a county road from the harbor towns to Montesano, then the county seat.[56]

The men who edited and published local newspapers had deep ties to lumbermen and the business class in general. In nearly every instance, editors joined and served important roles in business organizations. They founded and served as officers in chambers of commerce, commercial clubs, and development associations. They rubbed elbows with shippers, boss loggers, and manufacturers, collectively promoting dominant political, economic, and social agendas. Although the bigger newspapers sometimes differed over which major party to support, they agreed on the fundamentals: Grays Harbor's prosperity rested on unimpeded industrial growth overseen by lumbermen and their allies—elite white men drawn from the business and professional class. As the pages ahead show, these newsmen also published racist and nativist propaganda, nurturing and providing a quasi-intellectual basis for white supremacy. Some elite media figures also incited violence against workers of color and immigrants and even joined in extralegal attacks on immigrant laborers and radical unionists.

Three miles southeast of Aberdeen lay the small company town of Cosmopolis. Hardly the impressive city its name suggests, the little town of six hundred residents in 1908 was controlled by the managers of the Grays Harbor Commercial Company (GHCC).[57] (The large mill had been owned by Perry Lumber and Mill Company of Los Angeles until 1888, when it was sold to the Pope and Talbot Company, which renamed the mill the Grays Harbor Commercial Company.)[58] Like many American company towns, Cosmopolis was ruled through a mixture of paternalism and coercion. The company provided modern housing, schools, restaurants, general stores, and even a newspaper. Workers who lived in company housing paid four dollars per month for a private room, or two dollars and fifty cents for a place in the bunkhouse, and food at the mess house.[59]

Making famous the activities of the GHCC was the *Grays Harbor Post*, a labor newspaper that relentlessly condemned its management for running a company town and exploiting labor with long hours and low pay.[60] The GHCC dominated Cosmopolis, determining, in the words of one critic, "everything from its school affairs to the extortionate water system. The manager of the company controls the vote of the town."[61] A *Grays Harbor Post* editorial chimed, "Mr. C. F. White is the mayor, the council, the marshal, the school board, and the teachers."[62] Most of the attacks on the GHCC concerned its use of child labor, importation of "the shiftless and the criminal of the larger cities of the state," and opposition to the various wrongs collectively known as the "Cosmopolis Way" within their company's fiefdom.[63]

Criticism toward the GHCC came from harbor businessmen and journalists, unionists, and state and local authorities; labor activists even labeled it a "scab-hatchery."[64] Its myriad abuses ranged from its manner of securing labor to its poor record of workplace safety, its feudal control over everything within the town, and its managers' approaches to labor relations. Underlying the company's rule were the allegiances to open-shop principles held by manager C. F. White and his protégé Neil Cooney. When asked during his testimony before the 1914 US Commission on Industrial Relations what his attitude toward organized labor was, manager Cooney boasted, "We don't think it is practical, and we don't believe we can operate our plant with organized labor, and therefore we have made up our minds not to have organized labor."[65]

Whether in a company town like Cosmopolis or lumber towns like Aberdeen and Hoquiam, workers in Grays Harbor entered a corporate environment where they labored for wages on property owned by industrial capitalists. Although the three cities were home to industries other than wood products—fishing, canning, brewing, and shipbuilding—the harbor towns grew and survived as single-industry municipalities.[66]

Most Grays Harbor lumber operations were medium-sized businesses with between 100 and 300 employees. In Aberdeen, among the largest mills in the region were the Aberdeen Lumber and Shingle Company, and mills owned by S. E. Slade, Henry Wilson, and A. J. West. Across town in Hoquiam, George Emerson's North Western Lumber Company, the Lytles' Hoquiam Lumber and Shingle Company, and the Polson Logging Company each employed more than 150 laborers, while in 1914 the Grays Harbor Commercial Company in Cosmopolis employed approximately 600 workers at its saw and shingle mills. Both Aberdeen and Hoquiam boasted a number of smaller lumber and shingle mills, ranging in size from a handful of employees up to several dozen.[67]

Corporate mill and timberland ownership consisted of two major types: local and absentee ownership. Like much of the industrial West—including lumber operations throughout Washington—outside investors owned many Grays Harbor mills and timberlands. Residing in San Francisco, the Midwest, or the Atlantic Seaboard, absentee owners rarely visited their property. Although locals owned most mills, including the A. J. West, J. M. Weatherwax, and Henry Wilson operations, many of the bigger plants were part of larger corporate holdings. Newspapers ran articles noting investments in harbor lands by easterners, including "by a syndicate of Boston capitalists."[68] Californians owned and co-owned some of the largest mills in Aberdeen and Hoquiam, while the Pope and Talbot Company controlled the GHCC in Cosmopolis. Notorious local union-busters managed several of these operations.[69]

Lumber companies practiced vertical integration. Their holdings included logging camps, mills, docks, lumberyards, and ships. In 1900, Frederick Weyerhaeuser purchased 900,000 acres from the Northern Pacific at six dollars per acre. By 1903, Weyerhaeuser owned over 1.5 million acres of land in Washington. Through the twentieth century, the name Weyerhaeuser became synonymous with lumber. Loggers cut Weyerhaeuser timber, its railroads moved the trees to the company's mills, where Weyerhaeuser laborers turned trees into boards. The company owned 195,000 acres in Chehalis County (which became Grays Harbor County in 1915) by the first years of the twentieth century.[70] Like Weyerhaeuser, local corporations owned swaths of Washington timberland. Local owners operated several substantial lumber mills and logging camps. These families—the Polsons, Emersons, Weatherwaxes, Wilsons, Wests, and Lytles—formed interlocking directorates, jointly owning and operating dozens of local firms in logging, lumber, banking, grocery, and more. In 1908, the *Aberdeen Herald* ran several ads promoting the Union Bank and Trust Company being "backed by Sixty-two Leading Citizens of Aberdeen worth collectively over one million dollars," followed by a list of employers heading the firm.[71] Like many lumber companies, both the Slade Lumber Company and Wilson Brothers Lumber Company transported lumber on their own ships. By 1906, the Wilson company owned six ships, including the *Svea*, a three masted steam schooner capable of transporting 700,000 feet of lumber and worked by a crew of eighteen men.[72] The Grays Harbor Commercial Company transported most of its products by rail, selling lumber and shingles principally in the Midwest.[73]

Controlling these firms' day-to-day operations fell to locally based managers such as George Emerson of the North Western Lumber Company in Hoquiam and W. B. Mack, superintendent of the Slade Lumber Company, who oversaw the company's assets on the harbor and reported to S. E. Slade at company headquarters in San Francisco. Coming of age between the Civil War and World War I, these businessmen experienced what historians have called a "crisis of masculinity." Before taking their positions as managers and directors, some flocked to college where they might prove themselves on the football field—or, if they were truly lucky, as some of the student strikebreakers, since, in historian Stephen Norwood's words, "College students represented a major, and often critically important, source of strikebreakers in a wide range of industries and services."[74] Stanford University and the University of Washington proved popular destinations for children of the Northwest's elite. Once back on Grays Harbor, these young men had plenty of opportunity to prove themselves—including in physical fights against members of a class to whom the ivory tower's doors were closed.

Surrounded by hundreds of men who daily risked their lives amid fast-moving saws, axes, ships, and massive trees, lumbermen couldn't help but feel threatened at their absence of physical work—tasks oft-associated with manliness. Mill managers' jobs entailed varied tasks, including walking the grounds and hiring and firing workers. Much of their work took place in an office, at a desk, alongside secretaries. They spent their days producing reports, speaking with reporters and politicians, and placing orders. Managers sometimes failed to hide their disdain for "inferiors" in the working class. Emerson's privilege and perceived invincibility against society's "lessers" in the working class came through as the manager voiced his antipathy toward workers. As one of the "founding fathers" of Hoquiam—the first manager of a large lumber mill in the city—Emerson had years to hone his views of workers and unions. When workers weren't sufficiently deferential to the boss, Emerson advocated dealing with them "with a taut rein and whip in hand."[75] Elsewhere, he compared unionists to insects, arguing that it was necessary to "destroy . . . the caterpillars before they breed."[76]

Whether they owned their companies locally or from a distance, owners viewed timberlands, mills, docks, and ships as sources of profit and sought to maximize returns using whatever means available. Lumbermen and investors rapidly corporatized and mechanized the early twentieth-century Pacific Northwest lumber industry, turning the forest into a factory and transforming sawmills into more hectic, dangerous workplaces. Corporate tools—scientific management, speedups, machinery, and an imposing network of antilabor spies and foremen—led to a greater sense of alienation among loggers and growing hostility toward employers and their state allies who frequently came to their assistance.[77]

Corporate control over logging enterprises blocked opportunities for social mobility in the lumber industry. Having expropriated Native lands and ethnically cleansed most of the Northwest before Grays Harbor urbanized, scores of settlers established small logging outfits. Unlike the harbor's lumber manufacturing firms, which were mostly large corporations with sizable capital investments, during the 1880s and 1890s hundreds of loggers ran their own small concerns. In Grays Harbor, between 1891 and 1907, 263 new logging outfits began operations, an average of 15.5 each year. Before the turn of the twentieth century, dozens of small logging operators worked and lived alongside loggers, which helped to cultivate a shared identity between worker and owner, blunting working-class consciousness among the woodsmen.[78] In 1893, the Schafer family began logging the family property at the mouth of the Satsop River. By 1913, the firm had incorporated as the Schafer Brothers Logging Company with capital of $300,000; it also incorporated the Schafer Brothers Lumber and Door Company. During the 1920s, Schafer Brothers employed approximately 3,000 workers who ran the firm's camps, mills, and rail lines.[79]

Early loggers cut and transported trees using mostly human, animal, and water power: oxen pulled trees along skid roads from camps to mills, and splash dams facilitated log transport via rivers. As the waterside forests receded in the face of relentless cutting, Grays Harbor logging became a capital-intensive industry reliant on steam donkeys and railroads rather than oxen and skid roads, installing overhead cables to maximize logging production. Few workers could afford the equipment required for industrial logging; for those who could not, the opportunity to run their own logging firm dissolved. They either remained part of the permanent lumber proletariat or moved away—into town or away from the Northwest woods.[80]

In Grays Harbor, the number of new logging firms dropped dramatically from fifteen and a half per year between 1891 and 1907 to only nine annually between 1911 and 1919.[81] This sharp drop coincided with a major influx of new residents, as the county's population skyrocketed from 9,249 in 1890 to 15,124 in 1900 and 35,590 a decade later.[82] Opportunities for advancement and social mobility—hallmarks of the "American Dream"—shrank in the Far West as the great timber barons monopolized resources. Indeed, these figures indicate that even on the Pacific Coast in one of the most isolated parts of the country, the chasm between worker and employer paralleled trends across the country. On Grays Harbor, opportunity and prosperity were shared by an increasingly small percentage of the population while the number of wage-earning loggers climbed. With a lifetime of increasingly dangerous work facing them, Grays Harbor workers came to realize their best hopes lay in labor solidarity. During the first decades of the twentieth century, they came together in neighborhoods, halls, and eventually unions to improve their lives.

PATHS TO GRAYS HARBOR

From the mid-nineteenth century until the early twentieth century, most Grays Harbor residents were migrants new to the area. Drawing working people to the harbor proved a major decades-long project for local media, government officials, and employers. The migrants who built industrial Grays Harbor were not unique in North American history. In fact, industrial capitalism functioned in large part because of the work of migratory laborers that followed jobs across the country. "Finding jobs in industrial America required more than pounding the pavements; it required hitting the road," wrote historian Michael Bellesiles.[83] The perils of industrial capitalism pushed large parts of the US working class into poverty and homelessness. Such "indispensable outcasts" were critical to the operation of Gilded Age and Progressive Era capitalism, providing mobile labor that followed the work—or at least its promise.[84] Throughout these decades, approximately one-half of adult men in most US communities no longer lived there a decade later.[85]

Employers required this flow of working people and happily greeted an oversupply of labor they could use to drive down wages. But communities commonly expressed revulsion when migratory laborers—often labeled tramps, transients, vagrants, and hoboes—came to town. The

"Tramp Scare," in Bellesiles's words, came about from "the persistent depression" of the 1870s, which destabilized America, increasing unemployment and underemployment to levels never previously known."[86] Disgust toward and social marginalization of "tramps," however, did not cease with the end of the Long Depression of the late nineteenth century. Instead, it was a notable feature of community life throughout the early twentieth century.

States and municipalities across the United States regulated the poor, arresting and interning workers for a variety of crimes specific to their class. The territory and state of Washington criminalized unemployment and homelessness, using vagrancy laws to criminalize "wandering about and having no visible calling, or business to maintain themselves."[87] In practice, the law enabled police to arrest and expel unemployed laborers, particularly when they caused "trouble" such as organizing unions, refusing unpleasant job tasks, or lingering without work. In April 1906, the *Aberdeen Daily Bulletin* reported "Nine Vags Deported—During the past two days nine men have been arrested by the police upon vagrancy charges. The men included several hoboes, who were not needed here, so far as Chief Christensen could determine."[88] During periods of intense unemployment and poverty, Grays Harbor jails became little more than warehouses for the poor, with the caveat that, unlike homeless shelters, the poor who ended up in jails had their poverty criminalized.

An illustrative case came in April 1906, when police arrested a "one-armed vagrant" living in Aberdeen.[89] The Police Record for the City of Hoquiam is especially telling on this matter. In 1913, as the economy faltered and unemployment soared throughout the Pacific Northwest, the Hoquiam jail housed scores of impoverished workers under the charge of "vagrancy," "hobo," "bumming," "sleeping," or "bed." During 1913, the city jailed 365—or one for every day of the year—persons for these charges.[90] In a 1914 interview, an Aberdeen police sergeant demonstrated the cruelty of law enforcement's views toward people on society's margins. He counseled rounding up "vags" and forcing them to perform hard labor: "Put the vags to work and they will disappear. . . . A rock pile will solve the problem. Give the tramp free lodging and something to eat and he is sure to be a regular caller. Take him out at 7 o'clock in the morning and make him work on the rock pile until 6 o'clock in the evening, and he will not only cut short his visit, but will spread the news along the road, and those thus informed will steer for other cities."[91]

RUNNING THE WHEELS OF INDUSTRY

Criminalization and repression did little to slow the migrations of workers across industrial America. Each year thousands of migratory workers came to Grays Harbor's towns.[92] Workers followed a variety of paths to the harbor. Unions sometimes facilitated migration, both by dispatching members—such as seamen—to cities, and by informally advertising job openings and working conditions in union newspapers. Some companies brought in their own crews to perform work on the harbor. Rail companies brought construction crews—often immigrants—to the region.[93] For example, in early 1913, the *Aberdeen Herald* reported "twenty-six Dago laborers" had been induced to move from Spokane, Washington, to work on the Northern Pacific Railway, only to have "worked a week and not having been paid."[94] Although differing in detail, reporters peppered similar events throughout early twentieth-century papers.[95]

Grays Harbor's population followed chain migration, as family, friends, and neighbors followed one another from village or country into an adopted hometown. Migrants exchanged information in many ways, including through correspondence, as well as letters and advertisements published in newspapers. A 1980s nationality study for Grays Harbor explored the region's past through the lens of its immigrants and their descendants. Hundreds of children and grandchildren of immigrants returned surveys that provided the most detailed, although still incomplete, window into the area's early immigrant communities—particularly those like the Finns and Poles that retained a major institutional and cultural presence into the 1980s. Among many telling results, the surveys showed foreign-born migrants following relatives and acquaintances to the harbor. In 1892, John Branford, a young married man moved from Finland to Michigan's Upper Peninsula, where he joined the country's largest Finnish American community. Six years later, he traded mining for lumber when he moved to Grays Harbor for, in his granddaughter's words, a "Job-Better life." A year later, John's wife, Lisa, followed the well-worn path from northern Europe to Aberdeen.[96]

The largest group of Poles lived in west Aberdeen, where they controlled their own Catholic church, ethnic hall, and political association.[97] Arriving in the United States in 1906 from Russian-controlled Poland, Casimir (Charlie) Arciezewski settled in the west Aberdeen Polish enclave among dozens of Polish speakers—nearly all wage laborers and their families. In 1913, Charlie wed Paulina Kuklinski, who hailed from the same part of Poland as Charlie. The couple made a home in west Aberdeen and became naturalized citizens, ultimately divorcing during the 1920s. Charlie worked for decades in the harbor's sawmills; their son Edmont joined him there in the 1930s, and both "Archie" men joined the industrial union drive in lumber during the Depression, ultimately carrying union cards in the 1930s and beyond.[98] As for thousands of harbor newcomers, both foreign- and American-born, the lure of industry and the (for some) ethnic enclaves brought these workers to the harbor where they lived, worked, and organized in an emerging industrial region.

Chain migration alone failed to satisfy the harbor's need for lumber workers. To bolster their numbers and bring a sense of order to a chaotic market, lumbermen relied on private employment agencies. These "middlemen-businesses," in the words of historian Elizabeth Pingree, provided jobs to workers in exchange for a fee.[99] One laborer, who first worked in Cosmopolis in 1917 at age fourteen, recalled his experiences securing a job at the Grays Harbor Commercial Company:

> I was fourteen years old and had not worked out except in a small bean cannery. Labor laws restricting the employment of children around machinery were generally ignored. My mother, needing some income from my labor, took me to an employment office in the Skid Road section of Portland and signed me up for work with the Grays Harbor Commercial Company of Cosmopolis; the agency advanced me my railway ticket. The fee for my receiving this job was a modest one dollar, but the hidden factors which were probably spelled out in the fine print of the contract I signed made me a bound laborer until I could get out of debt to the company. Signed up at the time with me was a foreigner who spoke little

English and read none. We were to go together and report to the office of the Cosmopolis mill.[100]

Seattle and Portland boasted the Northwest's most employment offices—in 1903, approximately fifteen agencies operated in Seattle.[101] Agents in both cities contracted with Grays Harbor lumber operations. Disappointed by what they discovered in Cosmopolis, many workers did not last long in the company town. "The average stay of each man is less than 30 days," according to the *Grays Harbor Post*.[102] This was a classic example of the agencies' exploitative practices called the "job shark" system by labor radicals—notorious among workers because it kept "one man coming to a job, one man on the job, and one man leaving the job."[103]

Employment agencies existed throughout North America. They linked workers with jobs—including in rural and semirural areas across the West. For over a decade, though, Grays Harbor served as a case study in agencies' abusive practices. Although labor radicals opposed the agencies, criticism of employment agency malpractice was well within the Pacific Northwest mainstream—leading to a series of investigations by local, state, and federal governments, as well as those conducted by labor unions.[104] Private and government inquiries focused on the Grays Harbor Commercial Company (GHCC) in Cosmopolis. In 1903, in response to complaints "from the Grays Harbor district and directed against the Grays Harbor Commercial Company, located at Cosmopolis," the Washington State Bureau of Labor investigated mess-house systems and employment agencies. The report filled more than twenty-five pages of the bureau's biennial report, consisting of Cosmopolis workers' testimony delivered to the state's labor commissioner. Testimony focused on general conditions of labor and the use of a company store and payment in script. Some informants described how they purchased jobs and transportation to the workplace, and how employment agents misrepresented the conditions of labor. The GHCC employee Lee Rosen reported the agent "said it was a light, inside job, and that they would give board and everything like that"—an evaluation Rosen found to be dishonest. Shortly after his arrival in Cosmpolis, Rosen's work cost him two fingers and a thumb when a saw—owned, of course by the company—cut him badly. Rosen secured a lawyer "but thought it best to drop the case" when the company offered him fifty dollars for the permanent loss of his fingers.[105]

Although Cosmopolis was the major destination of workers hired through labor bureaus, job agents also shipped workers to the larger towns—including some cases where they sold jobs that did not exist. In March 1909, the *Aberdeen Daily World* condemned "employment agencies in outside cities sending men to Aberdeen under false premises." The city's police chief investigated the reasons why such "a large number of men have arrived in Aberdeen" and determined that agencies in Seattle, Tacoma, and Portland had sold jobs to the men—absent orders from local mills. The workers showed up in Aberdeen holding paperwork allegedly promising them jobs in Aberdeen mills, lured by advertisements in the Northwest's biggest cities. "Misleading Posters Announce that 'Thousands of Men are Wanted on Grays Harbor,' but No such Demand Exists—Men Pay Last Cent for an Illusive Situation—No Workmen Wanted," reported the angry journalist.[106]

WORKING-CLASS COMMUNITIES

Grays Harbor's population boomed during the first years of the twentieth century, skyrocketing from 9,249 in 1890 to 15,124 in 1900 and 35,590 a decade later.[107] Aberdeen's population more than tripled during this decade, as workers from across the globe moved to the harbor to fill jobs. Both Aberdeen and Hoquiam were home to complex webs of ethnic neighborhoods. During the first decade of the twentieth century, as Grays Harbor County's population swelled from 15,124 to 35,590, immigrants came to make up nearly one-third of its population. In urban centers, immigrants and the children of immigrants made up a large majority of the population. In 1910, 62 percent of Aberdeen's and 57 percent of Hoquiam's population were first-generation immigrants and their children.[108]

To cut the trees, transform them into building materials, and transport them globally, employers needed hundreds—and later thousands—of workers who daily risked their lives in the region's most dangerous industry. As in much of the industrial West, immigrants from northern Europe and Canada joined native-born whites in peopling the small but rapidly growing industrial cities. Before Washington became a state in 1889, thousands of white Europeans and Americans moved to the territory. During the 1880s, more than 230 Norwegians, Danes, and Swedes settled in the county, with scores more second-generation Scandinavians making up a large chunk of the area's population.[109] By 1894, that number ballooned to more than 350; hundreds more first- and second-generation Nordic immigrants moved to the area by the turn of the twentieth century.[110] With reputations for the physical strength useful in logging and sawmill labor and training from their premigration work lives, Scandinavians made up a large group of nineteenth-century lumber workers.[111] Many of these northern European immigrants settled in rural areas, but a sizable population put down roots in the growing urban areas, as Scandinavians built Grays Harbor's first ethnic enclave. Before the turn of the twentieth century, Scandinavians had established institutions, including Lutheran churches.[112] Many powerful individuals and institutions rolled out the red carpet for the Nordics. A front-page *Aberdeen Herald* article from 1905 described Scandinavians as "of Teutonic origin, blond, tall, muscular, and devoted to the Christian religion," as well as hardy and democratic.[113]

Few Pacific Coast locales featured the ethnic diversity of Grays Harbor's sawmills, as the families who made the region's economy run moved to the Pacific Northwest from all over the world. Thousands of Grays Harbor laborers hailed from southern and eastern Europe, primarily from rural homelands; most Croatian, Polish, and Greek laborers had little experience with industrial technology, but joined the ranks of the American industrial working class soon after their arrival. Most of these newly arrived men worked in manual-labor jobs, in sawmills, on the docks, and in railroad camps.

After selling his first Aberdeen mill, A. J. West established a company town called Junction City on Aberdeen's eastern border. Not incorporated, Junction City was one of Grays Harbor's many company towns.[114] West's 110 workers included an ethnically and racially diverse workforce—much like several mills in the region. From its opening in 1906 to at least 1910, West's mill employed large numbers of Finnish, Afghani, South Asian, and Scandinavian workers.[115] At the time of the 1910 census, Pashtu was, next to English, the most widely spoken language at the Junction City mill; relatively few in number across the country, workers from Afghanistan moved to the harbor for sawmill work, joining a polyglot workforce resembling the great industrial cities of the East and Midwest. Racial and ethnic conflicts were common among the workforce, boiling into physical fights and a handful of hate strikes. Matters came to a head in 1909 when "a fight between Hindus and a white man employed at the A. J. West mill" broke out. The *Aberdeen Herald* reported that "on account of the fight the Hindus left the mill; [on] the return of the Hindus to work, 25 white men left the yard, leaving the mill short handed."[116]

WHITE TOWNS

As across the country, northwest European immigrants and native-born white Americans constituted a host society on Grays Harbor, one where "whites" held all positions of power and influence. Through its early history, harbor residents did much to establish it as "white man's territory," one where whites—both American-born and those from northwest Europe—would be welcomed and praised, while those same whites met Asians with scorn and bursts of violence. Indeed, there was little disagreement that Aberdeen and Hoquiam were to be, in the words of *Washingtonian* editor and future congressman Albert Johnson, "White Man's Town[s]."[117]

Journalists like Johnson played important parts in establishing and maintaining the towns' whiteness. As employers and activists in business organizations, these elites articulated local versions of white supremacist beliefs so prominent among the upper crust of Gilded Age and Progressive America. In a characteristic editorial, the *Aberdeen Herald* declared "That the *Herald* is no friend of the Chinaman scarcely needs saying."[118] Mainstream newspapers seeded divisions along racial and ethnic lines. Reporters played upon racist caricatures of Asian and southern European immigrants, contrasting those groups' essentialized characteristics with the independent, hardy, and powerful members of the "Nordic race." Journalists warned of imminent invasions by immigrant workers—hordes coming across the Atlantic and the "yellow peril" moving from Asia. A November 1900 issue of the *Aberdeen Herald* devoted much of its front page to run a thick headline reading "Filipinos are Citizens," which was "A Decision That Throws Open the Pacific Coast to Asiatic Labor" and warning thus of "Malay Competition for American Labor."[119] Two decades later, the prominent *Aberdeen Daily World* praised the views of Congressman Albert Johnson, editor of the main Hoquiam daily, who insisted that Japanese people must be barred from American shores: "Their presence in this country in any measurable numbers means another race problem, and we have not solved the one we have now. We should be foolish in the extreme to take on another."[120]

Localities across the country matched national crusades against immigrants, mobilizing "citizenship" campaigns to keep Asian and "undesirable" Europeans out of communities. As Congress passed exclusionist legislation, from the 1882 Chinese Exclusion Act to the 1924 Johnson-Reed Immigration Act, localities practiced direct action exclusionism to keep hordes of "undesirables" away; when members of unwelcome groups arrived, employers and their media spokesmen collaborated to drive them out. To make Grays Harbor white, employers practiced elite forms of vigilantism, especially targeting Asian and southern European immigrants. Regulation sometimes fell to local officials all too happy to put up the guarded gate against the group they labeled "Celestials." The business-friendly press both incited those acts and defended them after the fact. The local press even glorified police and vigilante violence against "undesirables": persons of color, rebellious laborers, leftists, and "tramps." In February 1891, the *Aberdeen Herald* celebrated "Hoquiam's desire to rid herself of the Chinaman in all his dirty aspects" following a police roundup of "Hoquiam Celestials." The paper said "the police at Hoquiam had made a big killing, having bagged every Chinaman in Hoquiam drawing in the soothing smoke of the 'dope.'"[121] The Chinese were only the first of successive Asian American groups attacked by the harbor's whites—with their newsmen and police leading the attacks. In 1909, the *Aberdeen World*, the area's leading newspaper and a prominent Republican organ, ran a front-page article feting local officials for evicting Japanese residents of the town: "Exodus, Induced by County Attorney and Chief of Police Begins Today" ran the headline. Legal authorities had little interest in applying the law to these "Japs." The county prosecutor declared, "We are going after all these people. If they break the law, they must abide the consequences. We shall not wait for prosecution; we will merely give these folk a limited time to leave the city and we shall see that they leave within the limit."[122]

By the dawn of the twentieth century, the harbor's patterns of vigilante violence and racial exclusion was set in place, conforming to the methods used across the West. The harbor's Asian Americans suffered overt and violent oppression. Whites turned their hostility on the local Chinese, Japanese, South Asian, and Filipino populations. Following passage of the Chinese Exclusion Act, which forbid most Chinese immigration, many Chinese migrants passed into the United States via the US-Canadian border, "devising new cross-border migratory strategies and networks" and managed, in historian Kornel Chang's words, to partly circumvent immigration officials' efforts.[123] In May 1892, Aberdeen residents detained "several contraband Chinamen . . . on the beach"; customs officials deported the men to British Columbia, "whence they came."[124]

The number of Chinese on Grays Harbor would have been greater if not for Aberdeen's 1890 Chinese expulsion. In 1885, approximately thirty Chinese men lived in Grays Harbor. The 1889 territorial census showed thirty-six Chinese-born men working in Grays Harbor, with more than two-thirds working as laborers.[125] A year later, Grays Harbor's population included more than one hundred Chinese persons with forty Chinese immigrants living in Aberdeen—2.4 percent of the town's population.[126] In September 1890, a mob of whites demanded the Chinese leave Aberdeen. Unlike the Chinese expulsions in Seattle, Tacoma, and other western cities, the Aberdeen expulsion was an elite affair led by businessmen and professionals, supported by a business organization—the "best" people, according to the *Aberdeen Herald*.[127] The town's mayor ordered all Chinese residents to leave the town within a week. When the Chinese residents refused to flee, vigilantes took matters into their own hands. On November 8, the mob rounded up Aberdeen's Chinese American population, forced them to board the *Wishkah Chief* steamer, and expelled them from town. The vigilantes who perpetrated this act then demanded that the deportees keep moving.[128] Following the expulsion, the Hoquiam Furniture Company ran an advertisement making light of the vigilante action: "Furniture Must Go!! Whether the Chinese Stay or No."[129]

Aberdeen residents prevented Chinese from settling in the city for more than two decades.[130] In 1891, local whites expressed anxiety that the owner of a salmon cannery "will bring Chinamen to run the cannery"—fears stoked in the pages of the *Seattle Post-Intelligencer*.[131] In 1903, the *Aberdeen Herald* inflamed fears of Chinese domestic servants, reminding readers of the Chinese deportation "by a committee of its best citizens." The *Herald* continued, "Public opinion was unanimous that the Chinese were an unendurable nuisance, and their unlawful removal was winked at by the authorities, for the very good reason that the jury could not be secured to convict. To remove this ban, even for a few house servants, would be quickly taken advantage of by the Chinese, and in less than a year we could have a colony of Asiatics that would necessitate doubling the police force to take care of them."[132] These same newspapers reminded readers of the identification of the Chinese with opium and sex work. In a front-page article in May 1910, the *Aberdeen Herald* told of a drug bust in Hoquiam: "The seizure of two half-pound cans of opium and the arrest of Long Ling and Ching Lung, owners of a local Chinese noodle house . . . may lead to the seizure of a quantity of the drug in Seattle and the arrest and breaking up of a gang of coast smugglers."[133] Racist vigilantism paid dividends for Aberdeen's white town advocates: the 1910 US Census recorded no Chinese Americans living in Aberdeen.[134]

Run out of Aberdeen in 1890, Chinese workers persisted in the wider area, working in fish canneries, laundries, and sawmills.[135] According to the *Aberdeen Herald*, in the early 1890s a Chinese man named Chin Dock oversaw operations for the massive Grays Harbor Commercial Company's mess house—one of several Chinese employees at the Cosmopolis plant.[136] In 1900, twenty-four Chinese and twenty-five Japanese residents lived on the harbor. A decade later, that figure climbed to fifty-nine and seventy-nine, respectively.[137]

The expulsion and further harassment of the Aberdeen Chinese population pointed in an unsettling direction. Local elites, namely lumbermen, politicians, police, and journalists, understood the need to promote the region and recruit workers to build and maintain industrial Grays Harbor. But this same employing and professional class demanded that the region would advance on their own terms. When "undesirables" provided no clear material benefit or challenged managerial prerogatives, the elites responded with repression—the common target being persons of color, radicals, and vagrants. On the other end of the class spectrum from these attackers from above came thousands of working people who built unions and other workers' organizations to advance their class—and, commonly, their individual craft—interests. As seen in the next chapter, white workers sometimes adopted much the same bigotry as their fellow whites from the employing class. Lacking a democratic vision to unite the region's working-class majority, the harbor's union movement was divided and often incapable of challenging powerful and united employers.

2

THE "HOUSE OF LABOR"

MANY SMALL UNIONS

After eclipsing the two-million-member mark in 1904, trade union memberships stagnated, due in part to the open-shop drive of employers unified by membership in the National Association of Manufacturers, local employers' groups, and so-called citizens' alliances.[1] The float built and displayed by the International Shingle Weavers' Union of America (ISWUA) local for their 1906 Aberdeen-Hoquiam Labor Day parade was a local expression of the labor movements of the early twentieth century and a potent reminder of the struggles waged by unions across the country. Labor Day floats were often large, ornate displays, symbols of the craft and pride in skill of the union in question.[2] Unionists wore work uniforms, carried signs declaring their achievements, and marched in line reflecting a disciplined order. But the weavers' 1906 float also stood out for its overtly political themes. It featured a "bullpen," the name for the structures built alongside factories to house scabs during strikes. The weavers' bullpen bore a "neat and accurate likeness" to the one used by Robert and Joseph Lytle, owners of the Hoquiam Lumber and Shingle Company, to house scabs during a strike concluded only weeks before the parade.[3] For bosses and scabs, the bullpen represented a haven necessary to protect them from the weavers, who promised retributive violence against strikebreakers for their actions. To the weavers, the bullpen, and hence the float, was a symbol of the contest between shingle manufacturers and workers for control over the workplace, a struggle that, in this instance, played out in the streets for the entire community to behold.

Six months earlier, Grays Harbor towns hosted their first convention of the Washington State Federation of Labor (WSFL), the state branch of the American Federation of Labor (AFL), which was founded in 1886 by (mostly) craft unions. For several days in January 1906, some 230 delegates from dozens of unions met in Aberdeen to discuss the state of the labor movement, pass resolutions, and socialize among fellow labor brass.[4] Delegates, nearly all white men, patronized local unionized saloons and eateries, where bartenders, cooks, and waiters served them union-made beer while they smoked union cigars. Like the weavers' Labor Day exhibition would later in the year, the convention's political themes stood out. Delegates passed resolutions focused on bread-and-butter concerns that animate so much of labor organization, while also encouraging unionists to enter politics and advocating for the state to more aggressively regulate immigration—particularly from Asia and southern and eastern Europe.[5]

In retrospect, given the Northwest's status as a lumber center, the near-total absence of woodworkers' unions at the convention and parade was surprising. In the late nineteenth and early twentieth centuries, as their labor gave the harbor its claim to the title of lumber capital of the world, only a small percentage of the thousands of local lumber workers belonged to unions. Prior to 1910, other than a few short-lived Knights of Labor, AFL, and independent lumber unions, the only unionists in the lumber industry were the shingle weavers, a group of approximately 3,000 (mostly) men who manufactured shingles from western red cedar. Few in numbers, the region's woodworkers' unions nonetheless adopted militant approaches to labor relations, advocated for proworker politicians and policies, and carved out cultural practices that reflected a very damp and woodsy version of the Wild West. Like most trade unions of their era, early woodworkers' unions followed exclusive policies such as initiation fees and apprenticeships designed, in part, to limit available craftsmen and drive up demand for their work. However, guided by local and national experiences, and the work by radical unionists, the shingle weavers' union was among the first in the Northwest to advocate for and then practice industrial unionism. Weavers also engaged in electoral politics—chiefly through the Socialist Party of America.

SPLINTERED UNIONS

Beginning in the 1890s, Grays Harbor workers joined a nationwide labor upsurge; local union progress coincided with the growth of the American labor movement, as the number of unionists quadrupled between 1897 and 1903, when, in historian David Montgomery's words, "the American Federation of Labor (AFL) for the first time secured its place as the 'House of Labor.'"[6] The harbor's labor movement grew mostly unabated between 1898 and 1906, from a time when "the labor cause was dead" to become—according to state labor leaders—the most densely unionized workforce in Washington State.[7] The local labor movement had forty local unions affiliated with it at one time. Between 1904 and 1908, Aberdeen and Hoquiam contained a minimum of fifty-two labor unions, two central labor councils, two building trades councils, and the Grays Harbor Waterfront Federation.[8] Their two thousand members included workers from dozens of trades, and the movement's momentum spread labor organizations to new and uncharted territory: Hoquiam musicians organized, tugboat operators organized, and an impressive five new unions organized during a two-week period in March 1904.[9] The harbor towns hosted Washington State Federation of Labor (WSFL) conventions in 1906 and 1910.[10] In an address to the WSFL in 1905, John Gronow, then the fifth vice president of the federation, declared that "within the last few years unions on the Harbor have increased 300 per cent. till today Aberdeen and Hoquiam, the Grays Harbor cities, are one of the best, if not the best, organized cities of the whole state of Washington."[11]

Unions offered strike funds, sickness and death insurance, fraternal camaraderie, and a measure of security against arbitrary treatment by management. But the union difference was most obvious in workers' paychecks. Union weavers earned substantially more than their nonunion counterparts in Pacific Northwest lumber mills. Sawmill laborers in Aberdeen were frequently paid only a dollar and seventy-five cents per day during the first decade of the twentieth century, a meager wage that made survival difficult.[12] In contrast, during his tour of shingle mills on Grays Harbor, one ISWUA organizer "went through the Cosmopolis mills" and criticized managers for paying nonunion shingle weavers only two dollars and seventy-five cents per day, a sum far greater than was paid to most lumber workers but an amount the organizer called "scab wages."[13] Unionized weavers made an average of four dollars per day in 1909 and militantly defended those union wages against cuts.[14] Grays Harbor shingle weaver Harold M. Stilson explained the importance of collective security in an article describing his fellow unionists' response once they discovered he might have cancer. "I got this awful pain. I went to Grays Harbor General Hospital for treatment. The union would take as much care as they possibly could of anyone if he was in trouble, so they came in to see me. The secretary of the union went up to talk to the doctor, who told him that I wouldn't be going home because I had cancer."[15]

Craft unions made little sense in lumber, an industry with minor occupational differences within the logging and sawmill workforces. Still, building "one union in wood" was a decades-long project with imposing obstacles along the way. The core issue was the concerted and often violent employer opposition to unionism. Employers were especially opposed to industrial unions—those that offered the promise of uniting all workers within an industry into a single union, thereby potentially making employers' efforts to divide workers more difficult. Sawmill laborers spoke several languages, with some workplaces employing workers from a dozen or more countries. Labor radical Bruce Rogers added a bit of rhetorical flourish while describing the harbor's diverse lumber workforce:

> Came the foreign worker from the three hundred and sixty marks on the compass dial. By night they drank and fought in the saloons of the evil smells, each bellowing his patriot folk song. By day as the barons so wished they worked to excel, in the fool pride of race.
>
> But came a pay day when Ole asked Pierre and Zwobrowski and Garibaldi to have a drink with him down at "The Greek's." The night brawls ceased. Arms upon shoulders in a new emotion and that their rough voices might better chord they tried singing the Marseillaise together and found the hymn of revolt sounded even better.[16]

Although immigrant workers creatively organized to overcome linguistic differences in their union campaigns—including appointing multiethnic strike committees—remaining linguistic hurdles made building labor solidarity difficult, particularly among trade unionists who spoke only English. Compounding matters was the fact that labor leaders frequently espoused racist and nativist views—and spent their lives as urban craftsmen or bureaucrats, worlds apart from the rural proletariat. These men were unable or unwilling to devote the resources necessary to organize the industry in the face of sharp opposition from what radical lumber worker James Rowan called "the monopoly of the lumber trust," which, as Rowan asserted, was "controlling not only the industry, but also the local, and sometimes the state machinery of government."[17]

Throughout the country, the craft unions that dominated the early twentieth-century labor movement represented a small group of privileged workers in selected industries.[18] Indeed, the trade union movement did not represent the entire working class, nor was it built for that purpose. From 1902 to 1910, between 2 and 3 percent of Washington's labor force belonged to WSFL unions.[19]

AFL union leadership supported racist, chauvinistic, and nativist positions. Many individual leaders and the union officialdom supported Asian exclusion and immigrant restriction legislation; some also advocated excluding workers of color from union membership and opposed women's entry into the paid workforce.[20] Trade unions depicted and defended members' work as "skilled" labor, and "new" immigrants had far less access to these positions than native-born Americans and their counterparts from northwest Europe. But skill is a social construct that needed to be espoused and defended by those who claimed to be "skilled" laborers and sought the relative privilege conferred upon the "skilled" labor force.[21]

Unions and their members benefited materially from the construction of their trades as "skilled" because it enabled them to create labor shortages: employers could not pick freely from the "reserve army of labor" to fill positions that required skills that, ostensibly, required significant training. With much of the labor pool removed from competition for "skilled" positions, those with the requisite skills possessed some bargaining leverage with their employers. Those with a higher level of social power, namely white males, constructed the concept of skill by including their occupations within its fold, and those performed by "others"—women, immigrants, and racialized groups—as "unskilled." African Americans, Native Americans, women, and Asian Americans have throughout US history worked mostly in "unskilled" jobs in agricultural, industrial, and service work. In the early twentieth century, this was also true for southern and eastern Europeans, who employers usually hired into lower-paying "unskilled" jobs. Skill also bears a close relationship to training, although not only in the obvious sense of skill equating training. When large numbers of people have training in a job, then the price of labor can be driven down, regardless of the amount of skill needed to perform that job. Thus logging, a job that many northern European immigrants had some training in from their pre-emigration work lives, had a large surplus of laborers, thereby enabling employers to drive down wages.[22] The Grays Harbor workforce conformed closely to national patterns: jobs performed by "new" immigrants became classified as "unskilled" and hence nonunion, while those performed by their native-born counterparts were classified as "skilled" and union work.

Among the most glaring shortcomings of the Pacific Northwest's labor movement was the inability and unwillingness of its leaders to organize the tens of thousands of workers who made their living in its greatest industry: lumber. Unlike bosses—entirely white and male—who shared ties of kith, kin, politics, neighborhood, and fraternity, the industry's workforce was a diverse lot. Thousands of immigrants speaking dozens of languages worked in Pacific Northwest sawmills and logging camps, as did Indigenous workers—descendants of the area's original inhabitants whose families had worked the forests since time immemorial. Thousands of Finns joined thousands more eastern and southern Europeans in Washington's sawmills, where they worked alongside scores of East Asian and South Asian laborers. These workers expressed themselves in English—and in their native languages. Finnish-born workers who labored in Grays Harbor's mills, docks, camps, and homes recorded their experiences in thousands of articles for their press, while more than a dozen immigrant groups formed ethnic societies on the harbor.

The harbor's earliest lumber unions affiliated with the Knights of Labor.[23] Formed in 1869, the Knights sought to create a class-conscious industrial union movement, one that, ostensibly, had the capacity to draw in the entire working class: men and women regardless of race, ethnicity, or skill. The Knights popularized the phrase "an injury to one is the concern of all," but Pacific Coast Knights had no interest in unionizing all, instead constructing much of their union movement as white workers' clubs dedicated to Asian exclusion. In several western cities, the Knights were responsible for assaulting Chinese Americans, expelling them from towns, destroying their homes and neighborhoods, and threatening to act similarly if the "threat" returned.[24]

Lumber workers formed the Aberdeen and Hoquiam Knights years after the order's membership cratered in the Red Scare following the 1886 Haymarket Affair in Chicago; building unions continued to be difficult, too, because of high unemployment during the Long Recession of the late nineteenth century. Still, the Knights persisted in regions across North America. The Knights counted 100,000 members as late as 1890.[25] Formed in 1887, the Aberdeen Knights persisted until 1894 when their "twin city" of Hoquiam organized a second lumber workers' local.[26] The *Aberdeen Herald* indicated that approximately 200 members planned to join the Aberdeen Knights in December 1892.[27] But the organization must have lacked stability: in January 1893, a visiting Knights of Labor organizer who came to the harbor reorganized the Aberdeen local with fifty-one members.[28] In February 1893 the organization lived up to its motto "An Injury to One Is the Concern of All" when it issued a resolution in support of the San Francisco branch of the Sailors' Union of the Pacific: "We will use all honorable and legal means to help along their cause to a successful termination."[29]

Many Knights worked in the harbor's fast-growing lumber industry—especially its sawmills. The Hoquiam Knights' branch drew enough attention that the antilabor *Weekly Recorder* of Aberdeen complained, "There are 187 members of that organization and that a general strike is to be ordered on the Harbor if wages are not raised and certain objectionable employees of the North Western Lumber company removed."[30] Rather than negotiate with the workers, Hoquiam lumberman George Emerson responded to the strike threat by suggesting that bosses "starve" workers until they learned a lesson.[31] Possibly because of Emerson's threat, the strike never materialized, and one Grays Harbor Knight declared that the local's leadership—like the Knights' leadership as a whole—opposed the strike, preferring to function "as an educational organization formed for the purpose of educating the toilers on problems of political economy."[32] Although scores of workers joined the Grays Harbor Knights, they failed to form a mass movement or pose a significant challenge to the region's employers.

Few lumber unions fared better than the Knights. Before the 1910s, nearly all Northwest lumber unions folded after only a few months. They failed for several reasons: employers' union-busting; their officers' conservatism; their narrow, exclusive craft union practices that made little sense in lumber; an inability or unwillingness to utilize interethnic organizing strategies in an industry that employed a multilingual workforce; and organizers' persistent use of traditional urban trade union strategies for groups of industrial workers who worked and lived in the forest. Judging from the unenthusiastic response to calls to join these organizations, and workers' later support for unions with anticapitalist leadership and policies, it is fair to say that loggers and mill hands looked for more radical options.

Unsurprisingly, as was true throughout the Northwest, Grays Harbor's loggers' and sawmill workers' unions were short-lived and ineffectual.[33] In Grays Harbor, two branches of the Logger's Protective Union formed in April 1904, one in each of the twin cities, with 238 combined members "and a large number of applications . . . on hand." The unions held business meetings and smokers and appointed an organizer to travel throughout the region. These acts briefly increased the unions' membership, though the organized loggers never adopted anything but the most conservative trade union approach. Aberdeen local branch 11596 secretary A. E. Gagner described why, in his view, unions were unnecessary: "Now that we are getting well arranged, we recognize the fact that our employers' interests are identical to our own" and that "the boss loggers have paid more to the man in his employ, than any other employer on Gray's [*sic*] Harbor, and his profit has been least."[34] He wrote, "None of our so-called rights have suffered at the hands of our employers," advising "corporation employers of labor, come to the boss loggers and learn how to treat your employees and do away with all unions."[35] That a logger was referring to corporate bosses—meaning manufacturers—is a useful reminder of the large-scale industry developed around the turn of the twentieth century; unfortunately for the loggers, their branch of the industry was rapidly following the same path as the sawmills.

The loggers' opposition to unionism wasn't solely due to lack of class consciousness—or the fabled independent streak of loggers, who, according to some commentators, were too individualistic to be shackled by joining organizations.[36] Instead, union officials failed to appeal to the loggers' interests, and the rare appeals that they made hinted at unionists' ignorance of the differences between town and country. Both Grays Harbor loggers' unions formed in 1904 had headquarters in the city, far away from the logging camps and bunkhouses where loggers spent their time. Union activities occurred in Aberdeen, miles away from most logging camps. All of Grays Harbor's labor council executive officers for 1904–5 lived in the city, and the speakers chosen to address potential recruits were English-speaking urban workers who shared little in the way of life experiences with loggers.[37] The distinction between urban trade unionists and loggers was made clear by the dissolution of the two loggers' union branches "on account of non-attendance," a product of either potential recruits' lack of interest in the union or their inability to reach union gatherings held in the city.[38]

Even during their brief involvement with the labor movement, loggers must have noted the cultural differences between themselves and their fellow unionists. Loggers' own words were absent from articles written about their union.[39] The depiction of loggers' lives offered by AFL vice president James O'Connell before the 1914 US Commission on Industrial Relations in Seattle provides some idea of how city folk viewed the woodsmen. He reported learning of "a sort of cleaning up in the spring time, a general carousal on the part of the woodsmen, a general beating up of each other until the king lives among them." Recoiling from the suggestion that his fellow unionists should be lumped in with that sort of well-known caricature of lumber workers, union leader J. G. Brown responded that he hadn't seen "anything of that kind."[40]

WEAVING UNIONS, SPLINTERED WORKING CLASS

Labor organizations in the lumber industry during the first four decades after Washington became a state were almost exclusively those of the shingle weavers. Out of the approximately 100,000 workers who labored in the Northwest's forest industries, only the shingle weavers, a group that in May 1905 numbered only 2,400 members, belonged to labor unions.[41]

Weavers across the Northwest—concentrated in southwest Washington and the Puget Sound region—unionized during the late nineteenth century, but the International Shingle Weavers' Union of America (ISWUA) proved to be the first weavers' institution with staying power. After founding the union in 1903, the ISWUA affiliated with the AFL and moved decisively to spread the union to "every point in America where there are one or more shingle mills located."[42] ISWUA members organized dozens of locals between 1903 and 1906. The term "shingle weaver" originally referred to the men—and in the late nineteenth and early twentieth century, practically all shingle industry employees were men—who packed the shingles into bundles after cedar blocks were sawn into the thin strips known as shingles. The weavers' hands moved so rapidly during the packing process that it appeared they weaved the shingles into a bundle. As the "shingle weavers' union" expanded its ranks, so did the meaning of the term; by the early 1910s, "shingle weaver" included all workers involved in producing shingles.[43]

Weavers were among the most militant and radical members of the Northwest labor movement.[44] Hoquiam weaver J. G. Brown captured his union's socialist views, explaining why unionists "must ally ourselves with some political party that shall represent our interests as opposed to capitalist interests":

> Pure reason would seem to say that if we are spoiling for a strike, let us go after the eight hour day; call a district convention, as suggested by the *Shingle Weaver*. Make a move in the right direction! Experience has proven beyond a doubt that it is impossible for employer and employee to organize into a sort of "brother." Our methods lie apart; our interests

Shingle weavers at work in McCleary, Washington, ca. 1910. Polson Museum, Hoquiam, Washington.

> are in conflict, and men usually twist their logic to fit their interests. Our International officers may well go slow in this matter. And in no case should it be done without submitting the whole proposition to a referendum vote. Keep the power close to the rank and file.[45]

Brown was a leader of the Grays Harbor shingle weavers; those locals were among the most active and radical branches of the international union. Weaver activists had no qualms about antagonizing their employers in verse. In one poem, shingle weaver J. E. Elliot condemned Robert Lytle for using a bullpen to house scabs during a 1906 shingle strike:

> One mill man built a big bull pen,
> Its walls are standing still,
> And there he kept his working men
> Like beasts he meant to kill.[46]

ISWUA members also ran for political office as socialists, condemned capitalism, and in 1905 helped found the *Grays Harbor Socialist*.[47]

Many of the harbor's unions were fighting units with strong reputations for militancy. This was particularly true of the region's transportation and lumber unions. Grays Harbor shingle weavers struck almost annually between 1902 and 1917, striking for higher wages, control of the workplace and hiring, medical insurance, and the right to restrict the arbitrary authority of foremen.[48] When the ISWUA voted to stop paying the compulsory fifty cents per month hospital fee that was taken out of their checks, preferring to handle their own insurance fund, the weavers ordered the mills to stop collecting the insurance fee after March 1, 1905.[49] Only a single mill, George Emerson's North Western Lumber Company, refused weavers the right to create their own hospital fund, because its management did "not believe in unions" and "will treat with the men only as individuals."[50] For management's refusal, the weavers struck and the mill was tarnished in the mainstream and labor press as "short sighted" and guilty of committing a "monthly hold up" of workers' money.[51] After a few days, management capitulated, recognizing the union and meeting their demands. ISWUA official J. G. Brown celebrated, "We anticipated something of a fight here, but won just as e-a-s-y."[52]

RED CEDAR, RED POLITICS

Hoquiam shingle weavers stood at the head of the movement to expand organized labor and the range of the union's struggles to include mobilizing politically. In the union's early years, weavers kept their union a closely guarded white men's club. But by 1905 a new movement to expand the organization promised—or threatened—to end the unions' carefully guarded craft exclusivity. It came from Hoquiam ISWUA Local 21 radicals who looked with unease at the great power corporations held over governments and their use of that power to crush unions.

Grays Harbor socialists developed a strong and active local movement, paralleling the national Socialist Party of America (SPA), which formed in 1901, growing dramatically across the nation during the first decade of the twentieth century. Socialist ideas reached wide audiences. Party activists published newspapers, ran candidates for political office, and carried out social activities including socialist concerts, speakers' series, and mass meetings. In the 1910s, *The Appeal to Reason*, a socialist weekly, had a readership of 500,000, and the combined total of all socialist newspapers and magazines was in the millions during the early 1910s.[53] In 1912, at one of the party's peaks of influence, Eugene V. Debs, SPA candidate for president, earned more than 900,000 votes—6 percent of the nation's total—while voters elected more than 1,000 SPA members to office.

A strong socialist movement and growing socialist parties existed in Washington by the turn of the twentieth century. Within three months of its founding, the Socialist Party of Washington counted thirty-nine branches, including one in Aberdeen.[54] The local SPA drew members from the left wing of the trade union movement and immigrants—particularly Finns. Most SPA members agreed that capitalism was exploitative and political action was key to any effort to challenge that system.[55] The party's program included a wide range of demands, such as ameliorative planks designed to curb the rawest features of American capitalism, notably the abolition of child labor and injunctions in labor disputes, and the establishment of a state board of health "with full power for the inspection and condemnations of all unsanitary factories, tenements, etc."[56] The 1912 Socialist Party of Washington platform stated, "Our ultimate demand is the social ownership and democratic management of all the socially used means of production and distribution."

On Grays Harbor, significant blocks of socialists hailed from the shingle weavers' union and the local Finnish community. But unlike Finnish immigrants, who faced citizenship, gender, and age obstacles to voting, the weavers were well positioned to challenge political elites. Between their fellow weavers, fraternal lodge mates, and other unionists, the "labor vote" in cities like Hoquiam and Aberdeen could be considerable. ISWUA members even ran for political office, although before 1910 they usually lost elections.[57] In 1907, one Hoquiam weaver mourned the loss by a labor mayoral candidate by only fifteen votes, finding it "strange that the laboring men can not vote as they march."[58] A rare exception was the shingle weavers' union founding president, William Ingram, who won successive terms to the Aberdeen city council, although he was a county delegate for the 1908 Republican ticket after opening his own mill. In the next decade, however, socialists briefly built a winning electoral coalition on the harbor—as they did in hundreds of localities nationwide.

Many Local 21 weavers were socialists, writing, in J. G. Brown's words, of the need for "electing to public office, men out of their own ranks who will put an end to a system of barbarity and butchery."[59] But Brown was hardly alone. In nearby Raymond, Washington, shingle weavers held a simulated election for president in 1912; Debs was the overwhelming favorite, earning thirty-three votes, over sixteen-fold more than his nearest competitor, the future president Woodrow Wilson.[60]

The 1910s witnessed the tremendous growth of Grays Harbor socialism, as its members elected Aberdeen city council members and mayors in both Aberdeen and Hoquiam that were at least moderately sympathetic to the SPA. Many SPA actions took place in Aberdeen's three-story Socialist Finn hall, headquarters of the city's several-hundred-strong Finnish-American Socialist organization. The nightly musical performances proved so raucous that that the Aberdeen city council, *Aberdeen Daily World*, and a neighborhood committee collaborated to stop the "nuisance" that was the Red Finn hall.[61] In both Aberdeen and Hoquiam, the shingle weavers stood at the fore of the radical political movement. Unfortunately for the Reds, the weavers numbered too few to make much of a dent in the entrenched local parties, while state and federal election laws prevented other socialist-friendly groups—notably many immigrants—from exercising the ballot.

WEAVING A WHITE MEN'S LABOR MOVEMENT

For all their efforts to radicalize the Northwest labor movement, the ISWUA still represented the AFL's exclusionary policies, particularly its views on race, gender, and citizenship.[62] Unions and much of their leadership embraced white supremacy. Even as socialist weavers shouted "solidarity," they advocated Asian exclusion legislation and opposed employment of Asian Americans in shingle mills. Few figures straddled this divide between labor solidarity and fragmentation so completely as J. G. Brown. By early 1903 Brown was a committed socialist and industrial unionist. He climbed the ranks of the labor union bureaucracy, serving as president of the local in Elma, Washington, in February 1903; later he served in leadership for the Hoquiam local, and by January 1904 as ISWUA delegate to the annual convention of the AFL.[63] But Brown paired political and economic radicalism with white supremacy, specifically his belief in using labor unions to protect white workers' jobs. He declared that the "Shingle Weavers' Union has come in for its full share of praise for the prompt manner in which they recognized the danger of allowing the Japs to gain a foothold here, and the very energetic and effective methods they adopted to stop it."[64] W. E. Willis, Brown's close associate, stated that the Japanese and Korean Exclusion Leagues were "a step in the right direction and should have the moral and financial support of every Union in the Northwest."[65] Brown lambasted H. E. Richardson, an Olympia shingle manufacturer, for his plan to employ Japanese laborers, which would, in Brown's view, force "white workingmen to the point where they then must compete with cheap Cooley labor."[66]

Most unions and union federations were masculine institutions. Like Grays Harbor unionists at large, the overwhelming majority of weavers and ISWUA officials were men, while the rhetoric of both leaders and rank and file was masculine, focused on shop-floor struggles and male-dominated cultural activities. Brown reported on an April 1904 "monster open meeting" or "social session" in his monthly column to the *Shingle Weaver* that "one of the largest halls in the city was secured and a grand, free, happy, enjoyable time was had. . . . The lunch was then served, together with other refreshments, and was interspersed with some racy stories by Frank Reagan, the proprietor of the pool room resort. . . . About 300 cigars were donated."[67] Those few unions that included women members did so within gendered assumptions about women's labor and political activism, portraying them as important, if secondary, members of the union. At the 1907 Labor Day parade, for instance, male members of the Aberdeen clerks' union "took their chances on foot with the rest of the boys," while "carriages and automobiles were furnished for the lady clerks."[68]

Shingle weavers embraced and embodied working-class masculinity, but given their unique positions as the sole representatives of the official labor movement from lumber—perhaps the most famously rough

Laundry Workers of Hoquiam No. 133's horse-drawn parade float carries more than twenty people, mostly women wearing white blouses. Union members regularly paraded through downtown Aberdeen, Hoquiam, and other cities on Labor Day and the Fourth of July. Polson Museum, Hoquiam, Washington.

industry—they straddled the respectable and rough categories of masculinity.[69] As working men grew older, they often sought working-class respectability through marriage, stability within a community, proficiency in a craft, and involvement with a trade union. However, weavers' work made this path difficult; shingle weavers followed their industry as it pursued the dwindling western red cedar and moved farther into the forests. During the 1910s, more mills opened in the rural periphery of the Olympic Peninsula and southwest Washington; Grays Harbor's shingle weavers' unionists followed the jobs, becoming some of the region's first rural union members.

Many weavers were longtime members of local communities. They joined fraternities, owned homes, voted, and even ran for office. According to the 1910 census, forty-four out of the eighty-one Hoquiam shingle weavers were married. Wages were high enough for some weavers to purchase their own mills. Hoquiam weavers George Murray and William Brun built and operated their own shingle mill beginning in 1907, and former Hoquiam weaver J. G. Brown purchased a shingle mill near Tacoma in 1908.[70] Brown, too, noted the importance of the insurance benefits weavers received from their fraternities—the "Eagles, and Elks, and Moose, and that sort of thing."[71] The possibilities for the shift from wage laborer to management were most obvious in the case of William Ingram, a worker who arrived on the harbor before the turn of the twentieth century and in 1902 became the founding president of Grays Harbor's shingle weavers' union.[72] A longtime harborite, Ingram joined many blue-collar workers in the most popular men's social organization, the Fraternal Order of Eagles, and served as a trustee of a Pacific War veterans' association.[73] Ingram founded and served as both manager and president of the North Aberdeen Shingle Company, a small mill with twenty employees, incorporated for $30,000 in 1907.[74]

While many weavers dug local roots, recessions, mill closures, a dwindling resource-dependent industry, and workplace injuries meant that few weavers were ever economically secure.[75] This insecurity and the job dangers they faced motivated weavers to join and become active in their unions; making their workplaces safer—including their decades-long fight to shorten the workday—lay at the center of the shingle weavers' union movement.

Some weavers lived as itinerants, laboring in several different mills and towns stretched across the Northwest. Brown, for example, worked in Cosmopolis, Aberdeen, Elma, Hoquiam, and Raymond before settling into the life of the semipermanent labor bureaucrat, while editions of the *Shingle Weaver* carried regular notices of weavers' migrations.[76] Of the eighty Hoquiam shingle weavers listed in city directories and the *Shingle Weaver* between 1903 and 1907, only nine remained in the town when the census-takers surveyed the population in 1910.[77] During October 1906, at least eight shingle weavers moved to Shelton, Washington, to work in a new mill, and unionists forced two scab weavers to leave Grays Harbor during the same month.[78]

THE VIOLENCE OF INDUSTRY

A major cause of downward social mobility among weavers—and the wider working class—was occupational injury and sickness. The United States of this era was the world's most dangerous industrial country, with tens of thousands of workers dying on the job annually and hundreds of thousands suffering debilitating injuries. Although official records tell only part of the story, it's clear that workers suffered workplace deaths and injuries with, in historian Nate Holdren's words, "appalling frequency."[79]

Compounding workers' peril was the absence of an American workers' compensation system; even "progressive" Washington State didn't pass a workers' compensation bill until 1911.[80] Moreover, when labor advocated for legislation to cover hospital costs for workplace injuries, business organizations killed that legislation, as attested to by J. G. Brown: "The members of organized labor, the direct legislation league, and others introduced a first-aid bill in the last legislature. The provisions of that bill were that the employers and the employee should each stand half of the cost of that first aid. The employers were very bitterly opposed to it, and it failed to pass. Now we have a first-aid law among these initiative measures that we are trying to get submitted to the voters."[81] A laborer who lost a hand or broke his leg on the job could sue with the help of legal representation, but that was mostly a fruitless enterprise, as employers won a big majority of injury claim suits in court; only 10 percent of litigants won their injury claims in 1910.[82]

Although industrial conditions inflicted terrible injuries on workers from many industries, lumber stood out as among the most dangerous—an industry that could kill and maim workers in nearly countless ways. Finnish American logger Max Wilson put a number on it, recalling that there were "49 different ways to get killed in the woods." During one year logging for the Aloha Corporation, he recalled, "They must have killed about five men."[83]

Few workplace safety regulations existed in the late nineteenth and early twentieth-century United States. In logging, sawmilling, and shingle manufacturing, workplaces went mostly unregulated until the Great Depression. What few laws and rules made the books had little enforcement mechanisms and were flouted by employers, who operated in spaces distant from law enforcement bodies and culturally akin to the Wild West.[84] Given the nature of lumber workplaces, it was hardly surprising that logging and lumber manufacturing killed workers with virtually no consequences during this era, most often through what were and are conveniently labeled "industrial accidents" from falling trees, unguarded saws, exploding boilers, and broken cables.

But operators added to the pain through the far less "accidental" acts of refusing to provide adequate medical treatment to injured workers, refusing to replace faulty equipment, and paying spies and thugs to conspire against or harm labor unionists.[85] J. G. Brown reported the threat posed to loggers by poorly maintained boilers: "There was one boiler explosion last year in a camp on Grays Harbor. Two or three men were killed. Men working there told me that the boiler had long been known to be absolutely past the point where a large pressure of steam was safe in it."[86] Mill worker G. W. Thomas, who lost a limb at the Grays Harbor Commercial Company in 1906, swore out an affidavit against the company describing the chaos that ensued when injured employees sought medical treatment:

> I was formerly an employee of the Grays Harbor Commercial Co. at Cosmopolis, Wash. On the 29th day of July 1906, between the hours of 7 and 8 p.m. I happened to pass by the corner of F and First streets on my way from the doctor's office to church; I was then suffering from the loss of a limb an injury received in the mill of the said Company. A number of persons who had received injuries had collected on said corner. By actual count there were nineteen (19) injured and crippled persons collected on the said corner; that every one of these persons had received his injuries at the mill of said Company.[87]

The hospital Thomas referenced was, like many services in Cosmopolis, controlled by the Grays Harbor Commercial Company. The hospital staff was badly overtaxed by the number of "injured and crippled" workers, such as the "fourteen boys at one time on the streets at Cosmopolis, all crippled in the box factory."[88]

Workplace injuries and deaths were a grim reality in the lives of workers in lumber country. During the first three decades of the twentieth century, loggers died at a higher rate than in any other job on the Pacific Coast—five times as many workers died in lumber as in any other Washington State industry.[89] Con Murray perished in a "frightful manner" after a "sudden increase of speed on cable" trapped him between a swinging log and a tree trunk. Murray's death affected his fellow workers who observed the logs "crushing the heart and intestines," as the logger cried out "My God! I'm killed!"[90] Deaths such as Murray's were not inevitable but the product of specific technological innovations, long hours, highball logging, massive firms, and foremen and employers motivated only by higher production quotas. "As they are too fatigued by the hard and rigorous work of the woods to be alert," argued journalist Charlotte Todes, "and as they are being speeded up at a rate which makes it impossible for them to think of personal safety, accidents will continue to mount."[91] Local reporters gained significant experience describing workers' injuries and deaths, adding flair to their writing. In April 1913, the *Washingtonian* detailed the deaths of two loggers: "The tree held until the donkey was almost in place, but, when the donkey was being swung a little sideways the hemlock was uprooted and fell upon the crew. The skulls of Kerr and Crockett were crushed and their bodies severely bruised."[92]

Lumber workers knew they faced peril in the woods. In March 1914, the *Washingtonian* detailed "A Peculiar Accident" that ended logger Paul Everson's life: "He was struck on the head by a piece of stump hurled through the air by a sudden strain of the donkey engine, which was pulling on it with a cable. The blow knocked the man down and he fell upon a pointed root. Everson complained of severe pains in the stomach and died four hours after being removed to the camp."[93] Lumber worker and IWW organizer James P. Thompson assigned cause and effect for the deadly industry in his article "Murder in Lumber Industry." He laid blame for these so-called accidents to the capitalist drive to intensify production: "Speeding-up kills and injures more than all else."[94]

Like loggers, sawmill laborers worked ten hours per day as a rule in treacherous conditions for low wages. The men who worked these jobs were in constant danger from spinning saws, falling lumber, and sawdust filling their lungs. Lumber manufacturing was, after logging, the most dangerous occupation in the Northwest. Anvit Sidiy, a Greek American mill hand, lost his life when an edger man at the mill "placed a board in position, which caught in the saw, and was hurled over the saws, a distance of forty feet, striking the unfortunate man in the abdomen."[95]

These violent episodes told only part of the work-life stories of those who labored in Northwest lumber. Another threat came from what is often called slow violence, which "occurs gradually and out of sight . . . an attritional violence that is typically not viewed as violence at all."[96] Historian Erik Loomis analyzed many types of slow violence of the lumber industry, detailing the occupational hazards common to logging camps and lumber and shingle mills. For example, although many men died in the manufacture of shingles, it was workers' limbs that experienced most of the serious injuries. A longer-term threat came to the weavers' lungs, which were ravaged by the sawdust-filled air that caused cedar asthma, a respiratory disease common to shingle mill workers.[97] A journalist who observed shingle manufacturing reported, "Hour after hour the steel sings its crescendo note as it bites into the wood, the sawdust cloud thickens, the wet sponge under the sawyer's nose fills with fine particles. If 'cedar asthma,' the shingle weavers' occupation disease, does not get him, the steel will."[98] During a single month in 1907, six Hoquiam weavers received serious cuts from the saws, and local union president J. H. Cramer was forced to retire from the mills because of a respiratory ailment.[99] A 1918 Washington State Bureau of Labor study of health conditions of 297 shingle mill employees found more than one-quarter (79) of the men suffering from "continuous attacks of asthma," with another 21 workers "affected to a slighter degree." Elizabeth J. Davies, the nurse responsible for this report, issued several recommendations to improve shingle weavers' health, including "the elimination of hazard by accident thru the abolishment of piece work and speeding up."[100]

WEAVING MANLINESS

Like loggers, rural shingle weavers developed work-life practices that distinguished them from urban workers. Their "laborlore," folklorist Archie Green's term for workers' cultural practices and work traditions, differed dramatically from their urban counterparts.[101] And like other migratory unionists in industries across the country, rural weavers helped spread unionism. Specifically, weavers helped unionize the logging camps of the Olympic Peninsula and southwest Washington.

Weavers filled union newspapers with boasts of their physical attributes and abilities, while observers used martial terms to describe weavers' job—one prominent radical lumber worker declared that "shingle weaving is not a trade; it is a battle," while weavers' unionists framed their efforts at shorter hours and safer conditions as making "the lumber industry safe for democracy."[102] During strikes, unionists appealed to their fellow workers' manhood: "Don't listen to knockers, pessimists and paid spies. Be men. Stay in the fight. . . . We can cultivate the acquaintance and companionship of loyal union men in other industries and thus cement the bonds of brotherhood and fraternity among all classes of workers."[103] Aberdeen's *Shingle Weaver* correspondent Si Gotchy wrote in a downright seditious manner just after the US entered World War I, suggesting he might capture "a pair of wooden shoes . . . at the front," an unmistakable reference to sabotage that few 1910s lumber workers would have missed.[104]

Like many workers, weavers took tremendous pride in their speed and skill, maneuvering thinly sliced pieces of cedar at a pace so fast the eyes could barely follow. Paid by the piece, weavers had incentives to race at work, and both union and employers' association periodicals carried news of unofficial production records, including the May 1904 incredible feat where one unnamed weaver produced 91,000 shingles in ten hours.[105]

The weavers took note of their more tangible masculine abilities, notably their physical prowess. Grays Harbor's ISWUA locals enrolled amateur and former professional boxers, including Jack Parees, a former boxing champion from Wisconsin.[106] Fighting exhibitions proved great sport for their fellow workers, as they held boxing matches with proceeds going to union funds; the boxers too served in times of crisis, as these "homely

. . . bunch of pugs" were usually on the front of the picket lines to provide unfriendly greetings to scabs.[107] Indeed, few occasions activated masculine displays as did strikes, particularly when employers brought in strikebreakers and scabs to harm the union's cause—and take food from the union family's mouths. Employers, whose own masculine virtues were so often called into question by unionists, sometimes hired former boxers, wrestlers, and football players to serve as strikebreakers.[108] Hired toughs battled against the working-class men, who defied the dangers of the industrial workplace, during strikes.

For unions, having brawlers like Parees among their members to even the score with hired ruffians held real value. Union men encouraged one another to engage in physical combat with class enemies.[109] Unionists dealt out beatings and verbal harangues to strikebreakers; scabs' homes were sometimes unsafe places during strikes, with angry unionists bent on retaliation.[110] Unionists published scabs' names in the local and regional labor press, and when someone crossed a picket line, unionists communicated their name far and wide.[111] After Jent Butler scabbed during a 1906 strike, the *Shingle Weaver* responded, "Butler is absolutely devoid of even a shadow of principle, simply a slimy, crawling, unclean thing that is an eyesore to decent people everywhere. A traitor is, and should be, ever regarded with suspicion and treated with contempt."[112] When the "Carlisle Co. tried to land a crew from up the sound," noted Aberdeen ISWUA official M. P. Corbett, "some of us boarded the train that they were on at Aberdeen, by the time we got to Hoquiam, we convinced the boys that they were making a mistake, so they left the train, and the next day went back up the country."[113]

The personification of the weavers' rough manliness came in the form of Wormholes, an itinerant shingle weaver living in Grays Harbor during the 1910s. "Wormholes" was the nom de plume of Si Gotchy, itinerant shingle weaver, socialist, union official, pugilist, and frequent correspondent to the *Shingle Weaver*.[114] Wormholes was a prolific writer whose material ranged from news of shutdowns and strikes to agitating for the eight-hour day, to advertising his boxing matches, which he held partly to fund the local union treasury.[115] According to author Ralph Warren Andrews, Gotchy at one point held the "shingle mill championship" in boxing and he certainly attracted large audiences. In July 1916, he shared a boxing card with Billy Weeke, a champion boxer out of Canada.[116] Responding to the workers' successes at nearby Raymond, Gotchy claimed that all the men remained off the job, while only children and miscreants agreed to work: "Only two mills have had the gall to try and start. One of them has 24 scabs and the other, which normally has a force of 220, has only 50, including boys, cripples, degenerates and office crew."[117] On occasion, shingle weavers developed a penchant for growing beards, boasting over their "most luxurious growth of alfalfa."[118] Weavers basked in their unkempt appearance, a conscious rejection of the common urbane styles of collared shirt, tie, hat, and clean-shaven face. Gotchy, never shy about creatively boasting of his appearance or actions, opined that his "bazoo was adorned with the brush-broom style" beard.[119]

BARRING THE GATES

Few union tools proved as valuable as their press; writers in the *Shingle Weaver* and other media provided rich descriptions of working-class life. Labor media promoted unions, provided a rare lens into working-class politics and cultural institutions not rooted in condescension, and advertised the names of scabs to harass and unfriendly businesses to boycott. Critically, they sometimes challenged dominant narratives about American capitalism and mocked employers for their greed and depravity.

Labor journalists also intervened to stifle labor migration—both internal and international. For examples, labor reporters publicized strikes and ran "Keep Away" headlines to inform job-hunters about strikes, providing warning to not be lured by job advertisements.[120] Launched in 1904 by union official J. W. Clarke, and supported by the local labor movement, the *Grays Harbor Post* was among the most-popular periodicals in the early twentieth-century Northwest.[121] One of Clarke's main priorities was monitoring employment agencies; he ran an investigation into the Grays Harbor Commercial Company (GHCC) and the agencies that supplied it with workers. Labor newspapers advocated for ending the most exploitative of the agents' practices, including the notorious "job shark" method of procuring employment. These "sharks" sold jobs to prospective GHCC employees who were then shipped by rail to Cosmopolis, Washington. Misleading potential workers into paying for jobs that did not exist was, according to labor activists, not unusual. In 1914, the *Labor Journal* of Everett, Washington, one of the state's largest union periodicals, published a front-page cartoon illustrating agents' corrupt practices: selling jobs, rail transportation to those jobs, and purchasing room and board from the company hotel and store—followed by eviction from town by the boss.[122]

Cosmopolis even ended up on the radar of national political figures. During the 1914 US Commission on Industrial Relations, witnesses were questioned about the GHCC's practices. One of the commission's major takeaways from its investigation into the Northwest's lumber industry was a trove of evidence documenting abuses ranging from low pay to theft to fraudulent sale of jobs in the lumber industry—particularly by the GHCC. Cosmopolis resident Rudolph Distler testified, "When those men are sent by employment agencies—that is the greatest injustice ever practiced on labor," and reported on workers paying for nonexistent jobs and the practice of railroad companies holding onto workers' luggage to keep the defrauded workers from leaving town. Distler continued, "The railroad company keeps the baggage in their baggage room. If a man wants to take out his working clothes, he must leave his other clothes he wears in that baggage room."[123]

Much of labor's opposition to labor migration—both domestic and international—rested on genuine concern over exploitative workplace conditions. But immigration opponents also attacked the potential newcomers based on what they viewed as the undesirable characteristics of the migrants. Labor journalists helped lead the charge, condemning the "importation" of Asian and southern European laborers; the term "Greek Invasion" appeared in the trade union paper's pages.[124] Reveling in its status as a voice for white labor, in 1904 the *Grays Harbor Post* advocated a cross-class alliance of white locals to solve what it saw as the problem of "importation of Greek or Jap labor," asking, "Would but this be a good live question for discussion by the Chamber of Commerce?"[125]

The *Grays Harbor Post* joined other union voices in condemning padrones, a type of labor agent who brokered immigrant workers. Throughout North America, padrones established themselves as transnational agents who connected immigrant workers with employment opportunities. Attacks against the padrone system played on stereotypes of immigrants' essentialized characteristics, particularly those from southern Europe. Unionists used racist caricatures of Greek immigrants as reasons to discriminate against them. By 1910, approximately five hundred Greek men—and no Greek women—worked in Grays Harbor's mills and railroad camps.[126] Many arrived by way of California, where a padrone with Grays Harbor connections operated. In a lengthy front-page attack on the agency and on Greek immigrants more broadly, the *Grays Harbor Post* condemned G. Karonis, a Greek man who lived in Aberdeen, where he ran "an employment agency of his own. It appears that he imports his brethren and secures three dollars from each man he finds a place for." The *Post* had plenty of blame to spread around. It condemned "certain foremen of large mills" who, it alleged, received kickbacks for each Greek laborer given employment." In December 1904, Karonis asserted that fifty new Greek workers would soon arrive via Fresno, California, to work on the harbor.[127]

Attacks on southern European and Asian workers likewise represented immigration opponents' gendered perspectives. Union leaders, politicians, and reporters portrayed immigrants as, at best, young men who cared little for family or community and often as sexual deviants or violent miscreants. Southern European immigration shared another feature with that of its Asian counterpart: the lack of women, whether prohibited by law or custom, prompted native-born white residents to make racialized and gendered commentary about Chinese, Greek, South Asian, and Japanese immigrants. Police, journalists, and union leaders criticized race and ethnic mixing. In particular, they expressed concerns about the supposed cultural threats posed by immigrants' vices, including prostitution and drugs, and the corruption of children, especially young girls, by racialized immigrant workers.[128] A direct assault on Greek workers came in 1908, when a murder investigation of Clarence Poppas "brought out some revolting information concerning the Greek colony in East Aberdeen that will probably result in the strict police surveillance of those concerned, and it is possible that those to whom the testimony pointed will be ordered to leave the city." The *Aberdeen Herald*, a leading nativist voice, warned parents of the Greek threat: "The character of the crimes committed prevent their publication in a family newspaper, but it is such that every parent whose children come in contact with this bunch of degenerates should be advised."[129]

Unionists used similar rhetorical attacks on Greek and Japanese workers. The *Post* editorialized, "There are employers here as short sighted or selfish as those of Cosmopolis. They may favor the importation of Greek or Jap labor but public sentiment and the opinion of other manufacturers will not lend them aid or assistance."[130] Much of the press depicted Greeks as outsiders—single transients who contributed little to local communities. To sway public opinion against Greeks, in 1904 the *Grays Harbor Post* thanked employers who refused to hire Greek men, who, the newspaper claimed, cared neither for family nor community.[131] Those same newspapers sometimes fanned the flames of ethnic hatred in hopes of inciting anti-immigrant action. In 1907, the *Grays Harbor Post* more than hinted that its union readers should oppose Greeks from settling on the harbor: "Hoquiam has an invasion of Greek laborers. Aberdeen had one three years ago. A goodly amount of the right kind of publicity prevented the epidemic here. It will work at Hoquiam."[132]

J. G. BROWN AND THE PARADOX OF INDUSTRIAL UNIONISM

J. G. Brown closely studied the labor movement. What he found distressed the unionist, as he experienced in real time the power in the hands of coordinated capital. Few conflicts so decisively proved this point as did the Colorado "labor wars" of 1903–4. There, observed Brown, state and capital unified to defeat the Western Federation of Miners at Cripple Creek in the most brutal manner possible. For the shingle weavers, as for unionists nationwide, the Colorado conflicts had decisive ideological impacts, not unlike the effects of Chicago's 1886 Haymarket Affair, the 1912 Bread and Roses Strike in Lawrence, Massachusetts, or the 1914 Ludlow Massacre of striking miners in Colorado. At Cripple Creek, employers and police arrested, evicted from town, and assassinated strikers and their allies. One Hoquiam shingle weaver argued that "the treatment accorded union men in Colorado would make the cruelest Russian czar seem but an apprentice at despotism."[133] Grays Harbor weavers joined unionists across the country in pledging money and manpower, holding fund-raisers for the mine workers, and writing articles to inform the public of their cause.[134] To many Northwest weavers, the lessons of Cripple Creek and elsewhere rang clear for what they said about the need for greater working-class solidarity, a friendly government that wouldn't break strikes, and a self-activated union membership who kept "the power close to the rank and file."[135]

A rising star within the Northwest labor movement, Brown contended that the ISWUA must organize industrially before Pacific Northwest lumbermen followed the mine owners' path to destroy labor. Indeed, with Pacific Northwest employers arrayed "in a belligerent attitude against labor unions" and asserting "the 'divine rights' of employers to employ whomever they choose, regardless of their connection with societies or organizations," weavers needed to organize beyond their ranks to stave off their impending defeat.[136] In 1905 Brown joined fellow ISWUA radicals in proposing that the weavers organize an industrial union in lumber and in supporting a socialist political program.[137]

Brown and his allies faced stiff resistance from fellow unionists. Conservatives criticized industrial unionism—which opens unions to all wage laborers in a given industry—claiming that industrial unionism deprived "craftsmen" of their exclusive status. One critic attacking industrial unionism wrote that "the open union means a harbor for all classes of scabs, such as was afforded by the Knights of Labor."[138] Building industrial unions, according to one of Brown's critics, meant he wanted to "organize the Japs," using racist fear-mongering to build opposition to more inclusive unionism.[139] Opponents expressed outrage at Brown's proposal favoring industrial unionism that appeared to dilute their craft, refusing to "tolerate the disruption of trades unionism from within." Comparing Brown's plans to the radical sentiments issued from Chicago at the opening convention of the IWW, several weavers lashed out at the message and its messenger. J. E. Campbell, secretary-treasurer of the ISWUA, compared ISWUA radicals to the upstart IWW, arguing, "Brown's deluded following is a child of this nefarious scheme."[140]

ISWUA support for industrial unionism and socialism did not equate to support for interracial and women's-led unions. Some weavers who promoted socialism and industrial unionism were overt male chauvinists and committed nativists. And while industrial unionism is potentially less amenable to white supremacy and patriarchy than craft unionism, it was clear that unhinging the power of supremacy and patriarchy was not a priority for the radicals.[141] For instance, while advocating industrial unionism, Brown complained that local employers "may fill our places with Chinamen or Japs."[142] To these radicals, the ideal form of industrial unionism was one that struggled against capitalism by uniting white workers; challenging oppression in all its forms was peripheral at best, undesirable at worst.

The weavers thus simultaneously challenged the narrow, restrictive boundaries of AFL craft unionism through their advocacy of socialism and industrial unionism and undermined those views with an inability and unwillingness to adhere to a more inclusive type of unionism in practice. The fragmentation of the working class, as practiced by AFL unions, hindered the development of united workers' movements.

EXPANDING THE MOVEMENT

The year 1906 proved critical in Northwest union development as several of the region's most militant unions waged regional strikes. Notably, on Grays Harbor, the longshoremen aided the Sailors Union of the Pacific in a coastwise strike that closed down the great Pacific ports. Maritime unionists' solidarity proved decisive, and by autumn they had won a critical battle against the shipping companies.[143] On the other hand, 1906 also witnessed the shingle weavers' unions suffer a decisive defeat, as unified capital—including several Grays Harbor owners—defeated the militant weavers. One notable outcome of the ISWUA strike was that it radicalized much of the ISWUA's membership. Where J. G. Brown had once been too radical, he now had supporters who recalled his earlier prediction of capital's mission to "strike a crushing blow to organized labor." Where previously Brown had been attacked in verse, now his defenders turned to rhyme. Weaver C. T. Freese supported Brown and his politics:

Brown is a man we know that we can
Rely on his ability.
If elected to office by laws will abide,
And in J. G. Brown we all can confide.[144]

Lining up beside Brown were militant ISWUA branches, including those in Bellingham, Washington, and Brown's Hoquiam Local 21, which each rebelled against the international union, expanding their ranks to include all shingle mill laborers, including ostensibly unskilled mill hands. They thus became de facto industrial unions (for shingle manufacturing—not the entire lumber industry) and consequently grew into the ISWUA's largest branches.[145]

In 1907 ISWUA members elected Brown as international president. His years-long fight with other weavers over issues of industrial unionism and socialist politics had paid dividends; the victory placed him at the head of the only international union based in Washington State and gave him a platform to advocate for socialist politics and industrial unionism. Months earlier, in one of his last "Hoquiam" articles to the *Shingle Weaver*, Brown predicted great things to come for a united, radicalized working class:

> Individual craft organizations are no longer able, except under very unusual circumstances, to cope with the growing power of organized capital; and union men everywhere are becoming alive to this fact which each industrial conflict brings home to them with added force. One thing capitalists generally ought to keep in sight is that while they are booming trusts, combines, syndicates and mergers, the wheels of the car of progress are not chained in the other avenues of human activity. . . . The tendency of bringing the workers closer together and the general awakening to the need of united political action has been brought about by the tyranny of the heads of great industrial institutions on the one hand and the very partisan way in which the ruling class has been lashing the struggling workers with [the] whip of governmental power on the other. . . . Therein is room for vast possibilities.[146]

The "vast possibilities" Brown referenced meant building militant industrial unions capable of challenging the Northwest's most powerful group: the lumber barons.

Unrepresented by the official trade union movement, racialized, immigrant, women, and rural laborers shaped their class experiences and responded to union exclusion by forming their own institutions or joining radical movements capable of fighting for their class interests. Although a labor stronghold, Grays Harbor remained mostly nonunion with thousands of laborers left unorganized. The area's unionists, their elected union officials, and the wider movement all bore marks of white supremacy, male chauvinism, and the virility of the male leadership of the movement. The unions were at once working-class institutions designed to win gains for their members and white men's protective associations devised to preserve a monopoly over relatively good wage-earning jobs for their members. Pragmatically, too, the labor movement's exclusionism hindered them in their struggles with the bosses, dividing unions between those who supported more inclusive forms of unionism and those who adhered to the principles of craft unionism—leading to the labor radicals' well-known denigration of the AFL as the "American Separation of Labor." The following chapters analyze the harbor's diverse working-class movements as they expressed discontent and built a multilingual labor movement, pushing beyond the "Separation of Labor" into institutions and movements more reflective of the working class.

3

"AS ONE MAN"

EMPLOYER SOLIDARITY

Lumbermen were rabid anti-unionists. They declared their commitment to "open-shop" principles—a sharply effective euphemism relying on the language of liberty to mask the reality that open shop meant unorganized workers with little power to protect themselves—formed clubs to turn those principles into action, and waged war on workers who threatened their control over workplace and community. Despite their intention to eliminate unions from Grays Harbor, in the early years of the twentieth century the region's merchants and manufacturers lacked strikebreaking experience. As proven by the union successes from 1902 to 1906, local employers, without a concerted movement, could not contend with local unionists who affiliated with international unions, wielded strike funds, and enjoyed some successes with the use of the boycott and labor press. The growth of the harbor's early labor movement bears out this point, as dozens of unions represented workers in Aberdeen and Hoquiam.[1]

Most local employers coveted the open shop; making Grays Harbor an open-shop bastion, though, took significant resources. Few business owners had the money or power to bust unions on their own. To succeed they needed to form what historian Vilja Hulden calls "bosses' unions."[2] This chapter describes the early history of the employing class of Grays Harbor as they organized and institutionalized their anti-union campaigns.

Northwest employers had plenty of anti-union role models to follow across the country. By the turn of the twentieth century, employers and their allies had used all manner of tactics to weaken, if not destroy, the labor movement—from deploying federal troops and police to break strikes to spying on and blacklisting unionists. They coordinated much of the anti-union campaigns through institutions that could pool resources in defense of capital; employers formed citizens' alliances, the National Association of Manufacturers, and trade associations to defend their interests, which often meant fighting unions. The key object of organized employers was the open shop, and led by a group of open-shop militants, Grays Harbor employers waged similar struggles so that by 1910, several businesses were "open" and employers explicitly discussed the value of open shops. In 1914, union president J. G. Brown described lumber employers' antipathy toward unions: "I have never yet met a man who in the logging and sawmill branches of the industry expressed a willingness to see his men organized in any kind of union."[3]

Notably, though, Grays Harbor employers tolerated some unions, specifically those with conservative, class-collaborationist programs. Many of these unions represented service-sector workers—clerks, typographers, bartenders—at small businesses with a local working-class customer base. The *Aberdeen Herald*, which maligned strikes and radicals, ran lengthy front-page descriptions of the harbor's annual Labor Day festivities. "Labor Organizations Do Themselves Proud. 500 In Line" read one such headline.[4] Likewise, many businesses ran ads in the *Grays Harbor Post*, the local labor newspaper, which became the county's official paper as early as 1905, surely a sign of the cozy relationship between "respectable" labor and the region's political leaders.[5]

But employers had different views of unions in the region's dominant industry—lumber. Lumber reigned supreme as the Northwest's prime industry for several decades after Washington became a state in 1889; cutting, processing, and transporting forest products was long the main source of jobs and wealth in the country's northwest corner. Whereas managers sometimes tolerated unions in local industries owned by small businessmen with a handful of employees, they bristled at even a hint of unionism in mills and camps.

The tactics of anti-unionism were a well-known part of American employers' tool kits by the time Grays Harbor employers began organizing in haste around the turn of the twentieth century. Central to any anti-union project was the elimination of activists, chiefly radicals: those who successfully challenged management's rights to rule over the workplace.[6]

Employers and their allies in the state and press pursued this goal in diverse ways: terminating the most active unionists, arresting and prosecuting their leaders, intimidating them through violence or threats of violence, and disparaging them in the press. To better understand anti-union movements, historian Chad Pearson classifies three significant categories of union busters: the terrorists, the enablers, and the narrative-creators, the latter including authors, journalists, and religious leaders, those who "raised the status of elites while stigmatizing disobedient ordinary people."[7]

On the harbor, employer solidarity left its fingerprints on virtually every step of the region's history. Lumbermen used their collective power to achieve everything from influencing public policy to breaking unions—sometimes breaking unionists' skulls. Unfortunately, despite the massive body of evidence testifying to lumber manufacturers' collectivist practices, scholars of the Pacific Northwest lumber industry have spent nearly a century variously extolling and condemning the extreme individualism of the vaunted lumberman. Indeed, from boosters and propagandists to popular historians and seasoned academics, scholars writing from many points on the political spectrum have portrayed lumber employers as bastions of individualism, men who competed against each other in the "cut-throat struggle" of western capitalism.[8] This view suggests that lumbermen were individualistic actors who failed to unite around class to pursue common aims.

This chapter challenges the well-known narratives of Northwest lumber history, rooted in the actions of individual entrepreneurs who overcame great odds to carve out wealth and power for themselves. The myth of employers as "self-made men" is widespread in US history, nowhere more than in the rugged lumber industry. Those narratives ultimately rely on the stories employers told about themselves and their achievements and that, unsurprisingly, reached the public through friendly media and later through uncritical historical accounts.

A RULING-CLASS IDENTITY

Across Grays Harbor, wealth carried with it power, but whether in the company town of Cosmopolis, with its "monarchy," or in the industrial cities of Aberdeen and Hoquiam, in the years around the turn of the twentieth century, employers forged solidarity through collective action. Employing-class solidarity did not spring up automatically, created solely by employers' shared relationship with the means of production. Instead, merchants and manufacturers reinforced class bonds through connections of kinship, fraternity, race, gender, and community.

Beginning as early as the 1880s, the harbor's wealthiest settlers had established themselves in lumber, shingle, canning, and other industries. Early employers met at family and religious get-togethers, fraternal gatherings, and local government and commercial club meetings. They lived in the same neighborhoods, worshipped together at a few churches, and (mostly) voted as one—in the Republican Party, its policies reinforced by a Young Men's Republican Club that tapped into elites' youthful energies.[9] Unlike the workers employed in lumber, most local employers hailed from homogenous backgrounds and took great pride in their "Nordic" stock and 100 percent Americanness. For the most part, these white men spoke and read English—much the same as their favored politicians and newsmen. The harbor's lumbermen joined many of their western Washington comrades in advocating for the Republican Party and sometimes used threats of mill shutdowns to coerce employees into voting for the GOP.[10]

These men, too, gathered to discuss freight and log prices, coordinate mill closures, and fraternize with men whose interests and experiences mirrored their own. They formed "business men's protective" clubs and chambers of commerce as early as 1891, which, in their own words, were replicas of trade unions, in that they sought to "work together for the accomplishment of any purpose."[11] The Aberdeen Chamber of Commerce organized in February 1892 with fifty-seven individuals and firms signing the constitution and bylaws.[12] Trade groups also brought lumbermen together for political ends. In 1896, leading Grays Harbor companies signed onto a circular urging "the Loggers and Lumbermen of the State of Washington" to oppose the "Free Silver Experiment," a reference to the policy advocating the unlimited coinage of silver promoted by Populists and incorporated into the Democratic Party platform that year. The circular urged cross-class collaboration: "The interest of employer and employee are absolutely identical in this matter," because in the owners' view "it cannot but result in a disastrous calamity, and our business be forced into the greatest financial convulsion this country or the world has ever known."[13] Throughout the 1890s these organizations hosted events where employers and their families could socialize, sponsored fairs and parades to promote regional commerce, and lobbied legislative bodies for probusiness laws.[14]

Harbor lumbermen and bankers also formed and joined trade groups to advocate for and defend their interests. On this matter, lumbermen resembled bosses across the country who joined the National Association of Manufacturers, local citizens' alliances, and scores of regional and trade-specific groups. Dozens of local lumbermen belonged to the Pacific Coast Lumber Manufacturers' Association, Southwest Washington Lumbermen's Association, Interstate Red Cedar Shingle Association, Grays Harbor Loggers' Association, Grays Harbor Lumber Manufacturers' Association, Log Shippers' Association, and many others. These organizations fixed prices and regulated production and sales. According to the articles of incorporation for the Grays Harbor Loggers' Association, its purpose was "establishing and maintaining better and more familiar business relationships between loggers in Chehalis County and consumers of logs."[15] And "familiar business relationships" were exactly what harbor employers formed. They jointly owned and operated several mill companies, logging camps, savings and loan associations, and railroad companies.[16] Lumbermen also coordinated annual and semiannual mill shutdowns, which tossed thousands of lumber workers out of work for unpredictable stretches of time.[17] In January 1904, Washington's shingle manufacturers declared a statewide shutdown of shingle mills, then met and announced a general 10 percent wage cut throughout the industry.[18] Explaining the close-knit relationships among employers, Thorpe Babcock, a Grays Harbor lumberman and officer in the Pacific Coast Lumber Manufacturers' Association, wrote of the "delightful camaraderie among the managers and owners of the lumber companies on the harbor. We lunched at the country club, played golf together, and met under varying circumstances—business and social."[19]

Many of the businessmen who led open-shop offensives were themselves the second generation of Aberdeen and Hoquiam elites, owing their status to their privileged birth. This group included E. B. Benn, real estate magnate and Aberdeen mayor from 1909 to 1911; J. M. Weatherwax, town mayor and head of the Aberdeen Lumber and Shingle Company; Watson A. West, secretary, treasurer, and manager of his father's A. J. West Lumber Company at the age of twenty-two; and the children of lumberman George H. Emerson.[20] Following his education at Stanford University, Ralph Emerson returned to the harbor, where his father George bestowed him with the presidency and ownership of the Aloha Lumber Company, which operated the company town of Aloha, Washington, as well as its production facilities and surrounding timberlands.[21] Other employers owed their material success to "marrying up," wedding into a family that had already established its wealth and prestige. This was the "bootstraps" path of self-proclaimed self-made men like William J. Patterson, a cashier at the Hayes and Hayes Bank in Aberdeen. After marrying Frances B. Hayes, widow of bank manager Harry A. Hayes, William became the wealthiest man in Aberdeen.[22] As one historian correctly asserted, "On Grays Harbor, lumber, wealth, and power were synonymous."[23]

Family ties mattered as class interest coincided with kin, but on a day-to-day basis, few things tied employers together like their participation in fraternities.[24] Fraternal associations welded together a community of mutually interested men who met, dined, drank, and played together. In these groups, employers met their need for masculine bonding and companionship in an all-male world separate from both the domestic sphere and the workplace. Grays Harbor employers were vigorous joiners. Most belonged to more than one fraternal order; John Lindstrom, Aberdeen mayor from 1905 to 1906 and head of the Lindstrom Shipbuilding Company, who belonged to the Masons, Woodsmen, Redmen, Foresters, Hoo-Hoos, and Elks, was hardly unusual.[25] Frank H. Lamb, founding member of the Grays Harbor Logger's Association, even published a book entitled *Rotary: A Businessman's Interpretation*, in which he argued that "business is both the Alpha and Omega of Rotary, and any activity that does not concern business or which does not help business men to translate Rotary's ideals into service should have no place in a Rotary program."[26]

On the harbor, class influenced one's fraternal associations. Few fraternal bodies embodied the virility, elitism, and sense of community leadership better than the Benevolent Protective Order of Elks and the Concatenated Order of Hoo-Hoos. Owners and managers made up the membership in both organizations—and employers made business decisions collectively at these groups' meetings.

Membership in the Hoo-Hoos, a secret order specifically for lumbermen, mostly overlapped with the Elks. A secretive all-male society, the Hoo-Hoos founded their organization as an outlet for "the playful proclivities of lumbermen and those associated with the industry."[27] New recruits in the fraternity were labeled "kittens" by more senior "snarks."[28] Harbor lumbermen gained prominence in the Hoo-Hoos, a fact that enabled locals to host meetings, participate in rituals, and forge business relationships with lumbermen near and far.[29] Grays Harbor hosted Hoo-Hoo gatherings for visiting dignitaries from the lumber trust. At a regional Hoo-Hoo gathering in 1913, 150 members arrived by train and were met "by a strong committee of local Black Cats," who later showed the visitors "the big saw mills on Grays Harbor by the local Hoo Hoo."[30] But the Hoo-Hoos, like the Elks, was more than a social club; it also served as an expression of employing-class unity. Both groups provided spaces where businessmen could come together and vocalize complaints about their workers, complaints that, as often as not, they found they shared with one another. During strikes, the Elks club hosted employers' meetings where they discussed strategy and formed union-busting organizations.[31]

At the core of employers' ideologies were overlapping commitments to the sacrosanct nature of property rights and to Social Darwinism—hierarchical worldviews that deemed that those at the top of society were the most deserving. Employers justified their power and fortunes using Social Darwinism; workers, on the other hand, had lost that social struggle. Testimony before the 1914 US Commission on Industrial Relations of two of the most powerful and infamous Grays Harbor lumbermen, Neil Cooney of Cosmopolis and W. B. Mack of Aberdeen, provided a useful window into their beliefs. Asked whether sawmill workers could "live in an American manner" given the low wages paid at the mill, Cooney blamed workers for their failure to climb socially, asserting they could advance if only they "would hold their jobs better, and would save their money."[32] Boasting of his own rags-to-riches story, and claiming that workers "haven't the same capacity" as he had, Cooney concluded that a man of his capacity did not need unions: "I came to this country from Canada right off of the farm thirty-four years ago a common laborer, built myself up to the position I have, and had no education."[33] Lumbermen passed these views on to subsequent generations of their kin; articulating his pride in the "egalitarianism" of American capitalism, J. M. Weatherwax, whose wealth and prestige was inherited from his father, mill owner John M. Weatherwax, argued, "It is becoming increasingly evident that the destiny of the sawmill interest of the Northwest is to be a survival of the fittest and only by exercising the greatest economies of operation and the utmost efficiency can any unit of the industry hope to survive."[34]

These views were common among Northwest lumbermen. However, it was in struggles with workers when employers clung most tenaciously to the narrative that their success came from individual talents and determination. Thus, lumbermen demanded the open shop, asserting that it enabled workers to exercise the same independent spirit that animated their own actions. During his testimony, Cooney continued that his mill "has never been taken" by a strike. When asked by a commissioner, "How is [it] that" a strike had never succeeded at the Cosmopolis mill, Cooney claimed credit: "All the time I have been there I have run the place."[35] W. B. Mack concluded that only weak or inferior men needed unions: "Well, if he is of less than ordinary ability, I think that perhaps unionism might perhaps assist him. But if he is of ordinary ability or above it I think that it is a handicap to him."[36]

Cooney and Mack were hardly alone among employers in stating that unions transformed workers into weak, infantile individuals dependent on others for their survival. One boss logger opined that workers had become pampered, suggesting that only whiners were "susceptible to the radical IWW who were crying about everything, and nothing pleased him."[37] Edwin G. Ames, one of the Northwest's major lumbermen, mocked loggers' fragility, stating they "all want rooms with a bath, and Waldorf-Astoria fare."[38]

It's possible that at some level, employers like Mack and Cooney understood the hypocrisy and self-serving nature of this narrative, for when wage laborers entered into contracts as individuals, as their employers insisted, they were on an uneven playing field where employers had not only the judges, police, and financial resources on their side, but also the assistance of fellow capitalists who joined with one another to lower wages, shut down plants, and break unions.[39] Indeed, for every courageous act of individualism made by lumber manufacturers, from relocating to an area previously uncharted by industry to bucking the system by refusing to abide by lumber price controls, there were scores of meetings of chambers of commerce and the Hoo-Hoos, which in lumber country were all collective projects by and for capital.[40]

DIVIDE AND CONQUER

Climbing society's ladders—or being born on the top rung—was one thing; maintaining that position was another. Lumbermen and their allies developed cunning approaches to defeat challenges. Employers certainly recognized the truth of the phrase "strength in numbers" and hence sought to individualize their opponents: to keep workers divided and thus easily controlled. Managers made racial appeals to white—especially native-born white—laborers to divide the lumber workforce. Probusiness reporters highlighted perceived racial, ethnic, and religious differences among populations; for example, newspapers frequently published headlines decrying the criminal activities of working-class persons of color and southern Europeans, condemning the presence in town of "a Chinaman," "Japs," "Hindoos," and "dagos."[41] A more subtle approach came from newsmen who referred to—and warned against—actions of groups of immigrants, referring to people by their ethnicity, such as "Greeks" and "Finns," rather than individuals with names. As such, journalists and especially those who owned media outlets were not neutral observers simply reporting the facts. Class and politics influenced what content—and, critically, what perspective—made its way into print. Considering the composition of Grays Harbor's press—as middle- and upper-class white men with deep connections to the area's wealthiest employers—it's unsurprising that so much news content aimed, through both subtle and overt means, to divide the working-class majority.

Perhaps the most notable expression of employing-class white supremacy was their use of racialized wage scales and establishment and enforcement of a dual labor system that reserved higher-paying and more-prestigious positions for white men, while locking women and persons of color into lower-paid "unskilled" employment. Across the American West, bosses paid Asian (as well as southern European immigrant laborers) less than white native-born workers. According to the Washington State Bureau of Labor, Asian American workers made up a significant portion of the state's lumber workforce.[42] As a rule, Asian workers earned significantly less than their white counterparts. In 1901, the Labor Bureau reported that lumber millworkers and loggers employed in the state earned between $1.94 and $3.25 per day, but the "45 Japs" who earned only $1.33 per day were not included in these totals.[43] In 1913 the top daily wage rate paid to "unskilled" Asian laborers at Washington State lumber mills was $2.50, while "unskilled" white workers were paid up to $3 per day. At sawmills employing between ten and one hundred workers, the highest-paid "skilled" Asian laborers made $3.75, a full $1.25 less than the best-paid white workers.[44] Managers, whether in lumber or other industries, demanded the freedom to pursue any policies they wished, which included paying Asian workers less.

Managers hired immigrant workers in part to lower wage scales, only to reverse course if those workers unionized, struck, or challenged authority. Like Asian Americans, southern European immigrants earned less than native-born and northwest European counterparts. According to a 1909 study by the US Immigration Commission, on average US employers paid Greek and other southern European laborers a pittance—Greeks made an average of $8.14 per week; they made only a little more than half the pay earned by workers from Scandinavia and Scotland and approximately $3 and $5 less weekly than US workers born in Poland and Finland, respectively.[45] Italians, particularly those classified as south Italians, were likewise low-paid. Unsurprisingly, if they organized to demand increased wages, their employers responded with force. Reporting on a May 1905 expulsion of Italian laborers in Grays Harbor, the *Hoquiam Sawyer* reported, “Italian laborers got sick of their job and quit.” Responding violently, “the bosses brought several revolvers into sight and threatened to shoot,” until “the dagoes became very quiet and were put aboard of the gravel train” to Seattle.[46] Driving immigrant workers out of town was an extreme tactic, but it was hardly unique in the region’s history. After Aberdeen’s elite whites rounded up and expelled Chinese people in 1890; lumbermen and their allies used similar tactics to crack down on Greek and Finnish laborers during an immigrant-led lumber strike.

Driving out immigrant strikers was one of many tactics used to regulate the local workforce. During several early twentieth-century labor conflicts, employers discharged workers with “wild” or militant reputations, particularly the Finns and southern Europeans—groups commonly labeled by the colors “Red” (Finns) or “Black” (southern Europeans).[47] Managers sometimes denied employment to unmarried men and anyone unable to speak English; they also practiced outright discrimination against Chinese, Japanese, South Asian, Finnish, and Greek immigrants, as well as other ethnic groups. During a 1912 strike led by the radical IWW, the pro-business *Seattle Times* reported that the lumber operators refused to bargain with IWW strikers in part because of the union’s insistence that “color or race not be discriminated against,” a reminder that employers would fight for their right to divide and conquer workers.[48] The *Pacific Lumber Trade Journal*, principal organ of organized lumbermen, cheered a Hoquiam policy for paying more to “any so-called white labor, . . . with the idea of bringing to Hoquiam good American citizens, with families, if possible.”[49] Lumberman Alex Polson, a state senator, praised local “mill men” for “import[ing] men with families . . . and do[ing] away with the Finns and the Greeks.” He concluded, “We owe it to our country to do the same.”[50]

Employers also kept workers physically divided through segregated workplaces and company housing. In 1926, Filipino American lumber worker Philip Vera Cruz labored among an ethnically and racially diverse workforce in Cosmopolis. He recalled the all-white management dividing employees by race and ethnicity: “The day after we got there we went to present ourselves at the box factory. We didn’t choose our jobs—the plant manager decided where to place us. Besides the white workers, there were many foreigners who worked there—Greeks, Japanese, and Filipinos. The whites had the most important positions and the Japanese seemed to have the best positions among the foreigners."[51] Moreover, lumbermen sometimes segregated housing between white and nonwhite employees. At the Schafer Brothers Logging Company camps, for example, management established "Jap housing," apart from whites' accommodations.[52] Not even death on the job brought respect to Schafers' Japanese workers. The company's list of employees, published in a history, listed hundreds of workers' names—including several names marked "fatality." But the list records only "(Japanese worker)—section hand fatality" to identify the apparently anonymous Japanese workers who died on the job.[53]

Harbor employers found racism to be a tool for forming cross-class alliances with white laborers. Some lumbermen declared their hatred of Asians and support for Asian exclusion laws. On November 18, 1905, at a meeting of the Aberdeen Trades and Labor Council, a resolution asking for "co-operation in taking such steps as may be necessary to prevent the influx of Mongolian population into this Harbor" passed without visible dissent. What made the resolution significant was not its content—support for Asian exclusion was the norm among white workers—but that the labor council submitted it for approval to the Aberdeen Chamber of Commerce, a body that directed much of the harbor's union-busting.[54] This overt display of race-conscious class collaboration was but one of many such examples of the hostility local unionists—and employers—felt toward all nonwhite and not-quite-white laborers.[55] After receiving a telegram from a Seattle employment agency advertising "good and strong Japanese boys for the Yard, or cook, and dish-washer, etc.," William Ingram, Aberdeen shingle manufacturer and city councilman, said of Japanese immigrants, "Damn 'em. I wouldn't have one of them within a thousand miles of me if I could help it."[56] In the county seat of Montesano, ten miles east of Aberdeen, the chamber of commerce, the town's leading business group, passed a 1912 resolution calling for the exclusion of "undesirable foreigners" because of their supposed criminality. The *Aberdeen Herald* printed the resolution that Montesano businessmen passed: "The presence in the United States of America of the Hindoos, Turks, Greeks, and Italians has cost numerous and costly prosecutions under the criminal statutes of the state of Washington and elsewhere in the United States," and thus advocated that "the exclusion laws of the United States of America, by suitable treaties of congressional enactment, be extended so as to prohibit the landing in the United States of America of aliens from either of the aforesaid countries."[57]

THE "COSMOPOLIS WAY"

If violence was the stick of employers' methods of labor management, paternalism must have seemed like the carrot, for at least carrots did not shoot, arrest, or expel workers. Although often presented as a pleasant system paired with the word "benevolent," paternalism is a fundamentally unequal system that rests on social control and a subservient labor force. Paternalism showed itself most overtly in company towns such as Cosmopolis and Aloha, an Olympic Peninsula lumber and logging town where management owned all housing, banned unions and the construction of any saloons, and even required that all homes be painted white.[58]

Cosmopolis was the Northwest's most notorious company town. There, in the words of mill superintendent Neil Cooney's biographer, Cooney "stood in the living room gazing out of the spacious window down on the huge lumber operation over which he ruled with absolute power," while workers slept in small company homes or bunkhouses.[59] Cooney's predecessor, C. F. White got his first opportunity to enforce the open shop in early 1894 when members of the shingle weavers' union attempted to unionize the seven women employed at the Grays Harbor Commercial Company's shingle mill. According to the *Puget Sound Lumberman*, managers worried that union men were "about to make a sortie, marry the young ladies, and thus break up the only female shingle mill crew on the Pacific Coast." GHCC manager White relied on captive labor, keeping the women weavers locked up, thereby isolating them from male unionists. The *Puget Sound Lumberman* reported that White "gallently [*sic*] came to the rescue by locking them in during working hours."[60] In this struggle, both the unionists' and White's actions were deeply influenced by patriarchal ideals, as the male weavers sought to expand the labor movement by eliminating nonunion women from the workplace and replacing them with unionized male weavers, while White sought to control labor relations by confining the women weavers indoors and away from their unionized male counterparts. Unlike the weavers' union, however, White controlled the workplace and town—and used his power to structure a community reflecting his views on women's subordination. Given the manager's actions, it's little surprise that the Cosmopolis mill became widely known as the "Western Penitentiary."[61]

Cosmopolis was a bulwark of anti-unionism. Throughout the early twentieth century, its managers repelled the organizing efforts of unionists, earning Cosmopolis the title of "the scabbiest town on the coast" and a "scab-hatchery."[62]

GHCC manager White and his top lieutenant Neil Cooney had plenty of opportunities to test their union-busting strategies during the 1890s and 1900s. A concerted effort to unionize the GHCC came in early 1902. After a seven-month struggle, the newly formed Grays Harbor Shingle Weavers' Union No. 9618 unionized all the local shingle mills except for the GHCC.[63] Unwilling to deal with unions, White executed an open-shop strategy. Managers trained mill laborers in the weavers' craft, deployed police to guard scabs, and blacklisted union members. Describing the GHCC's antilabor views, Neil Cooney declared the company's policy was "to have nothing to do with union men at our mill."[64] And so it went for the next three decades. White and Cooney maintained the GHCC as a bastion of the open shop and established the standard for anti-unionism in the region, one both admired and copied by their fellow employers in the much larger lumber towns of Aberdeen and Hoquiam.

As the patriarchs of a company town, White and later Cooney remained culturally and spatially removed from the more contested labor relations arenas in Aberdeen and Hoquiam. Whereas in Cosmopolis the GHCC controlled the press, Aberdeen and Hoquiam residents published a wide variety of periodicals, including labor and socialist papers. In Cosmopolis, many workers lived in company housing and could thus be expelled from their homes during labor conflicts. Outside of Cosmopolis, many residents owned their own homes and were thus able to protest or strike without the fear of immediately being made homeless.[65] In seeking to control affairs in Aberdeen and Hoquiam, employers coped with ostensibly free institutions: elections, elected officials, a mainstream press, ethnic organizations, and labor unions. As a result, building solidarity among Aberdeen and Hoquiam employers proved to be a long-term project, one that relied on a small group of energetic bosses who understood the importance of acting together to protect their shared interests.

BUILDING AN EMPLOYERS' MOVEMENT

At the head of Grays Harbor employers' campaign for workplace, community, and civic control were several men who understood full well that their class interests were most secure when they cooperated. What distinguished them from others in their class was not simply their antipathy toward unions—opposition and hostility toward unions was never in short supply among lumber bosses.[66] Some employers, mostly small- and medium-sized businesses owners, preferred to deal fairly with unions. They favored the stability offered by collective bargaining over the chaos of strikes and importing laborers. Although some owners believed they could train "green" and scab labor to perform many mill and camp jobs, doing so risked conflicts and the likelihood that untrained workers would be hurt on the job. Perhaps most notable among this group was the lumber manufacturer A. J. West, a vocal advocate for the eight-hour day, even reporting to the *Grays Harbor Post* that "I stated to the West Coast lumbermen, at our last meeting, that the labor unions are the safe guards of the lumbermen of this coast and if the labor unions would only strike for eight hours in all the mills, in this manner curtailing the output, I would join a labor union."[67] That remarkable statement put West at odds with others in his class, but he was not the sole manager who bucked the trend of aggressive union-busting.

Thus, although anti-unionism was common among the harbor's employing class, the anti-union militants distinguished themselves from their fellow employers by their early and persistent assault on unions and their capacity for recruiting others to their crusade against organized labor. These men joined the most clubs, delivered the most speeches, held the most leadership positions, and were the most successful at persuading fellow employers to join their efforts. They comprised what historian Rosemary Feurer has called "the militant minority of employers," those "who urged fellow managers and owners to act collectively to control the labor market and to eliminate radical influences among workers."[68] Over the course of several battles fought against unions and radicals, the ideology of these militants spread to influence most of the local employing class.

Several harbor businessmen belonged to this "militant minority," and Grays Harbor's anti-union employers occupied practically every position of power in Washington State—and the western lumber industry.[69] At the core of this group, however, were a few leading lights who sought to change the ways business was done on the harbor. During the early years of the twentieth century, when the employers' movement was in its nascent stages, no one played as large a role in welding together his fellow employers as three men: William B. Mack and William J. Patterson of Aberdeen, and Robert F. Lytle of Hoquiam. During 1906–12, as the local expression of anti-unionism took shape, no other employers commanded so much attention for their campaigns to break unions. In the years ahead, employers adapted their approaches in response to new challenges and required government assistance to tame labor. However much those tactics changed, though, lumbermen's militant opposition to unions remained the same.

During the first years of the twentieth century a common joke on the harbor was that William J. Patterson, head of the Hayes and Hayes Bank in Aberdeen, was so wealthy that BPOE, the acronym for Benevolent and Protective Order of Elks, actually stood for "Billy Patterson Owns Everything."[70] Though it was an exaggeration, Patterson, cashier at the Hayes and Hayes Bank between 1906 and 1927, was one of the richest and most powerful men in Washington State. He was an avid gamesman and gambler, a future military officer, and a frequenter of clubs like the Elks and Grays Harbor Country Club.[71] Known among fellow employers as "Mr. Aberdeen," Patterson served as president of the Grays Harbor Railway and Light Company, the United States Trust Company of Aberdeen, the Aberdeen Savings and Loan Association, the United States National Bank of Aberdeen, and the State Bank of Centralia. He was also a leading booster for commercial interests, which elevated him near the top of every business association in southwest Washington.[72]

Realizing the threat posed by an assertive labor movement, Patterson encouraged his colleagues to aggressively oppose unions. In 1909, he assembled and presided over a citizens' committee—one of the anti-union groups masked behind the guise of good citizenship that were often called citizens' alliances. Representatives of 300 such groups met in Chicago in 1903 to form the Citizens' Industrial Association of America, a national organization to protect employers' interests—mostly by suppressing the labor movement. National organizations like the Citizens' Industrial Association of America assisted employers by supplying resources and sponsoring anti-union meetings and propaganda, but fighting western radicals was most often a local operation.[73] Employers on the Grays Harbor committee weaponized citizenship in a struggle against the region's maritime unionists, nearly all of whom were born abroad. The committee hired labor spies to break up the powerful sailors' union, raising approximately ten thousand dollars to finance their efforts.[74] In subsequent years Patterson further united business interests, serving several terms as president and trustee of the Aberdeen Chamber of Commerce as its membership ballooned. He also led the Southwest Washington Development Association and helped to mold it into "a movement for state-wide development which will mark an epoch in the material progress of the commonwealth." In 1911–12, Patterson directed the citizens' committees whose members beat, shot, arrested, and expelled Wobblies and other labor activists. He stood at the center of the Grays Harbor employing class; his skills at uniting members of his own class would be a match for even the best union organizers.[75]

Across town in Hoquiam, big business remained vested in an old guard of lumbermen, personified in the Lytle brothers, Joseph and Robert. Born in New York, Robert Lytle attended the University of Wisconsin before moving to Washington State, where he and his brother Joseph established grocery businesses in Fairhaven and Hoquiam. The Lytles belonged to the first generation of Hoquiam lumbermen, men who arrived on the harbor during the 1890s and who for more than a decade presided over local affairs with few challenges.[76]

In 1902, the Lytles opened their massive Hoquiam Lumber and Shingle Company.[77] In 1907, a lumber trade publication extolled the stature of the Lytles' mill, which employed 325 men and turned out 200,000 board feet of lumber on the ten-hour day shift and 125,000 on the night shift. Workers at the shingle mill cut 650,000 shingles per day.[78]

Robert, the mill's manager and point man on labor relations, had ample experience with unions and strikes during the first years of the mill's operation. In January 1906, following a sixty-day production shutdown, the Lytles refused to allow ISWUA official J. G. Brown his job back because of his reputation as an "agitator" and one of "those horrid socialists." In a typical move by the weavers, Hoquiam's ISWUA struck the Lytles' mill and placed it on the labor council's list of unfair employers. After four days, the Lytles agreed to rehire Brown. The labor council responded by declaring their "hopes that this will teach such corporations that a man has a right to speak as he believes, vote as he speaks, and claim a voice in the making of laws and in the choosing of rules."[79]

The militant defense of Brown's job was one of several successful shingle weavers' strikes waged between 1902 and 1906.[80] As the outcome of this strike showed, despite Lytle's professed adherence to the cult of individualism and his preference to "deal with the men as individuals," he lacked the ability to tame a union of the ISWUA's stature, with its more than two thousand members, large war chest, and the support of a statewide labor federation.[81] Because of Robert Lytle's increased prominence, shortly after weavers won a January 1906 strike at his mill, his fellow manufacturers elected Robert Lytle as first vice president of the Shingle Mills Bureau, which positioned him to lead the manufacturers against labor.[82] In the years ahead, as Lytle's status increased, he gained a reputation among AFL and Wobbly unionists as "the most vigorous and slimy foe of the Shingle Weavers' Union" and a man with "but slight regard for the provisions of a contract" and for "flagrantly" violating contracts.[83]

THE EMPLOYER OFFENSIVE

The biggest problem facing Grays Harbor employers was not that they failed to cooperate or coordinate their activities, but that they lacked the resources to individually defeat unions. Grays Harbor ISWUA locals won several strikes between 1902 and 1906. Seeing the potential for the ISWUA to interfere with managerial prerogatives, manufacturers organized to impose open-shop conditions on their industry. Members of the Shingle Mills Bureau recognized the potential for a trade association to function as what historian William Millikan calls "a union against unions."[84] Bureau members coordinated mill closures and production curtailment to drive up prices and jointly sued railroads to get better freight rates.[85]

Prior to 1906, the shingle weavers maintained their ranks and exacted gains from employers by following craft union policies. The limits of their craft unionism showed in 1906 when the harbor's weavers joined a statewide strike in support of the weavers in Ballard. Unlike earlier strikes, this time Lytle and most of his employer cadre were in no mood to compromise.[86] The Shingle Mills Bureau established a defense fund and declared that "manufacturers must cooperate for mutual protection against the abuses of organized labor. Contribute to the Defense Fund and do it now."[87] The *Seattle Times* reported, "The mills have been creating a fund for strike protection . . . to sustain a fight if what was determined to be an unjust demand was resisted by any subscriber to the agreement."[88]

The bureau proved to be a well-oiled machine, as its members routed the union. The strike began in Ballard in April 1906 as a contest over hours, wages, and the closed shop.[89] After more than two months of strike activity with little to show for it, the ISWUA declared a general strike in the shingle industry beginning on June 21.[90] Shingle manufacturers recruited scabs, including college students and unionists enticed to cross the picket lines. The bureau enjoyed press support, which, according to the ISWUA, were "lying reports" bought by a "big money barrel."[91] Boasting a war chest, the bureau enabled its members to import scabs from the southern United States, constructed bullpens to house strikebreakers, and funded a public relations campaign marked by glowing press coverage from several news outlets.[92]

Despite a few victories where shingle manufacturers signed contracts recognizing the union, most mills refused to bargain.[93] Grays Harbor weavers were the last to concede, but by mid-August all those ISWUA members who could return to work did so.[94] In September, the five largest harbor mills joined their counterparts throughout the state in issuing a resolution declaring their adherence to the open shop.[95] Defeated by a remarkable show of employer cooperation, the union lost members, while locals such as the Aberdeen branch disbanded. The strike devastated the union; the international nearly ceased operations.[96] Scabs retained their jobs and employers raised the open-shop banner. Crowing over the victory, North Western Lumber Company manager E. O. McLaughlin triumphantly said: "You can say through your paper that the North-western Lumber company does not forget its enemies. . . . We will not discriminate between men, but it is the open shop which we will now establish."[97] Demonstrating that a new era of employer solidarity was at hand, harbor shingle manufacturers issued a statement declaring "any discrimination against any of the undersigned [all large Grays Harbor mills] shall be considered as a menace to all."[98]

Manufacturers' success at crushing the weavers' strike was a blow to the harbor's—and the entire region's—labor movement. But as employers in one branch of the Northwest's main industry (shingles) won a decisive strike, those in shipping failed to break the 1906 maritime strike. Pacific Coast shippers, whose ranks overlapped with the lumbermen, conceded defeat to the Sailors' Union. The defeat required employers to pay higher wages, and labor retained control over hiring. This was a bitter pill to swallow considering that maritime unions were run by "foreigners," according to several press accounts. In the aftermath of the big 1906 strikes, employers focused on taming maritime labor. They imported labor spies, formed a citizens' committee, and redoubled their efforts to control local governments. By 1910, the once-powerful longshoremen's and sailors' unions had both been dramatically weakened by anti-union employers.[99] After working as a labor spy for the Thiel Detective Agency, L. D. Templeman became police chief in Aberdeen, the Northwest Coast's largest city. This marked a change in the region's government, for it installed an experienced professional antilabor operative from one of the country's chief strikebreaking outfits at the spear tip of a fight with labor radicalism.[100] Essentially, as the 1910s began, private industry asserted control over the ostensibly public responsibilities of government.

By 1910, employers had achieved a remarkable level of unity.[101] In the previous few years, lumbermen had united into a long list of clubs, ranging from fraternities to trade groups to anti-union associations. These groups had broken strikes among some of the region's most powerful and militant unions, and they used their power to manage both politics and the local media. These wealthy men practiced solidarity whenever their class interests appeared threatened. Indeed, as these antilabor successes showed, employers' mutual class feeling did not stop at the boundaries of glad-handing at the lodge or fighting for lower freight rates, but extended into the realm of labor relations, where its impact on wage earners and their families was greatest.

4

TOVERI AND *TOVERITAR*

GRAYS HARBOR'S IMMIGRANT LEFT

On July 18, 1905, sawmill laborers at the West and Slade Mill Company in Aberdeen struck, demanding a two dollar minimum wage. From the West and Slade, the strike spread throughout Aberdeen, eventually stopping production at six mills, as well as the Lindstrom shipyard, which closed for want of lumber. The conflict had implications far beyond a simple wage demand. Strikers held mass meetings, strike parades formed "in replica of a miniature Chicago teamsters' strike," and strikers insisted that their demands also include a nine-hour day. The strike required a great deal of coordination. Flying squadrons of strikers rushed into mills to convince workers to join the strike. Workers met regularly at the Aberdeen Finn hall.[1]

Finnish Americans constituted the militant wing of the strike force. In a letter to the socialist daily *Raivaaja* (*Pioneer*), based in Fitchburg, Massachusetts, socialist lumber worker Gustave Kinnunen praised the solidarity of his fellow Finns, along with the Swedish and Norwegian laborers who, to a man, remained on the picket lines until the strike's conclusion. Kinnunen had harsher words for his American coworkers who crossed the picket line—he called them scabs (*rikkurit*): "The Finns, Swedes, and Norwegians were unanimous throughout the strike and fought against the power/strength of the capital also for the benefit of the Americans. Six Americans joined in the strike but only 3 stayed on strike until the end."[2] Finns were not alone in their disdain for strikebreakers, but within Finnish working-class communities scabbing was an unspeakable offense, one that potentially carried with it banishment from community life. The Finnish-language workers' press excoriated scabs, even mocking "American workers" for their propensity to break strikes—in contrast to northern Europeans.[3]

Aware of the ethnic composition of the strike force, employers tried to purge the Finnish menace. On July 22, W. B. Mack, manager of the West and Slade mill but speaking on behalf of all the Aberdeen mill owners, offered to the strikers their proposed two dollar wage settlement but stated, "All right, but . . . I want men who can speak the English language," and hung up a sign at the mill reading "WANTED. 100 Men @ $2.00 and up per day. Only those who understand and speak the English language need apply. West & Slade Mill CO. W. B. Mack, Mgr." These were clear swipes at the Finns who led the strikers' ranks.[4] Practically no strikers returned to work at the mills, and at a meeting of some of the strikers, an eighty-six to thirty-eight vote repudiated Mack's discriminatory offer. Indeed, angered by receiving only the promise of future raises, as well as bosses' harangues against "a handful of irresponsible agitators, ignorant of the country and its language," the strikers rejected the agreement, demanding an immediate wage hike. Newspapers blamed the workers' refusal to compromise on "a few agitators" and the work of "hotheads who became intoxicated with their Saturday's success." The *Aberdeen Herald* attacked the Finns for their intransigence, writing that the lone holdouts in a compromise settlement came from mills that "employ the greatest number of yardmen, a majority of whom are Finns, unable to speak the English language."[5] Nonetheless, the strikers succeeded, returning to work under the two dollar minimum wage. Mack's efforts to use language restrictions to exclude the "agitators" and "hotheads," who he and the local press believed were responsible for the strike, failed. Employers weren't able to replace the immigrant labor and thus the requirements for English-only workers had little impact on the composition of Grays Harbor's workforce.[6]

Finnish workers made up a militant section of the labor-left in the harbor, much as they did across the northern United States in towns from Michigan's Copper Country to Butte, Montana, and from fishing villages on the Columbia River to Minnesota's iron ranges.[7] Still, it was not Finns alone who populated the Grays Harbor left. Radical organizations drew members of the region's many ethnic groups, including Croatians, Greeks, and Scandinavians. Indeed, shared experiences of class—similar jobs, bouts of unemployment and poverty, lack of workplace and community power—helped build solidarity among harbor workers who looked past their differences to pursue shared goals. In Aberdeen and Hoquiam, where immigrants settled into a complex web of ethnic neighborhoods, immigrant workers pioneered methods of interethnic labor activism, waging lumber strikes led by diverse groups similar to those fought by their counterparts in the Mesabi Range in Minnesota; in Lawrence, Massachusetts; and Paterson, New Jersey. In 1912, amid the largest Pacific Northwest lumber strike to that time, IWW strikers appointed a strike committee composed of two Greeks, two Finns, two Scandinavians, and two native-born Americans.[8] As with many lumber strikes, the most-detailed news coverage came from the Finnish-language socialist dailies, including the daily *Toveri* (*Comrade*) published in the nearby fishing and lumber town of Astoria, Oregon. Describing a parade and mass meeting at Electric Park on the border between Aberdeen and Hoquiam, *Toveri* wrote, "Reaching attendance up to thousands, the march proved that the increase of the police forces did not have a disbanding effect on the strikers, but quite the opposite! English, Polish, Greek, Austrian were all spoken in explaining the meaning of the strike."[9]

As these events suggest, the harbor's immigrants shaped its early twentieth-century left movements. The diverse groups of Grays Harbor workers, which included labor militants and socialists, had equally diverse methods for responding to—and in some cases reshaping—their working and living conditions in industrial Grays Harbor. The IWW rightfully received much of the credit—even admiration—for its militant efforts to form one big union of all workers. But in localities across the country, the roots of industrial unionism lay in immigrant communities who, before the Wobblies, responded with collective action to what they saw as exploitative working conditions and an oppressive society.

Often ignored by trade unions, harbor immigrants nonetheless challenged employers, declaring a series of nonunion strikes during the early twentieth century. Between 1904 and 1912, nonunion sawmill workers struck at least seven times at a total of fifty sawmills in the harbor towns.[10] These were among the first strikes on the harbor led "from below" by the lowest-paid immigrant workers and were likewise the first to unite workers in interethnic alliances. As this chapter and those that follow illustrate, it was the interethnic protests of laborers that animated the mass struggles in the Grays Harbor lumber industry during the 1910s, 1920s, and 1930s. Lumber, maritime, and an array of other workers expressed class solidarity—and discontent with both local employers and the wider American socioeconomic system—at their Finn halls and sawmill shop floors. Nourished by the Finnish newspapers and the impressive Finnish socialist cultural apparatus, that solidarity repeatedly burst into public view in the early years of the twentieth century.

FINNISH AMERICAN WORK LIFE

Finnish immigrants comprised the largest blocs of immigrant socialists in the United States. They formed the Finnish Socialist Federation (FSF) in 1906, one of the many language federations of the Socialist Party of America. By 1913 the FSF had 260 local branches and more than 12,000 members. At their height in membership, Finns represented a full 12 percent of SPA members, making them the largest language federation in the party. Their great numbers enabled the FSF to publish three daily newspapers, manage eighty libraries, and own at least seventy-six halls.[11]

Unlike other northern European immigrant socialists such as the Germans, Swedes, and Norwegians, all of which had thriving early twentieth-century socialist movements, the Finns occupied an in-between racial position. Like some other inbetween immigrant groups, notably the Poles and Italians, Finns had resources available on their paths to "white manhood" and "becoming American."[12] Some immigrants used politics or the police to advance their group's position in the United States; Finns had the labor movement, their fund-raising operations, and their halls. But unlike Italian, Jewish, Polish, or Irish immigrants, only a small group of Finns immigrated to the United States. Numbering more than 300,000 first-generation migrants who traveled across the Atlantic between 1870 and 1920, the Finns settled in large numbers in the Pacific Northwest and Upper Midwest. They settled primarily in medium-sized and small resource-extracting towns: mine towns of Michigan and Minnesota, lumber and fishing towns along the Pacific Coast.[13] Finnish Americans exercised influence well beyond their numbers. They mobilized what resources they possessed, including a long tradition of labor militancy and socialism on both sides of the Atlantic and the Finnish workers' halls and periodicals that served as significant institutions for the American labor movement in dozens of US cities and towns.

One view of the size and scope of the Finnish North American left appears in their socialist and IWW papers, which contained semiannual "Greetings" lists to their subscribers and supporters. The "Greetings" included the names and addresses of thousands of leftists. Aberdeen and Hoquiam—along with dozens of other western cities, from Astoria to Butte and Eureka, California, to Spokane, Washington—had lengthy "Greetings" sections, allowing the broader left to correspond and see the massive scope of left-wing support.[14] The end-of-year lists were especially useful for the diaspora population to remain in contact with friends and family members and for fund-raising among like-minded Finns.

The Finnish left possessed some unique attributes, notably their form of hall radicalism, their many daily publications, and women's leadership within diverse movements. Finns had power within local unions and left-wing political groups; an important source of that power often came from their lasting institutions—notably the Finn halls. These structures provided headquarters for labor and leftist groups and hosted political speeches and fund-raisers. Although many immigrant groups boasted their own ethnic halls, some of which were owned by unions and leftists, none could match the Finnish devotion to hall building and activities. In the early years of the twentieth century, the stronghold of the Grays Harbor labor-left was headquartered in the area's Finn halls.[15]

With movements deeply rooted in community spaces, it's perhaps unsurprising that women played critical roles in the Finnish American labor-left. Women were active in workers' societies in Finland throughout the 1890s and formed key pillars of support for the socialist movement in Finland during its early years.[16] Hundreds of Grays Harbor's Finns immigrated to the United States after the turn of the twentieth century and thus had direct knowledge of and experience with these events and involvement with radical groups.[17] The lively left-wing Finnish-language press kept its huge readership apprised of activities in the home country.

Spreading news about domestic and international workers' movements was one of the main occupations of the Finnish American socialist movement that stretched across the country; local socialist groups educated members using their own halls, libraries, and theaters.[18] While only a minority of Finnish Americans joined or supported workers' movements, all or nearly all read about events in Finland through the prolific Finnish American press. Between 98 and 99 percent of Finnish Americans could read their native language, which contributed to the proliferation of Finnish-language newspapers in the United States.[19]

The written word proved a key facet to building class solidarity, for although Finns had some background with socialism and labor solidarity in Finland, new conditions required new responses; labor organizers and journalists served as agents welding individual laborers into a movement. On the western side of the Atlantic, Finnish socialists published local news in *Raivaaja* (Massachusetts), *Työmies* (Hancock, Michigan), and *Toveri* in Astoria, Oregon. Each paper ran columns from socialist correspondents across the country, mixing local news with national and international stories. Professionally edited, the papers nonetheless included bottom-up and worker-run perspectives that also characterized the IWW's (and some other workers' organizations) publishing ventures. Many Finnish American socialist writers worked in industry, using their insider perspective to shine lights on the conditions that socialist movements endeavored to change.[20] These correspondents placed a working-class perspective in print, one that differed in style and substance from the news from professional journalists and the middle-class writers whose prose appeared in mainstream news organs. Grays Harbor's Finns were especially prolific contributors to *Toveri*; their reports covered topics—and provided perspectives—that never could have seen the light of day in probusiness papers like the *Aberdeen Daily World*, *Aberdeen Herald*, or *Washingtonian*. Finnish socialists detected the procompany bias of certain newspapers, seeing them as tools of management. During a 1912 sawmill strike, *Toveri* observed that mainstream journalists appeared to open their arms to immigrant workers so long as they obeyed management—and did not strike: "Until that very moment the local newspaper 'World' called them as patriotic Americans, but now they are filthy foreigners."[21]

One May 1910 *Toveri* issue demonstrated the impact of local socialist writers. It published a short article from Aberdeen titled "Ylioppilaat rikkureina" ("Students as scabs") about a group of Stanford students who joined professors in sailing to Grays Harbor to scab—they believed—in the logging camps, the "uninhabited remote wilderness," as the article sarcastically noted.[22] When they arrived, the college boys received a shock. Instead of a trek into the woods, they ended up at the S. E. Slade Lumber Company sawmill where they crossed a picket line. The students did not remain long and quit scabbing shortly after their arrival; the *Toveri* correspondent rejoiced, writing that "when they have found out that they were scabs, they left their jobs, and left the town."[23] Although the Stanford scabs' case appears to be an instance of miscommunication—intentional or not—with students ignorant of the malevolent purpose for their trip north, workers across the nation knew of employers' use of university—even high school—students as scabs.

With early twentieth-century higher education being the preserve of the middle and upper classes, few collegians sympathized with striking laborers.[24] In at least three strikes—in 1904, 1916, and 1917—children scabbed on striking Grays Harbor workers, actions that shingle weavers' union member Si Gotchy blamed on the educational system. He wrote, "Why did the high school punks scab on the shingle weavers in Ballard and also on the Grays Harbor longshoremen? Here is one reason: Fathers and mothers send their children to school and when they are old enough to pass the eighth grade all they know is what they hear there. The teachers are influenced in their teachings largely by the employing class, hence the children are taught nothing in regard to unions or unionism." At the Grays Harbor Commercial Company, the company secured replacement "boys" by forcing them "against their will to go scabbing by bringing official pressure to bear upon their parents. . . . Many of these boys be it said to their everlasting credit, have forsaken their homes rather than scab."[25] Indeed, the threat posed by employers who used children to break strikes was so persistent that W. C. Judson, an Aberdeen teamster, succeeded in passing a resolution at the 1908 Washington State Federation of Labor (WSFL) convention that condemned "the employment of young boys for strikebreaking purposes during teamsters' strikes, and praying the enactment of laws prohibiting such employment."[26]

Local correspondents likewise provided fresh perspectives into labor conflicts that the many mainstream and company-influenced papers usually condemned or treated as a nuisance standing in the way of community "progress." *Raivaaja* provided detailed reports of the 1905 sawmill strike mentioned atop this chapter, providing working-class perspectives on the scabs, police, and armed guards—a point of view left out of the news coverage written by lumbermen's allies.[27] Over a few issues in April 1912, *Toveri* readers learned from harbor correspondents that socialists had performed well in Aberdeen's municipal elections, dozens of lumber strikers had been arrested, and Aberdeen authorities closed down the Red Finn hall because the IWW used it as a strike headquarters.[28]

FINNISH HARBOR

The great majority of Finns arrived in North America after 1890.[29] Most Finnish Americans lived in northern states, particularly in the Upper Midwest, with large numbers of Finns settled in Massachusetts, New York, and the Pacific Northwest. Finnish American men worked primarily in resource-extraction industries such as mining, lumber, and fishing. Domestic service was long the chief form of employment for Finnish women. Particularly in the Midwest, Finns developed reputations for intense labor militancy and radical politics. The reputations of these Red Finns spread rapidly after the 1907 Mesabi Range strike in Minnesota when more than 10,000 largely Finnish mineworkers shut down the state's great iron industry for two months before being broken through the mass importation of strikebreakers.[30]

Between 1900 and 1910 Finns grew to become the largest foreign-born group in Chehalis (later renamed Grays Harbor) County. Hundreds of Finnish men worked in the lumber industry as loggers and mill hands; many others labored on the docks and in fishing boats. Domestic service was the largest occupation for wage-earning Finnish women: at least thirty-three Finnish women cleaned Aberdeen boardinghouses, hotels, and single-family residences in 1910. Some worked in the homes of the harbor's wealthiest residents, including lumbermen A. J. West and Robert Lytle and attorney W. H. Abel.[31] Finnish maids led the organizing of left-wing domestic workers' unions in the late 1910s and 1920s—a subject discussed in later chapters. Much as today, domestic work was among the lowest-paying jobs for women laborers.[32] According to Finnish American historian Ida Kari Smits, "Finnish cleaning women were in constant demand. They worked hard for low wages and were strong and dependable."[33] Finnish American radical musician Hiski Salomaa's lyrics described the frenzied work pace and abusive employers faced by domestic servants in her tune "Tiskarin Polkka" ("Servant girl's polka"):

> Those hags are yelling, eating and drinking
> Here I am only washing the dishes
> The coffee is nearly boiling over
> 'Cause I can't fly after everything.[34]

Although Salomaa's song does not hint at any acts of sabotage perpetrated by Wobbly domestic or food workers upon an employer's kitchen, tools, or food, the Wobbly musician Haywire Mac McClintock's song "The Hymn of Hate" affronts members of the ruling class with a haunting revelation that "when you dine in your gay café the waiter spits in your soup."[35] The lure of retribution against her boss must have been particularly attractive for Finnish Wobbly domestic worker Lempi Ellila, who worked in the home of Judge W. H. Abel, a labor-baiting attorney known for opposing workers in court.[36]

Despite their political orientations, most Grays Harbor Finns didn't belong to unions before 1910. This was not due to any explicit ban on Finnish membership in unions, but because most Finns labored in so-called unskilled jobs such as sawmill laborers and loggers, and workers in these occupations rarely belonged to unions. For instance, in Aberdeen's First Ward, which contained the highest concentration of Finnish immigrants in Chehalis (Grays Harbor) County, 243 out of the 383 Finnish immigrants who worked outside of the home listed their occupation as "laborer"; practically all these laborers listed their workplace as a "saw mill." With the sole exception of those who belonged to the IWW's revolutionary unions and short-lived trade unions, no Grays Harbor sawmill hands belonged to labor unions before 1912.[37] Still, the number of militant Finnish laborers helps account for the repeated strikes waged at Grays Harbor sawmills during the early decades of the twentieth century.

Some Finns did work in unionized trades and of these no doubt some paid their union dues and attended meetings of their local. For example, in Washington State in 1912, at the peak of state SPA strength, 121 of Washington's 1,062 Finnish socialists—roughly 11 percent—were union members.[38] Forty-four Finns living in Aberdeen's First Ward in 1910 worked as longshoremen, sailors, carpenters, teamsters, painters, and bartenders—all unionized jobs.[39] Ida Kanppa, an Aberdeen Finn, belonged to the local laundry workers' union until her "hand [was] crushed in machinery," forcing her to retire from laundry work and subsist on insurance funds provided by the union.[40]

Despite the long hours and dangerous working conditions, employers paid laundry workers like Kanppa and thousands of immigrant mill and dock laborers a pittance for their work. During the first decade of the twentieth century, Aberdeen mill hands earned between $1.75 and $2 per day—approximately half of what unionized blue-collar workers made.[41] Dr. Herman Titus, a prominent Washington State socialist, visited Grays Harbor and described the living conditions of the lumber workers' families: "I have seen children—sons and daughters of the working mill hands—come to the back yard of the hotel and pick old scraps of meat and bread from the garbage cans."[42] On the other side of the political spectrum, the archconservative lumberman W. B. Mack admitted that "it is practically impossible to live on $1.75 a day"—the pay his mill paid laborers.[43]

To make ends meet, workers depended on a family economy of multiple wage earners and significant (usually unpaid) caregiving and reproductive labor. Writing of Appalachian coal country, historian Jessica Wilkerson detailed some of the many tasks working-class women performed that sustained families, enabling (usually) male laborers to remain on the job earning wages: "raising and socializing children, caring for the elderly and disabled, caring for oneself, preparing food, cleaning living quarters, buying consumer goods, and maintaining ties of family and kin."[44]

As in mining regions, workers in lumber country suffered an array of debilitating injuries and diseases, adding pressure among family survivors—often wives and children—to get by.[45] The Laukkanen family of Aberdeen is illustrative. Following the death of Abel, a Finnish-born sawmill laborer, in 1930 five of the six household members—Amelia, widowed head of household, and four of five children—worked for wages outside the home.[46] Unsurprisingly, the harbor was home to dozens of widows who, like Amelia Laukkanen, survived by seeking out wage work. At least two of Amelia's daughters became leaders in the communist movement. Whether from seeing the struggles with wage labor, poverty, and early deaths among their family—or the inequality all around them—a sizable number of working-class widows joined and supported socialist, Wobbly, and communist groups.. For her support in 1912 of striking IWW mill laborers, "Mother" Carrie Walker, the proprietor of an Aberdeen barber shop, was among those arrested for "inciting to riot" for her leading role on the picket lines.[47] For her actions, police tossed Walker in jail and shut down her shop, all because, in the words of labor radical Bruce Rogers, "she stood up for the boys."[48] But Walker was hardly alone among widows drawn to the radical causes. Notably, the 1935 list of the IWW's *Industrialisti* "Greetings" contained the names of no fewer than thirteen widows.[49]

Caring for boarders was a common way for women—including married and widowed women—to earn money. In fact, for widowed women their home was often their only way to generate income. Boardinghouse keepers provided domestic support for their male boarders such as cooking food and cleaning laundry.[50] Hundreds of local laborers lived in large boardinghouses—often alongside others from their home country. The Johnsons, a Finnish American family, ran a boardinghouse on Marion Street in south Aberdeen. Evret Johnson, the father and head of the family, worked as a sawmill laborer, as did all seven Finnish boarders who lived in the Johnson household.[51] An even larger Finnish boardinghouse was built in Hoquiam during the early twentieth century, and in a commonly reproduced image, the three-story building is featured with its many residents posing on its porch and balcony.[52]

Few Finnish laborers found prosperity in the Grays Harbor mills, but

Boardinghouse on K and Ninth Streets in Hoquiam; fifteen names—mostly of Finnish Americans—appear on the back of the photo. Polson Museum, Hoquiam, Washington.

many were drawn to the radical socialist politics. Representative of these radical Finnish workers was Leonard Turi, a first-generation immigrant mill laborer who lived in an east Aberdeen boardinghouse.[53] Turi was a working-class radical, but like most politically active harbor immigrants from southern and eastern Europe, he was not a member of a craft union and he did not utilize the mainstream labor movement to advance his political aims. Instead, Turi served as one of the leaders of the Aberdeen socialist movement during the first two decades of the twentieth century.[54] Erkki (Erik) Himango, an east Aberdeen Finn and yardman at a local sawmill, followed a path similar to Turi's. Himango was one of five founding trustees for the Finnish Socialist Sick and Funeral Benefit Association of America, a leftist insurance organization based in Aberdeen. One of the association's stated purposes was "to unite fraternally for mutual benefit, protection, improvement, education, and for the promotion of friendship

At a funeral at the Finnish Socialist hall in Hoquiam, early in the twentieth century, members of a brass band appear on stage, above two caskets covered in flowers. These large halls provided indoor meeting spaces that could accommodate hundreds of people for funerals and diverse other gatherings. Polson Museum, Hoquiam, Washington.

and social intercourse, the male and female membership of the Finnish Socialist organization of America."[55] Like Turi, there is no evidence that Himango belonged to or acted under the auspices of a craft union, but instead operated in a political sphere that he and his fellow immigrants could mold to their own talents and interests.

The Aberdeen-based sick and benefit association that Himango helped found was one of several groups that immigrants formed to provide security while living in the world's most dangerous industrial society.[56] Thousands of Finns labored in some of North America's most dangerous industries, including lumber, mining, construction, and marine transportation. Finns—like all workers in lumber country—regularly came face to face with death, and even the rare laborers who escaped the mills, camps, and waterfronts unscathed had doubtless seen coworkers killed or crippled on the job. The harbor's Red Finns opened their halls to mourners and carried out funerals in the hall interior; no doubt this proved useful escape from the deluges of annual rain that fell on Aberdeen, making it one of the country's rainiest cities. One of the few surviving photographs of a Finnish socialist hall shows a band onstage looking out over two caskets and several ornate flower arrangements.

As scholars of working-class funerals have argued, these communal celebrations also "expressed the deceased's place in the local community" and enabled the local working class, or some segment of it, to take center stage in planning and carrying out the commemoration of their comrade's life and death.[57] Socialist funerals were community-building events where working people gathered with other members of their class, commemorated the life of the deceased, and assigned blame for the worker's death. Hosting large, often elaborate funerals ranked high on the list of priorities for trade unions, socialist organizations, and other radical groups. Thus, in May 1923 at the funeral of the IWW activist William McKay, Finnish workers led a parade through downtown holding a giant sign reading "Fellow Worker McKay. Murdered at Bay City Mill by A Co Gunman May 3rd, 1923. Trust. *A Victim of Capitalistic Greed.* We Never Forget?" The parade concluded at McKay's funeral where workers posed under the sign as they stood around McKay's grave.[58]

FINNISH "SAVAGES"

By marginalizing the large body of working-class Finns, the local labor movement reflected dominant racial ideologies of their era. Early twentieth-century social scientists regularly excluded Finns from the so-called Nordic races. The mainstream press and eugenicist propagandists transmitted ideas of the "essential Finn" throughout the United States. Local elites and intellectuals absorbed and repeated these ideas, which—judging from Finns' lack of acceptance in unions and non-Finn neighborhoods—were at least partly accepted by the native-born working class. Eschewing stories on the rich cultural production going on at the Finn halls, the four major Aberdeen and Hoquiam newspapers stuck to stories celebrating when Finnish "Foreigners Go Home" and referring to the numerous radically inclined Finns as "undesirables."[59] Indeed, Finns appeared in the press most often as the perpetrators of stabbings, the hapless victims of "industrial accidents," or alcoholics who fell off one of the harbor's docks to their watery deaths. To elites, Finnish American men appeared as "angry," "wild eyed," and strongly associated with drunkenness.[60] One news piece illustrates the treatment afforded Finnish Americans, whose individual traits were swallowed up inside the "essential Finn" caricature: "Julius Lehtonen cut the throat of a Finn. . . . Of four men arrested on suspicion in connection with the knifing of a Finn early yesterday morning, one has been positively identified by the victim as his assailant, and other evidence held by the officers makes the case complete."[61]

While Finnish American workers were lumped together as a single type of person, elites singled out Finnish leftists for abuse. Finnish American radicals, in fact, offer an illustration of the relationship in the United States between political radicalism and the racialization process. Across the nation, Finnish socialists were known as Red Finns, a reference to the color red in socialist flags, but also to the connection made in the minds of American elites between Finnish and Indigenous "savages."[62] Indeed, before 1910 it was common for social scientists to refer to Finns as a separate race, part of "Homo Mongolicus" and the Finno-Tatar "family."[63] After leading a strike at the Mesabi iron range of Minnesota, employers and middle-class allies castigated Finnish workers as "a race that tries to take advantage of the companies at every opportunity and are not to be trusted."[64] Finnish Americans were referred to as "Jackpine savages" and Mongolians.[65] The latter identification was so strong that in 1907 nativist employers attempted to halt Finnish immigration into the United States—thereby reducing the flow of radicals—by invoking Asian exclusion legislation.[66]

The 1920s immigration restrictions targeted Finns (as well as southern and eastern Europeans), making their entry into the United State increasingly difficult. But long before the 1924 Johnson-Reed Immigration Act and similar nativist laws blocked immigration, "looser and more local racializations of Finnish labor militants did matter, even at the level of governmental policies toward them," in the words of historian David Roediger.[67] Such policies mattered in Grays Harbor, where the Aberdeen municipal government repeatedly harassed Finns. Indeed, in Grays Harbor, to be a Red Finn was to be the target of special abuse by local employers and some members of the middle class. In one especially poignant example of the relationship between radicalism and otherness, Aberdeen Rev. Charles McDermoth linked the socialist Finns to "beer drinking" and even child molestation. When in 1906 the socialist Finns planned to break off from the Aberdeen Finnish temperance society to build their own hall, what eventually became the Red Finn hall, Reverend McDermoth, with support of the Aberdeen City Council, protested that the hall would "become a pitfall for young girls," who might "be led astray at a place of this kind."[68] After an indignant response from Finnish American residents, who argued that the new hall was to be used for political and social functions, the city permitted the socialists to build their hall.[69] Following a mass lumber strike in spring 1912, Aberdeen police shuttered the city's Red Finn hall because of the Finns' support of the strike.[70] In response, socialists requested a court injunction against the city, arguing that "great mental, moral, and spiritual 'suffering' has been caused by the act of the city administration in nailing up the doors of the resort."[71] But from employers' and strikebreakers' perspectives, closing the Red Finn hall made perfect sense. In one fell swoop, authorities shut down the centerpiece of the harbor's radical community and a fruitful training ground for labor activists. The hall was, after all, a place that Aberdeen mayor James Parks blamed for bringing about the 1912 strike because of "agitation carried on at the Red Finnish Hall on First Street."[72]

HALL SOCIALISM

Reverend McDermoth's campaign against the Red Finn hall reflected not only his concern with the plight of Grays Harbor youth. Instead, McDermoth knew that the members of the group he opposed were the Finnish socialists of Aberdeen, the best-organized radicals in the region. The threat posed by the radical Finns was so acute because no group in American history has been more strongly attracted to socialist and syndicalist ideas, joined radical organizations in greater numbers, and struck as often as the Finns.[73]

Red Finns also threatened employers' interests in Grays Harbor because they established a strong base in the community through their political activism. By supporting and running socialists for local elected office, making their own literature and material culture, staking their claim to public space by building halls and holding street meetings, and striking regularly, these radicals mounted public challenges to employer control in Grays Harbor. In their official history, Aberdeen's Finnish socialists recalled that hall activities were so popular that they pulled workers away from "the most notorious booze-joints by the riverside." Thus, for any employers hoping to keep workers drunk and distracted rather than focused on collective action, Finnish workers' halls posed a threat, for "as soon as the program starts in the hall, the bar becomes empty."[74]

Members of a Finnish temperance society built the harbor's first Finn hall in Hoquiam during 1903. The "temperance Finns" rented the hall to the socialists until Hoquiam Reds purchased it six years later. The first meeting of Finnish American socialists in Aberdeen came on July 25, 1904, when fifteen members formed their own Finn socialist organization. By that time, Hoquiam's Finnish socialist local was already more than a year old. Both groups joined the Finnish Socialist Federation (FSF) after its August 1906 formation.[75] Within two years of its founding the Aberdeen local reported 116 members.[76] They built the famed Red Finn hall in 1906 and enlarged it in 1909.[77]

Peak membership for the national FSF came in 1912 when the federation reported 167 locals; four newspapers, three of which were dailies; and ownership of the Work People's College, a radical workers' college in Duluth, Minnesota.[78] That same year the Aberdeen local counted 301 members, while those in Hoquiam had 120, making the Grays Harbor locals the largest and fifth-largest FSF branches in Washington State.[79] Showing that their community presence extended well beyond even these impressive figures, a 1911 photograph prominently featured in one national FSF publication of an outdoor gathering of Aberdeen's Finnish socialists showed hundreds of picnickers seated on a hillside.[80]

The Hoquiam and Aberdeen Finnish Socialist halls played substantial parts in Finnish workers' lives; they attended theater and concerts as well as funerals and speeches in their hallowed halls. In these radical spaces Finnish workers met several times per week, discussed jobs, community events, and politics, and formulated responses to a political and socio-

A picture postcard shows the Finnish Socialist ("Red" Finn) hall in Aberdeen, towering over a neighboring residence. This hall was the center of Grays Harbor's labor-left throughout the early twentieth century. Vigilantes and police raided the hall on several occasions. Polson Museum, Hoquiam, Washington.

economic system that did not work in their interests. Music and theater were routine parts of Finnish social and political meetings, as the groups gathered in their halls dozens of times each year. The Aberdeen Red Finn hall even housed a Sunday school.[81] The Hoquiam local boasted a musical group that played at social functions—and when left-wing luminaries, including Eugene V. Debs and William "Big Bill" Haywood, visited the harbor.[82] When Haywood, a leading figure in the American socialist and industrial union movements, toured the harbor in 1909, the FSF brass band greeted his arrival in Hoquiam, playing two consecutive performances of "The Marseillaise," among other numbers.[83]

The Finnish hall was one of several socialist institutions founded by immigrants on Grays Harbor. The harbor's Finnish socialists also ran a bookstore and news agency. Opened around 1911, the Toveri Bookstore sat at 409 East Wishkah in Aberdeen, near working-class spaces—homes, saloons, eateries, sawmills, and docks.[84] Formed during a difficult period in the region's history—vigilantes and police ransacked leftist spaces — the bookstore held down valuable Aberdeen real estate for over a year before closing amid the suppression of all socialist and IWW activities. Operated by the socialist movement, the bookstore sold Finnish- and English-language books and newspapers, stationery, refreshments, and tobacco. The harbor's socialists must have thought a great deal of the bookstore: they fashioned picture-postcards of the store's entrance.[85]

With a deep tradition of involvement in social and political movements in their home country, Finnish American women eagerly joined Finnish socialist locals in the United States. Unlike the national Socialist Party of American, which included only a small percentage of women members during the 1910s, large numbers of women joined the FSF and its constituent locals.[86] In 1920, 41 percent of FSF members were women, an especially high number considering that only approximately 35 percent of the Finns who moved to the United States between 1880 and 1914 were women.[87]

Large numbers of Grays Harbor women, men, and children supported the FSF; entire families entered the movement together. Of the 421 Grays Harbor FSF members in 1912, 103—roughly one in four—were women.[88] One significant site of women's leadership in the movement was their work with *Toveritar (Woman Comrade)*, a women's newspaper of the FSF published in Astoria. Grays Harbor women found a receptive audience for their writings in *Toveritar*.[89] Founded in 1911, *Toveritar* had by 1915 boosted its subscription list to five thousand, and in the words of historian Mari Jo Buhle, the "publication [was] not merely one for women but women's own paper."[90] Indeed, female Finns were not ancillary to the "real" socialist movement, but integral parts of the whole.[91]

Finnish radicals' halls and their abilities to raise large sums of money made the Finnish left indispensable to segments of the local, regional, and even national left. Finns donated large sums to founding national leftist periodicals, notably the *Daily Worker*, which grew to become the most famous American Communist periodical.[92] Beyond that contribution, from the 1910s to 1930s Finnish Wobblies and socialists donated thousands of dollars to IWW defense and class war prisoner collections, proving vital to the many legal cases that occupied so much of the labor-left's resources during the early twentieth century. But the Red Finn fund-raising machine could also prove to be a lifesaver for workers living in a country without any social safety nets. When, in October 1912, a newcomer to the harbor found herself hopelessly in debt, the "female comrades of Hoquiam held a soiree" to raise relief funds; the comradely event raised almost thirty dollars.[93] Like the halls themselves, Finnish fund-raising operations persisted for decades on the harbor. Thus, the perseverance of Finnish radical institutions, which thrived in many places into and even beyond the Great Depression, mattered for the wider left. In many locations, Grays Harbor included, without the Finns the left would likely have withered far earlier.

OUT OF THE HALLS AND ONTO THE PICKET LINES

Workplace militancy and interethnic solidarity were as important to immigrant workers as was their activism within socialist organizations. In logging and lumber manufacturing where so many Finns earned their living, there were no trade unions to slow militancy—and the AFL showed only sporadic interest in lumber worker unions. Stepping into that void were immigrant socialists and labor militants who developed traditions of community-based and interethnic solidarity outside of traditional union structures.

Still, ethnic identity can compete with class loyalties, and fragmentation during organizing campaigns and strikes is every bit as prevalent in the historical record as are the stirring examples of interethnic solidarity. Employers have had a long history of drawing upon ethnic and racial differences to keep workers divided. Foremen played on "natural rivalr[ies]," getting ethnic groups to compete against one another at work, thus maximizing production.[94] Disunity plagued Grays Harbor, as immigrants competed over jobs and physically fought one another.[95] Although reporters sensationalized ethnic conflicts to sell papers and sow fragmentation, the brawls were real—and sometimes based around real ethnic disagreements. In a notable but by no means unique incident, a 1908 conflict resulting in "Eight Scandinavians Routed by Two Japs" in Aberdeen made front-page statewide news with one paper reporting, "A Japanese war on a small scale took place aboard the big dredge *Pacific* one evening this week and the little brown men came off victorious, two of them putting to rout eight Scandinavians after a pitched battle."[96]

Although stories of working-class fragmentation garner attention, some workers—particularly laborers drawn to one big union ideas—were more interested in building solidarity. In both English- and Finnish-language radical publications, Wobblies and socialists expressed sympathy and appreciation for South Asian workers' class solidarity. In *Toveri*, an Aberdeen worker discussed the interplay of employers and the press, as they attempted to deceive South Asian workers into scabbing, only to be thwarted by an insatiable need for more scab labor. "Those ten Hindus who have (thus far) worked in Wilson and Donovan mill(s) have joined the strike. None of them could understand a single word of English, so they could not be explained how things (really) were. Then the mill owners made the grave mistake of bringing in another group of Hindus here and amongst them was one, who could speak the language. And when the Hindus realized they were scabs they left their positions immediately. . . . Until that very moment the local newspaper '[Aberdeen Daily] World' called them as patriotic Americans, but now they are filthy foreigners."[97] When in 1913, South Asians formed Ghadar, an international revolutionary organization dedicated to overthrowing British rule in India, they did so at Astoria's Finnish socialist hall, choosing an immigrants' headquarters with its anticapitalist politics instead of any of the dozens of other meeting halls.[98]

While the Finns' militancy aggravated harbor employers, it impressed their fellow workers, including members of the IWW. Detecting among the Grays Harbor Finns the seeds of an IWW movement, Wobbly organizer Fred Heselwood stated, "In the matter of organization in the northwest for the coming year, I believe the most effective work can be done among the lumber workers, both in the woods and in the saw mills. The Pacific coast especially offers the greatest inducement, owing to the great number of Finnish workers employed, and as a great majority of these men are revolutionarily inclined, they are very susceptible to industrial unionism."[99] The *Timber Worker*, news organ of the AFL industrial union in lumber, likewise praised the harbor's Finns: "The Finnish workers on Grays Harbor are going to join our movement in great numbers, and there are no better or more class-conscious workers anywhere than are the Finns who are in the lumber industry."[100]

Between 1905 and 1914, the center of immigrant militancy was the S. E. Slade Lumber Company, Aberdeen's largest mill and one that employed scores of Finnish men.[101] Mill manager W. B. Mack had a well-earned reputation as an anti-union roughneck who used any means at his disposal to keep workplaces nonunion. Whether because of low wages, Mack's notoriety, or the presence of Finnish ethnic solidarity complementing their shared class experiences, Slade mill hands were the most militant group of nonunion workers on the harbor, leading strikes in 1905, 1909, 1910, and 1912—all of which escalated into wider conflicts.[102]

Like the Finnish-led strike mentioned at the beginning of this chapter, the sawmill strikes in 1909 and 1910 began when lumber workers demanded higher wages. In May 1909, a strike wave initiated by Finnish mill hands swept through Aberdeen, closing twelve mills and bringing 2,500 workers out on strike. They struck to reverse a pay cut that reduced wages to one dollar and seventy-five cents a day for "common" labor—twenty-five cents lower than at Hoquiam's mills.[103] On May 26, mill hands walked off the job at the S. E. Slade Lumber Company. Within two days strikes had closed the Slade and American Mill Company plants, and by May 31, two large south Aberdeen mills sat idle.[104]

From the opening strike call, this appeared to be more than an isolated protest against low wages. After stopping production at the Slade mill, strikers, many of whom were Finnish leftists, swept across town to the American and Western Lumber Company mills, forming roving pickets and encouraging a citywide mill strike. The interethnic solidarity registered with the public. The *Grays Harbor Post* observed that "the Finnish workers of the north side were joined by the Austrian [Croatian] workers of the south side Monday and Tuesday when the men went out at the Union mill and Aberdeen Lumber & Shingle Co.'s plant."[105]

Shortly after the first walkout at the Slade mill, strikers formed a bargaining committee that met with local and state officials, organized mass meetings, and voted as a body on the mill owners' proposed settlements.[106] To accommodate the large strike force, they met in Aberdeen's Red Finn hall. To reach the large and diverse workforce, strike leaders addressed groups in Finnish as well as English.[107]

Responding to the strike, the harbor's leading lumber firms formed the Aberdeen Manufacturers' Association, a trade group to coordinate employer action. In an effort to suppress the strike, employers at twelve mills stopped operations—locking out the city's 2,500 sawmill workers and promising to close their doors until July 4.[108] In the words of A. P. Stockwell, manager of the C. E. Burrows Lumber Company and spokesman for the local lumber manufacturers' association, none of the mills "had come anywhere near breaking even for the past year or eighteen months, and all of them are only too glad of the opportunity to close down until the market conditions are better."[109] Practicing solidarity, mill owners were "acting in concert," determined to form a permanent lumber manufacturers association on the harbor.[110] This was not a coordinated and violent strikebreaking effort of the type that both preceded and succeeded this strike. But it did illustrate the deep solidarity that, by 1909, unified harbor lumber manufacturers. While the mill hands were strategic in their choice to strike only the mills paying the lowest wages, their bosses saw the seeds of a much wider conflict, with its roving pickets and skilled-unskilled alliance. Lumbermen saw their class interests threatened by a wave of working-class militancy that might get out of hand.

The sawmill laborers lost the 1909 strike. But as in 1905, the strike also demonstrated the potential of workers to build solidarity across ethnic divisions and outside of a trade union movement. Indeed, for the first time on the harbor, Croatians played a significant role in this strike. Like the Scandinavian and Finnish populations, many Slavic immigrants—especially Poles and Croatians—had permanently moved to Grays Harbor and established ethnic institutions like churches, fraternities, and shops. On Aberdeen's south side lay the city's South Slav district. More than one thousand Croatian, Slovenian, and Serbian immigrants settled in Aberdeen and Hoquiam; many worked in south Aberdeen sawmills.[111] By 1912, the harbor's South Slavs had built several ethnic institutions, including a workers' organization and a mercantile; the Croatian Workingman's Company, which they incorporated in 1910, housed a "Workingman's store."[112] During a 1912 lumber strike, the IWW held meetings at the Croatian Workingman's Company when it allowed the Wobblies to use their hall; the hall was valuable considering its location in south Aberdeen amid a heavily immigrant population.[113]

The Croatian Workingmen's Grocery and Meat Market was established by Croatians in south Aberdeen, where hundreds of Croatian Americans lived and worked. Polson Museum, Hoquiam, Washington.

Not discouraged by their strike defeat in 1909, a coalition of "new" immigrants struck Grays Harbor's sawmills less than a year later. In May 1910, a group of mostly Greek and Finnish workers at the Wilson Brothers mill in Aberdeen struck and demanded raises; each of the mills paid between a $2 and $2.50 minimum wage, and in each case strikers demanded a raise of twenty-five cents per day.[114] From the Wilson mill, workers spread the strike to the notorious Slade operation.[115] In addition, dock workers at the Slade mill halted work, and the strikers received support from the Aberdeen local of the IWW. W. A. Thorn, secretary of the Aberdeen IWW and a longshoreman, wrote to the *Industrial Worker*, "Keep away from Grays Harbor if you believe in better conditions. Saw mill men are on strike at several mills."[116]

The 1910 strike ended in defeat for the mill workers. Writing that "present market conditions will not permit of any raise" and "there is nothing to warrant an increase," harbor lumbermen refused to grant the increase, and by May 23 enough of the strikers had returned to work for the plants to restart.[117] But their defeat in 1910 was more of a temporary setback than a decisive failure for the immigrant strikers, and both the militancy and interethnic solidarity of 1910 was manifested in a far larger conflict two years later. In the spring of 1912, during a strike begun by mill hands in Hoquiam, one Wobbly confirmed that the Greeks had firmly established themselves in the militant wing of the harbor's immigrant working class:

> The Northwestern was the first mill to bring Greeks to Hoquiam and now they want them to leave. Greeks are too revolutionary. Not one of them is scabbing. They repudiate the idea with scorn.
>
> The bosses think they can use the scissorbill to scab on the Greeks and then use the Greeks to scab the scissorbill out of existence, but there is nothing doing. All the strikers realize that the only foreigner they have to fight is the boss.
>
> Yesterday morning four of our pickets were arrested at the Northwestern and the captain, a Greek, had his head split with a hammer in the hands of a scab.[118]

The quotation lauding the Greeks' militancy came during the well-known "War of Grays Harbor," the weeks-long strike of lumber and maritime workers and their allies led by the IWW that shut down practically every sawmill and dock in Grays Harbor and nearby Pacific County.[119] These alternate currents of radicalism forged by immigrant laborers, rather than the "official" labor movement of craft unions, provided the foundations upon which the IWW built its movement. Indeed, the immigrants' socialist organizations, hall culture, and interethnic mass militancy all contributed to the Wobbly movement as it developed on the harbor during the early 1910s. On the harbor, the roots of interethnic radicalism and militancy resided deep within the world of the immigrant worker.

5

BUILDING THE "W" CITY

COMMUNITY-BASED RADICALISM

On March 31, 1912, eight thousand striking workers and supporters gathered at Electric Park on the border of Aberdeen and Hoquiam to present a united front against Grays Harbor employers in what was growing into a major regional strike. The park, however, could not contain this crowd, which spilled onto the surrounding streets. Near the crowd's center, atop a soapbox, rose an illustrious lineup of "speakers in many different languages."[1] Workers listened to speeches, sang and played "revolutionary music," and carried signs reading "We Are Striking for Living Wages."[2] The mass meeting itself followed two parades, one from Aberdeen, the other from Hoquiam, both a "half mile long," which had descended upon the overflowing park. Red Finn women and members of the Finnish socialist band led both parades. Marchers included children, striking lumber and maritime workers, and supporters drawn from other sectors of the community.[3] Inspired by the militancy shown during the initial walkout and impressed with the public presence of the strikers, workers from a diverse cross section of ethnic and occupational groups flocked into the harbor's Industrial Workers of the World branches.[4] Longshoremen, shingle weavers, sailors, and electrical workers all struck alongside the mill hands in what had fast spread beyond the Hoquiam sawmills where it started, rapidly escalating into a region-wide conflict.[5] Men and women remained on the picket lines for two months in Aberdeen and Hoquiam, often enduring beatings for their efforts. More than 1,500 strikers crowded into the Hoquiam Finn hall during one meeting, and the workers needed the Aberdeen and Hoquiam Finn halls, south Aberdeen's Croatian hall, as well as their own IWW hall in order to accommodate the crowds.[6] The

Striking workers and their supporters march through Hoquiam during a 1912 strike. The sign near the middle of the photograph reads "Longshoremen Striking for Better Conditions." A band marches at the front of the parade. Polson Museum, Hoquiam, Washington.

strike spread into Washington logging camps, drawing an estimated five thousand loggers at fifty camps in the Grays Harbor and Puget Sound regions.[7] One enthusiastic Wobbly captured the spirit of the strike by writing, "This struggle is no longer a Hoquiam strike, but a general tie-up of the Grays Harbor lumber industry. It's catching and the longer it lasts the farther it spreads."[8]

Two weeks before the meeting at Electric Park, the strike began when Hoquiam sawmill laborers struck, demanding an increased pay scale for all lumber workers, including a minimum wage of two dollars and fifty cents and union recognition for the IWW. The conflict escalated, eventually shuttering much of southwest Washington's lumber industry.[9] On March 20, the strike closed four mills; by March 22, nine Aberdeen mills were closed; six days later nearly twenty mills sat idle.[10]

The IWW had a substantial presence in the Northwest lumber industry; over the course of the 1910s and 1920s the Wobblies forged a community-based radical movement rooted in Grays Harbor's working class—particularly among the immigrant sawmill laborers. Lumber workers joined the IWW for a variety of reasons. First, the Wobblies built industrial, rather than trade, unions and prioritized direct action over elections. Loggers, sawmill laborers, and Grays Harbor Finns joined the IWW en masse. Finnish radicals in other parts of the country had long voted for prolabor candidates and found elections—without unions—to be lacking. Wobbly direct action held a special appeal for the lumber workers, men who saw electoral politics as a farce, one in which they could not participate. While the United States broadened democratic participation throughout the nineteenth and early twentieth centuries, its scope failed to include most Northwest lumber workers either because of the itinerancy of the job or because they, as non-naturalized immigrants, failed to meet voting qualifications. Grays Harbor elections were exceptionally unrepresentative and corrupt. In 1912, during the big IWW-led lumber strike, Hoquiam's vigilante employers' organization forced a recall vote against the prolabor socialist mayor and simply ousted the socialist city clerk—an official in the local labor movement.[11]

Second, American unions had long histories of ethnic, race, gender, and skill exclusiveness that kept lumber workers on the outside. Wobblies openly challenged those distinctions and asked workers to unite into industrial unions where class—or at least industry—were organizing principles. This appealed to many Grays Harbor workers, who joined the organization by the thousands. Although best known for their revolutionary politics and creative challenges to elites, Wobblies also fought for bread-and-butter improvements—higher wages, shorter hours, safer conditions, and sanitary reforms like clean bedding and toilets.[12] The IWW did not sign contracts with employers, but they did make strike demands that promised to improve working families' lives. Ignored by the traditional unions, loggers and sawmill laborers saw their chance at a union in the IWW.

Third, in an industry where occupational differences within the logging force and within the sawmill force were minor, industrial unions were the only ones that made sense. As historian Philip S. Foner noted, "The industry . . . included many different trades, each of which, if organized separately, would have had only one or possibly two or three members in each camp."[13] In 1913, the *Timber Worker*, organ of the American Federation of Labor industrial union, editorialized, "This paper will stand for industrial unionism as indicated and provided for by the new constitution formulated by the delegates to the Portland convention of the International Shingle Weavers' Union."[14] But the AFL's position on industrial unionism came only after several years of disinterest in, and opposition to, organizing loggers and sawmill laborers. The IWW's *Industrial Worker* urged lumber workers to remember the AFL's views: "We ask loggers and mill workers to look up the record of every organization fostered by the American Federation of Labor. We guarantee that you will find, with scarcely a single exception, that they are all formed so as to give the employers the best of it." The author then contrasted the revolutionary industrial unionism of the Wobblies with the AFL Timber Workers "that can openly organize, under police protection, in the Grays Harbor District—a district that has made its threat that no union shall be allowed to exist among the lumber slaves."[15]

THE WOBBLIES IN AXE-HANDLEVILLE

In the wake of the open-shop drive, highlighted by the defeat of the shingle weavers' union, the attacks on maritime unions, and a compromise settlement with their "unskilled" sawmill laborers, Grays Harbor employers faced a new challenge from the IWW. The Wobblies had formed two branches on the harbor in 1907 and recruited a small membership among Aberdeen and Hoquiam shingle weavers and mill hands. By mid-1911 the Wobblies had forged several radical outposts within Grays Harbor manufacturing and transportation workplaces, those industries with recent histories of union-busting and practically no history of industrial union organization by the AFL.[16] Between October 1911 and May 1912, harbor employers faced off in a series of battles against workers who joined or sympathized with the IWW. The Aberdeen Free Speech Fight and Grays Harbor lumber strike, as the conflicts were popularly known, witnessed a new style of employer offensive for the region, one waged by an employing class devoted to eliminating radicals from the community.[17] Supplemented by anti-union media and police, employers based their campaign on physical force. During their drive against the Wobblies, local employers formulated and utilized a model of anti-unionism based on cooperation with each other, violent direct action against workers, and heavy assistance from the state and the media.

As radicals, Wobblies posed special problems for employers. They relied on direct action at the point of production and mass community pressure to achieve their aims. As employers made clear during earlier open-shop campaigns, they wanted little or nothing to do with unions. Moreover, most employers saw the IWW as both a union and as a "red menace," a revolutionary "horde of men" who imported chaos into communities that the employers' organizations claimed as their own.[18]

IWW membership grew during the Aberdeen Free Speech Fight of November 1911 to January 1912, when local and itinerant Wobblies joined harbor socialists in a successful effort to overturn a city law banning speeches in Aberdeen's downtown.[19] Municipal governments passed these laws in response to IWW's street-corner organizing. In the words of geographer Don Mitchell, these speech battles were really over turf within a community. He wrote that that "the streets and parks of American cities were the most important organizing ground. . . . 'If denied the right to agitate there, then they must remain silent.'"[20] The most famous fight brought Spokane and the Wobblies national attention during 1909–10 as radicals battled Spokane's elite—city government, employers, police, and courts—over the city's law banning radical speeches. The famed "Rebel Girl" Elizabeth Gurley Flynn joined fellow workers in challenging the law. Like scores of others, Flynn ended up behind bars when she challenged the law, to "fill up the jails" and drain municipal coffers by demanding individual jury trials. Radicals flooded into Spokane intent on defying the law in perpetuity. Whether because of the negative publicity or the cost to continue the fight, in March 1910 the Spokane government rescinded the speaking prohibition.[21]

The victory lifted IWW sails, and Grays Harbor, because of its large socialist population and reputation for labor militancy, grew into an important Wobbly outpost. In mid-1911, Wobblies began delivering speeches on the streets of downtown Aberdeen. In November 1911, for instance, Wobblies William Thorn and James M. Train launched into speeches denouncing "the national administration, the local administration, the millowners, the business folk, the union officials, and the local police."[22]

IWW organizing poked the bear of lumber manufacturers and boss loggers, who responded with a six-month-long attack on the radicals. On November 24, 1911, five hundred businessmen and allies met at the Aberdeen Elks club to plot their strategy to defeat the IWW, whose recent "invasion" of the harbor towns had raised the specter of anarchy in the region. Hours after the meeting where its participants had vowed to "render . . . any assistance within our power in their efforts to preserve order and uphold the laws," members of the newly formed Citizens' Committee armed themselves and surrounded a group of IWW members as they waited to enter the Empire Theatre, the site of a rally planned for that evening. What followed next was a bloody rout. Hundreds of newly deputized police, mostly businessmen, fell upon the unsuspecting Wobblies, beating the workers about the head and body as they passed. For the next two months, the Citizens' Committee coordinated street patrols, guarded the town entrances, searched trains entering Aberdeen, and visited nearby towns and farms to ask their residents to evict the radicals from the county's rural periphery.[23]

Employers across the country organized citizens' committees to wage anti-union campaigns. Formed in November 1911, the Aberdeen Citizens' Committee rounded up and jailed activists, used fire hoses to disperse their meetings, sought to starve out strikers by refusing them credit at local merchants, imposed exorbitant fines for minor criminal offenses, kidnapped activists and ran them out of town, assaulted them with clubs and firearms, and raided and closed their halls. During the lumber strike in spring 1912, the Hoquiam Citizens' Committee armed itself with shotguns and clubs and formed a cavalry to ride down the strikers.[24]

Workers' halls were the centers of the IWW movement—places where families sang and played, ate, socialized, and organized. As the symbolic and strategic centers of the Wobbly movement, IWW halls became prime targets for repression. Grays Harbor employers were aware of the importance of the IWW's halls, a fact that no doubt contributed to their desire to remove them from their communities. The physical destruction visited upon IWW halls the nation over was remarkable. Aberdeen employers, vigilantes, and officials were at the vanguard of this pillaging. Police and vigilantes raided Grays Harbor IWW halls on no fewer than eleven occasions between 1911 and 1922.[25] These acts of vandalism were the source of admiration for anti-unionists who recognized the merits of dealing with the labor movement through violent direct action. One such imitator was one of the men who planned the raiding of the Centralia IWW hall on Armistice Day 1919. He argued, "The only way to handle the IWWs in Centralia is to do the same thing done in Aberdeen. Clean 'em up, burn 'em out."[26]

The *Aberdeen Daily World* complimented the Citizens' Committee for its bold actions, writing, "The city will not place [the IWWs] in jail, nor will meals be furnished them. They will be shipped out by the carload or train load, if necessary, and as soon as enough of them have been collected to make up a shipment."[27] During one expulsion, Citizens' Committee member L. G. Humbarger confessed that they operated outside the law in his warning to deportees: "What we have done we did by taking the law in our own hands. You men go and never return. God bless you if you remain away, but God help you if you ever return."[28] Municipal police and elected officials worked alongside the committees and even participated directly in acts of violent anti-unionism. To disperse a crowd of protestors, police chief L. D. Templeman turned the city fire hose on them, hitting women with baby carriages and children standing beside their parents. The *Industrial Worker* reported, "The fire hose was brought into play and thousands . . . were drenched for being 'rioters.'"[29] Temp's aggression endeared him to at least some elites; during the summer of 1912 the police chief ran for county sheriff, although he dropped out because "his first duty lies toward the city [Aberdeen] and that he must service its interests before his own."[30]

While harbor business owners insisted on calling themselves a committee of citizens, Wobblies exposed the class-based nature of the Citizens' Committee. To the Wobblies, the Citizens' Committee was a "slugging committee of the business men," a group of "piratical masters," "'law and order' thugs" a "gang of scab policemen," and a "bunch of middle-class scissor-bills who are but acting in the interests of the lumber trust." "Their particular names in this instance," wrote IWW cofounder and leading journalist C. E. "Stumpy" Payne, included "Banker Patterson, who has 80 per cent of the business houses of Aberdeen and Hoquiam under his thumb," and Robert Lytle, "one of the most vigorous and slimy foes of the Shingle Weavers' Union." For its employers' actions against the IWW, the city of Aberdeen received the nickname "Axe-Handleville."[31]

Wobblies published the names of known Citizens' Committee members. The committee united employers as a class—men joined its ranks from across ethnic, political, religious, and, perhaps surprisingly given the emphasis on "citizens" in their title, even citizenship lines. At the head of the group were officials and ex-officials from the Aberdeen Chamber of Commerce and Elks club.

Most committee members were businessmen, including real estate agents, saloon and theater owners, and proprietors of grocery and clothing stores. By committing public acts of violence against the Wobblies, small businessmen opened themselves up to boycotts that Wobblies enthusiastically carried out in December 1911, just in time to hurt Christmas sales.[32] Editors from Grays Harbor's four largest local mainstream newspapers served as enthusiastic mouthpieces for the Citizens' Committee.[33] In response, Wobblies declared the press to be "another wheel in their machine of suppression . . . which, true to their harlot like nature, lay themselves at the feet of any who will buy."[34]

The Wobblies' free speech fight brought national attention. For two months, the *Industrial Worker* ran news from Grays Harbor across the front page. IWW, socialist, and trade union locals across North America channeled hundreds of dollars and supportive resolutions to the harbor free-speech fighters.[35] By January 1912, local IWWs assembled more than a hundred free-speech fighters prepared to violate the ordinance and go to jail and face other forms of punishment. Many of the visiting Wobblies awaited the demonstrations in Hoquiam, making use of the relatively prolabor administration of Mayor Harry Ferguson, a preacher elected earlier that year with strong union and women's suffragist votes; Ferguson later became a prominent socialist and claimed he attended

IWW meetings but did not join "because he is not a working man."[36] Faced with this determined opposition, Aberdeen municipal officials compromised. Stumpy Payne, who was jailed during the fight, declared the IWW received everything it had demanded in negotiations and that "the Free Speech in Aberdeen passes into history as a clean-cut, unqualified victory for the Industrial Workers of the World."[37] The city council allowed street speaking without a permit on most of Aberdeen's streets. In return, city officials and employers asked only that the Wobblies "not crow and brag" over their victory, "owing to [employers'] sensitive feelings." Within a month of the repeal of the speaking ban, Grays Harbor workers had formed three Wobbly locals, which hosted nightly street meetings and weekly hall lectures.[38]

By early 1912, the IWW had established beachheads in Grays Harbor workplaces and the wider community, posing threats to both capital accumulation and elite rule over public spaces. In fact, employers' responses to the IWW were influenced nearly as much by the perceived threat to their dominant positions within the community as by employers' hostility toward unions. John Carney, editor of the *Aberdeen Herald*, left little doubt as to this fact, writing, "The issue is not free speech; it is not whether or not street speaking be permitted or denied, but who shall control Aberdeen, its resident citizens or a bunch of irresponsibles gathered under the red banner of anarchy by a small coterie of grafting officials parading under the high sounding name of the Industrial Workers of the World."[39]

The IWW grew rapidly in the wake of the free-speech fight. It organized a lumber workers' local in Hoquiam and a branch of the Marine Transport Workers' Industrial Union (MTWIU) in Aberdeen.[40] But while employers and their allies conceded to radical workers the right to organize in public, they refused to consider the possibility of a contested control over their workplaces. In the years ahead, the harbor experienced repeated clashes between local workers and the coordinated efforts of employers to prevent this from happening. Jay Fox, anarchist editor of the *Agitator* and a future lumber union organizer, responded to the free-speech fight by connecting employer power to their class solidarity: "The bosses act as one man. There is no question whose business is attacked. Nobody sulks in his tent. 'All for one, one for all,' is their motto, stolen from us. They have a better title to it. Let us get together and prove ourselves worthy of what we preach."[41]

A WORKING-CLASS ORGANIZATION

In early 1912, Grays Harbor Wobblies hosted nightly street meetings and weekly hall lectures. They helped to organize a sawmill strike during the spring of 1912—a conflict that some IWWs appropriately called the "War of Grays Harbor."[42]

The strike was a mass effort that combined thousands of workers in a struggle for a host of demands, including increased wages and an eight-hour day. Strikers also demanded that employers hire all loggers and mill workers from a union-controlled hiring hall. Worker control over hiring was, as sociologist Howard Kimeldorf notes, an example of "syndicalist impulses," one that saw workers challenge owners over their most sacred principle: managerial control over their own businesses.[43]

Strikers built upon earlier foundations of interethnic solidarity, as European immigrants—Finns, Croatians, and Greeks—struck in tandem with native-born Americans and immigrants from northwest Europe and Canada. The strike force also included East and South Asian workers, challenging not only the view among some unionists that the Asians represented a "scab race" but also employers' decision to pay Asian workers less than whites. Wobbly organizer F. H. Allison wrote, "Hindus are out of the mill and bosses are trying to get negroes to act as scabs. We are gaining ground every hour. All attempts to break the strike are futile. The mill whistles are barely operating." The *Industrial Worker* provided context for Allison's statement, concluding, "The reason the Hindus worked in the first place was because there was no way in which to explain the situation to them. When an English speaking Hindu was found he made the situation clear to his countrymen and they all quit. The strikers are going to send a Hindu delegation in to persuade the Americans to quit scabbing."[44] On the strike's second day, Grays Harbor's IWW formed an eight-person strike committee composed of two Finns, two Greeks, two Scandinavians, and two English speakers.[45] The committee had more than token importance. With the rank and file in control of their own affairs, immigrant workers emerged as leaders, giving speeches in their own languages, guiding fellow workers along picket lines, writing strike reports in their native languages, and rooting the conflict in their ethnic enclaves and halls. Strike reports from the harbor written in both Finnish and Italian reached immigrant working-class populations around the country.[46]

Community allies turned out to support the strikers. Finnish socialists proved to be the IWW's main source of support. When the small IWW halls could not accommodate the group's members and supporters, Wobblies turned to the large halls owned by their supporters among the Finns of Aberdeen and Hoquiam and the Aberdeen Croatian Workingmen's Association. Leftist Finnish workers joined other prostrike groups to establish soup kitchens in Aberdeen and Hoquiam, "feeding the unmarried men, while provisions are being given out to men of families." Vigilantes responded by attacking the strikers' soup kitchens. One Finnish worker reported that the "union grubhouse was attacked by the hounds on the night before the 23rd [of April]. They beat up one man severely, and others less seriously, and in general raised hell."[47] With little sympathy in the press, Wobblies penned articles for the *Industrial Worker* and *Solidarity* and published local bulletins.[48] The first of these was the *Workingmen's Bulletin*, a daily strike report edited initially by Herman Titus and later J. S. Biscay and published by the Grays Harbor IWW during the 1912 strike.[49] Harbor Wobblies also published their own leaflets during the 1912 lumber strike. One of these was a satirical advertisement for a fictional employment agency called "Catchem, Fakeum, Skinum, and Shipum Employment Assassination," which specialized in providing "hungry slaves" and "men to break strikes."[50]

Police, professional strikebreakers, and a 1,000-member citizens' committee composed of local employers organized violent mass resistance to the strikers. Some newspapers, particularly those from outside Grays Harbor, where media had fewer ties to local lumbermen, publicized the violence. One strike report told of the violence committed by an owner of the Anderson and Middleton Mill: "Mill owner Anderson, swinging a heavy club and brandishing a revolver, urged his thugs to shoot down the workers. . . . He had shot a workingman who had come after his pay and who was leaving the vicinity of violence. Shot from behind. He may recover."[51] In one article, the *Oregonian* reported that "a citizens' police force of 200 men . . . armed with shotguns and part mounted and all carrying clubs and some kind of guns" had been dispatched so as to "preserve order."[52] Hoquiam police chief Theodore Quinn beat and hanged Wobbly prisoners; memories of the tortured IWW members remained so strong in the region that more than two decade later local communists condemned Quinn in the *Voice of Action*: "Under his direction strikers were lashed up by their wrists in their jail cells."[53]

Besieged by strikebreakers, the male strikers left the picket lines only to be replaced by their wives, daughters, and female acquaintances. By early April, women bore the brunt of very dangerous picket line duty.[54] Photographs of strike parades feature long lines of women in prominent positions, usually marching alongside their children at the front of parades or demonstrating in women's-only picket duty.[55]

Children, including infants, accompanied their mothers on picket line duty. Their presence represented potent symbols of the strike as a family-based movement to win "living wages."[56] But the presence of children and infants on picket duty placed them in the line of police and vigilante violence. A local *Strike Bulletin* reported strikebreakers' brutish acts; it told readers that an "infant in baby carriage is nearly drowned" after "deputies turn the hose on a group of women and small children when they attempted to speak to scabs on the street." The local IWW also tried to appeal to "the citizens of Aberdeen" to stop "allow[ing] even women and babies to be attacked by thugs" because "the authorities refused to protect working women on the streets of Aberdeen."[57] Police arrested picketer Manda Niemi, the mother of a two-month-old son; Niemi's supporters brought the infant to jail so she could care for him.[58]

Photos of women picketers, including those nursing injuries, reached thousands of readers through the *Seattle Star*, which dispatched staff to Grays Harbor.[59] Hoping to control the narrative, police abused journalists; when a *Seattle Star* photographer snapped pictures of "the squad of special officers" guarding Aberdeen mills, police arrested him and held him in custody until he agreed "to keep his camera in his grip until he returned to Seattle."[60] Later, the Aberdeen police chief told one *Star* reporter, "The less you people say about us the better it will be for you. You are forbidden to take pictures anywhere."[61]

The size of the IWW movement, its community support, and its rank-and-file leadership could not stave off defeat at the hands of a unified employing class with support of the state and local media. From the strike's early days, management painted the strikers as outsiders unwelcome in the community before then importing actual outsiders into the harbor towns to break the strike. On March 15, Al Kuhn, manager of the Hoquiam Lumber and Shingle Company, blamed "blacks" for the strike. Angered at seeing "blacks" picketing outside the mill, he asked that they be replaced by "white men with families."[62] After two months of advertising for scabs "from the Atlantic coast as well as from near by," constructing housing and finding permanent homes for the replacement workers, and guarding the scabs' every move, the lumbermen broke the strike at the end of April. They offered "white labor" a new minimum wage of two dollars and twenty-five cents per day.[63] By making the offer only to "whites," harbor employers divided and conquered the once-unified local working class. Employers tried to eliminate "black" and "foreign" workers, especially the Greek American mill hands who were active in the strike.[64] Press outlets cheered the lumbermen's victory, declaring that the "Revolution on Harbor Fails" and proclaiming that "Hoquiam Is to Be a White Man's Town."[65] The *Industrial Worker* picked up on this fact, scorning "the press of the plutocracy united in their exclamations of glee over the defeat of the IWW."[66]

Local businessmen and newspapermen, however, moved to eliminate the IWW to make sure the harbor had no places of refuge for radicalism. Employers fixed much of their rage on Hoquiam Mayor Harry Ferguson, blaming him for the IWW's successes in Hoquiam and urged his removal—contending that by not acting decisively to break the strike, he was unfit for office. In fact, the day after Ferguson's 1911 election, seven months before the strike, the *Washingtonian* editorialized that "on the street yesterday was frequently heard . . . in six months the people would require a change."[67] Although the editorial counseled patience with the preacher-mayor, the suggestion of a possible coup was hard to miss. At the end of March, Hoquiam employers demanded Ferguson quit office; the mayor refused.[68] Hoquiam's businessmen had an even brusquer method for punishing the city's leading labor politician: Harry Kress, the city clerk and socialist president of the Hoquiam labor council. On April 10, the Hoquiam City Commission removed Kress from office for supporting the strikers.[69] Aberdeen's voters elected two socialists to the city council in elections held during the strike, including the sawmill laborer E. E. Wieland, who alleged that vigilantes threatened his life unless he left town.[70] An elite lumbermen's periodical even cautioned its national readership that if Ferguson remained in office, the IWW "troubles were to start on August 1st."[71] In June 1912, businessmen took their shot, sponsoring an ultimately successful recall election.[72] Ferguson's experiences at the center of a violent class struggle gave him new insights into the workings of American capitalism. Leaving office, the former mayor affiliated with the SPA and became a socialist orator, arguing that "capital should be rolled up and shipped out of the country and labor would be just as well off."[73]

The Wobblies lost the 1912 lumber strike. They declared the strike at an end on April 27, 1912.[74] Through beatings, arrests, evictions, the blacklist, and attempts to replace "foreign" labor with "All American" crews, employers drove many radicals from the harbor.[75] However, neither their defeat in the strike nor the expulsion of well-known organizers ended the IWW movement on the harbor. Instead, by 1912 the Wobblies had developed roots in Grays Harbor's working-class community, particularly among immigrant laborers. These workers continued to meet, write, publish, and agitate for better working conditions throughout the mid-1910s before reemerging as part of a revitalized Wobbly movement during the latter part of 1916. The strikers, especially the women picketers who took so much abuse, gained legendary status among Northwest unionists. In 1936, more than two decades after the "War of Grays Harbor," a special Labor Day edition of the *Timber Worker*, official periodical of the industrial union movement in lumber, cast the 1912 picketers as heroic working-class women whom future workers should emulate.[76]

AFL UNIONS IN TIMBER

AFL leaders came around to the fact that Pacific Northwest loggers and mill workers wanted to unionize and that craft unionism made little sense in lumber. In 1911–12, shingle weavers took the lead in creating an industrial union in lumber, an alternative to the IWW. International Shingle Worker's Union of America president J. G. Brown had long advocated unionizing the region's sawmills and logging camps. In January 1913, at the ISWUA convention, the shingle weavers adjusted their constitution to become an industrial union and enlarged their organization to form the International Union of Shingle Weavers, Sawmill Workers and Woodsmen (IUSWSWW).[77]

As with the IWW, labor radicals sparked the IUSWSWW's creation. Led by socialists such as Brown and syndicalists such as Jay Fox, former editor of the *Agitator* at the anarchist colony at Home, Washington, the IUSWSWW drew thousands of Northwest lumber workers into its fold.[78] The 1913 Fourth of July holiday witnessed a flood of loggers into Grays Harbor's new labor unions. Union officials used the concentration of loggers in Aberdeen and Hoquiam during the holiday to organize:

> Let's throw our headquarters open to them, hold mass meetings, hire bands, urge them not to get tanked up and throw all their money over the bar. . . . Three mass meetings were held, all of them splendidly attended. Men came to headquarters, singly and in groups, to hear more about this movement, and seldom did they go away without enlisting for the war. . . . Here were men, literally hundreds of them, eager to hear the message of co-operative effort. Not a jangling, disputatious set of know-it-all wiseacres, but a body of men, filled with a burning sense of social and industrial injustice and anxious to find the way to right their wrongs.[79]

The Syndicalist, organ of the Chicago-based Syndicalist League of North America, reported the success of the Aberdeen and Hoquiam IUSWSWW locals, concluding that the locals' membership would soon "reach the 500 mark."[80] Five Grays Harbor timber workers' locals marched at the 1913 Labor Day parade in Aberdeen, "occupying several blocks, two abreast."[81]

In January 1914, the IUSWSWW estimated its membership as 31,000 (likely exaggerated), including 2,600 members in Aberdeen Local 10 and another 2,100 from Hoquiam Local 21.[82] The union took a more manageable name in 1914, becoming the International Union of Timber Workers (IUTW), known as the Timber Workers' Union.[83]

The Timber Workers' Union was a radical organization. At its opening convention, the union passed a resolution supporting the SPA and the union officially endorsed socialist policies and politicians. The first issue of the *Timber Worker*, the Timber Workers' union newspaper, ran a front-page reprint article from the *National Socialist*.[84] At the 1913 convention, the annual report given by union president J. G. Brown predicted that a socialist society lay in the future: "Returns from the last election ought to encourage all thinking members of organized labor to believe that the day of final reckoning, where labor shall come into possession of the means of production and distribution is perceptibly nearer."[85] Union writers peppered the *Timber Worker* with socialist material throughout the organ's two-year run. One unionist wrote that the organizing of the timber workers "shall mean the hastening of the time when the workers of the world shall be fitted to take over the machines of production."[86] Much of the discussion around the new union focused on the role of the Shingle Weavers' Union as the core of the larger lumber workers' movement. A poem by unionist Arthur Jensen read, in part, "The Shingle Weavers' Union has been placed in the ground. From this seed is now sprouting the International union of Shingle Weavers, Sawmill Workers, and Woodsmen."[87]

With the IWW under duress during and after the 1912 strike, some Wobblies and supporters joined the seemingly safer AFL timber union. The leading presence of socialist J. G. Brown and his friend William Z. Foster meant a variety of radical influences were at work in the union. As early as 1912, Foster asserted that the ISWUA was full of Wobblies: "the rebels are probably enuf to run the 'Shingle Weavers' Union."[88] After trying and failing to convert the IWW to his position that a "militant minority" of radical workers should bore from within AFL unions, in September 1912 Foster formed the Syndicalist League of North America and traveled the continent forming syndicalist leagues. Foster also convinced Jay Fox, himself a former lumber worker, to move the *Agitator* to Chicago and rename it the *Syndicalist*. With his experiences in the Pacific Northwest, Foster went to work with the timber workers in March 1914, just as the organization planned an industry-wide strike for the eight-hour day.[89]

Foster and other syndicalists viewed the IUTW as a hotbed of syndicalism, writing in a memoir, "In this union League forces were strong; Jay Fox, our national editor, was a Vice-President, and I myself became an organizer of the union for a few months in the summer of 1914. I was in the midst of one of my periodic hobo agitation trips and was induced to help in the eight-hour day campaign in the woods and mills, which our forces had done much to stimulate."[90] One shingle weavers' unionist declared, "I have been getting Syndicalism started among the members of our union . . . The *Syndicalist* is our paper, so let's boost for it."[91] As organizer for the Seattle branches of the Timber Workers' Union, Foster organized a Seattle Loggers' Union and opened up a Loggers' Union headquarters along Seattle's Skid Road, "right in the heart of the 'slave market,'" where unemployed loggers purchased jobs from employment agents. In April 1914, Foster and other militant timber workers picketed the Skid Road employment offices when they recruited scabs to break a loggers' strike. He described, "The work of our pickets was easy. So fine was the spirit of the loggers that, although there are thousands of them out of work, all we had to do was simply notify them there was a strike on. They would then turn back and cover the scab herders with imbrecations."[92]

As historian Alexander Saxton argues, racist and exclusionist policies can be more difficult to sustain in industrial unions than they are in craft unions.[93] Shortly after its formation, the Timber Workers' Union articulated their "one purpose," building "one union in the timber industry."[94] Because of their numbers in the labor movement and commitment to radicalism, Northwest Finns received warm greetings from the Timber Workers' Union. *Toveri*, the Astoria-based socialist daily, pledged the support of Pacific Coast Finnish Socialists to the new union, and in 1913 Santeri Nuorteva, editor of *Toveri*, became an organizer for the union.[95] Still, racism was rife in the union—and the timber workers' industrial unionism was not the same as the IWW's antiracist revolutionary unionism. At the 1913 ISWUA convention, delegates adopted a resolution opposing efforts to change a Washington State law that banned Asian immigrants from owning land, stating that this effort at reform was "a cunningly laid scheme to make it possible for Asiatics to own land, driving out eventually other nationalities."[96]

The IUTW's institutional racism connected it to other Pacific Coast trade unions. But the timber workers were far more supportive of socialism and anti-imperialism than were their peer unions. The Timber Workers Union pushed the Aberdeen Central Labor Council to the left, even convincing the council to pass a resolution attacking President Woodrow Wilson and "the international capitalist class" for committing a "capitalist outrage" by sending troops to Mexico. The leftward tilt of the council upset the Aberdeen Carpenters' Union, a bastion of business unionism on the harbor. Determined to prove that they were "not that kind of men," the carpenters quit the labor council after the resolution's passage.[97] Still, plenty of evidence shows local trade unions' leftward trajectory persisted throughout the Timber Workers' Union years within the movement. The US Department of Labor maintained records on Grays Harbor's union support for the left. The feds were especially concerned by the letters and resolutions, submitted to President Wilson in support of the IWW victims of the November 1916 Everett Massacre, penned by Aberdeen trade unions condemning the "murderous attack . . . made on a passenger boat, landing at the dock, by armed citizens of Everett, for no other reason than there were members of the I. W. W. aboard, and many peaceful, law-abiding citizens were killed and wounded."[98]

WOBBLIES IN HARD TIMES

Between 1913 and 1916, the main locus of Grays Harbor radicalism lay in the lumber workers' unions and the Socialist Party of America, but at no point during the 1910s was the IWW removed from Grays Harbor, even if many of its best-known organizers remained at a safe distance from "Axe-Handleville."[99] In July 1912, three months after the collapse of the IWW strike, the head of the Thiel Detective Agency estimated that there were still more than one thousand IWW members working in Grays Harbor.[100]

In September 1912, Big Bill Haywood wrote, "The filthy jails of Hoquiam and Aberdeen are filled with our men."[101] IWW branches in Hoquiam and in neighboring Willapa Harbor functioned long after the end of the strike, while Wobblies found new ways to communicate in Grays Harbor after the strike.[102] Though the *Industrial Worker*, primary organ of the western IWW, halted circulation on September 4, 1913, Grays Harbor Wobblies met, often in secret, and circulated local newspapers.[103] The first, called the *Greek*, was a short sheet printed briefly by a group of Wobblies expelled from the town of Raymond during the 1912 lumber strike. These radicals settled at the site of a boys' reformatory camp along Grays Harbor's south beach, took over the camp, and issued the newspaper.[104]

During the mid-1910s, the largest source of IWW membership on the harbor came from radical Finns. A schism among Finnish leftists broke open in 1914–15 when fifty-five Finnish Socialist Federation branches, and three thousand members left the FSF to join the IWW. The breakaway branches included three of Washington State's largest FSF locals: Seattle, Spokane, and Aberdeen; the large harbor local brought approximately two hundred leftists into the IWW.[105] Elsewhere, as in Hoquiam, leftist Finns quit the FSF to form Finnish Marxist Clubs. These clubs withdrew support for *Toveri*, then under control of socialists and AFL union supporters in Astoria, and invested in the *Sosialisti*, a Finnish-language daily printed by Duluth socialists with IWW support.[106] Grays Harbor radicals eagerly embraced this new Finnish-language IWW newspaper, and a December 1916 issue listed 225 Aberdeen and Hoquiam residents as supporters of the radical sheet. The *Sosialisti* specifically addressed Grays Harbor's Finns, urging them to join the IWW.[107]

Despite the IWW's perseverance on the harbor during the mid-1910s, they failed to crystalize into a mass movement. Their troubles stemmed in part from the recession of 1913–15, when high unemployment made union organizing of any type difficult.[108] Between late 1912 and mid-1916, as the lumber industry contracted, labor produced, in the words of Cloice R. Howd, "little profits for any of the mills."[109] Across Washington, businesses folded and workers lost their jobs. Many available jobs provided only part-time work. The Washington State Bureau of Labor concluded in 1914 that at least 20 percent of the state's employees were a "transient mass of workmen who constantly patronize the employment agencies and form this state's 'army of the unemployed.'"[110] The year 1914 proved especially tough, with lumber and shingle prices bottoming out from mid-1914 to late 1915. On the harbor, the closures of the S. E. Slade Lumber Company and Bay City mill only added to the workers' troubles.[111]

The mid-1910s also saw an offensive by lumbermen against unions, including the Timber Workers' Union. Employers locked out unionists at dozens of mills in 1915, and the IUTW lost much of its membership in the process. The *Timber Worker* shifted from a weekly to a bimonthly in 1915, and IUTW membership cratered throughout the year, with only a handful of locals in existence at the start of 1916.[112]

Wobblies were also the targets of repression. Labor spies tailed the rebel workers and intercepted their mail, dutifully forwarding it to their patron lumbermen. W. S. Seavey, spy for the Seattle branch of the Thiel Detective Service, informed major employers that the "'Wont [*sic*] Work' gang has guilty knowledge of the burning of the seven sawmills the last three months on Puget Sound" and maintained a file on Wobbly John Pancner, who remained locked in the Aberdeen jail throughout much of late 1912.[113]

Sustained by a small group of activists during the recession of 1913–15, the IWW gained new life during the economic recovery of 1916. The state Bureau of Labor described how World War I improved labor market conditions for workers in the state, writing, that "general industry, accentuated by war demands, has expanded to an unlimited extent . . . creating demands for labor far beyond supply of available workers remaining unmolested by national draft call."[114] With little in the way of job competition preventing union organization, the "labor movement in this state," continued the Bureau of Labor, is "in the possession of the largest measure of prosperity which it has ever enjoyed."[115] Unions of the Washington State Federation of Labor grew dramatically during the war years. The 1917–18 WSFL Report declared that the growth of Washington's unions "has been beyond all precedents, financial receipts indicate a most healthful condition of affairs."[116]

SOCIALIST HARBOR

Economic conditions during the 1916 recovery boded well for the IWW's organizing activities. Also, from 1912 to 1917, some parts of the state apparatus became contested terrain with moderate and prolabor candidates entering office. This was most visible in the composition of the Aberdeen city council, with socialists winning several municipal elections.

The socialists' big breakthrough in Grays Harbor came in April 1912 at the tail end of the lumber strike when, in a protest against the collusion between employers and the state, socialist candidates for Aberdeen city council seats captured 34 percent of the total votes and won two of six races.[117] From 1912 to 1919, socialists controlled either two or three seats in the twelve-member council.[118] In other elections, socialists used their votes strategically, as during the 1915 Aberdeen primary election, when a large, if indeterminate, number of socialists voted for Republican mayoral candidate J. M. Phillips, pushing him over the top in his race against the incumbent mayor Eugene France, who, "because of the position he holds among men of wealth, has been inclined to favor the interest of business, sometimes to the great detriment of the workers."[119] A Native American who attended the Carlisle Indian School, Phillips later earned a law degree at Dickinson College and played college football. Moving to Aberdeen, he worked as a union hod carrier and served in union leadership, before running unsuccessfully for state legislature on the Progressive ticket.[120] As he set up his law practice, Phillips earned a reputation for representing "the little guy," including injured workers seeking compensation from recalcitrant owners. Although Phillips was not a socialist, his support for labor earned him the backing of the labor movement, including from some radicals.[121]

Election successes of the Grays Harbor SPA mirrored those of the state and national party.[122] Like the larger organizations, the harbor's SPA drew much of its strength from trade unionists and immigrants. Socialists had always represented an important minority of membership in the harbor's trade union movement, especially in the lumber unions. During the mid-1910s, SPA activists controlled several trade union positions and institutions, including top spots in the labor bureaucracy and control over the *Southwest Washington Labor Press*, the region's weekly labor newspaper.[123]

As evidence of the American government's intention to join the Great War mounted, Grays Harbor Wobblies and socialists joined millions of workers organizing to prevent American involvement in the bloodshed. The drums of war signaled the SPA to mobilize, which they did in every municipality, company town, and unincorporated township throughout Grays Harbor. Harbor leftists' protests connected them to the international workers' movements, as they argued that "the United States . . . throw[ing] herself into this vortex of hate, rapine and murder would be the height of madness." The radicals made far-reaching critiques of imperialism, capitalism, and the oppression of their fellow workers.[124] J. H. Shroyer, secretary of Hoquiam's SPA branch, summarized the relationship between their electoral successes and America's recent declaration of war in Europe: "The entrance of the US into the European conflict is making sentiment here. Seems like something like this was needed to awake the workers. We initiated ten new members at yesterday's meeting."[125]

Nationally, the IWW did not fight the war with as much vigor as did the socialists. But Wobblies did oppose the war, both as an immoral act of violence and as a diversion from the class struggle. In 1914, the IWW issued a resolution reading, "We as members of the industrial army will refuse to fight for any purpose except the realization of industrial freedom."[126] Once the United States declared war in April 1917, most members of the IWW and the institution itself refused to endorse American involvement in the war.[127]

A MASS IWW MOVEMENT

Socialist city council members delivered results for local radicals. Wobblies and other strikers operated in public for part of the war, as Axe-Handleville's bosses sheathed their blades. In 1917–18, Wobblies operated at least four halls: two in Aberdeen and one each in Hoquiam and Copalis Beach.[128] Wobblies opened the first of these halls in October 1916. Antilabor groups did not raid, destroy, or otherwise attack the structures before September 1917, when federal authorities raided the

Aberdeen and Hoquiam halls—along with most Wobbly offices across the country.[129] The absence of attacks on the IWW sites indicated at least a grudging acceptance by local government of the Wobblies' presence in the community. Wobblies likewise believed that some city officials could be counted on as allies. Writing to IWW lawyer George Vanderveer, two Aberdeen Wobblies noted that they had "a talk to one of the Aldermen here and he said he is at the command of the defense [for the *United States v. Haywood, et al.* trial] and would furnish a statement outlining the condition here prior and during the strike."[130]

Although economic conditions and supportive officials opened the door for greater organization, it required both the self-activity of workers and a union capable of advancing workers' real interests to make such organization a reality. In spring 1916, the *Industrial Worker* returned to print. By June 1916 the radical newspaper recorded the presence of several IWW organizers working among the mill hands, loggers, and ship carpenters in Aberdeen, Hoquiam, and the surrounding "jungles." Wobblies planted themselves in the harbor towns and camps. The IWW also shifted its organizational strategy for Northwest lumber workers, urging Wobblies to organize on the job, including in the logging camps, rather than in the cities.[131]

In September 1916, Aberdeen Wobblies organized a local of the National Industrial Union of Forest and Lumber Workers.[132] The Forest and Lumber Workers Union was succeeded by the more successful and well-known Lumber Workers' Industrial Union (LWIU), founded in Spokane during a March 1917 convention.[133] The radicals achieved some early successes, immediately certifying six credentialed delegates and "more of the fellow workers are waiting only till blanks [delegate credentials] arrive."[134] Still, the IWW's true growth came close on the heels of the Everett Massacre of November 1916.[135]

On November 5, 1916, in the midst of a free-speech fight to support a shingle weavers' strike in Everett, 250 Wobblies boarded the steamship *Verona* in Seattle and traveled north toward Everett. They planned to confront that city's law enforcement officers and vigilantes, the men responsible for brutalizing IWW members and supporters for weeks prior to the *Verona* sailing. The scene that followed is as renowned as any in the history of the Wobblies. As the boat neared shore, Snohomish County Sheriff Donald McRae called out to the Wobblies, "Who's your leader?" The workers replied, "We are all leaders."[136] After refusing to back down, the Wobblies were met with a flurry of gunfire from the shore. The sheriff's forces killed at least five IWW members. Many more were seriously wounded, and perhaps a dozen others fell or jumped off the ship in terror and were drowned. Forced to retreat to Seattle, seventy-four Wobblies were arrested and put on trial for murder.[137]

The Wobblies' response to tragic events in Everett generated enthusiasm for their movement. Workers gathered on Grays Harbor, as around the nation, to collect money for their imprisoned fellow workers' defense. They held mass meetings in metropolitan centers like New York, Chicago, and Seattle; in mill towns like Aberdeen and Hoquiam; and in company towns and work camps. IWW orators visited the harbor during their national speaking tours to collect money for the legal defense. Elizabeth Gurley Flynn's May 1917 speeches reached large audiences—in Aberdeen, the IWW had to rent the large Finnish Socialist hall to accommodate all those who wished to attend. Thousands more read translations of her speeches in the IWW's new daily Finnish-language periodical *Industrialisti*. At the Aberdeen speech, Flynn condemned "Everett's bloodhounds" for its crimes against the IWW and welcomed the blossoming IWW movement, providing "lessons about how important it is for the workers to get organized into One Big Union."[138]

The Everett Prisoners' Defense Committee campaign mobilized Pacific Northwest workers, as thousands donated money for the prisoners' defense.[139] The state brought charges against IWW member Thomas Tracy, one of the seventy-four workers arrested for his involvement in the *Verona* incident. The prosecution failed to demonstrate that Tracy had fired any shots from the boat, and the jury acquitted him on May 5, 1917. Failing in this test case, the state released the remaining seventy-three Wobblies without trial.[140]

Although printing Finnish translations of Flynn's speech might in retrospect appear like an obscure way to reach a large audience, publishing it in Finnish in the *Industrialisti* ensured her words would reach thousands.

Like their Finnish socialist counterparts, Finnish-language IWW organs, particularly *Sosialisti*, *Industrialisti*, and *Tie Vapauteen* (Road to freedom), were all popular periodicals read by IWW members and their supporters.[141] Most important of these was the *Industrialisti*, a daily published in Duluth beginning in March 1917. The *Industrialisti* served as an official Wobbly newspaper between 1917 and 1919 and retained a close affiliation with the IWW until it ceased publication during the 1970s. Other Finnish-language IWW publications, including *Tie Vapauteen*, *Luokkataistelu* (Class struggle), and *Ahjo* (The forge), also found eager audiences.[142]

Like other IWW newspapers, the *Industrialisti* published a range of voices; its columns included news, opinions, advertisements, editorial cartoons, jokes, sections written by local correspondents across North America, and a youth page. Staff penned articles and editorials, but more representative were the correspondents' reports that came from across North America. Grays Harbor Wobblies published semiweekly news between the 1910s and 1930s in the "Länneltä" ("From the West") section.[143] Reports ranged from relatively mundane information concerning donations to defense funds to reports of Flynn's May 1917 speeches in Aberdeen and Hoquiam.[144] Scores of Aberdeen and Hoquiam Finnish American businesses advertised in the *Industrialisti*, which carried a weekly "Grays Harborin Ilmuituksia" ("Grays Harbor advertisements") section.[145] The section contained anywhere from a dozen to more than thirty business notices.[146] Although Finns owned many of the advertisers, large harbor companies such as the department store J. C. Penney and Aberdeen Motors paid to advertise in the IWW paper.[147] These advertisers helped sustain the *Industrialisti* as a daily for much of its history, something the English-language periodicals failed to do.[148] The *Industrialisti* also printed a "Young People's Section," a part-English, part-Finnish page that included news articles, literary reviews, and witty treatises on scabs. Junior Wobblies, including Grays Harbor youngsters, read and wrote to the *Industrialisti*, thereby remaining in contact with IWW locals across North America and contributing their own unique perspective to this new organ.[149] The *Industrialisti* found an enthusiastic readership on the harbor. In July 1917, a mere four months after the founding of the

Industrialisti, Grays Harbor Wobblies had "broken all records for a single amount raised by any part of the IWW for the support of the press," in their feverish rush to support the new Finnish-language IWW organ.[150]

RANK-AND-FILE RADICALS IN WARTIME

The guns of World War I began firing in the summer of 1914; by 1915 the war boom kicked off as Northwest lumber fueled all sides of the war machine raging in Europe. Spruce from the Northwest coastal regions took on special importance, used for airplanes by both the Allied and Central powers; workers shipped tens of millions of board feet of spruce to the warfront.[151] The federal government signed millions in contracts with Grays Harbor lumber companies. As historian Robert E. Ficken writes, "Mills on Grays Harbor sent an estimated 750,000 feet of spruce a month by rail to Atlantic coast ports for export to England."[152] Lumbermen accumulated tremendous profits during the war and had little intention of sharing their spoils with labor.[153]

In the winter of 1916–17, Pacific Northwest loggers seethed with discontent. Described as "more deadly than war," loggers' working conditions shocked observers. They worked ten-hour days in cold, wet, dangerous conditions. Their "rewards" for long, hard days of labor was to return to crowded, stinking bunkhouses—their bedding crawling with vermin. Loggers endured cruel "straw bosses," foremen who sped up production through high-ball logging methods and blamed victims for their own workplace accidents. Those who protested could be—and were—fired for their dissent and placed on blacklists that kept them from earning a living.

While conditions such as these were nothing new to the "timberbeasts" of the Northwest woods, their patience had come to an end. Within a month of the LWIU's founding in March 1917, loggers in eastern Washington and Idaho waged sporadic strikes, limiting the timber reaching sawmills. The LWIU set a strike date in eastern Washington for July 1, but when loggers walked off the job by mid-June, it caused the Wobblies to move their strike date up to June 20.[154]

The IWW, the largest and most dynamic labor organization in the Pacific Northwest woods, led a second regional lumber strike in the summer of 1917, demanding improved camp conditions and the eight-hour day.[155] The strike, coming mere months after America's entry into war, disrupted the flow of lumber—a vital war material—needed for the construction of American airplanes, ships, and sundry weapons of war. It began in the logging camps of Grays Harbor, whose loggers pulled off the shutdown in the face of employer and state repression.

With the economy thriving and Wobbly organizers and periodicals spreading throughout the region, the Wobbly movement of the war years eclipsed anything in Grays Harbor—indeed in Pacific Northwest history—as thousands of workers from several industries followed the call into the one big union.[156] By early June 1917, it appeared that nearly everyone was joining, as one IWW maritime union official declared that Aberdeen was "now generally regarded as the strongest wobblie town for its size on the coast."[157] By July, the Wobblies had at least six locals in Grays Harbor, representing clam cannery workers, fishermen, construction workers, and domestic workers, along with the core membership of lumber and maritime workers. By mid-1917, thousands of Grays Harbor workers had flocked into the one big union. According to a letter written to the Finnish-language IWW newspaper *Industrialisti* by Wobbly Jurnun Veli, five thousand people attended an IWW meeting in early July hosted by the IWW in Aberdeen.[158]

A significant moment in the history of the Grays Harbor IWW came on July 1, 1917, when nearly one thousand workers traveled by boat to the beach community of Westport for an IWW picnic. By design a massive affair, the picnic featured food prepared by Wobbly domestic workers, music by the twenty-piece IWW band, and a keynote speech by *Industrial Worker* editor J. S. MacDonald. Boats left the harbor towns at 6 a.m. and the Wobblies arrived on the scene wearing red tags and carrying large banners, one of which read, "Raise High the Blood Red Banner, the Only Flag We Know," a provocative singing choice considering that era's jingoistic fervor. From the moment they first boarded their ships until late into the night when the last boat left Westport, the air was filled with sounds of workers singing IWW songs and talk "of what was going to happen to the boss after the holidays." Through the feasting, festivities, and casual chats while "resting with their friends among the trees," there resonated a sense of the greater purpose of the day, for this was not simply a picnic, but an event hosted by a revolutionary organization whose members stood on the precipice, ready "to grapple with the lumber trust for an eight hour day."[159]

The July 1 picnic was "the largest ever held on the Pacific Coast by the IWW," noted MacDonald, who continued, "It is . . . certain that this picnic has broken all records for a single amount raised by any part of the IWW for the support of the press."[160]

Each of the groups that formed the constituencies of the resurgent IWW wove their own distinct cultures into the movement. By early 1917, the Wobblies had become so firmly entrenched on the harbor that some workers patronized only those restaurants employing Wobblies, such as the No Graft Restaurant.[161] IWW members also worked on the infrastructure projects undertaken by the city and county during the prosperous war years. On the job, these radicals refused to work at anything other than a casual pace for eight hours per day.[162] When contractors failed to raise wages beyond the three dollars per day paid in early July, Wobblies "called a meeting with the result that all men began to take out cards and turn the fight over to the Sure Winner." Four hours later, the boss conceded to the Wobs, raising wages and agreeing to union control over hiring for his firm.[163]

Maritime workers, with their well-known reputation for radicalism, ran their own IWW hiring hall in 1917. On the waterfront, the IWW exercised de facto job control; one IWW official proudly declared that the Wobbly hall was where "the bosses are coming . . . now for help."[164] At the four shipyards in Grays Harbor, fifty Wobblies helped organize thousands of shipyard workers.[165] In fact, shipbuilders were the first to strike in July 1917. After settling their own strike, shipyard workers refused to handle lumber from the struck mills operated by scabs.[166] All told, between 1,500 and 4,000 Grays Harbor workers took out their red cards during 1917 and 1918.[167] Few could fault Agent 31, a labor spy from the Washington State Secret Service, for predicting that Aberdeen might become a "W city."[168]

Strikes at several timber camps followed. The early center of strike activity was in North River, a logging section about twenty-five miles south of Aberdeen. On July 13, workers walked out at three camps, including one operated by the Anderson and Middleton company. A camp manager remained adamant in his opposition to the union, noting that "wages and hours would remain the same, and that if they cared to quit, they could do so." Loggers demanded fifty-cent raises for all camp employees, regardless of position. But bosses at the Anderson and Middleton camp attempted to divide and thus conquer the strikers by offering the full increase only to buckers, a compromise twenty-five cent raise to chokermen, and nothing to "flunkeys" and kitchen workers. Refusing this proposal, loggers remained on strike, the first of what would be hundreds of strikes at logging camps and mills across western Washington.[169]

The rank-and-file Wobblies' militancy caught the IWW's top officials off guard. For many in union leadership, the strike was poorly timed and likely to fail. Yet pushed into action by rank-and-file woodsmen, Wobbly officials were forced to slowly accede to the demands of the workers. On July 13, after receiving messages from Aberdeen and Hoquiam indicating that it was "impossible" to stifle the strikers' momentum, the IWW's district office in Seattle wired back to its Grays Harbor offices, "If You Can't Hold Them. Let Her Go." As the message reached union headquarters, "twenty-five hundred loggers, three thousand mill men, two hundred ship yard men and one hundred tub makers" were already hitting the skids.[170]

The "Complete Close-Down [of] Grays Harbor" made state and national news.[171] Charles R. Griffin, an IWW logger employed two miles outside of Tacoma read, in his words, in "big black headlines the news of a big strike on the Harbor."[172] Word of the strike spread through strike bulletins, mainstream newspapers, and the mouths of rank-and-file IWW delegates whose travels took them into the deepest and darkest parts of the Washington woods. The news reached an eager audience among the loggers, who responded en masse. "Practically every camp in the county" was shut down by the strike by July 17, which brought upward of three thousand workers out on strike.[173] The *Industrial Worker* said a great deal about conditions in Grays Harbor, running a headline that declared, "All out except the bosses, and they are out of their heads."[174]

6

PERSISTENT WOBBLIES

THE IWW AND REPRESSION IN WARTIME

Employers' inability to permanently dislodge the Wobblies from Grays Harbor in 1912 illustrated the IWW's importance in the timber towns. When some IWWs left voluntarily to join other struggles, or were removed by force, the movement did not die; instead, it continued to hold a stake in the community. IWW membership varied from one year to the next, and it is difficult to pinpoint exact figures. But unionists recorded a membership of 1,060 in 1912, to between two thousand and four thousand in 1917–18, to two thousand in 1919.[1] In May 1917, before the upsurge in IWW membership, the Finnish daily *Industrialisti* reported that "in Grays Harbor, too, we have (well) over a thousand members and more troops are coming in with every meeting."[2]

During World War I (July 1914 to November 1918) and its aftermath, left-wing movements burst forth with general strikes, socialist political victories, and attempts to spread revolution across the globe. As the IWW struck in the Northwest's big war industry, the radical organization came under fire from employers, strikebreakers, labor spies, state officials, and most of the press. In the face of these assaults, Wobblies fell back on their community support, as many locals rallied to aid them.

Grays Harbor Wobblies and other radicals were also inspired by rage as they witnessed their fellow workers and comrades lynched, gunned down, and arrested across the United States. The November 1916 mass killing of Wobblies in Everett and the August 1917 lynching of Frank Little in Butte, Montana, outraged American radicals, who responded much the same as IWW leader Big Bill Haywood, who declared: "We never forget. Organize and act."[3] With unemployment low, American workers unionized and struck in record numbers. Some workers—and their AFL unions—observed the federal government's no-strike pledge during the war, but following the November 1918 Armistice, the dam broke with labor militancy rushing forth. The next year, 1919, witnessed a high mark for both strikes and number of striking workers, as approximately one-quarter of all US workers engaged in strikes. Not all work stoppages emerged from IWW locals, but in the Northwest, where Wobbly strength was greatest, the radicals led, or contributed to, strikes in lumber, maritime, shipping, and agriculture.[4] And historian Cal Winslow's words about wartime Seattle were likewise true of Grays Harbor: the city was "at once a strike center and a radical center, a stronghold of working-class socialism with a vision of a better world."[5]

LABOR IN WAR AND VICTORY

The United States entered the war in April 1917, and on July 17, 1917, lumber union delegates met in Seattle and sent out a strike call. Starting in the camps of Grays Harbor, loggers struck, and both the IWW and the AFL sent out organizers to get loggers and mill workers to join the strike. The strike spread rapidly from the woods of Grays Harbor to most of the logging camps and lumber mills west of the Cascades. By the end of July, the strike closed between 75 and 90 percent of western Washington mills and camps.[6] Throughout the summer of 1917, practically the entire lumber industry west of the Cascades remained at a standstill.[7]

Leading the strike were Wobblies and members—including many socialists—of the shingle weavers' and timber workers' unions. AFL and IWW unions remained at loggerheads throughout the strike, and their members had different strike aims. The IWW, shingle weavers, and timber workers each made demands for work-life improvements that included the eight-hour day, increased wages, and sanitary reforms. But while the trade unions contented themselves with shorter hours and higher wages, the Wobblies saw the revolutionary potential for the strike. The *Industrial Worker* described it as a contest for power between "industrial overlord[s]" and a working class becoming aware of its power: "The lumber trust, secure in their power in the past, are now up against a new condition. They are learning that the power of the 'Bums' is a power greater than their own. Any worker in the strike area, who is not on strike is a traitor to his class. The line is distinct. Either a worker stands for his interest or he stands for the interest of the industrial overlord."[8]

On July 21, the *Grays Harbor Post* printed news of what was already clear on the streets: "The strike movement appears to be largely conducted by the I.W.W., whose membership many times outnumbers the combined shingle weavers and timberworkers."[9] In spite of the disparaging remark about the size of the AFL shingle weavers and timber workers, those unions expanded at a healthy rate during and immediately after World War I. Paid-up membership in the Washington State Federation of Labor (WSFL) grew from 15,093 in 1916 to more than 55,000 in 1919. By the end of the 1910s, more than 9.5 percent of Washington workers belonged to WSFL-affiliated unions—while some unions were independent of the WSFL.[10] Formed in 1917, the Aberdeen local of the shipyard laborers boasted 400 members during the war, a powerful contingent of laborers in a critical war industry.[11] Approximately a hundred boilermakers working at the shipyards unionized in October 1918.[12]

While the addition of the harbor's four shipyards provided unionized jobs for hundreds of workers, the bulk of Grays Harbor's workforce lay in the region's mills and logging camps. Many shingle weavers were socialists, but the International Shingle Weavers' Union of America (ISWUA) saw the strike as an opportunity to win the eight-hour day rather than a fundamental challenge to the socioeconomic system. Weavers remained remarkably on message, using practically the entire space of their newspaper to make repeated calls for the eight-hour day.[13] J. G. Brown, the socialist president of the ISWUA and future national Farmer-Labor Party leader, urged his fellow weavers to "take no bluff. Stand pat. This is our opportunity to gain the shorter work day."[14] The *Shingle Weaver* ran lists of "Mills Operating 8 Hours A Day" to remind readers of their numerous successes and used the epithet "ten hour rats" for those who worked in mills not on the list.[15]

Following the demise in 1916 of the short-lived Timber Workers' Union, the International Union of Timberworkers (IUT) formed in late 1916 and early 1917 to unionize lumber; headquartered in Aberdeen, it was another effort by sawmill laborers and other lumber workers to unionize industrially—outside of the IWW.[16] The IUT's paper, the Aberdeen-based *American Timberworker*, proclaimed, "Now brothers of the International Union of Timber Workers, let us do for the logging camps and sawmills, what the United Mine Workers union has done for the coal miners' camps."[17] IUT members struck at the same time as, but not in coordination with, the Wobblies, pulling thousands of lumber workers into the great struggle for the eight-hour day. J. G. Brown praised labor's solidarity: "Entering the third week of the strike sees the lumber industry tied up tight, the greatest protest ever heard against unjust conditions in this backward calling. The men where the owners have not yet conceded the eight-hour day are standing firm and it has been hard to get workmen to accept the work offered even in eight-hour concerns." He concluded, "The world of labor is watching the workers in the lumber industry in this hour. We shall not disappoint them nor betray ourselves."[18] Thousands of IUT and ISWUA members joined thousands more Wobblies in shuttering the Northwest's largest industry.

In August 1917, the IUT, then based in Seattle, took out its charter with the AFL; in March 1918, the Timberworkers union merged with the Shingle Weavers' union.[19] During the IUT's five years (1917–22) of existence, it chartered more than 170 locals, including more than 50 Northwest union branches and dozens more in the Midwest and South.[20] Between December 1917 and April 1918, three Aberdeen timber locals affiliated with the WSFL; lumber workers in neighboring cities took out IUT charters in 1918.[21] Early twentieth-century social scientist Cloice R. Howd estimated the union peaked at around 15,000 members in 1919.[22] The IUT's newspaper attributed the union's existence to the efforts of socialist activists within organized labor who built the movement; union officials included socialist unionists, including its first international president, E. E. Wieland, an Aberdeen mill worker and socialist city council member.[23]

Significantly, the IUT also differed in its perspective on interracial and interethnic unionism from the overtly racist views and actions of earlier lumber workers' trade unions—and most of the labor movement at large. The opening statement atop the *American Timberworker* read, "It is the purpose of the International Union of Timber-Workers to unite in one organization, regardless of creed, color, or nationality, all workmen eligible to membership who are engaged in the production of lumber on the North American continent."[24] Acknowledging the thousands of immigrant workers in the region's lumber mills and the occasional difficulties faced by non-English speakers in influencing English-language-only union activities, the IUT embraced the policy of immigrant workers forming their own locals and conducting business in their native language.[25]

After a long history of support for Asian exclusion, at least some shingle weavers came to realize the value of interracial unionism. J. G. Brown, who earlier condemned "Jap" labor, wrote an article in the *Shingle Weaver* expressing a change: "The Chinese of British Columbia, the Japanese in the state of Washington, together with the many and various nationalities are standing regardless of racial and national differences as one man for the eight-hour day, recognition of the union, and humane working conditions."[26] IWW and shingle weavers' unionist Andy Raynor praised the solidarity shown by Chinese and Japanese weavers during the strike: "I see here every other day white men and Chinese meeting in the same hall. I see men from the Orient clasping hands with men of the Occident, striving as best they can, according to their understanding, to establish the brotherhood of men."[27]

Both the harbor's left-wing unionists, particularly the timber workers and shingle weavers, and more conservative unions in the building trades used their wartime and postwar growth to increase their political influence. Brown and Wieland, international presidents of the ISWUA and the IUT, respectively, were socialists with Grays Harbor roots, and the ISWUA delivered strong endorsements to local, state, and national Socialist Party of America candidates during the war.[28] Even Aberdeen's labor council, long a bastion of trade union conservatism heavily influenced by the building trades, endorsed labor candidates for political office, including Aberdeen's former mayor, J. M. Phillips, the Farmer-Labor Party candidate for Washington State Attorney General.[29]

To AFL unions, regardless of their views on socialist politics and industrial unionism, the IWW was an enemy, different from but nearly as "dangerous," as the boss. Trade unionists leveled full-throated assaults on the Wobblies. In May 1917, as workers flocked into the IWW, the Aberdeen Central Labor Council passed what the *Aberdeen Herald* deemed to be "perhaps the strongest resolutions ever adopted against the Industrialists by a labor organization." The resolution read, in part, "This council unqualifiedly condemns any interference with the bonafide unions of this city by the antagonistic, ununion, unAmerican organization styling itself the Industrial Workers of the World."[30] At the March 1918 convention, where the IUT and ISWUA merged, the unified organization agreed to "start a campaign to oust all IWW from the camps and mills in this district."[31]

WOBBLIES AND THE COMMUNITY

ISWUA, IUT, and IWW strikers won community support—at least from several small proprietors who depended on labor's purchasing power. Banker William J. Patterson, the man who as head of the vigilante citizens' committees in 1911–12 had attacked the Wobblies, conceded that by 1917 the IWW had won widespread support on Grays Harbor. He noted that "there were men in Aberdeen, good, prosperous citizens, who wanted to go back to the old vigilante tactics. 'Run them out, kill the anarchistic traitors,' and all that. But the town was not with them. . . . It was a question of the justice of their more important immediate demands. And on this question the town was overwhelmingly with the strikers and against the operators."[32] Even the *Grays Harbor Post*, ever hostile to the IWW, acknowledged, "The great bulk of the strikers are members of the IWW."[33] W. F. Hall, an AFL union organizer, concurred, stating that "in almost every window" of the "merchants and business people" were hung signs supporting the eight-hour day.[34] Business owners delivered material assistance to the IWW; it's unclear whether this was support for the Wobblies' radical politics or an effort to retain goodwill among working-class customers, but the support was there all the same. According to the *Industrial Worker*, Aberdeen businesses donated a "great number of prizes" to the IWW for the union's use at a July 1917 mass meeting.[35]

Community, including middle-class, support for the strikers had three main causes. First, shopkeepers, bankers, grocers, and other business owners relied on working-class customers to make their living. The harbor's largest industry was lumber and most workers earned their wages in the industry's camps and mills. By July 1917, the entire industry was shut down. At least one labor spy made the connection between business owners' support for the IWW and other strikers with working-class purchasing power. After researching the Wobblies' presence in Aberdeen, one labor spy reported disturbing findings to his superiors: "I learned that not only the IWW but other Unions as well are well organized in this section. No man in business here would openly declare against the Union, on account of business. In practically every store along the main streets in windows will be seen signs reading 'We are in favor of 8 hours,'" concluded the spy.[36]

Second, as Patterson's comments suggested, at least some harbor elites felt shame and embarrassment over actions in 1911–12. The shock at being labeled vigilantes by the IWW and trade unionists, as well as middle-class progressive journalists, likely contributed to the fear that working-class shoppers might punish anti-union businesses. Third, in 1911–12, employers and their allies in the press had depicted the strike as the product of outside agitators. That claim was more difficult to make in 1917, given the size and scope of the strike—and that the strike was led every bit as much by longtime residents as by migrants. Still, community support went only so far. Patterson's fellow business owners did not disclaim all vigilantism, only the unpopular type. Had the town been with those favoring extralegal repression, the harbor's citizens' vigilantes would have mobilized again—as they would months later.

WARTIME REPRESSION

Threatened by the IWW's support in the community and disruption of war materials, employers and state officials attacked IWW members and community spaces, while journalists and other public figures incited violence. This antilabor action mirrored the 1911–12 anti-Wobbly crusade—except that the wartime emergency brought the full power of government into coordination with local officials, strikebreakers, and vigilantes. One Grays Harbor newspaper summarized the wartime clampdown: "These are busy days for investigators for city and federal governments. Charges of disloyalty are pouring in, suspicious cases are being looked into and officers are finding all their time occupied. I.W.W. members are receiving particular attention, two of these being hauled to police headquarters yesterday. H. V. Collins of the intelligence bureau interrogated these men and found them Wobblies of the faithful kind, but not offenders under the existing laws as he interpreted them."[37]

During the war, public officials and private companies effectively merged, as lumbermen and their antilabor forces held sway over local governments—and private employees (often labor spies) did double duty in the government. Indeed, Grays Harbor's history of lumber and labor in wartime shows the lengths to which all parts of the state would go to make the lumber world safe for profits.

Threats of violence against strikers were ubiquitous during World War I; public officials did little to quash these threats. Some government officials joined journalists in fueling jingoistic anger. In August 1917, vigilantes warned of the drastic actions they had planned for the radicals. They hanged an effigy of a logger, with its head covered by a black bag, from a tree near Montesano. Coming only three weeks after the infamous lynching of Frank Little in Butte, Montana, the lesson was clear: radicals and their ideas were not welcome in Grays Harbor. For anyone who missed the threat, those behind the hanged effigy affixed a sign to it; one side read, "I Won't Work," a nickname for the IWW, while the other read, "Take This Effigy at How it Looks." In November 1917, Grays Harbor gained national attention for its citizens' terrorist activities. A group formed in Grays Harbor called itself the Black Robes and issued a threat to tar and feather Hoquiam Wobblies. The group broke a window out of the IWW headquarters with a brick and an attached note warning, "Remember the boys in France. Feathers are light and tar is cheap. This is for the IWW." Fearful that his property was to be destroyed, their landlord evicted the Hoquiam Wobblies shortly after the Black Robes issued their threat. Considering the many roundups, beatings, and even murders of radical lumber workers in the years to come, it's clear now that the threats were serious.[38]

Municipal police and the county sheriff's officers arrested more than one hundred striking Wobblies in July and August 1917 on charges of unlawful assembly, picketing, vagrancy, and the dubious charge of being an "IWW agitator." Local authorities also enforced injunctions. From July 20 to August 5, the Grays Harbor Superior Court repeatedly enjoined the "Industrial Workers of the World, International Union of Timber-Workers, Lumber Workers Industrial Union No. 500," and a list of picketers. The injunction barred IWW members and trade unionists from picketing the plaintiffs' mills and camps, "coercing and intimidating" scabs, or even using the words "scab" or "scabs" to harass the strikebreakers.[39] Police arrested other Wobblies for being "slackers," the pejorative label for those men who refused to register for the draft. Police arrested IWW member Frederick Meischke ostensibly for threatening to assassinate the president, although his "crimes" of holding a red card and a German surname were likely the causes. Some reporters urged authorities to take decisive action against the IWW, claiming that its members represented but a minority of the strikers and were able to shut down the mills only through intimidation. Throughout the strike, Aberdeen police received complaints from local mill owners that IWW pickets used "vulgar language." These complainants promised to meet the radicals' strike with violent retaliation.[40] With the political establishment calling for eliminating the IWW, police rounded up radicals with little or no cause—and the persecution outlasted the strike. In May 1918, police arrested two loggers when the men refused to donate to a Red Cross campaign. The *Washingtonian* noted that one arrestee had IWW credentials.[41]

While Wobblies did not advocate assassination or support the Germans during World War I, their revolutionary ideology, industrial unionism, and militant labor tactics all threatened the business-friendly status quo of the United States, particularly during wartime. For good reason, the IWW's and other unions' demand for the eight-hour day in lumber remained central. But a shorter workday was not the Wobblies' sole demand. They also called for workplace safety and sanitation improvements and union control over hiring.[42] Furthermore, the Wobblies' class-based demands and advocacy of industrial unionism threatened to reverse the separation of American workers into small, easily divided groups in AFL-style trade unions. In the summer of 1917 Wobblies threatened not only the lumbermen's routine profit-taking, but the accumulation of enormous war profits. Thus, lumbermen labeled Wobbly unions and strikes "un-American" and "treacherous" not only for disrupting profits but also, supposedly, harming the efforts of brave soldiers in Europe.

Heading the antilabor forces was a group of lawmen in the sheriff's office, most prominently deputy sheriffs H. D. McKenney and John A. McBride. Between 1917 and 1919, the two men arrested scores of Grays Harbor Wobblies. A physically imposing brute with a long history on the harbor, McKenney threw his weight around to intimidate picketers. The *Washingtonian* reported, "The crowd was somewhat sullen at first but one of the women pickets who had been stopped created a diversion by delivering a series of addresses which caused considerable laughter. H. D. McKenney engaged in a little controversy with one of the pickets and it looked as if trouble was imminent, but Mac's size and vigor of language, etc., won and nothing further happened."[43] Mac proved so popular among employers that they lobbied for the then-deputy sheriff's promotion to constable; the employers' "committee explained McKenney has been doing a considerable amount of investigating of the I. W. W. strikers, that it is highly important he should have a legal commission so he can do his work as a special officer properly," reported the *Washingtonian*.[44] McKenney and McBride also served as informants, spies, and scab herders—seemingly public employees who recruited "replacement workers" for struck companies. Their wartime "service" included positions as special agents for the Lumbermen's Protective Association, an employer's organization formed by lumber operators dedicated to maintaining the ten-hour day and keeping the industry union-free. As part of his duties, McBride went undercover as a member of the IWW's Marine Transport Workers' Industrial Union (MTWIU) and "immediately set about spying on its meetings" and searching for "an inner circle" of IWW militants, which he reported up the chain of command. McKenney submitted his reports to A. J. Morley, an Aberdeen-based officer in the Lumbermen's Protective Association and president of the Saginaw Timber Company. However, McKenney's greatest contribution to the anti-IWW crusade came as a spy for the US Army. He issued reports to military officers that included lurid details of "the Wobblys' methods which are getting worse and very hard to combat." According to McKenney, these methods included the use of "acid in shoes and cow-itch" and the destruction of tools and machinery.[45]

McBride traveled to the great IWW Chicago trial of spring and summer 1918—where more than one hundred Wobblies were charged with interfering with the war—to testify about his experiences. Intent on impugning the IWW members' characters and demonstrating their seditious acts, McBride claimed to have heard Wobblies proclaim, "Do all in your power to defeat conscription" and "Do not allow the United States to send food to the allies, for that will prolong the war five years."[46] McBride was one of several Grays Harborites who made the long trek to Chicago to help the state dismantle the IWW. In November 1917, Aberdeen police chief Dean had traveled to Chicago to assist the prosecution in crafting their side in the *United States v. Haywood, et al.* case. Fully aware of the chief's lengthy history as an ally of employers, Aberdeen Wobblies J. F. Rhodes and Walter Horace Margason wrote to "counsel for the damned" George Vanderveer in Chicago warning about Dean: "If he confined his statement to facts it will be of no use to them, but from what we know of him we think he said or will say what he is told."[47] This case served as the legal centerpiece of the federal government's offensive against IWW officials in which 101 Wobblies were convicted and sentenced to up to twenty years in prison and fined, collectively, two million dollars for obstructing the war effort.

Lumber operators upped the violence to beat the radicals out of the woods, mills, and communities. During the 1917 lumber strike, Cosmopolis management had repelled IWW pickets with armed guards and an electric fence. Threatening to revive the ax handle brigade of 1911–12, the manager of the Western Lumber Company telephoned Aberdeen police in late July 1917 to threaten that if the lawful authorities did not remove the pickets, "the Mill would not be Responsible, for any Trouble that might Occur." Aberdeen Wobbly Walter Margason declared that picketers dared not venture out alone or in groups of under fifty men because of the widespread knowledge that "there were a lot of gun men carrying clubs and beating them up."[48] Police did little to discourage—and sometimes encouraged—private violence. Hired as a mill watchman during the strike, John Dunn received a billy club from police to assist in his duties; he kept the club as a souvenir after his work ended. Police eventually confiscated the weapon after arresting Dunn for using the club to beat his stepson; as in many of the era's conflicts, private citizens could freely commit violence against strikers, while authorities rarely charged the brutes for their violent deeds.[49]

STRIKE ON THE JOB

In the face of persistent attacks, IWW leaders changed their strategy. Instead of staying out on strike with dwindling resources and offering targets for repression, in mid-September 1917 the Wobblies took their strike back on the job, their term for returning to work but utilizing a variety of tactics—slowing down, feigning ignorance of work processes, closely following safety regulations, and sabotaging machinery—to minimize production. Striking on the job had advantages for the Wobblies. With workers on the job, employers had difficulties securing scabs, and strikers could continue to earn wages while taking direct action at their workplace. The strikes sometimes proved effective at winning concessions, partly because they were so unpredictable. As radical lumber worker James Rowan put it, the IWW "advocated that the strike should be transferred to the job while the union was still intact, and the fighting spirit of the men unsubdued; or in other words, that the strikers should go back, and work no more than eight hours a day, or if at times they found it necessary to stay on the job ten hours, they should work slow so that no more than eight hours work should be done in ten hours."[50]

Wobblies also used "quickie strikes"—small-scale and unannounced walkouts to catch operators off guard—to bring about or enforce the eight-hour day or to respond to the discharge of an IWW agitator. Close study of IWW and government sources shows that Wobblies carried out at least forty-two quickie (sometimes called "intermittent") strikes in the Grays Harbor woods between September 1917 and March 1918. These walkouts became so common that the C. H. Clemons Logging Company reported that thirty men were quitting work every day. One typical report was delivered by Wobbly No. 261357, which stated, "I was working on a

IWW loggers on a picket line near Elma, Washington, in 1917 hold copies of Wobbly newspapers *Industrial Worker* and *Solidarity*, which ran frequent news of their massive strike. The strikers also carry IWW banners reading "One Big Union." Washington State Historical Society, Tacoma.

pile driver singing 'Dump the Bosses' Off Your Back' when the straw boss, Austin, told me to go and get my time. 'Did you get me?' he said. I told him I did and that the rest of the crew would get him, too, which they did, as the whole crew accompanied me to the office and kept the timekeeper busy writing checks until there was no one left on the job but the boss and he was swearing to himself the last we saw of him."[51]

THE MILITARY IN THE WOODS

Because of these ongoing threats to war production, the federal government took a direct role in crushing unions. Troops converged on the harbor in July 1917 as part of a program to round up anyone suspected of being a delegate, agitator, or "in any way a leader."[52] The *Washingtonian* showed how the antilabor war in the woods reflected the war in Europe, writing of one July logging camp picket line, "Soldiers are putting all agitators under arrest, and they also are arresting all I.W.W. members who are of German nationality. All freight trains are searched and men beating their way are arrested." Troops helped to break the strike by guarding mills and camps.[53] According to historian Philip J. Dreyfus, use of the troops succeeded, as the "strikers offered no resistance to the soldiers, and picketing practically ceased as the troops surrounded the mills and the city's employment offices."[54]

The federal government also rolled out a vast surveillance network during the war. The Department of War's military intelligence operations tracked unionists, radicals, and anyone they suspected of harboring radical sympathies; reports included the names and descriptions of numerous Wobblies, as well as information on workplace conditions, strike activity, and acts of real or imagined sabotage. A military intelligence report dated December 14, 1918, included summaries of letters from Grays Harbor Wobblies to Seattle IWW official George Williams with news of "lots of good members, mostly Finns," in Aberdeen, but "it is not possible to hold a meeting with these Finns, because they do not understand English." Along with specific revelations about labor activities, reports such as this reveal federal agents surveilled the US mail and passed it up the military intelligence command chain.[55]

Like local authorities and vigilantes, federal officials raided Wobbly halls during the war. On September 5, 1917, federal agents raided IWW halls throughout the nation. Local and Washington State officials joined their federal counterparts in late-night raids of the Aberdeen and Hoquiam halls when no members were present to mount a resistance. Perhaps to show their defiance in the face of such overt repression, the Aberdeen IWW branch threw a dance following "the regular street propaganda meeting" shortly after the raids while their halls were out of commission.[56]

While the conventional strike by the IWW and AFL unions had caused significant problems for the lumber operators, job strikes represented a danger because worker-strikers could carry them on indefinitely and it made using scabs more difficult. After all, if the strikers were at work, who would the scabs replace? Lumbermen considered the IWW's new strategy a grave threat. Fortunately for the lumbermen, their status as war manufacturers allowed them to tap the government for help. In October 1917, the US Army Signal Corps, responsible for acquiring the raw materials required for the war effort, assigned Colonel Brice Disque to "mediate" the labor dispute and return the spruce harvest to full capacity. To accomplish this, Disque created two new organizations: the Loyal Legion of Loggers and Lumbermen (known as the Four Ls) and the Spruce Production Division. Disque ranks high in the history of Northwest strikebreaking; he "closed the woods to labor organizers and trade union members by organizing a company union . . . with practically compulsory membership and a no-strike policy."[57]

The Spruce Production Division was a branch of the army that sent soldiers into the woods to procure the lumber needed by the military. It achieved three major tasks for the lumber operators. First, the soldiers functioned as scabs doing the work of the strikers. Second, they worked as guards for the lumber interests, intimidating union organizers and dissident workers. Third, the presence of the soldiers created another opportunity to jail strikers, as promoting work stoppages or slowdowns to federal troops could be construed as interfering with the war effort. The presence and activities of the Spruce Production Division were so effective in breaking the IWW strike actions that operators who were previously not engaged in defense production quickly began doing so to get troops sent to their camps.[58] Cloice R. Howd, in his bulletin of the US Bureau of Labor Statistics on West Coast lumber and labor, wrote, "Leaders of the Timber Workers complained that officers of the Spruce Production Division, from Colonel Disque down, opposed their organization in every possible way and made it almost impossible for them to secure new members."[59]

The largest and best-organized efforts to defeat the IWW in the Pacific Northwest came from the Four Ls, a unique form of "workers' organization" that combined a company union with the military—and thus support from the federal government. Formed to break legitimate labor organizations in the Northwest, the state-sponsored military company union was almost unique in its potential to harness coercion—and violence—against unions. While other company unions might compel membership through the threat of lost jobs or access to company housing, the Four Ls was the military—its means of coercion included the state's ability to use violence. In fact, the Loyal Legion of Loggers and Lumbermen proclaimed that it "is not a labor union in the common acceptance of that term, but is purely a patriotic association of both operators and operatives engaged in this essential war industry."[60]

Formed in November 1917 as the wartime need for wood products peaked, the Four Ls constitution declared that "its objects are to promote a closer relationship between the employer and the employee." As an organization designed primarily to secure sufficient war materials from the woods, and rid those woods of the IWW menace ("stamp out sedition and sabotage"), the Four Ls considered the Grays Harbor region a priority. By December 1917, legion officers and troops organized across the harbor cities and woods, recruiting loggers and running unionists out of the camps. Four Ls membership had its appeals. The legion's constitution included the main measures it hoped to achieve, including "accident, health, and other insurance" plans and "cooperative hospitals for the care of the sick and injured, and medical attention to the families of members."[61]

An appeal of membership was that members could avoid the brutal treatment meted out to resisters. Military recruiters used violence against lumber workers who refused to join. Four Ls officials forced dissenters to run the gauntlet, while unionists from outside the Four Ls faced beatings and tar and feathering from Loyal Legionists.[62] The *Washingtonian* recorded the dangers faced by labor radicals—and Germans: "Lawrence Kalb, member of the I. W. W. of German parentage, was given a sound thrashing and covered with a coat of tar or creosote by a number of Aberdeen men at a point near the Northern Pacific railway crossing east of Montesano, about 11 o'clock last evening. He says he was warned not to go back to Aberdeen on fear of death . . . Kalb declared the same bunch of men have been taking one man out every night. He doesn't know what became of the men."[63] Loyal Legionnaires also took part in IWW hall raids, continuing the harbor's long history of vigilantism with a tacit endorsement from public officials.[64] Wobbly George Harper received threats from a "Four Hells" lieutenant at the Aloha camp, who suggested that before allowing Harper to leave camp he should be "mark[ed] up as a remembrance." The lieutenant also offered his advice for dealing with other intransigent loggers: "If they won't line up, *knock their blocks off!*"[65]

Mixing coercion with patriotic appeals and promises of future improvements, the Four Ls organized practically the entire lumber industry, with its peak membership reaching somewhere between 110,000 and 130,000 workers. In Grays Harbor, the Four Ls organized 103 locals and more than 8,000 laborers by the summer of 1918.[66] Four Ls membership seems less impressive since it wasn't consensual. Refusal to join the Loyal Legion could, unsurprisingly, lead to a spot on the lumber companies' blacklists. Writing to the *Industrial Worker* in early 1918, one Wobbly described the induction methods of an Aberdeen Four Ls recruiter: "The officer sizes up the weakest looking men and bulldozes them first and when he forces their signatures he uses them to break down the other men. Those who refuse are put on the blacklist."[67] Three years after one of their members was tarred and feathered at the company town of Aloha, the IWW still issued reports about the perpetrators, one reading, "Chas. Collins, 4 feet 4 inches, weight about 180, a little stoop-shouldered . . . This fink carried a gun in 1917, also was one of the leading guys who tarred and feathered a fellow worker at Aloha, Wash., in 1918."[68]

In his book *The Centralia Conspiracy*, Wobbly Ralph Chaplin relates that a band of Four Ls had lynched an IWW near Montesano, the Grays Harbor County seat.[69] It's unclear which worker Chaplin refers to—since no one was prosecuted for murder and more than one worker's body was found hanging in the late 1910s. But he was most likely referring to William Lindgren, a Wobbly logger who refused to join the Loyal Legion.[70] After refusing to join the Four Ls and drawing his one hundred dollars in back pay in March 1918, Lindgren went missing; four months later, a logger discovered Lindgren's decomposed remains hanging from a tree near Montesano. Authorities and the press suggested Lindgren died of suicide.[71] While it isn't certain that Lindgren was lynched, it's clear that the era's wartime belligerence, stoked by hateful antilabor rhetoric, created the conditions ripe for murder. And to at least some radicals, Lindgren's death was a lynching. Moreover, throughout the war, anti-Wobbly groups had threatened to lynch unionists and strikers.

"CURING" WORKERS OF THEIR RADICALISM

The Four Ls was not alone in its efforts to cultivate belief in an identity of interests between workers and bosses. Complementing the efforts of reactionary lumbermen and state officials to dismantle the IWW by force were those who preferred to contain the radicals using the "softer" union-avoidance methods of welfare capitalism: the practice of companies providing welfare such as insurance and retirement plans and rewarding "loyal" and "productive" workers with bonuses. Beginning in the 1910s, Grays Harbor employers had created employee representation plans; company-sponsored athletic, picnic, and musical events; and bonus systems designed to speed up production, silence worker dissent, and foster loyalty among productive laborers.[72] Like the Four Ls, the Schafer Brothers Logging Company, Posey Manufacturing Company, and other firms sought to harmonize class relations through paternalism.[73] Posey Manufacturing in Hoquiam created a mutual benefit society, an early welfare capitalist scheme originally founded in 1911. The society's stated goal was to bring "unison . . . between employee and employer" and provide health insurance for the workers.[74] To cultivate loyalty among workers, Posey also published a newspaper, the *Poseygram*, and funded sports teams and holiday parties for employees.[75] The Grant-Smith-Porter Shipyard Company in Aberdeen produced a company newspaper called *The Propeller* designed to "foster the morale of the yard and . . . chronicled the various yard activities, both as to industrial progress and as to social and athletic happenings."[76]

Elites used every tool in their belt to "cure" workers of radicalism, which they often saw as pathological, something that just needed the correct treatment. With wartime patriotic fervor running high, diverse groups joined in the anti-Wobbly crusade. Mainstream Christian groups joined itinerant preachers in the quest to exorcise the IWW from the woods. The Aberdeen Presbyterian Church leafleted town in December 1917 with literature trumpeting its program of "IWW: Its Cause and Cure," which consisted of the minister's "knowledge of a plot to paralyze the industries of the country in the coming months," along with the more traditional service and a performance by the church choir.[77] Meanwhile, "Three-fingered" Jack Godwin, a reformed "ex-hobo, ex-IWW, ex-gambler and gambling house proprietor," toured the region during December 1917 providing lectures that detailed how he single-handedly converted eight thousand IWWs to the teachings of Christ. During an address in Aberdeen he claimed to have personally torn up 135 IWW red cards during the previous week and was not shy about claiming responsibility for destroying the IWW on the harbor.[78] J. G. Anderson, "corpulent, threadbare and shiney," who had a history of testifying against radical political prisoners, toured the mills and camps of Grays Harbor in late 1919 "under the guise of evangelism," passing out Christian literature and using his time among the workers to collect information on agitators.[79] In Aberdeen, T. H. Simpson of the Presbyterian Church became convinced of the need for "a logging pastor [who] should have a definite status in the camps like that of a chaplain in the army." Thus convinced, Simpson became the first of many "industrial chaplains," designated to many camps in the region to "bring to bear the spirit and point of view of Christ." He pursued this goal by showing the workers films, holding courses in "English and Americanization," and promoting discussion in the camps to combat the "one sided and fanatical social propaganda" of the Wobblies.[80]

STATE SPIES

Washington State officials acted decisively to help federal officials in their war on the Wobblies. State legislatures across the country passed legislation criminalizing IWW membership; these criminal syndicalism statutes gave police and prosecutors a valuable antiradical tool.[81] Also valuable—if less well known—were the public labor spy groups created in states such as Washington, which created secret service bodies to infiltrate, investigate, and break up radical organizations. Washington officials used both syndicalism laws and public spy agencies, but Governor Ernest Lister refused to sign the criminal syndicalism bills passed by both houses of the state legislature in 1917, and Washington's criminal syndicalism bill didn't become law until 1919. Still, Lister, no civil libertarian, turned to labor spies to assist local authorities in disrupting the movement, as well as federal authorities who were already gathering information on the Wobblies' activities.[82]

For fifteen months, from August 13, 1917, to November 1, 1918, the Washington State government employed the Washington Detective Bureau, a New York City–based labor spy service headed by C. B. Reed. Because of the IWW's strength throughout the state, the agents spread throughout Washington.[83] Agents monitored and reported to local authorities on bootleggers, sex workers, and enemy aliens, but their focus was on the IWW. Of the 697 investigations undertaken by the agents, 362, or about 52 percent, pertained directly to the Wobblies, while another 61 cases involved investigations of specific job sites and sabotage. All told, the agents arrested 87 workers they classified as "IWW Officers, Organizers and Delegates" and confiscated four hundred "Seditious Volumes." Agents served in Grays Harbor between November 1917 and February 1918. Due to what the agents perceived as their successes at stifling "IWW activity and also more or less labor difficulties in connection with the IWW organization," a year into the war Lister reduced the force to only four agents.[84]

Their four months on the harbor were fruitful for the agents. Agent 31 was the principal spy assigned to Aberdeen. While there he infiltrated the IWW, formed a friendship with an Aberdeen IWW branch secretary, and gathered information about numerous strikes and cases of alleged sabotage at local logging camps. He reported the presence of thousands of IWWs working in Grays Harbor and noted that hundreds of them attended the daily meetings in Aberdeen and Hoquiam. He gathered and reported the names of those Wobblies in Aberdeen he deemed worthy of special surveillance. One brief but typical report went as follows:

> At midnight last night I met Grady, one of the IWW organizers of this district and learned from him that after New Years they are going to have assistance from other men not members of the I W W in closing all mills and camps, unless 8 hours are granted.
>
> I received verification from one Ed North, who is an active member of the LLLL and is a former W., from Idaho and Montana. He is down on them now and will not even be seen speaking to one (at least I have heard him claim). Anyhow, from what I pick up it is sure to come. The Climax had another break down yesterday and it looks odd but I can't do anything, as Mr. Scott's partner, _____ Fox is rather inclined to believe that his men are O.K. When I pointed out a W. to him he wouldn't believe me, saying I'm mistaken. Of course I did not insist but let it go and admitted a mistake in identification.[85]

Agent 31 was so deeply entrenched within the union that he reported to headquarters of his imminent assignment as either "one of the flying squad or an active delegate." But shortly after reporting to his boss C. B. Reed of the possibility that he had been outed by harbor residents (a major danger faced by labor spies), Agent 31 left town and issued no more reports. A second agent, called S-7, came to the harbor in early 1918. He wrote Reed, explaining how prominent Wobblies "asked me to start to open up a hall here big enough to hold the Wobblies and wants me to be the main speaker, having me speak one night at Raymond and the next in Centralia."[86]

Wobbly activism persisted during the war despite the surveillance and violence. In November 1917, an anxious member of Lister's Secret Service made this report:

> Conditions in Hoquiam are about equal to those in Aberdeen. The names of agitators would be hard to get as each man here is an active agitator and all are asking for credentials and lining up new members in the camps about. The names of those I obtained are ones who I've met and talked to: J. J. Connolly—Semple—O. Neva, J. Rhodes (Sec.) also learned that there are fully 2000 Wobs in Aberdeen section. Starting Wednesday a lot of new Wob delegates are going into the camps and try and organize, and I've been asked to go and do my share. From Rhodes I learned that the majority of the business people are helping all they can, and he expects to make this a W city.[87]

In May 1918, one Wobbly reported his success during the previous week while working secretly. He described the organizing strategy that proved so successful, stating, "A delegate goes ahead and feels out the prospective member whereupon, if latter is sympathetic with the IWW and desirous of joining," the delegate steers him to "a second party working under cover who is carrying the supplies necessary to writing up the members and giving them credentials." The new members continued by holding secret meetings "to avoid the activities of the police."[88]

State, federal, and private repression impacted the lives of countless labor radicals across the country. Walter Horace Margason, a Grays Harbor logger, camp delegate, and chairman of the Aberdeen strike committee during the summer of 1917, experienced firsthand many of these strike-breaking tools. Hailing from Oakland, Illinois, Margason had worked for two decades in the woods "west of the Mississippi River nearly every place," before joining the IWW in June 1917. Labor spies described him as "5'9", 200 lbs., red face, fat, and talks as though his mouth was full of spit, is a bad man." A dedicated organizer, Margason worked at several Grays Harbor camps during the war, but he "couldn't get started to work for a while until I would get run away." Margason's fellow workers valued his creative organizational skills. They elected him secretary-treasurer of the Lumber Workers' Organizational Committee in late 1917. His actions and influence earned him the title of "the most persistent agitator in the IWW" from one federal labor spy.[89]

MOB VIOLENCE

In Grays Harbor, mob violence hit a brutal crescendo in April 1918 during raids of Northwest Wobbly offices and attacks on individual IWW members. On April 6, a mob of six hundred ransacked the Aberdeen IWW hall, dragged out four cartloads of paper, and initiated what mob members termed a Liberty Loan bonfire in the street.[90] Later that night, Wobblies and allies received threats of lynching and vigilantes raided restaurants and hotels frequented by IWW members. They also kidnapped IWW member R. C. Quint, tied a rope around his neck as they drove him from town, and made him ride the rail and run the gauntlet.[91] Mrs. H. W. Sampson, an Aberdeen hotel owner, reported that the mob took a nineteen-year-old boy "out of his room and the house to about a mile east of town and beat [him] up and told [him] not to return or he would get what Frank Little got." Sampson mocked and condemned the mob's actions: "Tuesday night they came again, took a man out of the office and beat him up, and we are told he is in the county hospital. I see they put handcuffs on him, as a mob of about 100 small men could not handle him."[92]

Police also raided workers' homes in search of radical literature, and arrested workers for their actual or suspected radical beliefs.[93] Wobblies blamed the violence on Aberdeen police chief George Dean, who "issued an order that all hotels be searched—by a bloodthirsty gang of maniacs—for 'seditious literature.' The idea, of course, was to drag out for the amusement of the mob anyone found to have IWW literature in his room."[94] Chief Dean had earlier helped frame union official William Gohl for murder—and during a later term as chief, from 1939 to 1940, he looked the other way as vigilantes destroyed the Red Finn hall and murdered Finnish union activist Laura Law.[95] In April 1918, Dean refused to protect the IWW members and anyone who considered reopening the IWW hall or small businesses raided by the mob. According to the *Aberdeen Daily World*, Dean said one "would have to take his chances, that Aberdeen workingmen and citizens had been provoked to a high pitch of anger against the IWW and that the mobs which had been at work here twice were too large for local authorities to control."[96]

Mob violence continued—with support of local government and encouragement from the press. On April 10, 1918, vigilantes raided an Aberdeen rooming house, rounded up six IWW members, and threatened them with a tar and feathering. The right-wing mob then seized more IWW members and made them kiss and swear allegiance to an American flag. Vigilantes seized one Wobbly and forcibly tried to extract information on a comrade's whereabouts. "When the prisoner refused a rope was called for," according to one press account.[97] Local elites were not shy about inciting violence; instead, those with power over municipal and county affairs—from police to elected officials to journalists—encouraged solving the "labor problem" with violence. In April 1918, this became clear when Congressman Albert Johnson's *Washingtonian* ran the headline "More Work Yet for Aberdeen Vigilantes" and concluded that "the general impression is that the vigilante leaders believe they still have work to perform and will keep their men together. So far the mobs have been quiet and have dispatched their work quickly."[98] All told, vigilantes and police raided and vandalized Aberdeen and Hoquiam halls at least four times in 1917 and 1918.[99]

1919 AND THE BIRTH OF A NEW ERA

Some prominent reactionaries who thrived in wartime ascended to even greater heights during the war's aftermath as the nation's officials and business elite coordinated a nationwide Red Scare aimed at—in the words of one popular magazine article—"Rooting out the Reds."[100] Employer and state tactics—both the velvet glove and iron fist—emerged in response to the growing and militant wartime and postwar labor movement. The number of strikes and workers involved in strikes surged during the war. But as the November 1918 Armistice brought some measure of international peace, labor war broke out in 1919 as workers steered the greatest strike wave in American history. In early 1919, the general strike, long a tactic urged by Wobblies and other labor radicals, became a reality in Seattle, the Pacific Northwest's largest city—and spilled over beyond the city. The conflict emerged in Seattle's vast shipyard industry. During the war, shipyard workers failed to gain wage hikes despite severe inflation. The end of the war brought little in the way of gains for "skilled" shipyard workers, no gains for "unskilled" workers, and the likelihood of shipyard closures. Outraged with employer and state intransigence on the wages issue, 35,000 metal trades workers struck on January 21, 1919.[101]

In a show of solidarity, the thirteen Grays Harbor shipyard locals, representing 2,500 workers, declared a strike in solidarity with their fellow unionists in Seattle.[102] Grays Harbor unions appointed their own police to maintain law and order among the strikers and convinced Aberdeen mayor Roy Sargent to deputize the unionist specials. Sargent's acceptance of these unionists for, in the words of the anti-union *Aberdeen Daily World*, "maintaining order in the city," gave the unions an unusual amount of power in a city embroiled in labor conflict.[103]

The Seattle Central Labor Council, one of the nation's most radical labor institutions, agreed to strike in support of the metal trades workers. Pushed forward by a large group of radicals, including many dual unionist Wobblies, large and influential portions of the Seattle Central Labor Council had long agitated for a general strike to demand the release of Tom Mooney, a political prisoner convicted of throwing a bomb during a San Francisco Preparedness Parade in 1916. On January 22, 1919, the president of the Seattle Metal Trades Council requested a referendum vote by Seattle Central Labor Council unionists on whether to call a general strike in the city to support metal trades strikers. One hundred and ten Seattle unions voted to strike; it would begin February 6.[104]

Unionists throughout Washington coordinated strike actions to spread the conflict beyond Seattle. On February 5, Tacoma's unionists approved a strike vote in sympathy with their Seattle fellow workers—ushering in the Tacoma General Strike.[105] But in Grays Harbor, the strength of that region's conservative building trades unionists—long a thorn in the side of the local working-class left—dashed the hopes for bringing about a greater shipyards strike.[106] Aberdeen's building trades unionists continued working at the shipyard, crossing the picket lines.[107]

The Seattle General Strike began on February 6, 1919, when 25,000 union members struck alongside the 35,000 metal trades workers. To handle the problems that arose when an entire city was shut down, the General Strike Committee organized the management of essential services by workers. Working-class power was certainly on the mind of *Seattle Union Record* reporter Anna Louise Strong when in her famous editorial she wrote:

> Not the withdrawal of labor power, the power of the workers to manage, will win this strike. . . . The closing down of our industries as a mere shut-down will not affect those eastern gentlemen much. But the closing down of the capitalistically-owned industries of Seattle while the workers organize to feed the people, care for babies and maintain order—this will move them, for this looks too much like the taking of power by workers.[108]

Experiencing the power of labor to manage was what Strong saw as the biggest gain from the strike and the reason that Seattle workers went back to work "proud of themselves for the way they had come out," in one of the biggest general strikes in American history. Seattle Mayor Ole Hanson attacked the strikers as Bolshevik agents. The US War Department ordered troops from Camp Lewis to Seattle to help "keep order."[109] AFL leaders joined in the attacks, speeding to Seattle to demand unionists end the strike.[110] After four days, the general strike movement collapsed as workers returned to their jobs, and much of the city functioned as normal by February 10.[111]

The Seattle General Strike and the repression used to end it coincided with the resumption of legislative efforts to outlaw the IWW. If lawmakers needed encouragement to criminalize the IWW, capital was happy to oblige. Washington lumbermen had led efforts in 1917 to get a criminal syndicalism enacted. They began lobbying for the bill when the first states—led by Idaho—criminalized membership in the IWW. In Grays Harbor, where labor militancy had been a problem for employers for more than a decade, the response was especially rapid and enthusiastic. Lumbermen with strong political connections, including state lawmakers Alex Polson, president of the Polson Logging Company of Hoquiam, and Mark Reed of Shelton, considered the bill a compromise piece of legislation. Some of their colleagues preferred to completely outlaw strikes instead of the more "moderate" criminal syndicalism bill. During four days in March 1917 alone, Governor Ernest Lister received no fewer than seventeen requests from Grays Harbor lumbermen and employers' groups that he sign the syndicalism bill. Polson, one of the bill's champions, wrote the governor an urgent letter, arguing the criminal syndicalism law "is a sabotage bill, and which nearly everyone except the IWWs are in favor of."[112] N. J. Blagen of the Grays Harbor Lumber Company offered a violent alternative, should the bill not be passed:

> Five years ago we had a very serious experience with the IWWs on this Harbor which no doubt would have had terminated in serious destruction of both life and property had it not been for the strong hand with which it was handled by the authorities, and even at that it looked pretty serious for a couple of weeks. We have every reason to believe this is to be repeated this spring and summer if these people think the conditions are right for it. Therefore we think there is a special need of such law as above referenced to, especially in view of the experience Everett had lately with this lawless element.[113]

Despite Blagen's assertions, the effort to pass the syndicalism law was not some civic-minded effort in pursuit of the common good; instead, it was employers acting in their class interest to fight labor with new and ever-more-potent tools.

Legislators passed the syndicalism bill in 1917 and again two years later. But Governor Lister, while no friend to workers, understood the dangers of the bill and vetoed the criminal syndicalism bills in 1917 and 1919.[114] In response to the failure to pass the law at the state level, a handful of Washington municipalities, including the northwest Washington towns of Anacortes and Sedro-Wooley, passed ordinances outlawing IWW membership, while Hoquiam passed a law "aimed at IWW activities" and immigrants, according to the *Washingtonian*, that "will provide drastic measures for regulating the Wobblies and all other persons who by word or action are unpatriotic. The main feature of the ordinance will be control of public utterance in a foreign tongue."[115] A week after announcing the anti-IWW ordinance, the Hoquiam newspaper described the city's policy of expelling Wobblies: "IWW members have been receiving orders from the local police to move on. Seeing the handwriting on the wall they have been complying with the order."[116] Even without their coveted state law on criminal syndicalism, Grays Harbor lawmen arrested workers for suspicion of belonging to the IWW—during both the 1917 lumber strike and for years thereafter.[117]

However, the bill became law in January 1919. Passage of the Washington State criminal syndicalism statute marked the high point of antiradical lawmaking activity by the lumber industry–dominated Washington State Legislature.[118] Although lumbermen had long exercised power in the state capitol, the criminalization of the IWW was their prize. It allowed lumbermen and other Northwest employers to focus on the business of making profits, rather than fighting street battles against radical workers.[119]

But the state's syndicalism law didn't go into widespread use until after the Armistice Day Tragedy in the town of Centralia, an important lumber center halfway between Seattle and Portland, site of a small but vibrant trade union movement. A small contingent of IWW members had organized in Centralia since at least 1912, and the surrounding woods contained scores of radical workers throughout the 1910s. Employers, police, and wealthy vigilantes (members of the American Legion) came together to rout the Centralia Wobblies—mirroring the antiradicalism in nearby Grays Harbor—on November 11, 1919, the first anniversary of the end of World War I, then known as Armistice Day, today as Veterans Day. American Legionnaires joined several other groups in a planned parade through downtown Centralia. The parade, ostensibly designed to celebrate the end of the "war to end all wars," in fact proved to be a cover for the belligerent veterans to attack their IWW foes.

As they reached the IWW hall, the parading Legionnaires paused before calling out, "Let's get them!" The veterans then rushed the Wobbly headquarters, broke down the door and front window, and entered the hall. Waiting on the other side of the door was a surprise for the veterans: armed IWW members willing to protect themselves and their hall with lethal force. As the first round of Legionnaires entered, a flurry of bullets met them, scattering the frightened, injured, and dying men. After regrouping, the mob reentered the hall and rounded up several Wobblies, while a second group chased down IWW logger Wesley Everest who had escaped through the back door. Chased down at the banks of the Skookumchuck River, Everest traded shots with his pursuers before finally capitulating and being hauled off to his jail cell. Later that night, a mob abducted Everest, tortured and lynched him, and shot his body full of bullets while it was slung off the side of the Chehalis River Bridge.[120]

The entire establishment—politicians, press, employers, military, church, and more—condemned the IWW in the harshest terms, while ignoring or celebrating the American Legion's vigilante raid on the Wobbly hall and their lynching of Everest. If there was any doubt about the Four Ls' official policy—from the top down—on violence against radicals, the company union dispelled it on the front page of its December 1919 newspaper. Printed on red paper, the *Four L News* published this about the American Legionnaires killed and injured on Armistice Day: "They symbolize the heroic minute-men of Lexington, and those who fell on the blood-crowned Bunker Hill; they signify the men locked in death grapple at Gettysburg, who fought that America might be preserved [as] a nation. In them cries again from the ground the blood spilled at Chateau-Thierry, at St. Mihiel in the Argonne." The paper continued: "It is rebellion. It is treason, if these assailants were nominal citizens of the republic. It was an attack upon society."[121]

The Wobblies' violent self-defense at Centralia provided state agents and vigilantes with all the reason they needed to aggressively enforce the new criminal syndicalism law. "The aim" of these laws, as legal scholar Ahmed White writes, "was to destroy the IWW and punish its members, and the laws were put to these purposes."[122] The Washington law, which was one of twenty similar state laws, gave the police a broad scope with which to direct their attacks. The law stated that "whoever shall (1) Advocate, advise, teach or justify crime, sedition, violence, intimidation or injury as a means or way of effecting or resisting any industrial, economic, social or political change," along with those who helped to "organize, give aid to, be a member of or voluntarily assemble with," and anyone who printed, published, edited, issued, or sold material advocating the above, was guilty of violating the statute.[123]

The law brought a crackdown against Wobblies. Authorities sprang into action in the IWW stronghold of Aberdeen. On November 11, 1919, Centralia authorities notified Aberdeen police of the parade violence. On November 12, Aberdeen police raided the town's IWW hall, evicted its tenants, and nailed the place up tight. Materials police seized gave an indication of the local movement's diversity. They included "English, Swedish, Finnish, and Russian stickers," detailed reports on members and activities, and conditions of the area's lumber camps.[124] The harbor's men in blue responded much as they had earlier in the decade: they filled jails with Wobblies and other leftists.[125]

Grays Harbor County prosecutor George Acret led the drive to enforce the syndicalism law, a fact that Wobblies stated was due to his "political ambitions for a higher job." Regardless of his motivations, Acret proved an enthused partner in what Wobblies called the "lumber trust's orders for revenge." Police arrested dozens of IWW members in Grays Harbor between November 12, 1919, and April 5, 1920. The dubious honor of being the first criminal syndicalism victim on the harbor fell to Charles Riddle, a "logger transient," whose crimes of being "suspected of being an IWW" and blaming the "capitalist class" for the Centralia Tragedy earned him time in the county lockup.[126]

In Grays Harbor, as in so many places, public officials joined employers and vigilantes in going to great lengths to crush the Wobblies. Although the national version of this story is well known (at least among historians and activists), peering into efforts to eradicate an IWW community reveals the cooperation between state, capital, and vigilantes—as capitalist America came to resemble the right-wing authoritarian state of Jack London's 1908 novel *The Iron Heel*.[127] And frankly, a century later, it's remarkable how many tools went into this antiradical crusade. Although it's possible to get a read on IWW history by studying its headquarters in Chicago, as so many have, examining a diverse and loose-knit organization from the top down masks as much as it reveals. In some Wobbly strongholds like Grays Harbor, local labor radicalism and a history of militancy continued, even thrived, in the face of repression.[128] That the Wobblies persisted in 1920s Grays Harbor, a major center of political and cultural reaction, makes this history even more relevant.

Congressman Albert Johnson, the longtime editor of the *Washingtonian* who served in Congress for twenty years, was in both positions a leading right-wing activist who opposed immigration and labor radicalism. Written on this photo is "Albert Johnson, Washington State Elks Association, Vancouver, Washington, August 17, 1920." Polson Museum, Hoquiam, Washington.

7

ALBERT JOHNSON'S GRAYS HARBOR

1920S NATIVISM, LABOR, AND THE RIGHT

On May 26, 1924, President Calvin Coolidge signed the Johnson-Reed Immigration Act. It placed restrictions on annual immigration based on national quotas, which limited any nationality to 2 percent of the number counted during the 1890 census. Designed to limit the arrivals of "new" and "undesirable" immigrants, particularly the southern and eastern Europeans maligned by eugenicists who exercised so much power in the early twentieth century, the act also excluded from entry anyone born in a geographically defined "Asiatic barred zone," which included all of Asia except the Philippines. A final section of the act banned immigration by groups ineligible for naturalization, a category that included the Japanese.[1] The law's consequences exceeded even its most optimistic supporters' expectations. Between 1924 and 1947, only 2,718,006 immigrants came to the United States, a mere fraction of the millions who had arrived during the previous two decades. Senator David Reed of Pennsylvania, one of the bill's cosponsors, opined in the *New York Times* that "America of the Melting Pot Comes to End," while Congressman Albert Johnson described the act as "America's second Declaration of Independence."[2] The act, writes historian Adam Hochschild, "placed the most severe restrictions on immigration in American history."[3]

Three thousand miles away from the nation's capital, Congressman Johnson's newspaper, the *Washingtonian*, had spent years congratulating its owner for achieving his life's work by passing immigration restrictions. The crosstown newspaper, the *Aberdeen Daily World*, greeted the triumphant Johnson as he returned home, remarking that the congressman had "international fame by reason of his immigration measure."[4]

The Aberdeen daily had eagerly anticipated the bill, writing in late 1923 of its potential to "prevent undesirable aliens from entering the United States."[5] The Hoquiam congressman's popularity was peaking, as supporters flocked to his speeches, while "News of Congressman Johnson's arrival on the Harbor spread rapidly in Hoquiam and he had to forego necessary slumber to meet all who sent cards to his room."[6] A Seattle daily greeted the bill's passage with glee, writing "JAP BAR SIGNED" in large font atop its front page.[7]

Gratitude rolled in for Johnson's work. Secretary of Labor James Davis explained that Congress passed the law to homogenize the US population: "We are more and more coming to realize the propriety of making this nation a homogenous one. We have discovered that certain racial characteristics lend themselves better than others to assimilation with the stock of the original founders of the Republic."[8] Further to the right, the Ku Klux Klan lavished praise on Johnson and what it called "the Johnson Law." The *Wisconsin Kourier*, a Klan newspaper, celebrated the new law and condemned Johnson's opponents. In December 1924 it wrote, "Colonel Sprague, Defeated Roman Catholic Candidate for U.S. Senator from Illinois, joins with Italians in Criticism of Congress for Protecting America from Influx of Diseased Immigrants—Is the United States to be ruled by Alien Groups or By American Citizens who refuse to be dictated to by a foreign potentate?"[9] The law proved popular in Congress and with many elites, but its overtly racist intent and impact drew condemnation, particularly from immigrants, Jews, Catholics, and labor radicals. *The Survey*, a progressive periodical, criticized the law, writing, "This immigration bill would throw the wholesome social evolution in America into violent reverse. The United States is made to declare for discrimination."[10]

Congressman Johnson in many ways embodied 1920s America. A native-born Midwesterner and lifelong Republican, he moved west, settled into some of the Northwest's biggest cities (Seattle, Tacoma, Hoquiam), and operated a small business before jumping into politics. A Babbitt to the core, Johnson was an all-around bigot: a violent nativist, jingoist, and antiradical whose politics seem extreme a century later. But during his congressional career, he sat comfortably in the center of the nation's white Protestant majority. Having purchased Hoquiam's daily newspaper in

1909, which he also edited, Johnson rode his anti-immigrant (especially Asian) and antiradical actions into a Congressional career—winning election months after he incited (and likely committed) violence against IWW members in 1911 and 1912. He then founded a second newspaper, the *Home Defender*, in 1913. As its editorial policy stated, the *Home Defender* was "devoted to a denunciation of radical, revolutionary socialism."[11]

Johnson was a traditional Republican of his era. He allied with the William Howard Taft side against the "progressive" Theodore Roosevelt wing that divided their party. Most important, he was a strong supporter of business—a chamber of commerce official and a vocal mouthpiece for business talking points. Johnson's politics intersected with his era's two dominant wings of the business elite: the lumbermen, bankers, news editors, and others in the citizens' committees and chambers of commerce in the early twentieth century, and the emergent nativist—even proto-fascist—movement of the 1920s, best represented by the Ku Klux Klan and American Legion, and whose leadership and policies were shaped by businessmen and professionals. Both the traditional business right and their upstart challengers saw Congressman Johnson as their champion. For much of the 1920s, the previous era's right-wing businessmen who handled labor problems with strikebreakers, spies, and vigilantism were joined by the Klan. Like the citizens' committees, the KKK's leadership included many businessmen, had close ties with some members of "law enforcement," and sought to position themselves as representatives and defenders of their community. In the 1920s—as Northwest unions eschewed radicalism and ignored lumber workers, the Wobblies turned inward and focused mostly on sociocultural activities, and the communists got off to an abortive start—it was two branches of the right-wing elite that took center stage in Grays Harbor and national politics.

THE TWENTIES

Johnson and the wider nativist movement spent years pursuing immigration reforms. They succeeded during the early and mid-1920s, a period of political and cultural reaction long identified with the ascendant political right. Conservatives passed immigration restriction and dominated national politics; rightists, too, supported their armed proto-fascist movements. The 1920s witnessed the dramatic growth of the Second KKK as a large national movement, the mostly successful suppression of the labor-left, and an end to mass immigration from southern and eastern Europe. Unlike the earlier Klan, founded by Southerners in the former Confederacy during Reconstruction to terrorize the black population, the KKK of the 1920s was a national movement with deep wells of support in the Midwest and Pacific states. Although trade unions persisted, and in some cases thrived, during the 1920s, "labor" was a far tamer movement. Much of its leadership and rank and file embraced "identity of interests" between labor and capital and bought into a "labor capitalism" of supporting union-owned businesses.[12]

Bridging the 1910s and 1930s, two decades identified with labor militancy and industrial unionism, the labor movement of the "lean" 1920s was dominated by craft union principles, antiradicalism, and nativism. Like in 1920s Seattle at the center of historian Dana Frank's study *Purchasing Power*, Grays Harbor's trade unionists rejected industrial unionism and focused most of their energies on consumer campaigns such as union labels and cooperating with management. An editorial in Grays Harbor's labor press spoke volumes about local union priorities: "A remarkable spirit of cooperation exists between the employers, the business men and the trade unions of this locality. . . . The American Legion is a loyal friend."[13] Many successful 1920s unions represented service workers—chiefly those from small businesses that depended on working-class customers and benefited from union wages. Lumbermen fought unions in the 1920s much as in earlier decades; management had no interest in treating with organizing mill and logging camp laborers.

The Red Scare decade kicked off in 1919 with a series of epic conflicts across the country—with the northwest corner of the United States taking center stage. The wheels of change rolled through Grays Harbor during the decade after World War I. During the 1920s, Grays Harbor County was the state's fastest-growing large county, as its population grew by a third, to 60,000 residents, making it Washington's sixth largest.[14] By the early 1920s, Aberdeen and Hoquiam's combined population surpassed 30,000. The edges of the two cities ran together, blurring Aberdeen and

Hoquiam into a single large industrial entity with separate governments. The cities continued to grow during the twenties; by 1930, the "twin cities" population hovered around 35,000, making it the largest coastal population north of San Francisco.[15]

As in earlier decades, Aberdeen's population had a large foreign-born young population—locals who kept the city running but who had little say in its governance. Many Americans have an exaggerated view of their country as a bastion of democracy. The reality is more complicated—or, rather, the reality is that elections in the United States have never been all that democratic. Women won the vote in the Evergreen State in 1910. However, the electorate remained unrepresentative of the population with immigrant, migratory, and young people largely excluded from the polls. In 1924 Aberdeen, the booming city of between fifteen thousand and twenty thousand residents, a small minority of 4,500 voted in the municipal elections; the new mayor received 2,562 votes—considered by observers a high turnout. A paltry percentage of residents supported the new mayor, but of those (mostly native-born older white adults) who had the vote and the time to cast a ballot, the far-right proved popular.[16] This small suffrage exposes the hole in the argument—common among liberal and conservative historians—that suggests electoral politics present accurate windows into Americans' belief systems.[17] With such a restricted franchise, two branches of the American right dominated Grays Harbor's politics in the 1920s: the merchants and manufacturers who had long controlled local affairs, and the proto-fascist movement that turned out native-born white Protestants on election day and in the streets. The two groups merged in support of many Republican politicians, namely Congressman Albert Johnson.

The forest-products workforce also changed during and after the Great War, expanding from nearly all-male in 1910 to include a significant number of women workers in wood-products plants. World War I provided the greatest impetus for this shift, with thousands of women going to work in lumber. From 1910 to 1920, the number of women working in saw and planing mills nearly doubled, from 3,732 to 7,225, with many women entering the logging workforce as waitresses and cooks.[18] Some of the harbor's leading radicals, notably Jennie Sipo, Laura Luoma (later Law), and Hellen Niemi worked in the area's camps as waitresses. These camps connected women radicals to male workers and fellow unionists—and not solely as family members and auxiliaries.[19]

A second major change in the workforce came in 1925 with the formation of the Harbor Plywood Company in Hoquiam, which, by 1931 employed 200 men and 90 women.[20] Scores of women had long worked in wood-products manufacturing plants such as the Grays Harbor Veneer Company in Aberdeen and for the Henry McCleary Timber Company in the company town of McCleary.[21] But the construction of Harbor Plywood and other plywood plants made this change permanent. Sex segregation pervaded wood-products industries.[22] Indicative of the forest-products industry segregation was the married couple Dilmar and Zinie Sharp, who in 1930 both worked as mill laborers, but with Dilmar working in lumber, Zinie in plywood. However, in plywood and veneer plants, men's and women's jobs overlapped. Viviana Rice, a Minnesota-born divorced twenty-two-year-old woman living near the Chehalis River in Aberdeen, made the same commute to the same job at an Aberdeen plywood factory as her neighbor Alex Chouinard, a fifty-three-year-old son of Canadian immigrants.[23] In the 1930s, though, as plywood laborers joined their sawmill and logger comrades in organizing industrial unions, women took leadership positions. Agnes Brewer served as treasurer for a 1,300-strong plywood union local, which during the mid-1930s represented plywood workers at five Grays Harbor plants.[24]

The lack of lumber unions during the 1920s limited public exposure of gender discrimination and abuses that women experienced. But by the end of the decade, as conditions deteriorated and labor radicals expressed their voices in print, more workers struck, unionized, and detailed specifics of women's workplace conditions. In May 1929, workers at the General Package Manufacturing Company in Aberdeen, where workers manufactured buckets and other wooden objects, unionized and struck over low wages, speedups, and abusive foremen. A reporter going only by "Aberdeen Worker" reported that "several workers have complained of the treatment that the women receive at the hands of unscrupulous foremen, who know that the worker's livelihood depends upon her job. Slave women have never been forced to stand for more insulting treatment that have the girls in this plant."[25] The reporter provided no specifics, but it was common in all US industries for male foremen to sexually harass women workers.[26]

BOSSES UNITED

Business ruled 1920s America—a fact attested to by President Calvin Coolidge, who famously said, "After all, the chief business of the American people is business. They are profoundly concerned with producing, buying, selling, investing and prospering in the world."[27] The Schafer Brothers Logging Company was a prototypical 1920s business. Emerging as a small family-run logging outfit before the turn of the twentieth century, the company flourished. Managed by the Schafers themselves, it became a multimillion-dollar corporation with vast holdings in land and equipment.[28] The company had a mutually beneficial relationship with the federal government—and the Great War helped make the family rich. Both Albert and John Schafer testified against the IWW during the *US v. Haywood* trial in 1918. Having traveled across the country, the lumbermen got their money's worth; John contended that IWW members committed sabotage by destroying the company's saws because these saws were, in fact, patriotic tools of war. As Albert testified, the IWW's actions were responsible for slowing spruce production, thus depriving the doughboys in Europe of needed war materials.[29] The Schafers used wartime profits to expand their holdings. Indeed, the Schafer Brothers Logging Company, headed by one of the leading timber families, spent lavishly during the decade. In the mid-1920s, the company paid $3.5 million for all timber, land, railroad, and camps from the Wynoochee Timber Company.[30] Thousands labored in Schafer operations, and their camps and mills became central to the era's budding labor movements. As a measure of its wealth and prestige, the company hired Stewart Hall Holbrook, the country's best-known chronicler of logging and lumber, to pen its official history.[31]

Standing atop the lumbermen's ranks did not mean the Schafers stood alone. Indeed, lumber operators never abandoned their commitment to solidarity. They used tried-and-true practices that had served them so well in earlier decades. They belonged to trade associations that coordinated sales and marketing campaigns, exchanged information about wages and conditions, and instituted industry-wide shutdowns and wage cuts—dealing with labor problems as a class.[32] At the 1920 Red Cedar Shingle Congress meeting in Seattle, 200 manufacturers came together in the interest of "promoting shingle markets," given that the year ahead "would present many problems to solve." Showing Grays Harbor's importance, the manufacturers elected Aberdeen lumberman E. C. Miller as president. Seeing power in class solidarity, the shingle group's committee on labor committed to cutting wages by twenty-five cents and demanded that "100 per cent efficiency should be required from those employed."[33] Lumbermen also pursued joint investment opportunities, uniting supposedly "highly individualistic" employers into new firms beneficial to all investors.[34] To increase access to Atlantic markets, in December 1925 Grays Harbor lumber manufacturers announced organization of the Eastern Terminal Lumber Company, shipping from Wilmington, Delaware, "to maintain a steady and growing market on the Atlantic Coast for Grays Harbor lumber," in the words of one trade journal. That column of the trade journal could plausibly have been titled "Cooperation." Next to news about the Delaware port appeared a story of "the latest group to organize a red cedar shingle selling agency," a group of Grays Harbor shingle manufacturers; the story's framing suggests that its readers were familiar with lumber bosses acting in concert.[35]

Lumbermen came together to secure markets and influence government, but it was labor's threat that convinced those at the top of the lumber economy to act decisively to protect what was theirs. In discussing the decline of the IWW during the mid-1920s, historian Richard Rajala cited the widespread use and success of blacklists. These had long been a basic feature of industrial relations in lumber; thus, when lumber workers struck, they demanded an end to blacklisting unionists.[36]

Lumbermen on the harbor and elsewhere in the Pacific Northwest used devious methods to oust agitators from their ranks. In one version of the blacklisting operation, out-of-work loggers were required to produce their time-check cards from their previous job, a card that contained the phrase "This Statement is subject to correction and payable at the

Company's Office in Aberdeen, Washington." Unbeknownst to the prospective employee, the card "carries with it a blacklist that is far reaching and actually is the means of supplying the record of every man that works in the logging camps on the Pacific coast." How the scheme worked was made clear in a letter from owners of the Grays Harbor Lumber Company to camp foreman Dan Peterson, in which the secret code on the card was exposed. "When a man quits underscore the words of the code which will give us the information why the man is getting his time," read the letter. If the word "This" was underlined, the logger had been discharged from his previous job; if "payable" received an underscore, then he was fired for showing up drunk at work; if "to" was underlined the card holder was designated a "poor workman"; and if his bosses underlined "the," then the card's receivers knew him to be an "agitator." The result was, in the words of one Wobbly, "a spy system that outdoes anything that was ever concocted in the fertile brain of the oppressors of Russia."[37]

Although blacklisting was rarely advertised by employers, they sometimes left evidence of this practice. During a 1927 shingle strike, bosses at the Schafer mills taunted strikers with the blacklist, telling eight strikers they'd "never be able to work for that company again."[38] To skirt blacklists, workers sometimes changed their names. Reporting on their years in the Northwest lumber industry, in 1929 Aberdeen lumber workers attended a Communist meeting in Cleveland, where they reported on the tragic loss of identity suffered by workers who ran afoul of employers. One logger—a Delegate Pitkin—reported, "Many of the loggers of the northwest have had to change their names so many times they couldn't tell you their right name if you asked them."[39]

As shown by their widespread use of surveillance, employers knew that information was power. In the 1920s and 1930s, lumbermen joined the national trend in labor relations, using employee registration systems to collect information and track workers. The goal was, in the words of historian Andrew Parnaby, the "accumulation of knowledge" about workers and to use information—required to be provided by workers as a condition of employment—to track them, keep loyal and productive workers employed, and weed out radicals.[40] Given the spread of unionism in the lumbermen's open-shop stronghold, employers endeavored to track workers as they moved between jobs—especially significant among the itinerant loggers' workforce. In other words, lumbermen forced workers to register for employment, tracked those employees, and used that information to implement new and sophisticated spying and blacklisting systems.[41]

Formed in World War I, the Seattle-based Loggers' Information System (LIS) advertised its services to lumbermen; they developed employee registration cards that required job seekers to provide identifying information. Management kept the card, used it to record worker performance, and mailed it back to the LIS offices so that it could serve as a clearinghouse for management. Employment cards included basic information, as well as workers' nationality and job history. Ideally, in the words of the LIS, "Any information you can give us regarding this man's service while in your employ other than that shown on the front of this card, please write on the back. . . . Such information will be confidential but used for the benefit of our members."[42] LIS services were only part of an effort to modernize labor relations in lumber—to potentially defeat labor with the brain and card index rather than through vigilantism and state intervention.

Management gathered intelligence and populated blacklists in part through spies—private and publicly funded detectives. E. B. Benn, scion of Aberdeen's founders and former union-busting mayor, used his prominence within the Republican Party to secure an appointment as federal marshal. Given his history in Grays Harbor's labor wars, it's unsurprising that he investigated the IWW, reporting that "the radical element have control of the State Federation of Labor and most of the officers of the local railway unions are radical and believed to be members of the IWW." Benn encouraged the US Attorney General to keep marshals assigned to guarding scab labor against the violence of strikers because, in his words, "new men working for the railroads are frequently assaulted after they leave the shops."[43]

BOOMING PRODUCTION, BOOMING VIOLENCE

Employers like the Schafer brothers stood in a powerful position in the early 1920s. They had a pliant local government, labor spies prowling workplaces, and a potent tool in the criminal syndicalism law—all of which proved useful in the postwar roundups of Wobblies. Lumber production and profits climbed during the twenties, as lumber retained its spot as Washington's largest industry. Grays Harbor boasted the largest amount of privately owned timber of any county in the state, and the Schafers, Polsons, and others expanded operations to cut as much lumber as possible before the federal government restricted Olympic Peninsula logging.[44] Washington's sawmill payrolls climbed from less than $25 million in 1921 to more than $32 million the next year. An even larger increase took place in logging. In 1921, Washington's logging payrolls hit $22.2 million, while a year later they reached $34.47 million.[45] In 1922, Grays Harbor County counted sixteen Class I sawmills—those producing over 100,000 board feet daily—far more than any other part of the state.[46] Approximately four thousand loggers worked in Grays Harbor's woods in 1923.[47] Victor Beckman, longtime official in lumbermen's trade associations, declared that the county's lumber workforce had the highest lumber payroll—nearly $17 million for 1923—in the state.[48]

Much of that lumber traveled to Japan, the Northwest's greatest lumber purchaser; during the first half of 1923 (before Japan's terrible earthquake), 53 percent of all Washington foreign shipments went to Japan.[49] *The Timberman* published articles reading, "The opinion is rather widely expressed that, from a business standpoint, the earthquake in Japan will be a good thing, in the long run."[50] The Chicago-based *American Lumberman* reported on Grays Harbor, "That the catastrophe in Japan will undoubtedly have a strengthening effect on the lumber market seems to be the consensus of the manufacturers on the Harbor."[51] The harbor played a pivotal role in that rebuilding, and reports of record-breaking lumber shipments filled lumbermen's news columns. In 1924, Grays Harbor became the first port in the world to ship over a billion board feet of lumber. In the years ahead, the camps would keep running and the mills keep cutting—in 1926 harbor mills cut 1.56 billion board feet of lumber, an astonishing figure that shocked contemporaries.[52] *The Timberman* reported, "Grays Harbor was the first and only port to ever ship a billion feet of lumber in one year. In 1924 the port barely succeeded in topping the billion mark and in 1925 the mark was almost a billion and a quarter.

In December 1924, Grays Harbor became the first US port to ship over a billion board feet of lumber by water. Left to right: Lytle Logging Company treasurer L. W. Taft, Grays Harbor port commissioner Frank H. Lamb, and Port Commissioner C. N. Wilson. The sign on the timber reads, "This stick contains the billionth foot shipped in 1924—from Grays Harbor, Wash.—by water." Jones Photo Historical Collection.

Last year's mark was approximately a quarter of a billion feet in excess of that of 1925."[53]

As lumber production and shipments boomed, so did the number of workplace deaths among those who made the harbor's record-setting industry possible. Indeed, accompanying these production feats of the 1920s were scores of lumber workers who paid the ultimate price.[54] At the Aberdeen-based Saginaw Timber Company in 1924 were John Pesola, an IWW logger, killed after a log rolled over him; Ole Rasanen, killed at a logging camp when a knot from a tree spar struck him; and Ernest Lehto, who died in October 1924 after his skull, face, and thigh were fractured by a rolling log.[55] A year later, more than one hundred Grays Harbor loggers lost their lives on the job.[56] Straining under the pressure from the increased population of disabled workers, the Finnish American fraternal organization United Finnish Kaleva Brothers and Sisters Lodge No. 9 in Aberdeen was forced to increase its fund-raising activities to cover "the sick benefits [which] became a heavy burden," particularly for those who "were crippled for life."[57]

Workers and labor activists who studied the industry discussed the relationship between productivity and workplace dangers. Radical writer Charlotte Todes was particularly adept at illustrating the relationship between the drive for profits and violence in the lumber industry. She criticized the speedup, which "results in over-fatigue, exhaustion and a greater toll of injuries and deaths"; paradoxically, as fewer workers were required to perform a job due to mechanical improvements and the speedup, accidents in both lumber mills and logging camps rose dramatically during the 1920s.[58] Shingle weavers, whose jobs were sometimes compared to "a battle," had articulated for decades the relationship between job speed and dangers. As war demands led to increased production, trees, saws, cables, and rail cars killed and maimed hundreds of workers. In his exhaustive study of workplace deaths in the lumber industry, historian Andrew Prouty demonstrates that the industry killed more lumber workers in 1917 than in any other year during the 1910s.[59] The dangers of logging amid wartime pressures were apparent in accidents like that of Finnish logger George Wilson whose head was crushed between two logs while on the job.[60] Indeed, lumber workers framed their struggles to organize unions as an effort to make "the lumber industry safe for democracy."[61]

Employers, state officials, and mainstream journalists sometimes blamed the victims of these so-called industrial accidents, declaring the violent acts to be the result of stupidity, drunkenness, carelessness, or even suicide. For example, local authorities declared that Steven Wash, a twenty-seven-year-old planerman at the Grays Harbor Commercial Company, committed suicide after he "was crushed in a planing machine."[62] The *Aberdeen Daily World*, the county's largest newspaper, ran a long article in January 1924 attesting to Aberdeen's record as a safe city, specifically noting that "births outstrip deaths for 1923."[63] Worse yet must have been hearing a Washington State Department of Labor and

Industries official's speech, where he contended that "eighty per cent of the accidents were the result of carelessness! The majority of those 409 men killed last year are in their graves because someone was careless."[64] This statement assigned no responsibility to employers or to capitalist relations of production for these workplace deaths. Instead, the state official implied that workers were themselves responsible for dying on the job—a ghastly suggestion that certainly fueled worker discontent.

Unlike their employers and the many reporters who saw industrial violence as either unfortunate accidents or caused by worker negligence, unionists and radicals argued that these deaths were the fruits of a violent capitalist system. Wobblies were from their inception among the most vigorous opponents of industrial violence. In September 1916, Wobbly Walter Harris wrote an article entitled "Murder in the Lumber Industry" for the *Industrial Worker* in which he condemned the speedup, which "kills and injures more than all else." Harris also expressed a distaste for those "workers trying to save the bosses from destruction" and who did not seem to understand that when "the boss loses tools or timber, he does not lose anything that he has worked for," while "our body is all we have; and we should protect it against accident."[65] When a Grays Harbor worker known as Fellow Worker Holmes died on the job, the IWW declared he was a victim of the speed-up system.[66]

Workers, subjected to production-pushing foremen and the high-ball method of logging, perished at new and frightening levels during the 1920s. So-called industrial accident rates skyrocketed in the lumber industry during that decade. The 1920s saw at least 1,767 Washington loggers die on the job; another 493 sawmill and shingle mill workers paid the ultimate price. A total of 2,260 combined loggers, mill hands, and shingle weavers died due to "industrial accidents" during the twenties—63 percent more than the previous decade. Deaths among mill workers nearly quadrupled from 127 during the 1910s to 493 the next decade.[67] Wobblies didn't mince words; workers who died in the woods and mills were "dead to feed profits" and "another victim of capitalism."[68]

DECLINING HOUSE OF LABOR

One reason why lumbermen encountered little resistance as management increased production was labor's weakness and conservatism. Indeed, the events of Armistice Day 1919 and the IWW roundups that followed constitute an appropriate starting point to a period marked by what historian David Montgomery called "the fall of the house of labor." In the twenties, membership in unions and radical groups cratered. Mirroring national trends, WSFL-affiliated union membership went into a free fall, dropping from a high of 55,257 in 1920 to only 39,910 the next year. Seattle's union membership dropped from more than 60,000 in 1919 to 18,000 in 1927.[69] Unions also declined in Grays Harbor. In 1919, twenty-one Aberdeen locals belonged to the WSFL; three years later, the WSFL counted only fifteen Aberdeen affiliates.[70] In April 1927, the "Directory of Grays Harbor Unions" listed twenty locals; notably, none represented lumber workers. Labor's only "movement" in the twenties was backwards; for Labor Day 1925, unions could muster only a dance and a "labor booth" at the county fair and a dance at a Moose hall, a far cry from the raucous union parades of the previous decade.[71]

One of the major reasons for labor's impotence was the near-absence of industrial unions—as legitimate lumber workers' organizations withered and disbanded amid the open-shop campaigns and postwar recession.[72] The International Union of Timberworkers lost nearly 90 percent of its members between March 1920 and February 1921. In May 1922, the WSFL suspended Aberdeen Local 22 of the IUT for not paying its per capita tax, as the lumber workers who had birthed the international union shuttered their local. In March 1923, the IUT disbanded and closed its office.[73] Although lumber workers unionized and frequently struck during the decade, they failed to create lasting institutions until the early 1930s.[74]

The decline of legitimate unions—those formed by workers themselves—had many causes, including repression and the existence of a military-company union: the Loyal Legion of Loggers and Lumbermen (the Four Ls). As a company union backed by capitalists, the Four Ls advertised that its hiring hall, registration systems, and information compilation were all created for the "sole purpose of ridding the industry of organizers and agitators . . . to prevent a recurrence of the recent strike by the IWW."[75]

The Four Ls shifted to a civilian operation after World War I but continued to enroll workers *and* bosses, while Colonel Disque remained Four Ls president—hardly the stuff of legitimate unions. The Four Ls, seemingly labor organization, used much of its influence to assist capital. The Loyal Legion instituted wage cuts, and elsewhere proclaimed that "labor must be prepared to realize the necessity of rendering a fair day's work for a fair day's pay."[76] Furthermore, in a demonstration of its subservience, the Four Ls celebrated a logging company's record-breaking production. Its newspaper bragged that "the greatest log production record for one side ever attained on Grays Harbor, it is claimed, was made by Camp 5, Schafer Brothers Logging company, Sept. 29, when 35 cars of logs were yarded and loaded in eight hours. Heretofore, even in war time, production of 25 cars was considered a good day's work."[77] How these achievements benefited the workers who remained in the Loyal Legion was left to readers' imaginations. Between its loss of government backing and its support for managerial prerogatives, the Legion lost members—membership declined by more than 90 percent between 1918 and 1921.[78]

The impact of labor's weakness and conservatism reverberated throughout Grays Harbor. Without the radical politics championed by lumber unionists, harbor union leaders collaborated and communicated a perceived "identity of interests" with capital. Signs of labor's subservience to capital and efforts to form "partnerships" were evident in trade union media and celebrations. In February 1926, the Montesano Carpenters' Union voted to place a representative in the chamber of commerce.[79] The AFL and other unions condemned Communism and the wider left. Founded by socialists in the 1910s, Grays Harbor's own labor newspaper, the *Southwest Washington Labor Press*, which had long served as the official paper of the harbor's trade union movement, became a leading voice for anti-Communism.[80] In one way, the Grays Harbor labor paper came to a literal end with the conclusion of the 1920s; the longtime union newspaper switched its name to the *Grays Harbor Press*. The paper had lost even a sniff of challenges to the establishment, present during the 1910s, long before it changed names; however, losing the word "labor" in the title mirrored the change in content: the newspaper included ads for local businesses, but nary a mention of unions.[81]

One casualty of this rightward drift was the dearth of voices questioning labor leadership's entrenched white supremacist and nativist views. The AFL and many of its affiliates supported Congressman Johnson's immigration restrictions; he bragged that hundreds of unions supported him, including a Hoquiam local that expressed its "appreciation for the good work, just completed in passage of the Johnson immigration bill."[82] AFL President Samuel Gompers wrote, "Every trade union in America ought to register its support of the Johnson bill."[83] The *Southwest Washington Labor Press*, before its name changed, enthusiastically supported Johnson. It proclaimed, "The ballot in the coming election carries a name honored the country over and particularly honored in this district which its owner calls home, the name of Congressman Albert Johnson. . . . He is labor's friend."[84] Nonunion whites likewise found much to celebrate in the bill. *The Poseygram*, a company organ published in Hoquiam by the Posey Manufacturing Company's mutual benefit society, said of the bill that it was "one of the greatest efforts ever made toward maintaining the standard of American living that makes the good old USA what it is. . . . So as someone has said, 'Let us have America for Americans first, last, and always.'"[85]

Few Grays Harbor unions had Asian or black members during the 1920s.[86] Several trade unions forbid Asian Americans from membership.[87] When, in 1922, a local Moose fraternity started its own blackface minstrel touring group, the *Southwest Washington Labor Press* ran a front-page article praising the show as a "fine evening of enjoyment."[88] A more frequent target for the *Labor Press* attacks were Asian workers, who unionists portrayed as threatening to "white wages." A front-page article condemned "Jap Growers" from the Puget Sound, who sold crops on the harbor, acts described as an invasion by the Aberdeen labor council.[89] In January 1923, an organizer from the Journeymen Barbers' International Union of America addressed the Aberdeen Central Labor Council on matters of immigration, stating, "The large employers of labor are trying to break down the bars of the present immigration act; they are trying to flood the North American continent with the uneducated workers from Southern

Europe. . . . Many large employers are not concerned with the Americanization of the immigrants. What they are seeking is cheap labor."[90]

The labor movement's reactionary positions showed in other ways as well. Some trade unionists allied with right-wing organizations. AFL unions celebrated their alliance with the American Legion, a right-wing veterans' organization notorious for attacking union halls. The *Labor Press* ran front-page articles celebrating the American Legion and advertising Legion events. The labor paper dubbed the Legion "a loyal friend," while boasting that "a remarkable spirit of cooperation exists between the employers, the business men, and the trade unions of this locality."[91] In 1926, the local labor council accepted fraternal delegates from both the police and fire departments.[92] Occurring shortly after local police arrested and beat unionists—mostly Wobblies, but also trade unionists—the labor council extended "brotherly" greetings to police, a clear sign of the drift of local labor away from the working-class militancy that so animated its history.

KLAN CITY

By the start of the 1920s, Congressman Johnson was famous; his well-earned reputation as a hard-liner on immigration connected him to many of the nation's leading eugenicists. Johnson remained rigidly opposed to the leftism of the IWW and emerging communist movement. Indeed, Johnson blamed radicalism on mass immigration, particularly from eastern and southern Europe. He therefore saw restricting immigration as the best way to stop radicalism, for in nativists' minds, immigrant "bomb throwers" were responsible for the nation's ills. From the halls of Congress, Johnson advocated violence against the IWW. In 1918, as the IWW came under attack from the federal government and vigilantes, Representative Johnson took to the House floor to say the IWW was a "mob, which makes contracts only to break them, which goes into mills only to watch the chance to burn and destroy them, and into the mines for the same purpose."[93] Johnson's own daily newspaper told thousands of readers much the same: "Mob law is not a thing to be admired, but it has always proven effective. . . . This means of meting out justice is being applied to the pro-Germans and the pro-German IWW organization leaders."[94] During an April 1919 visit to Centralia, Johnson urged violence against leftists, stating, "Don't get the idea that this country will be run by Bolsheviks. . . . We will let them go so far; then we will rise up against them."[95]

Johnson's biggest achievements came in restricting immigration. In 1919 he became chair of the House Immigration and Naturalization Committee. Johnson's immigration laws gained wide praise from a cross section of the native-born white Protestant American population. Particularly enthusiastic was the Ku Klux Klan. The national KKK organized in haste after Atlanta-based William J. Simmons revived the order in 1915. During the early and mid-1920s, KKK membership boomed; by 1924 the Klan had millions of members stretching across the country. The hooded order appealed to the racism, anti-Semitism, anti-Catholicism, xenophobia, and antiradicalism of large swaths of white Protestant America.[96] As historian Trevor Griffey suggests, the Klan of the 1920s was right at home in the Northwest: "The massive attendance at Klan rallies also demonstrated the everyday quality of white supremacy and Christian nationalism in the Pacific Northwest. They showed that the politics of intolerance could be made remarkably palatable by simply dressing it up as a form of entertainment."[97] In Seattle, the Northwest KKK newspaper *The Watcher on the Tower* ran the slogan "The Klan, the Konstitution, and the Kross Shall Be Our Faith, Our Hope, Our Creed of Liberty" on its cover.[98]

In Grays Harbor and beyond, the KKK pushed for rigid enforcement of dry laws, a ban on religious schools, and immigration restrictions, among several other planks. Klansmen saw a ban on "undesirable" southern and eastern European immigrants as a necessity, and they campaigned furiously for it. The national Klan was so supportive of Johnson and his racist quota system of "National Origins" that when issuing their platform for 1926, it included the "Renomination and re-election of Representative Albert Johnson of Washington, so he can continue to be Chairman of the House Committee on Immigration and fight for restricted immigration laws."[99]

As historian Linda Gordon argues, the Klan adapted its messaging and program to diverse regions, catering to regional audiences. Along the Pacific Coast, with its relatively large Asian population and persistent IWW presence, the Klan devoted considerable energies to attacking Asian immigrants and radicals—Wobblies and Communists.[100] The KKK built from its Northwest base in Oregon, which had the smallest immigrant population of the Pacific Coast and where in the twenties the hooded knights dominated politics. Its largest locals were often in major metropolitan areas, including Seattle and Portland, but some of the strongest Klaverns—the Klan's name for its local units—were in the state's medium-sized cities like Bellingham, Yakima, Aberdeen, and Hoquiam. Klan members organized branches across western Washington, boasting Klaverns in Aberdeen and Hoquiam.[101] By the summer of 1921, news reports began to mention that a Klan organizer who resided on the harbor found enough success "to warrant launching of one or more branches of the Klan here in the near future."[102]

The Wobblies knew they were in the Klan's crosshairs, and in 1921, the IWW's *Industrial Worker* compared the Klan with Italian fascists: "The fights that have been going on in Italy between the Fascisti, the Ku Klux of Italy, and the communists, socialists, and trade unions has reached its height."[103] An article in the July 1921 *Industrial Worker* reported that the KKK paraded through Hoquiam alongside the American Legion.[104]

Somewhat unique among local Klans, Grays Harbor's KKK retained its presence for over a decade; their reemergence in the 1930s fight against the industrial union and communist movements caught the attention of national observers. The employer base of the harbor's Klan helps explain its persistence in the area; the merchants and manufacturers who donned KKK robes for parades in the 1920s a decade later used the Klan as a terrorist tool against the leftist industrial unions—which were led, as they often were, by immigrants and radicals. Notably, the most prominent Klansman on the Washington coast retained his place among regional elites and served as head of the business groups during the thirties—as business declared war on labor. In Grays Harbor, as across the United States, the Klan had its greatest appeal among small merchants, skilled laborers, and public officials—"middling men" as historian Nancy MacLean calls them.[105] After observing the local Klan, a Grays Harbor IWW claimed that the Klansmen hailed from the "gentry."[106] The Klan agreed with this assessment. In 1921, Kleagle (the title for a Klan officer and recruiter) W. D. Norris spent four weeks recruiting in Hoquiam; he announced that most of the new members were businessmen.[107]

Norris's assessment spoke volumes. Although Klan membership was private and included hundreds of anonymous members, it's possible to trace a composition of the organization based on those leaders who made their membership public. As in many areas of Klan activity, Grays Harbor's most-active KKK members included small businessmen and professionals. Moreover, like many other groups formed by managers and professionals, the Klan demonstrated its class character as Klansmen pledged to fight intoxication, thus maintaining a sober, punctual, and hard-working labor force.[108] The organization, too, ranked among the nation's most dedicated fighters against the "red menace" of the IWW and communists. The Klan championed a form of respectable middle-class Protestant masculinity focused on "flag, faith, and family." Promoting traditional gender, race, citizenship, and class hierarchies, the KKK argued that social pressures arising from urbanization, immigration, and industrial capitalism, as well as the feminist and labor-left movements, weakened male authority over the traditional family.[109]

The harbor's best-known Klansman was Ransom Minkler. A prolific joiner, Minkler enjoyed the networking and socializing common to fraternities and employers' associations. By 1918, he led the Grays Harbor Dairyman's Association; in later years he led the area's chamber of commerce and an automobile dealers' association.[110] He, too, performed a great deal of "public service." In 1914, he ran unsuccessfully as a Republican for a spot on the Chehalis (Grays Harbor) County Commission.[111] Although not a lumberman, Minkler was undoubtedly a member of the elite. The twenties was a dynamic period with fortunes made in the automobile industry, and Minkler cashed in. In 1927, he started the Sunset Oakland Automobile Company in Aberdeen, paying $20,000 for a Hudson dealership; the next year he spent another $6,000 for land to expand operations. He kept the dealership for over two decades, eventually selling the business in 1950.[112]

Klan members' resources undoubtedly aided their efforts to build

Ku Klux Klan parade at Eighth and Simpson Streets in downtown Hoquiam on July 4, 1925, with a large crowd of onlookers on all sides. Klansmen and the horses pulling their float appear in KKK white robes and hoods. A small building on the float represents a schoolhouse bearing a sign that reads, "Education." Several children ride inside the building. The banner on the side of the float reads, "Americanization through Education Is One of Our Objects:. The Klu [*sic*] Klux Klan." Polson Museum, Hoquiam, Washington.

and sustain the movement. KKK messages reached audiences through its parades and mass meetings. In 1923, state Klan leaders held a mass meeting in Grays Harbor attended by "between 900 and 1,000 members, according to an estimate given by members who were there." Members of the Aberdeen and Hoquiam organizations gave the "king kleagle of the Aberdeen klan" a gold knife, "in recognition of the work he is said to have done for the organization on Grays Harbor," according to the *Aberdeen Daily World*.[113] On July 4, 1925, the Klan turned out for the Hoquiam Independence Day parade, donning white robes for members and the horses pulling their float, as well as a large sign reading "Americanization through Education is One of Our Objects: The Klu [*sic*] Klux Klan."[114]

Klan parade floats provided lenses into the Klan thought, including its gender ideology: proper roles for men, women, and families. At the 1925 parade pictured, five robed men stood at the front, publicly championing the Americanization cause. The Klan constructed a small building atop a float; the building sported a sign reading, "EDUCATION" atop its door. Several women clad in white dresses peered out from behind the windows and door, symbols of white women's importance as upholders of "Americanization through Education." As the Klan's statement of principles and purposes articulated, "Patriotism and Christianity are preeminently the moving principles of the Knights of the Ku Klux Klan. The Flag, the Constitution and the Holy Bible are the keystone of Klan principles."[115]

The Ku Klux Klan had strong allies in law enforcement. Far from impartially upholding the law, police concerned themselves with maintaining white supremacy, regulating vice, arresting strikers, and monitoring radicals—four concerns that united police with the Ku Klux Klan, whose membership sometimes overlapped. Political leaders such as lumberman and Washington State Senator Alex Polson had long argued that Finns made up a "fifth column" within the lumber industry and western Washington; he questioned their loyalties, writing that the Finns "were never citizens of the United States and . . . are in sympathy with the Germans, from the girl who works in our home to the man that works in our logging camp."[116] Those attitudes filtered to local police, who singled Finns out for special attention. According to the reports compiled by the Aberdeen Police in the mid-1920s, which tracked arrestees' nationality, Finns were arrested more than any other group—far disproportionate to their numbers in the population.[117]

Aberdeen's police force kept close watch over Asian immigrant men, as well as other persons of color. Reports of the activities—even local presence—of Filipino, South Asian, and Japanese men filled the police records during the twenties. Police likewise corresponded with fellow law enforcement to oversee the movements of African American men. In June 1924, Aberdeen police were told to keep a watch out for a "N——," who was wanted by Seattle police "for assaulting a Seattle Policeman."[118]

Reactionaries also monitored the local Filipino population. The 1924 Johnson-Reed Immigration Act had extended the "Asiatic Barred Zone" to include Japan, widening the area to cover all of Asia except for the

Philippines, which as a US colony was exempt. Approximately 45,000 Filipinos—almost exclusively workers—lived in the United States by 1930, with two-thirds settling in California and Washington, where they labored in the West's resource economy: agriculture, lumber, and canning. Outside of the Seattle area, Washington's largest Filipino community was in Grays Harbor; by 1920, approximately 400 Filipinos lived on the harbor—the county's largest Asian immigrant group.[119]

Filipino workers developed reputations as dedicated unionists. Along with Finns, in fact, Filipinos lay at the center of Clara Weatherwax's award-winning proletarian novel *Marching, Marching!* Set on the harbor during the 1930s, Weatherwax's book adhered closely to historical record; in fact, in an innovative literary section, the author included real news articles in her text to demonstrate that the outlandish methods of propaganda her book described were based on actual anti-labor print-media writings.[120]

Weatherwax had extensive evidence of Filipino workers' class consciousness. Historian Dorothy B. Fujita Rony's study of Filipinos in the transpacific West includes several illustrations of Filipino men drawn to Grays Harbor for work. Jose Acena accompanied other young men to Montesano where he worked for a month. Mike Castillano's work life on the harbor was typical of Filipinos: he mostly worked at a sawmill but also moved between jobs at a box factory, on farms, and in the railroad industry. Al Bautista caught a ride to Cosmopolis in search of work. In the mills, he encountered a hiring system similar to the "shape up" common to the era's dockworker hiring practices. Fujita Rony writes, "Workers would line up, hoping to be chosen for the membership. To 'look tough,' Bautista rolled up his sleeves, even though it was snowing, and earned a chance to make $2.50 per day working at the mill." Treated with hostility by union leaders and some other whites, many Grays Harbor Filipinos retained their support for labor solidarity. Filipino lumber worker Roman Simbe remembered a 1924 sawmill strike in Montesano, which earned him and other strikers "a little bit more respect" from local whites.[121]

Although engaged in union-busting and race-baiting, the police concentrated on regulating the social lives of Grays Harborites, especially immigrants and workers. For example, in July 1924, Aberdeen police raided the city's Balkan Club and arrested 300 people on gambling charges.[122] Cracking down on consumption of liquor, along with the production and distribution of intoxicating beverages, occupied police time while liquor offenders filled jails and courts. In November 1924, Aberdeen police made 645 arrests; 157 of them were for drunkenness.[123] This reflected the views of capital—particularly major lumbermen—who favored a sober labor force to speed production. Lumberman Alex Polson took out an advertisement in the *Southwest Washington Labor Press* to impart his views on liquor to a working-class audience, crediting Prohibition with "a wonderful prosperity" where "laboring men are building more homes, and prohibition is the greatest cause for it. . . . They are building more homes today, where in years gone by, it was spent in drinking and as time goes by it will be more pronounced than ever—the bootlegger and moonshine will have to go," concluded Polson.[124]

AN ELECTION, A KLAN MAYOR, AND A COUP

The Klan was an explicitly Protestant organization and its membership and values connected it to the temperance movement. Klansmen prioritized enforcing laws that outlawed "vices" such as consuming liquor, gambling, and prostitution. Enforcing the Eighteenth Amendment, outlawing alcohol, was a high-profile and often dangerous business. According to one estimate, nationally more than 1,300 persons were killed during the 1920s, "in which it is known that prohibition enforcement was directly at issue. In every case one or more sworn officers of the law or their agents were involved as principals, either as the killers or the killed."[125]

The KKK's campaigns against booze and prostitution distinguished it from some other right-wing business-led organizations—notably the citizens' committees, which were more "big tent" employer operations. Those groups enrolled businessmen from diverse backgrounds; what really mattered to the citizens' committees like those formed in Grays Harbor was that employers were willing to unify to break unions—using any means necessary.

Grays Harbor had its fair share of sensational dry raids; some ended in bloodshed. Klan-affiliated police directed some of the raids on moon-

Hoquiam police display confiscated liquor, ca. 1920s. Polson Museum, Hoquiam, Washington.

shiners' homes, destroyed stills, and lobbied politicians to strictly enforce Prohibition.[126] At the center of Grays Harbor's legal and extralegal battle against the "demon rum" was the notorious "phantom dry squad" run by a prominent Klansman, an octogenarian Civil War veteran and constable named Albert G. Hopkins, a longtime prominent Grays Harbor resident.[127] In 1922, Hopkins tried his hand at politics, running for Aberdeen mayor. Although he lost to the incumbent mayor, shingle manufacturer H. E. Bailey, Hopkins earned nearly 40 percent of the votes cast, a strong showing considering Bailey's incumbency and support from local elites.[128] Two years later, as Klan strength peaked and some locals grew frustrated by what they perceived as the city government's unwillingness to regulate vice, Hopkins ran again. First, however, he spent two years in the public spotlight enforcing dry laws.

The Grays Harbor county attorney created the dry squad to carry out a "clean-up campaign," appointing men such as Hopkins as constables. The press referred to the Hopkins operation as a "phantom squad," likely a reference to the similarity between Klan and ghost costumes.[129] Dry-squad activities generated dramatic news stories. In 1923 and 1924, Hopkins led armed raids on private homes and businesses across the harbor; these sometimes led to confrontations between law enforcement and the public officials ostensibly tasked with upholding the law. In November 1923, Hopkins gained notoriety when he raided a house owned by Aberdeen mayor H. E. Bailey—his recent opponent.[130]

Although dry raids were common, violence by Hopkins and his squad outraged segments of the public. In January 1924, Hopkins led a raid on an Aberdeen pool hall; there, officers shot two suspected bootleggers. A front-page *Seattle Times* headline screamed, "Mob Foiled in Aberdeen!" It continued, "Immediately after the shooting, mobs of South Aberdeen citizens gathered in groups and started to march upon the city jail in Aberdeen, where Wilbur Hollingworth, special officer who did the shooting, was being questioned. Threats to storm the jail and lynch the special officer" led to Hollingsworth's removal to the county jail in Montesano.[131] Hopkins largely avoided this type of backlash as he conducted months of liquor raids; in fact, his brash tactics in defense of "law and order" won him fans among the voting public.

When it came to local politics during the Roaring Twenties, in most cases the far right and farther right vied for supremacy. In November 1924, the hooded knights succeeded when their chosen candidate, Albert G. Hopkins, became mayor, unseating Bailey, the incumbent, in the primary and winning the general election by more than 500 votes a month later.[132] To aid in the election, the KKK had organized a front group called the Aberdeen Civic Betterment League that ran advertisements and campaigned for Hopkins; Klan locals regularly organized auxiliaries such as the Aberdeen Civic Betterment League to turn out the vote and provide a facade of civic-mindedness to the hate group's activism.[133] With Ransom Minkler at the helm, the campaign generated mass enthusiasm, especially with dry activists. On the day of the primary, the *Daily World* recorded that "unusually large crowds for a city election gathered at various places where returns were received."[134]

Few parts of the Klan's 1920s history in Grays Harbor were exceptional.

Nationally, Klansmen exerted control over numerous local governments during the decade and maintained a stranglehold over elected officials in states such as Oregon.[135] But Aberdeen was no mere backwater; in the 1920s it remained one of the Northwest's largest and fastest-growing cities, and its public affairs regularly turned up in major metropolitan dailies.

The election of a Klan mayor made statewide news, proving an embarrassment to some of the city's elite who worried that the Klan mayor might lose them tourism and investments. Banker William J. Patterson led the opposition to the new mayor. Patterson was one of western Washington's wealthiest men and a decade earlier had organized a series of citizens' committees that used vigilantism to brutalize labor activists. Hopkins, Minkler, and the wider Klan had a base among local business groups, but summarizing the non-Klan business groups' opposition to Mayor Hopkins, Patterson reported that "Aberdeen would like to devote its interest to the things that will contribute to its growth and to the development of Grays Harbor country in general."[136] Expressing these views, the *Seattle Star* wrote that many businessmen "charged him [Mayor Hopkins] with causing the town to lose its former prosperity."[137]

Another charge was that the elderly mayor was doddering and frail, unable to overcome the many hurdles opponents put in his way. Patterson claimed that "the duties of the office of mayor had become too strenuous for a man of Mr. Hopkins' age." Moreover, the new mayor violated political norms by replacing appointed officials with his supporters. Klansman Minkler served as campaign manager, and Hopkins rewarded him with a municipal position. Opponents charged the KKK political duo with stacking the police force and city government with their Klansmen pals. For good measure, Mayor Hopkins crafted new police regulations, including an authoritarian measure—the mass fingerprinting of anyone charged with traffic or parking violations.[138]

The final disagreement between Hopkins and sections of the business elite was likely the most serious because it threatened businessmen's finances. Indeed, some businessmen formed a citizens' committee and a Tax Payers' League, a common euphemism for opponents of public spending, to fight the mayor's support for the Wynoochee Plan, a project to harness the Wynoochee River for public use. To fund the Wynoochee public water project, voters went to the polls in March 1925 to decide on a $700,000 bond. According to contemporaries, the water project was the first step. Once harnessed, the Wynoochee could be used for public power.

The Wynoochee project (both its water and power components) was enormously popular and supported by labor; by the Farmer-Labor Party, a third party that garnered considerable support on Grays Harbor—and across the state; and by much of the political establishment, including the Aberdeen City Council and its former mayor J. M. Phillips (a future Superior Court Judge). The Wynoochee Plan was, in fact, the main policy advocated by the *Southwest Washington Labor Press* during the mid-1920s. The Aberdeen Civic Betterment League, the local Klan's auxiliary front group, also came out in support of the Wynoochee Plan, placing two well-heeled and well-organized groups of Grays Harborites on opposing sides. Hopkins joined the city council in support, writing, "The People should vote for the water because there is a need for the water, and also because it will be the first step in the development of power."[139] Federal Marshal E. B. Benn, a former mayor whose citizens' committee eliminated union activist William Gohl from the harbor, emerged to head the Tax Payers' League. As he had two decades prior, Benn formed a citizens' committee of (mostly) wealthy locals to represent their class interests. Benn's group resolved, "We, the undersigned citizens of Aberdeen, have become alarmed by the proposed extravagant expenditures for an additional water supply for Aberdeen as proposed in the bond issue."[140]

The conflicts between the harbor's two pillars of the elite led to an exceptionally chaotic term for Hopkins, dubbed "a bitter political strife for months" and a "civic war" by the *Seattle Star*. The mayor's wealthy opponents spent weeks organizing to counter his political maneuvers—with the goal being the mayor's ouster. The *Seattle Star* summarized the period, saying, "This town is in the throes of one of the bitterest political fights it has ever had." This was quite the statement considering the area's long history of bloody conflict.[141]

The *Daily World* and *Grays Harbor Post* opposed the Klan and Mayor Hopkins in print, although the *World* routinely muted its criticism, ostensibly providing a just-the-facts reporting that never applied to stories on the Wobblies and other labor radicals. J. W. Clark, editor of the *Grays Harbor Post*, condemned the Klan in the harshest language possible. His newspaper featured front-page headlines and lengthy, biting editorials condemning the Klan as "an unlovely thing that has no place in the United States of America" and an "unhealthy mental epidemic" that "every other intelligent citizen and right minded man" should help in "blotting out."[142] Harsh feelings were apparently mutual; one issue of the Seattle-based Klan paper *The Watcher in the Tower* featured a front-page article attacking the *Post*: "Does the editor of the *Grays Harbor Post* really know what an American is? He is like a lot of the present day editors, who have a limited knowledge on certain subjects and when these are presented, makes what he thinks is a bright retort, for an answer, that stamps him for what he is quicker than any branding iron ever could."[143] Displeased at the attack, Clark used the entire editorial page of his weekly to issue a sharp rebuttal to the Klan.[144]

Like many critics, Clark derided the KKK's cowardice since they "hide their identity" and "wear sheets." He also condemned their use of "direct action," which he defined as to "take what you want when you want it." One irony of Clark's attack, however, was that in Aberdeen, the KKK gained power through an election, while newspapers like the *Post* and *Daily World* worried that the "hooded order is active in election."[145] Moreover, Clark and his fellow employers had long used direct actions—sometimes violent types—to further their interests. Four months after the December 6 election, a group of businessmen hostile to Hopkins again used force to get their way.[146]

On April 3, 1925, the "town fathers" had had enough. That night, a group of prominent citizens—described by the *Seattle Star* as "business men, bankers, and the 'open town' element"—took the aged mayor to the Morck Hotel in Aberdeen. The *Star* set the scene: with "armed deputy sheriffs standing guard," the mayor "sat dumbfounded, with no friends to counsel or cheer him" as "nearly 100 leading businessmen" hurled charges at him for four hours. After the lengthy period of "third degree methods, . . . a paper was thrust before him to sign. It was his resignation." Hopkins complained of being "forced to quit."[147] The soft coup's architects and its main spokesman was the banker Patterson, an old hand at dealing with sticky problems through extralegal solutions.

As in earlier decades with business-led vigilantism against immigrants and labor radicals, the harbor's businessmen got their way through coercion. In the mid-1920s, however, employers' interests motivated them to target a right-wing hate group—or at least their elected representative. The Klansmen's reputations—and potentially their commitments to enforcing Prohibition and other political issues—threatened investments and statuses of the other businessmen who undoubtedly wanted to keep their city out of the headlines.

Like the KKK's outlandish costumes and customs, the improbable story of Aberdeen's Klan mayor's rise and fall should not distract from the Klan's significance. Fundamentally a racist and nativist organization, the Klan embodied the culture wars of the 1920s and was right at home in the Northwest. The Klan was representative of a large swath of the nation's (and Grays Harbor's) white Protestant population, and as across the country, many of Grays Harbor's elites had power in the hooded order. Indeed, three of the area's leading citizens—Congressman Albert Johnson, Mayor A. G. Hopkins, and (future) chamber of commerce president Ransom Minkler—were either Klan members or strong advocates for KKK platforms. Johnson even played an important part in turning Klan beliefs into public policy; generations of migrants turned away from America's guarded gates are part of that legacy.

Former Mayor Hopkins's reputation and influence were barely (if at all) diminished by his disastrous term. The 1930 census showed Hopkins still employed as a constable.[148] Reporters sometimes turned to Hopkins for his political opinions, while a decade after his brief mayoral stint, the *Seattle Daily Times* celebrated Hopkins's birthday, reporting, "Aberdeen's Lone G.A.R. Man is 90."[149]

More significant support went to Minkler. His years of Klan activity had done little to dampen his reputation—quite the opposite—as he continued to exert considerable influence. In the early New Deal, he served as chair of the Aberdeen Better Housing Program Committee, a local unit of the Federal Housing Administration; a decade later Minkler served as a trustee of Grays Harbor Junior College.[150] A decade after his time as political advisor made statewide news, his fellow businesspeople chose Minkler as president of the Grays Harbor Chamber of Commerce. In 1940, as Grays Harbor again rose to national infamy for vigilante attacks on labor, Minkler served in the vanguard as a director of the controversial Grays Harbor Business Builders, an employers' organization blamed for the vigilante violence against industrial unionists that brought national attention to the harbor.[151]

Nationally, the Ku Klux Klan's strength waned as the 1920s wore on. Weakened by charges of political and sexual corruption, the KKK declined from a membership in the millions in 1924 to numbering around thirty-seven thousand by 1930. But in some parts of the country, the "secret empire" maintained itself into the 1930s. Historian David M. Chalmers views the harbor as the KKK's main base of strength in the Pacific Northwest during the late 1930s: "With the exception of the Aberdeen, Washington, Klansmen, whose stones rattled the windows of the town's union halls, the only active realm in the West was California," notes Chalmers.

Thus, while early twentieth-century Grays Harbor witnessed waves of labor-left movements, as Wobblies, socialists, communists, and assorted industrial unionists pushed to expand equality and workplace democracy, politics and business affairs were firmly in the hands of men like Johnson, Minkler, and Hopkins. They had tremendous support from the minority of locals who voted and ran businesses. Indeed, when "the people" could choose their representatives, they selected elites who adhered to nativist, antiradical political views. On the other end of the class and political spectrum, radical workers continued to be harried and pressed by the powerful men who proved that they could even oust the mayor of one of the Northwest's largest cities. As the next chapter shows, however, leftists remained a vital force among the area's working class, organizing on the job and in their halls, carrying memories of the one big union idea through the 1920s and into the Depression decade.

8

HALL RADICALISM

FINNISH WORKERS, COMMUNITY, AND THE IWW IN THE 1920S

On the weekend of October 31 to November 2, 1924, hundreds of IWW members and supporters crammed into a massive new wooden hall constructed during the previous several months with funds raised by the Finnish Workers' Association of Aberdeen, an IWW-affiliated organization. A year earlier the *Industrialisti* described in detail the careful planning necessary to erect what they intended as an enormous home for the movement. Having spent $1,600 for land at the edge of one of Aberdeen's Finn Towns, they needed thousands more to build the structure, but the group's coffers were dry since members had funded "IWW peoples court cases constantly for [a] few years" and had $250 on hand pledged to aid the Centralia IWW prisoners. Ultimately, the hall—called the Uusi Halli (New Finn Hall) or IWW Finn Hall—cost approximately $25,000 to build, an immense sum accessible to workers only through collective pursuits. The *Industrialisti* writer discussed the fund-raising potential of speeches, theater performances, and bake sales; the big hope was that the movement's hundreds strong would donate at Christmas—thus avoiding taking out loans.[1]

The hall proved to be a tremendous asset—a reflection of the thriving radical movement that had survived years of attacks. The finished product included an auditorium, theater stage, balcony, library, business offices, restaurant, and apartments.[2] The October 31–November 2 weekend's activities signified the local character of the IWW movement culture as it existed on the harbor during the 1920s and early 1930s, one with a family-friendly nature and the movement's rootedness in the community. *Tie Vapauteen* (*Road to Freedom*), the IWW's monthly Finnish-language magazine, reported that those in attendance witnessed a play, a banquet, a dance, poetry recitals, and political speeches. To commemorate the event, Grays Harbor Wobbly Antti Maki penned a poem entitled "Puolesta Joukon Miljoonaisen" ("On behalf of a group of a million strong"):

> Thus, as one we must procure information,
> And begin this work of light.
> Who has gotten lost will be guided
> By showing light into the night.
> The power of tyrants will be stricken down
> The work will be raised into honor.
> We demand freedom for slaves
> Even if we must purchase it with blood . . .
> —Wonder if the chest filled with glee endure
> When the moment of freedom arrives—:
>
> When the cold chains of the slave are broken
> And our victory journey has begun . . .
> Thus, welcome, children of oppression,
> Beginners of a new era.
> Young, and the gray-haired,
> Carriers of a heavy load:
> Welcome, a thousand times welcome,
> Are you to celebrate here.[3]

Indeed, throughout the 1920s and 1930s, the Finnish IWW hall served as the nucleus for the Grays Harbor IWW movement as its members organized strikes, raised money for Wobbly prisoners, and further developed what was by 1924 already a rich movement culture.

Maki's provocative language about "the power of tyrants" and purchasing freedom "with blood" was not mere hyperbole. Instead, Maki and much of the harbor's working class recalled the bloody conflicts they had waged against employers during the previous two decades. Many of them lived on Grays Harbor during the 1911–12, 1917–18, and 1923 conflicts, raised money to support those harmed during the conflicts, and passed down their memories to newer generations.

The opening of the Aberdeen Finnish IWW hall in the autumn of 1924, and the impressive level of planning and the detail needed to fund-raise for and construct a hall large enough to house hundreds, showed that the IWW was not teetering on the edge of oblivion during the mid-1920s.[4] Indeed, the history of the Grays Harbor Wobblies throws cold water on the suggestion that the Wobblies were a "cult of spontaneity," incapable of long-term planning—as communist enemies on the left suggested.[5] Instead, the IWW had deep roots in Grays Harbor, and the radical workers exerted tremendous energies to build and maintain a movement that could withstand the "iron heel" of repression.[6]

The radical union was particularly vibrant in the Pacific Northwest, where the Wobblies followed their 1923 general strike with smaller conflicts in the succeeding months. In 1924, the Lumber Workers' Industrial Union (LWIU), with an active membership in Grays Harbor, claimed more members than any other IWW industrial union.[7] Between 1923 and 1930, Grays Harbor Wobblies formed and maintained locals of the LWIU, Marine Transport Workers' Industrial Union (MTWIU), General Construction Workers' Industrial Union, and Foodstuffs Workers' Industrial Union (FWIU).[8] Grays Harbor Wobblies formed several auxiliary organizations that provided financial and moral support for local and national IWW activities. To raise money for the defense and support of political prisoners, harbor IWW members hosted dances, picnics, and mass meetings featuring prominent radical speakers. In the 1920s and 1930s, Finnish Wobblies also met under the auspices of an education club that sponsored fund-raisers and propaganda meetings in members' homes and workers' halls. As late as 1931, the group hosted lotteries to help fill its coffers.[9] Young Wobblies formed their own organizations that sponsored social activities. The Grays Harbor IWW sponsored a band, choir, theater troupe, and athletic club, while during strikes harbor IWW members formed their own relief and medical committees.

The Wobblies' ongoing significance helped shape the 1920s labor movement, keeping the militant, radical flame lit during a period of labor's general decline. The IWW movement won real gains for the region's workers. They challenged criminal syndicalism laws in the street and courts; as a result, in 1922, after more than 100 local arrests, local authorities ceased enforcing the law. The IWW also waged strikes that led to increased wages in lumber and maritime—reminding employers of the potential to strike if wages and conditions deteriorated. But their influence didn't stop in the early 1920s. Instead, as this chapter and the next show, current and former Wobblies exerted influence on the lumber and maritime workers' movement in the Pacific Coast's greatest lumber port during the emergent "Radical Thirties."

The "fall" of labor in the 1920s is rightfully viewed as a period of reaction—and a transition period between the class wars of the 1910s and the Radical Thirties. But workers persisted during the 1920s, forging radical traditions in an era and region dominated by the right. During a tough decade, working-class families passed down memories of the epic strikes of the 1910s and forged institutions to sustain the movement. Although historians have long denigrated western Wobblies as little more than a band of agitators that "invaded" communities and concluded that the movement ceased in the 1910s, the reality in the forests and bustling lumber towns of Grays Harbor was a Wobbly movement based in working-class communities and families. Indeed, much of the labor-left that developed in the 1930s had roots in the family-centered IWW of the 1920s. Grays Harbor workers retained their place as a militant, radical core of the Northwest's lumber workforce—easily Washington and Oregon's largest industry. Dozens of the lumber, maritime, and other workers who steered the Northwest's organizing drive in the 1930s came from and lived in Grays Harbor, a place that both nurtured and suppressed radical working-class activism. These workers led one of the nation's greatest campaigns of the Depression decade, when they won union recognition and improved conditions from the lumber bosses, the most powerful men in the Pacific Northwest.

Those who lived in or traveled to the harbor during the 1920s reported on the local Wobblies' influence. During a 1925 sawmill strike in Aberdeen, IWW newspapers such as the *Industrialisti* and *Industrial Unionist* declared that the Wobblies had organized and led the conflict. Recognizing that Grays Harbor was a historic IWW stronghold, the *Industrialisti* wrote that Wobblies led the strike from its outset, while IWW Delegate L-5-1017 kept that newspaper's several thousand subscribers up to date on the strike.[10] Nonmembers of the IWW agreed on the group's importance during the 1925 strike and on the harbor in general during the 1920s. Egbert S. Oliver, a tallyman at one of Donovan's lumber mills who scabbed during the 1925 conflict, recalled that it had been "fostered by the IWW," whose "rag-tag picket lines and small groups of men at the entrance to the mill vocally harassed workers reporting for work."[11] Eight years later, Seattle Communist Party organizer Sidney Bloomfield ran into similar problems with the Northwest's Wobblies. He wrote, "In our most important organization, the TUUL [Trade Union Unity League], we have several comrades who are too old to reorient themselves away from their IWW past, and altho [*sic*] they are sincere comrades, it is extremely difficult to work with them as it is almost impossible for them to develop along the correct line of the Party."[12] The lifelong Communist Gordon "Brick" Moir, who worked in shingle mills and logging camps in Grays Harbor during the early 1930s, recalled that at the start of his career everyone in the woods carried an IWW red card.[13]

The IWW presence in Grays Harbor was particularly visible in the organization's press. Wobbly newspapers such as the *Industrialisti*, *Industrial Worker*, and *Industrial Unionist* featured regular news about IWW and other labor activities in the harbor towns throughout the 1920s. To gain funding and readership for the Wobbly newspapers, harbor radicals competed in subscription sales contests and established an IWW auxiliary called the *Industrialisti* Support Circle. Announcing the Support Circle's May 1918 formation in the *Industrialisti*, IWW activist Hellen Niemi wrote, "The radical women of our town held the founding meeting of the 'Industrialisti-support circle' on May 7, and decided to start sewing in order to support our paper," before signing the announcement "Yours for industrial freedom."[14] The harbor's Finnish Wobblies had a knack for fund-raising. On the afternoon of July 6, 1924, hundreds of Wobblies packed up and took an excursion to a local riverside for a picnic. IWW members participated in athletic events, sang alongside the Wobbly songbird Katie Phar, listened to a talk delivered by IWW soapboxer Arthur

Boose, and raised nearly two hundred dollars for IWW publications, while giving away one hundred dollars in prizes for athletic events.[15] Additionally, during the mid-1920s, the Aberdeen IWW ordered weekly bundles of 350 copies of the *Industrial Worker*, an impressive figure considering that Aberdeen's population was only around 20,000. Finnish-language Wobbly organs *Industrialisti* and *Tie Vapauteen* registered more than ten thousand and six thousand North American subscribers, respectively; in the middle and late 1920s, the *Industrialisti* issued hundreds of "Greetings" each year to workers in Grays Harbor, nearby Pacific County, and Seattle, as well as Butte, Montana; Portland, Oregon; Vancouver, British Columbia, and other western locales.[16] These official figures can hardly account for the full readership of the periodicals, as dog-eared secondhand copies were doubtlessly shared among workers who used the libraries housed at IWW halls.

POSTWAR IWW GROWTH

Across the United States, Wobblies faced tremendous difficulties in the 1920s. Vigilantes and local authorities harassed them, criminal syndicalism laws in Washington and several other states criminalized membership in the organization, and the company- and military-sponsored Four Ls enticed members with offers of potential benefits and threats of violence if they refused.[17] Still, throughout the late 1910s and early 1920s, the IWW carried on in both secret and open activities, planning strikes and calling spontaneous—or quickie—strikes in the woods and mills of Grays Harbor. The early 1920s was a time of organizational gains for the IWW on the harbor and in the wider Northwest. In 1922–23, the IWW's US membership reached nearly its high mark attained during the First World War, a fact that is often ignored or dismissed by some historians of the IWW.[18]

Repression during the war years took a toll on the IWW in lumber, but it did not eliminate the Wobblies. During the early 1920s, the IWW drew its membership primarily from two unions: the Agricultural Workers' Industrial Union and LWIU Local 120. The Aberdeen branch of the LWIU was one of the, if not the, largest locals in the industrial union. Between October 1920 and June 1921, the *Industrial Worker* and *Lumber Workers'*

Bulletin listed delegate and branch reports for each of the locals within the Seattle district of the LWIU, including Aberdeen. More than a dozen delegates worked in the Aberdeen district alone, collecting between sixty-five and several hundred dollars each week in initiation fees and dues in the midst of the first recession of the interwar period.[19] Wobblies retained a core of camp delegates on the harbor: twelve in October 1920, ten in May 1922, nineteen in July 1922, while in October 1923 the *Industrial Worker* announced that clearances for twenty-four Wobbly delegates had arrived at Aberdeen headquarters. Evidence of the growth of the IWW in the Pacific Northwest woods came at the 1923 LWIU convention when it was announced that the industrial union had "doubled in numbers" during the previous year. In Aberdeen, 900 Wobblies and supporters attended a September 1923 talk by Wobbly Arthur Boose and donated $69.31 to the local movement.[20]

Oiva Carl Wirkkala, a Finnish American IWW member who worked in the Grays Harbor woods during the early 1920s, recalled that although the Wobblies "were under pretty heavy attack by 1921," they still retained a large presence in the logging camps and could call strikes practically at will. At one camp, IWW delegates had been hired and after six months of holding Wobbly-style concerts and discussing camp conditions in the bunkhouse, one day delegates exchanged secret correspondence calling for a strike. The next morning, according to Wirkkala, "It was 'roll out,' to work, you know, nobody went out. That's how quietly it was pulled."[21] The strike described by Wirkkala occurred in the early 1920s after the worst of the post–World War I repression had abated.

Rank-and-file IWW activism continued throughout 1921–23. When IWW members entered the workplace, they came armed with radical literature. After an early August 1921 police raid on the Aberdeen IWW hall, the *Aberdeen Daily World* registered some shock that "75 pounds of radical literature was seized" from the wrecked hall. When the newspapers were not seized, they reached an eager audience that used them to advertise working conditions and debate union policies. One Wobbly delegate at a Humptulips Logging Company camp reported that despite such creature comforts as "bunks are good, all lower" and the presence of "a bath house, and electric lights," this was "a good camp to sell papers in."[22]

WHO WERE THE GRAYS HARBOR WOBBLIES?

In 1971 historian William Preston argued, "What kinds of men and women joined the Wobblies is, of course, extremely significant to the overall judgment eventually made about radicalism."[23] To determine the composition of the IWW on Grays Harbor during the 1920s and 1930s, I compiled lists of Wobblies and those who supported the radical organization strongly enough to be listed in its publications. The sources for these lists include court and jail dockets, newspaper accounts, local union charters and dues books, petitions, newspaper subscription and fund-raiser contribution lists, and the lists of "Greetings" published annually by the IWW's *Industrialisti*.[24] The list totals more than 1,300 names of those affiliated with the Grays Harbor IWW between 1921 and 1935. Cross-checking these lists with census data, city directories, and mortuary records, I uncovered a significant amount of demographic data for 599 of the radicals.

The IWW of the 1920s was a diverse group, comprising first- and second-generation immigrants, native-born radicals, and workers steeped in the local radical traditions built on the harbor during the first two decades of the twentieth century. Working-class families and others rooted in local communities fueled the IWW movement of the 1920s. Additionally, the demographic composition of Grays Harbor's radical movement changed in the years after World War I. Often portrayed in the 1910s as a rural movement based in the region's forests among rootless single young men, by the 1920s the Grays Harbor IWW had become a predominantly urban movement composed of men, women, and children.

Wobblies maintained a strong presence on the docks and fishing boats and in the lumber mills of Aberdeen and Hoquiam. Scores of IWW members labored in the harbor's lumber mills, forming and maintaining locals of the LWIU in Aberdeen throughout the 1920s and early 1930s. Wobbly lumber workers William Randall, Tom Murphy, Bob Pease, Gust Casperson, and Matt Johnson rotated between leadership positions in the Aberdeen LWIU from 1922 to 1926. These men organized and maintained the Aberdeen LWIU, wrote job reports published in IWW newspapers, collected donations for the IWW, and, during the early 1920s, served time in jail for their activism in the union.[25] Randall, the branch secretary of the Aberdeen LWIU during 1923–24, directed several Wobbly fund-raisers during his term in office, collecting and relaying a substantial sum to the IWW Publicity, Defense, and Jail Relief Committees.[26] Although the harbor's LWIU shrunk during the 1920s, local lumber workers continued to meet, raise money, and even publish educational materials for the IWW. This group included Iver Johnson, a Norwegian-born laborer at the American mill in Aberdeen. He served as chairman of the LWIU General Organizing Committee during the late 1920s and early 1930s and published the *Bulletin*, a one-page newsletter for the LWIU in 1933.[27] Local IWW members also published short educational articles advocating militant industrial unionism and improved wages and conditions as they joined non-Wobbly lumber workers in building the "one union in wood" during the thirties.

Wobblies also worked along shore and aboard ships. These men provided much of the labor necessary to sustain Grays Harbor as the "lumber capital of the world" during the 1920s as its annual lumber shipments exceeded one billion board feet.[28] Their persistence on the waterfront during the 1920s, years of unprecedented lumber shipments, enabled the Aberdeen branch to emerge in the late twenties as one of the largest locals of the MTWIU in the nation. Many longshoremen were dual unionists who also belonged to the International Longshoremen's Association.[29] At least fifty-six Grays Harbor longshoremen from the 1921–35 period belonged to or associated with the Wobblies. Many of the maritime workers who formed the International Longshoremen's and Warehouse Union (ILWU) in 1937 had longtime affiliations with the IWW. Of the 416 longshoremen listed as having worked on the Grays Harbor docks between 1935 and 1938, at least seventeen of them carried both their ILWU and red IWW cards.[30] These dockworkers formed and maintained locals of the IWW's MTWIU throughout the decade, and in a 1984 interview the famed longshoremen's leader Harry Bridges recalled that there was a major presence of Wobblies on Pacific Coast ports during the mid 1920s. Maritime unionist and historian Ottilie Markholt noted that the IWW had tremendous influence in both the Grays Harbor and nearby Raymond dockworkers' unions, and they maintained the dockside militancy in the years leading up to the 1934 maritime strike.[31]

Robert Benson, Aberdeen longshoreman and second husband of

Finnish American IWW organizer Jennie Sipo, was a longtime IWW member; following the "Big Strike" of Pacific Coast maritime workers in 1934, he rose to major leadership positions, most notably as vice president of the Maritime Federation of the Pacific Coast, an organization of Pacific maritime unions formed in 1935. Benson was a noted anti-Communist and opponent of longshoreman Harry Bridges, who, following Benson's refusal to induce the cannery workers to return to the federation, joined other Communist maritime workers in attacking Benson at the 1938 Maritime Federation of the Pacific Coast convention, labeling him a traitor, and passing a motion condemning his actions.[32]

The heavily Finnish IWW of the 1920s stood upon a solid foundation of radical Finnish American women who had a substantial place in the Pacific Northwest left throughout the early twentieth century. Finns retained their spot in the center of the Grays Harbor left—in the Socialist and Communist Parties and IWW, particularly the Finnish branches. Indeed, wage-earning and unpaid female laborers stood at the center of the later Grays Harbor IWW movement. Of the 275 adult women identified in my sample, 129 worked in the home, providing the domestic labors necessary to sustain and reproduce families and communities.[33] Many of these women worked outside the home as maids or waitresses prior to marriage. This number included such activists as Hellen Niemi and the sisters Stella and Irma Hendrickson, who worked as logging camp waitresses and founded the Domestic Workers Industrial Union Local 122 in 1917. The most prominent female Wobblies on the harbor were the rebel maids and servers, women who labored in the food and domestic service industries during the mid-1920s. Women led and served as rank-and-file members of the Foodstuffs Workers' Industrial Union (FWIU) Local 460, a mixed-gender local formed in Aberdeen in October 1923. Women, including Finnish Americans Emily Koski, Lydia Kuusisto, and Signe Heikkila, numbered fourteen of the twenty Grays Harbor Wobblies who formed the FWIU.[34] Lydia Heino, a charter member of the Aberdeen FWIU, moved to Grays Harbor from Butte, Montana, after her husband Victor's health problems forced him out of the mines. While the institutional life of the FWIU in Aberdeen proved to be fleeting, Lydia's family's involvement in the IWW long outlived that union. The Heinos' names appeared in the pages of the *Industrialisti* as late as 1935.[35]

The FWIU's membership rolls also included one of Grays Harbor's most prominent Wobblies, Jennie Sipo. During the war, Sipo moved to Aberdeen with her miner husband, John Sipo, who passed away from the flu pandemic shortly after their arrival.[36] By the early 1920s, Jennie emerged as a leading force in the harbor labor movement, becoming a restaurant workers' union (FWIU) delegate by 1922. She headed the list of the union's charter members a year later when IWW headquarters issued the Aberdeen FWIU local their charter.[37] During an IWW free speech fight, waged to challenge Washington's criminal syndicalism law, police arrested Sipo along with more than twenty other Wobblies on charges of syndicalism.[38] The *Industrial Worker* noted that Sipo was charged with "having in her possession the minute book of the meeting" of the IWW, an indication that she had earned a measure of responsibility within the union.[39] Some of the political prisoners received an early release from jail, but Sipo refused such treatment, earning her the honorary title of "a real rebel girl" from the free speech fighters' jail committee.[40] Sipo dropped from prominence in the mid-1920s, but she passed the radical torch to her niece Emily Kaiyala, a second-generation Finn whose family migrated from Butte's mines to Washington State in the early 1920s. Emily remained a longtime Wobbly, taking her organizing talents to IWW headquarters where she worked as an official.[41]

Maintaining a several-hundred-member leftist organization with a vast set of social, cultural, and political activities required the labors of numerous women. Wobbly women used their domestic skills to craft products for sale at local fund-raisers. Aberdeen's IWW Finnish sewing club hosted entertainments and sold handmade goods in 1919 to support class war prisoners. The *Industrial Worker* recorded how the IWW put these crafts to good use in July 1923 when organizer Jennie Sipo donated a pillow that local Wobblies auctioned off for $39.86 to help with the defense of the Centralia prisoners. The IWW's General Office Bulletin kept detailed records of the various IWW auxiliaries' fund-raising efforts. Grays Harbor IWW auxiliaries such as the Finnish Workers' Association,

Jennie Sipo (top) joins her second husband, Robert Benson, and children for a family photo. On Grays Harbor, families such as the Sipo-Bensons provided the backbone of radical movements, including the IWW, that enabled them to persist in the face of state and private repression. Photo courtesy of Lauren Love.

Aberdeen Support Club, Finnish Women's Circle, Education Club, and *Industrialisti* Support Circles in both Aberdeen and Hoquiam raised hundreds of dollars for the IWW.[42] Some IWW women including Hellen Niemi and Hulda Laine also proved to be skillful sub hustlers, selling subscriptions to the *Industrialisti* and *Tie Vapauteen* to their fellow workers on the harbor.[43] Few, if any, fund-raisers equaled Niemi, a top national Wobbly salesperson for at least two decades who brought in thousands of dollars; she was such a prolific salesperson that in March 1935 the *Industrialisti* printed her name and sales record atop a list of eighty Finnish American IWW newspaper sellers.[44] Along with Hellen Niemi and her husband, the names of scores of Grays Harbor families—with the wife's name listed first—appeared in the annual *Industrialisti* "Greetings" lists each December.[45]

The family-friendly IWW welcomed children, and indeed youths also contributed to the lively cultural traditions of the IWW. They wrote letters to the *Industrialisti*, spoke and performed at meetings, attended the

IWW's Työväen Opisto (Work People's College) in Smithville, Minnesota, and stood alongside their parents and fellow workers during demonstrations.[46] IWW "children" and "girls" took part in all types of radical activity, ranging from funeral parades to picnics, political speeches to strike demonstrations.[47] IWW activist Guy Askew described the participants in these festive celebrations as the "cutest bunch of girl and boy Junior IWWs you could ever want to meet or hear its songs." He observed a group of children during a gathering at the IWW's large hall in Seattle during 1928 and wrote, "These wonderful little Junior Wobblies sang 5 or 6 songs at each show and they was given free lunches and candy bars for their wonderful cooperation."[48]

Young Grays Harbor Wobblies, particularly first- and second-generation Finnish immigrants, organized IWW auxiliaries and cultural events. These youth groups represented a local—and Finnish American—version of the IWW's Junior Wobbly movement. Formed in connection with the 1927 Colorado coal strike, Junior Wobblies organized local branches in many parts of the United States, attended summer classes at the Work People's College in Minnesota, and published a newspaper called the *Young Recruit* in Chicago.[49] In Grays Harbor, radical children organized their own youth organization known as the Finnish Workers' Association League of Youth. In the late 1920s, the group held meetings every Friday night, as well as occasional picnics and dances, including the "moonlight and confetti dance" on August 25, 1928. Violet Nurmi, an eleven-year-old member of the Finnish Workers' Association League of Youth, wrote of the group's activities in the youth department's page in the *Industrialisti*: "At the hall the children have a club. About 40 belong to it. The name of the club is F.W.A. League of Youth. We held a dance and are going on a Weenie roast."[50]

The daughter of Finnish immigrants, Hilja Karvonen, an Aberdeen Wobbly who studied at the IWW's Work People's College, straddled the line between the mostly Finnish-speaking world of the Grays Harbor IWW and the wider English-speaking world she grew up in.[51] Born in 1913, Karvonen became active in the IWW as a teenager, attending the Work People's College in 1928. Apparently impressed with the mixture of activism and scholarship that characterized a Work People's College education, she returned to Aberdeen from Minnesota to continue her schooling and involvement with the local Wobblies, penning verse about working-class life on the harbor and writing letters to and articles for the "Nuorten Osasto," the children's page of the *Industrialisti*. In a July 1928 letter published in the "Nuorten Osasto," Karvonen expressed hope that future generations of workers would mobilize to challenge capitalism: "I get such enjoyment out of reading this column that I feel I should contribute a letter every now and then . . . Then too when I write I grow more enthusiastic about the working conditions which is precisely the thing that inspires organization, the vital factor of a worker's life. We younger ones will soon be the older ones, whereas the responsibilities will then rest upon our shoulders. It is better that we be prepared by starting early to have sympathy with our fellow workers."[52]

As these cases illustrate, the presence of many women, children, and married men with families in the Grays Harbor IWW contradicts the view of the Wobblies as a band of migratory male hoboes without families or homes, the "bindlestiffs" and "timberbeasts" of Wobbly lore.[53] In fact, during the 1920s and 1930s many working-class Grays Harbor families came together to support the IWW, helping to root the movement in the local community.

Finns comprised the largest part of Grays Harbor IWW membership from 1912 until the late 1930s; their funds and fund-raising activities sustained the movement as it withstood repeated blows of state and employer repression between 1911 and 1923.[54] Beginning in 1917 when the Finnish-language IWW newspaper *Industrialisti* began publishing annual Christmas "Greetings" lists, it is possible to observe with some precision the makeup of the Grays Harbor Finnish Wobbly movement. In its first year, the organ sent greetings to 162 men, women, and children in Aberdeen, another 138 in Hoquiam, and 9 more in the nearby beach community of Grayland. Evidence of the movement's continuity and growth is seen in the fact that by December 1921, 513 harbor residents received greetings from the *Industrialisti*. The size of the movement increased dramatically during the early 1920s so that in 1924, the year local Finnish Wobblies built their hall, the *Industrialisti* issued more than 750 greetings to Grays Harbor residents. Participation in the movement dwindled, albeit slowly, during the remainder of the 1920s and 1930s, so that the December 1935 "Greetings" issue of the *Industrialisti* still listed the names of more than 600 Grays Harbor residents.[55]

The *Industrialisti* must rank as one of the, if not the, most complete sources for information about the IWW during the decades it was published, including four decades (1917–50s) of daily publication. A radical publication that ran Wobbly and general working-class articles, the paper's writers catalogued a vast array of activities, ranging from IWW strikes to fund-raisers in one of the many Wobbly and Finn halls, to letters penned by working-class children commenting on everyday experiences. Even so, *Industrialisti* content, written mostly in Finnish, has remained locked away from most IWW scholars, leaving labor scholars ignorant of much of the movement.[56]

Finnish American Wobblies crafted their own, in some ways distinct, brand of Wobbly culture, one that blended the revolutionary syndicalism and industrial unionism of the IWW with "hall socialism."[57] The new hall proved to be both the literal and figurative center of the Grays Harbor IWW movement.[58] Located at 110 North F Street in Aberdeen, the hall was in east Aberdeen's Finnish ethnic enclave. IWW members' and supporters' homes, as well as dozens of small businesses that advertised in the *Industrialisti*, surrounded the hall. No fewer than forty-six businesses located within a six-block radius of the Uusi Halli placed advertisements in the *Industrialisti* during 1928.[59] As a result, it took harbor Wobblies only a short walk from their hall to a variety of cafés, grocery stores, saunas, or several businesses that advertised in the *Industrialisti*.

Based at the Uusi Halli and other meeting points throughout Grays Harbor, the local IWW movement experienced something of a cultural renaissance during the mid-1920s. Inside the halls, Wobblies and their guests enjoyed a range of cultural activities, including theater performances, athletic competitions, music, dances, potlucks, poetry, operas, literary clubs, movie showings, and talent shows.[60] In 1923 and 1924, harbor Wobblies hosted four meetings per week, including Sunday-night mass meetings open to the public. Harbor workers also received a long line of IWW speakers, including the well-known orators Ralph Chaplin, James Rowan, Elmer Smith, James P. Thompson, and Arthur Boose.[61]

The Uusi Halli provided radical Finnish workers with a large meeting hall, library, theater, gymnasium, and offices to conduct Wobbly business. As with many other Finnish American radical movements, Grays Harbor's Finnish IWW culture centered on the production, performance, and viewing of workers' theater. Those Finns who staged the plays came from working-class backgrounds and thus crafted dramatic shows of, by, and for Finnish workers themselves.[62] Finnish American radical Reino Nikolai Hannula spoke to the significance of workers' theater to Finnish immigrant leftist movements: "Show business was the first item on the agenda in the Finn hall. The class struggle, basketball, and other matters had to wait in the wings of all Finn halls—the IWW hall, the socialist hall, and the communist hall—until the drama society was done."[63]

Grays Harbor Wobblies had a long history of putting on theatrical performances produced and performed by local drama groups.[64] On June 22, 1923, a crowd of five hundred witnessed an Aberdeen IWW performance of *The Kangaroo Court*, a "one act burlesque" by IWW Walker C. Smith, which provided a semifictional account of the nation's criminal syndicalism cases.[65] These radicals were intensely devoted to their dramatic pursuits, trekking across town to practice six days per week, often on top of their already demanding work schedules.[66] The local Wobbly troupe put on regular performances at the Wobbly Finn hall, including a three-act "workers' play" entitled *Kaivantokylassa* on December 25, 1924.[67]

IWW theater at the Uusi Halli served two main goals. As a workers' theater, the troupe put on plays with explicitly class-based themes for didactic purposes. Audiences gained entertainment while learning about labor history, the significance of industrial unions, and the brutality of capitalism. But these were paying audiences, and knowing that some in the local Finnish community preferred to view mainstream shows, local radicals performed a varied repertoire to increase the group's take for their performances and thus raise greater revenue for their movement. To appeal to a wide audience, local Finnish Wobblies widely advertised the four-act play *Attila*, based on the history of the Huns, in the pages of the *Industrialisti*. According to the Finnish Wobbly newspaper, the show's producers spared no expense in building the sets for the show, which they hoped would be received by an audience of several hundred spectators.[68] One October 1928 *Industrialisti* advertised two comedies, including "one of the funniest plays in the world," no doubt trying to expand their regular audience.[69]

Theatrical performances drew in dozens of actors, directors, and stage crew who put on shows for hundreds of spectators. Ida Randall and her husband, Armas, both Finns, took a special interest in Aberdeen's IWW theater. On September 8, 1929, the Randalls joined twenty-one of their fellow actors onstage before a large crowd at the hall for a performance of *Tuhlaajapoika* (*Prodigal Son*).[70] Recalling his parents' time in Grays Harbor, the Randalls' son Tom wrote that his parents "were both very active in Finnish theatricals at the Finn halls of Aberdeen and Hoquiam. Armas played leading men, Ida portrayed mother types in serious dramatic roles."[71] The harbor's theater caught the attention of Finnish-born playwright Felix Hyrske, one of Finland's greatest dramatists, who spent much of the 1920s and 1930s living and producing plays among Aberdeen's Finns before his death in 1939.[72]

DEFENDING WORKING-CLASS FAMILIES

Working-class families and communities maintained the IWW; in turn the Wobblies devoted much of their post–WWI energies to the defense of working-class families who suffered under what historian Bryan Palmer labeled "capitalism's punitive essence."[73] Indeed, the perils of industrial capitalism were everywhere in the lives of workers, particularly radical activists who suffered under repressive laws, police, and courts; received condemnation from antilabor journalists; and were harassed by strikebreakers, labor spies, and employers.

A principal threat for early 1920s radicals came from Washington's criminal syndicalism laws—a potent tool in the hands of local authorities in Grays Harbor as they arrested and jailed more than a hundred harbor residents. The Wobblies were old hands at fighting to free political prisoners, and in the early 1920s they turned to an old tactic—the free speech fight—to combat the continued abuses of state-directed union busting. Using mass pressure to gain publicity, bankrupt municipalities, and secure workers' rights had long fallen out of favor with much of the

IWW, including those who, like John Pancner, argued that fights were better at organizing "the bourgeois, the street moocher and the saloon soak" than the "wage slave."[74] But as IWW historians have pointed out, much of the former leadership of the IWW was in prison, marginalized, or dead or had departed for greener pastures by 1921, and the discussion of tactics were again debated.[75]

Wobblies waged free-speech fights across the Pacific Northwest in 1921 and 1922. Wobs launched these latter-day struggles in defiance of the criminal syndicalism laws that made their organization illegal.[76] Direct action retained its place as the chief weapon in Pacific Northwest Wobblies' arsenal to free their fellow workers during the early 1920s. Declaring "Come one, come all! You're needed," the Wobblies declared free-speech fights in 1921 and 1922 to pressure local judges and prosecutors to cease criminal syndicalism prosecutions and free the scores of men and women held in city and county jails for their involvement with the IWW.[77]

The May 1922 arrests of J. M. Johnson and Claude McAlpin in Hoquiam for violating the criminal syndicalism statute triggered Washington's largest free-speech battle of the twenties. Police arrested nineteen IWW members for the same offense during the next week. As in earlier battles, Aberdeen Wobblies sought to overwhelm the local authorities with a mass show of support from IWW members around the region. In a piece that could have appeared a decade earlier, the *Industrial Worker* ran an announcement proclaiming "Volunteers Wanted" to make "it safe to Organize in Grays Harbor Country!" The same issue contained a letter from Bob Pease, Aberdeen branch secretary, who reminded readers, "This is the same old story. . . . We must stop this thing here, as well as elsewhere. . . . Let's fill their jails. Yours for the IWW." Answering the call, Wobblies held branch meetings in Seattle, Portland, and Aberdeen to support the fight and collected defense funds from "many points in Washington and Oregon." In keeping with their tradition of local autonomy, Wobblies formed a committee inside the jail, which took responsibility for making all decisions regarding their defense. The jail committee called for direct action, issuing "requests that you do not write to these men, but come and help in the fight." They also used the *Industrial Worker* to antagonize the "able-bodied bourgeoisie" who persecuted their organization, arguing that the American Legion had "been duped to further the schemes of the lumber barons."[78] Even those IWW members jailed during the fight managed to bring their message to the streets. During "an outing to the beautiful little city of Aberdeen," authorities took IWW prisoners from their jail cells in Montesano and loaded them in the back of a truck headed to Aberdeen; the Wobblies sang renditions of "Hold the Fort" and "Solidarity Forever" to the "waving hands and hankerchiefs by sympathizers among both workers and business men."[79]

A late October 1922 edition of the *Industrial Worker* triumphantly reported, "Free Speech Fight Won, Syndicalist Law Ended." The fight succeeded at freeing the fourteen IWW defendants and restricted the state's use of evidence in all future syndicalism cases in Grays Harbor. Their attorney, "the fighting Wobbly Lawyer from Centralia" Elmer Smith, based his argument on the fact that most criminal syndicalism prosecutions relied on literature written by non-IWW members as evidence. This included "the writings of authors and poets, some times dead for many years," several of which "would be disclosed as standard books on the library shelves."[80] The free-speech fight victory, while based more on legal than direct action, gave the local Wobblies ample cause to celebrate. After years of public and private harassment had kept them underground, in 1922 the Wobblies waged a very public free-speech fight. With Washington's syndicalism law no longer widely enforced, the Wobblies carried their program to the next level by planning for a general strike in spring 1923.

The general strike was the central piece of the IWW's revolutionary strategy, a tactic designed to prevent capitalists from extracting profits from workers, thereby paralyzing corporations and the state apparatus dedicated to their defense. Wobblies viewed these strikes as the best way to bring about a social revolution. Big Bill Haywood declared, "All the workers have to do is to organize so that they can put their hands in their pockets; when they have got *their* hands there, the capitalists can't get theirs in. If the workers can organize so that they can stand idle they will then be strong enough so that they can take the factories . . . whether the capitalists like it or not; when we lock the bosses out and run the factories to suit ourselves. That is our program. We will do it."[81]

By October 1922, once it became clear that President Warren G. Harding had no intention of freeing the Wobblies held in federal prison, planning began in earnest for the general strike to free IWW prisoners. Wobblies intended the strike to begin on May Day. In Aberdeen on April 15, thirteen IWW delegates from the Grays Harbor district voted to coordinate the strike with their fellow workers on Puget Sound, all while making it clear that "the main issue in this upcoming strike shall be the release of the class war prisoners."[82]

The IWW struck early, leafleting the Northwest with declarations of "The Strike Call For April 25, 1923." That day, reports came "into the Seattle headquarters in a steady stream," announcing that forty-eight logging camps in western Washington were closed by the strike. On April 26, 600 IWW members in good standing met in Aberdeen to celebrate what had already been accomplished and plan their next moves. The *Industrial Worker* told how one group of loggers brought about the strike at their camp: "Aberdeen, Wash.—Saginaw Camp No. 1 . . . We held a meeting here on April 16th with 35 members present in good standing and 30 nonunion men present. A collection of $27.65 was taken up for the strike fund. A strike vote was taken and every one present, sixty-five in number, voted to go out when the strike call comes for the release of class-war prisoners.—(LU-224)."[83]

Responding to the call, loggers at thirty Grays Harbor camps struck. In addition, groups of longshoremen and sailors struck and picketed the docks. According to one IWW member's report of the union's waterfront actions, "As fast as the ships come in, the crews are notified that the General Strike is on for release of Class War prisoners, and so far 75 per cent on all boats have quit."[84]

One IWW success came at the Grays Harbor Commercial Company, the only mill that had remained in operation during the 1912 and 1917 strikes. Following the 1923 IWW strike call, approximately 85 percent of the mill's workers walked off the job. Shocked that the mill, often called the "penitentiary," succumbed to the strikers, the *Seattle Union Record* celebrated the closure of this "infamous company" that was "known for long hours and short wages." In all, somewhere between four thousand

and five thousand mill workers, loggers, longshoremen, and clam diggers walked off their jobs in Grays Harbor during late April and early May 1923.[85]

Employers worried that the strike might reach proportions of earlier IWW conflicts and responded to this threat by putting aside log price negotiations until the strike had run its course. At the May 2, 1923, meeting of the Douglas Fir Exploitation Committee, one official registered their concern, noting, "This is a strike, not for wages, but to show their power and ability to call strikes and call out men. The IWW are active, and old leaders are appearing who have not been seen for four or five years." Grays Harbor lumbermen intimidated and attacked picketers. They hired gunmen to guard the plants. Stoolpigeon Jackson, the night watchman at one mill, allegedly yelled at a group of workers that "if my son joined the IWW I would shoot him."[86] Tragically, Grays Harbor gunmen proved willing to back up these threats. On May 3, a Bay City Company gunman shot IWW William McKay in the back of the head, killing him. The gunman escaped punishment when authorities dropped charges, deeming the killing an act of self-defense.[87]

Local Wobblies met violence with solidarity and community support. On May 8, 1923, a massive and diverse crowd of more than 1,000 marched across Aberdeen in a funeral parade paying tribute to McKay.[88] The parade and funeral were extraordinary for both their size and the explicitly political messages of its participants: the *Seattle Union Record* described the affair as the "most imposing funeral ever held in Grays Harbor."[89] The parade ran through the streets of downtown Aberdeen bearing a large sign that read "Fellow Worker McKay: Murdered At Bay City Mill By A Co. Gunman May 3rd, 1923, A Victim of Capitalist Greed We Never Forget?"[90]

If the parade and signage were displays of militancy, the funeral and IWW commemorations of the event pointed toward the family and community bases for the movement. At the head of the funeral march were two young Finnish American sisters, Taskia and Ellen Jarvinen, who dressed in white outfits and posed for photographs in front of McKay's grave. The girls' conspicuous presence in the day's affairs were pointed reminders

The funeral parade for IWW member William McKay, who was killed while picketing at the Bay City Company mill in Aberdeen, extends far down the street. This huge group of Wobblies and supporters marched through Aberdeen mere days after McKay's death to protest the murder. Polson Museum, Hoquiam, Washington.

A picture postcard features an image of William McKay's funeral on May 8, 1923, in Aberdeen. The sign at the center of the photo reads "Fellow Worker McKay. Murdered at Bay City Mill by a Co Gunman, May 3rd, 1923. *A Victim of Capitalist Greed.* We Never Forget?" The question mark at the end of the sign can be seen as a challenge to future generations to remember the sacrifices made by McKay and others who fought in the era's labor wars. From the author's collection.

of the scores of children, including McKay's own, left without parents as the result of class violence. Indeed, families were ubiquitous at the funeral and in IWW representations of the events: Jennie Sipo and her soon-to-be husband, IWW longshoreman Robert Benson, marched and stood prominently in the funeral lines and posed for pictures in front of the large "Fellow Worker McKay" sign reproduced for international audiences.[91]

While Wobblies devoted much of their energies to cultural and social activities during the 1920s, they also mobilized to fight for improvements for workers in Grays Harbor and beyond. Renowned for their commitment to direct action, IWW members regularly spilled out of their halls to take up positions on picket lines and speak at street meetings.

Wobblies positioned themselves as defenders of working-class families against bootleggers and gamblers who peddled their services to striking workers. Knowing that strikers occasionally spent what little money they had on alcohol and that liquor often bred trouble on picket lines, the Wobblies closed saloons in communities experiencing labor trouble.[92] They also argued that some striking workers wasted their money on booze, which forced them "to go back to the point of production immediately, regardless of conditions and pay, for they are in no position to demand. They must take what they can get and by doing this they are lowering the standard of wages."[93] Put more bluntly, the radicals proclaimed that "You can't fight the bottle and the boss at the same time." Wobbly Guy Askew remembered the toll taken on workers' lives by the bottle: "So many of the unfortunate wage slaves are victims of that foul social disease called 'chronic alcoholism.' . . . The winos in time became nothing but human wrecks. It is capitalist poison for the wage slaves; as they can't fight the booze and their capitalist masters at the same time."[94] Despite the imposition of Washington State and federal Prohibition measures in 1916 and 1920, respectively, working people continued to suffer the effects of alcoholism.[95] Between 1917 and 1929, at least twenty of Grays Harbor's Finnish American workers died from the effects of chronic alcoholism.[96]

IWW members implemented their "de-horn movement," the term applied to the IWW's practice of shutting down saloons during strikes. Wobblies boycotted, picketed, and ran negative news articles condemning merchants who sold liquor during strikes.[97] In July 1923, IWW William Randall wrote to the city councils of Aberdeen, Hoquiam, and Cosmopolis requesting that local officials "do all in their power to close gambling and drinking places in these cities, and by any and all means endeavor to find and prosecute those responsible for the liquor traffic and gambling in these cities."[98]

Wobblies brought mass community pressure to bear against Grays Harbor's notorious saloons, gambling dens, and eateries that served scabs during strikes.[99] "Carrie Nation direct action," as IWW historian Fred Thompson calls it, began in Aberdeen during the lumber strike of 1917, when a committee of twenty-five Wobblies shut down the city's entire bootlegging industry.[100] A large IWW dehorn squad forced all Aberdeen saloons to shut down during the 1923 general strike, an action reflected in contemporary IWW news reports and even the fictionalized account of the strike provided by IWW activist Joe Murphy, one of the organizers of the general strike. At one saloon, a physically imposing bouncer harassed the "Murphy" character and tore down the flyer he had posted. After punching out the bouncer, "Murphy" carried on with his work, reposting the notice and moving onward.[101] "The night before the strike the Committee notified all the restaurant men and hotel keepers," noted Aberdeen IWW James Pezzanis in the midst of the 1923 general strike, "not to raise the prices on board and room, and also the bootleggers not to do any business with the strikers."[102] Arguing in December 1929 that the "price of a gallon of rotten booze will get you an IWW card stamped a year in advance," one anonymous Aberdeen Wobbly penned a poem reminding workers that they had much more to gain through organization than drunkenness:

Oh, dehorn, why don't you get wise?
Cut out the booze and organize,
A sober mind will win the day,
The One Big Union points the way.[103]

In May 1923, the strikers' dehorn squad shut down many of the illegal taverns and casinos in Grays Harbor. In celebration, Wobblies ran a front-page story in the *Industrial Worker* proclaiming that in Aberdeen, "Feeling among the townspeople is favorable to the IWW."[104] Aberdeen resident Josephine Smith agreed, writing to the antilabor *Aberdeen Daily World* to praise the "honest working men" of the IWW who were "helping them [the police] to clean up Aberdeen's Filthiest dope and Gambling joints."[105] The Grays Harbor IWW's dehorn activism showed that the union and its individual members did not confine their efforts to workplace struggles. Instead, they extended their class-based critique and activism into the community as they sought to address concerns of workers that were not necessarily based on the shop floor.

The harbor's IWW also waged a two-decades-long struggle to support class-war prisoners. There is some truth in historian William Preston's contention that the scope of repression suffered by Wobblies forced them into becoming—at least partly—a defense organization, as much of the group's work went to hosting events to raise money for legal aid and prisoner relief.[106] On the harbor, defense and relief funds went mostly to Wobblies prosecuted under the Washington State criminal syndicalism law and the "eight men buried alive"—the Wobblies convicted and imprisoned for their roles in the Centralia Tragedy. Efforts to support the Centralia Wobblies remained constant from their initial arrest in late 1919 until 1939 when Ray Becker, the final Centralia IWW to be released from prison, gained his freedom.[107]

As the strongest left-wing movement in the Pacific Northwest at the time, and the one directly involved with the Armistice Day Tragedy, the IWW took the lead in political-prisoner defense. At the head of the IWW's defense efforts was the General Defense Committee. Founded in October 1917, the General Defense Committee coordinated national defense efforts and authorized the creation of local defense organizations to assist the national body. With the General Defense Committee's efforts aimed toward the release of federal prisoners and the Centralia victims sorely in need of full-time assistance, Wobblies and supporters formed the Centralia Publicity Committee (CPC). Both the General Defense Committee and CPC held rallies, raised money for the prisoners, and issued news articles and pamphlets on what was fast becoming known among radicals as the "Centralia Conspiracy."[108]

Wobblies and IWW auxiliaries channeled resources to the cause of their imprisoned fellow workers, contributing to what was by the early 1920s a well-organized fund-raising operation. During the 1920s, harbor Wobblies raised money for the CPC, the bail and bond committee, and general defense, press, propaganda, and hospital funds.[109] On the fourth anniversary of the Centralia Tragedy, Aberdeen Wobblies held a memorial meeting to honor the memory of IWW martyrs Wesley Everest and Joe Hill, which included singing, piano tunes, and violin numbers, and a collection for legal defense.[110] The radicals redoubled their fund-raising efforts during the holiday season. Several Grays Harbor radicals donated money to the IWW's 1923 Class War Prisoner Christmas Fund, while a year later Aberdeen Wobbly Hellen Niemi sent in fifty dollars for prisoner relief around the Christmas holiday.[111] Local Wobblies also raised money to support local, national, and international labor struggles. Funds raised among Finnish immigrant workers assisted Finnish maritime workers during a 1928 maritime strike in Helsinki.[112]

Support also came from small-business owners and middle-class professionals who attended Wobbly events and donated money to the IWW. Whether feeling guilt over their complicity in earlier antilabor violence or hoping to appeal to working-class customers, local merchants proved willing to donate money and time to help liberate the IWW prisoners.[113] In November 1924, the proprietors of the Brooks and F Street Cafés contributed money to the IWW. That same month IWW organizer John McCarthy toured all boardinghouses, poolrooms, and cigar stores and collected funds from the customers of Cars Cigar Store, the Pioneer Royal Cigar Store, and Peto Wilson's lunch counter. Local merchants also donated heavily to collections for workers outside their immediate locale. Following a September 1933 dance held at the Finnish IWW hall to raise funds for the defense of Yakima agricultural workers imprisoned during a hop and fruit growers' strike, Wobbly lumber worker Iver Johnson wrote, "The business men are quite liberal and have donated quite a sum for the Yakima defense."[114]

The movement to free the Centralia prisoners convinced even some hardened antiradicals to change their views on the IWW. Heading up this list was Edward Coll, World War I veteran, insurance salesman, and head of the Hoquiam post of the American Legion.[115] In large part due to the tireless speaking tours of Elmer Smith and other IWW activists, a number of veterans refused to join the Legion, and those who did often refused to discuss their fellow veterans' violent acts in Centralia in 1919.[116] When Edward Coll moved to Hoquiam and took over leadership of the local American Legion, he discovered a group of Legionnaires who were ashamed of their own complicity in the Armistice Day Tragedy.[117] Upon learning in 1928 of the ample support among Grays Harbor veterans for the Centralia prisoners, Coll investigated the case. He learned that "many ex-service men refuse to join the American Legion on account of our reputed attitude towards the never-to-be-forgotten killings in Centralia on Armistice Day, 1919."[118] He joined forces with Elmer Smith and the IWW's CPC. For several years, Coll gave speeches, wrote letters, and petitioned Washington State Governor Roland Hartley on behalf of the prisoners.[119] The large *Industrialisti* audience read a detailed report on Colonel Coll's investigation and judged it "will have a tremendous effect (meaning) for the fight to free those workers who were sentenced."[120]

W. H. Abel, one of the prosecutors at the Centralia trial, changed his view of the Wobblies' role in the Armistice Day Tragedy years after helping to convict the men. He visited IWW members in prison and offered apologies and promises of support.[121] That Abel served as the attorney for E. I. Green, the man who murdered IWW logger William McKay in May 1923, made his support for the Centralia Wobblies all the more remarkable.[122]

The cross-class alliance clearly aggrieved Grays Harbor lumbermen. Voicing concerns over this type of cooperation between the middle class and unionists, lumberman Alex Polson warned his business partner R. D. Merrill that the "Reds are bending every effort under the sun now to re-organize, and I suppose that you are aware that this main strike on the railroad is brought about by the IWWs and it would astound you to know how many wealthy people are contributing towards them, and some of them close to home."[123] Polson may have been writing about the most prominent middle-class supporter of union organizing on the harbor, the left-wing Methodist minister Aaron Alan Heist, an ally of national progressives and Marxists such as Clarence Darrow and W. E. B. DuBois.

Ministering in the early 1920s at one of Aberdeen's venerated churches put Heist face to face with wealthy families who opposed unions and saw treachery in the eyes of every radical. He delivered prolabor sermons for the congregation, while penning news pieces for labor newspapers as well as mainstream press organs with bitterly antilabor records.[124] A Methodist social service organization praised Heist for his advocacy "for the release of political prisoners, free speech, and the repeal of the Anti-Syndicalism Law." They credited Reverend Heist for moving public sentiment in favor of the IWW on the harbor and helping to convince local judges to cease enforcing the criminal syndicalism law.[125]

Polson's frustration spoke to the fact that by the 1920s, the IWW had become a fixture in the community with a broad base of local support. Whereas earlier, local employers could mobilize much of the local employing class and police to repress the IWW, in 1922 he found some elites supporting the Wobbly cause. Polson must have recognized that the Grays Harbor IWW of the 1920s remained a potent movement capable of shutting down saloons, raising large sums of money for prisoner relief, and even turning out hundreds of supporters for hall activities and parades. Still, despite their local strength, the harbor Wobblies were not immune to the changes taking place among the nation's radical movements, nor could they hide from lumbermen's and other employers' mostly successful efforts to bolster production and bust unions during the 1920s. With its base shifted into its halls and thus away from its members' workplaces, the once-powerful Grays Harbor lumber workers' movement splintered into several competing groups affiliated with the IWW, AFL, Communist Party, and several independent union organizations. By the middle of the 1920s, the groups directing the majority of lumber and maritime workers' activism lay largely outside of the IWW's sphere, as the Wobblies divided into two competing organizations; Communists channeled new resources into organizing in the Pacific Northwest; many Finnish socialists shifted allegiance to the Communists; the migration of Finns into Grays Harbor (and the United States) dried up, depriving radical groups of new recruits; and employers continued to stymie worker organization through a combination of paternalistic welfare programs and repressive labor spying and blacklists. Maintaining their decades-long record of red-baiting, in the mid-1920s Aberdeen police kept track of IWW members in the city, while the former labor paper *Grays Harbor Post* compared the Wobblies to the Ku Klux Klan—a century-old example of reporters spouting nonsense about the similarities between far-left and far-right groups. Amid these difficult times, Wobblies continued to meet on the harbor, stoking radical flames and youthful energies for times riper for the labor-left to build militant working-class organizations capable of transforming industrial America.

9

ORGANIZE!

THE DRIVE FOR A MILITANT UNION

On the evening of July 25, 1933, more than 1,000 striking mill workers and loggers turned out to Aberdeen's Red Finn hall to protest police abuses and share strike news. They committed to continue picketing mills, blamed the strike on the "unfair practices of logging and mill operators," and issued a resolution to Governor Clarence Martin demanding the recall of the state patrolmen dispatched to Grays Harbor to quell the strike.[1] For the first time in a decade, Grays Harbor mill workers and loggers struck in concert against the region's lumbermen. Strikers replicated much of the community-based unionism that lay at the heart of earlier upsurges. They issued demands including the six-hour workday, a fifty-cent hourly minimum wage, the abolition of the speedup and blacklist, and workers' control over hiring.[2] Merging with the strikers was a network of community groups connected to Communists, highly trained at organizing and fund-raising. This "alternative unionism" of the early 1930s resembled the revolutionary activism of the 1910s and early 1920s. Gone were the free-speech fights and dehorn squads. But the hall events, flying picket squadrons, radical rhetoric, and street meetings returned to the harbor in force as the region's workers stood as the vanguard of Depression-era militancy.

In the historiography of lumber and labor, the key ingredients to bringing about the militant strikes of the 1930s were the federal legislative victories enacted by the labor-friendly Democratic Party. In this version of events, Northwest loggers, mill hands, and shingle weavers were paralyzed by the Depression. Workers were unorganized, quiescent, and relatively powerless until President Franklin D. Roosevelt opened the door to unionization with Section 7(a) of the National Industrial Recovery Act in 1933 and the National Labor Relations Act (NLRA) two years later, allowing workers to form unions of their own choosing.[3]

The reality was more complex, as labor militants responded to the desperation of the early Great Depression by organizing in the community and workplace. From 1930 to 1932, miners, teamsters, and indeed lumber workers built networks of shop-floor and community solidarity across the country. A militant core of lumber and maritime workers joined unemployed activists to demand change across society and to build local institutions to put pressure on employers and politicians.[4]

Grays Harbor workers did not wait for any legislative dictate to provide salvation from above. Repeatedly across the early twentieth century, lumber workers had struggled with their bosses. In the homes and halls of Grays Harbor, radicals had kindled the flames of class struggle that had been stifled during the Red Scares and Klan years of the 1920s. Proclaiming "Fight or Starve!" and "Organize and Fight: Against Wage Cuts! For Decent Conditions," Communist and IWW radicals were at the center of these struggles.[5] But it was not leftists alone who joined these efforts and launched the unions they spawned. Instead, a penchant for militant direct action on the shop floor and picket line was at the heart of rank-and-file lumber workers' unionism during the early 1930s, much as it had been during the previous three decades.

During the late 1920s and early 1930s, two groups emerged among Grays Harbor lumber unionists. The first was a community-based radical movement with support from the Communist Party and its auxiliaries. It also drew inspiration and members from the Wobblies, whose militancy and self-directed leadership continued to inspire. This movement embraced leadership from women, men, and children; organized in both the workplace and wider community; and used a confrontational, militant form of unionism. This movement fought for relief, support for those most harmed by the Depression, civil rights and equal pay for equal work, higher wages, and improved working conditions. It also engaged in electoral politics, backing progressive and leftist legislation and politicians.

The second group was a more traditional trade union that resembled the AFL unions that thrived a decade earlier. This union was rather conservative, male dominated, and focused principally on the workplace. During the early 1930s, it had little community outreach and in many ways resembled a fraternity—for instance, by meeting at the Moose and Eagles' halls, rather than the available workers' halls. This conservative movement established institutions, trained union leaders, and financially supported strikers. They also battled Communists, had a cozy relationship with old-style craft unionists, and avoided conflict with employers. In 1935, the two parallel groups merged—albeit temporarily—into a fighting labor movement with ambitious demands, a base in the community, diverse leadership, auxiliaries, and leaders trained by both the CP and older union movements.

At the heart of the harbor's community-based unionism were Communists and Wobblies. The presence of revolutionary unionists in the local labor movement influenced the forms of class conflict waged during the Depression era. In fact, a marked feature of this period's labor activism was the refusal of the picketers to confine their critique to wages and hours.[6] For so many harbor workers, accustomed to wave after wave of joblessness, underemployment, and workplace injuries, it was not wages alone that they sought, but deep, intrinsic change. Radicals carried banners demanding free milk for babies alongside signs that read "Fight capitalism" as the system itself came under fire.[7]

Grays Harbor was a hotbed of radicalism during the Depression that coincided with a national upsurge in union organizing, striking, and radical activity. Southern textile workers joined nut pickers in Saint Louis, Missouri, and woodworkers in Grays Harbor in forming community-based, horizontally organized, militant working-class institutions. Scholars on this topic have attributed the rise of this "alternative unionism" to a wide range of sources, including the leading roles played by Communists, socialists, Trotskyites, and "individual Wobblies or former Wobblies" in local and regional labor struggles. Based primarily on the work of activist historians including Staughton Lynd and Len DeCaux, this concept rests largely upon the argument that the IWW exerted a residual impact on the struggles after its own demise through the activism of former Wobblies and those influenced by earlier IWW actions. As Lynd argues, regardless of its sources, the new unionism of the period bore a stark "Wobbly resemblance." Surprisingly, few scholars have traced this resemblence to the Wobblies to a likely source: the Wobblies.[8] But in Grays Harbor, of the several thousand workers who participated in the strikes of the early 1930s, many retained institutional and ideological affiliations with the IWW.[9] This fact was shown most explicitly in the opinions of Communists, who excoriated what they viewed as the "IWW ideology among the strikers" and the "syndicalist (mostly IWW and ex-IWW) leadership of the unemployed movement in the district."[10] Thus, active red-card holders, and not just ex-Wobblies, were at the fore of strikes waged during the 1920s and 1930s in lumber country.

THE DEPRESSION IN LUMBER COUNTRY

The Great Depression officially began in late 1929, but the Pacific Northwest lumber industry went into decline during the mid-1920s. The region's slide into the Depression, as well as the lumber industry's previous busts, provided workers with experience critiquing the ills of capitalism.[11] Anticipating the crash by six years, Wobbly Floyd Hyde addressed a large crowd of Aberdeen workers in December 1923, casting an alarming omen for future years:

> A greater panic is coming than the world has ever seen, the whole system of production is going to collapse. He gave many economic reasons why this should be, such as inflated currency, overproduction here, and Europe's inability to buy our surplus products. There is no power on earth that can stop the hard times from coming, and when the capitalist system shall have ceased to function, that is to fail to furnish food, clothing and shelter for the people, then shall the workers of the world step in and do what has to be done, namely, operate industry for the good of the people.[12]

Predictions of the imminent self-destruction of capitalism did little to prepare Americans for the tragedy of the Great Depression. Even longtime residents of the harbor, so accustomed to the booms and busts of the lumber industry, were unprepared for the misery that befell the nation in the years following the October 1929 stock market crash. Aberdeen mill worker Mickey Orton, a Communist who, during the middle and late 1930s, became one of the West's top union leaders, recalled workers' suffering during the Depression and indifference of government officials: "Our experience during this trying period of great unemployment, suffering, and misery was that public officials in Grays Harbor County showed less concern and were definitely more hostile to pleas on our part for greater and more adequate relief than in any other county in the northwest. They showed a callousness and brutal lack of concern over the starvation, illness, and inadequate or no housing of workers and their families unequalled anywhere in the lumber industry in our experience."[13]

The impact of the Depression fell hard on the harbor, where, according to the US Department of Agriculture, 40 percent of gainfully employed workers labored in forest industries, while another 40 percent labored in related industries.[14] In 1932, the worst year of the Depression, Grays Harbor County welfare expenditures ran to more than $446,000, a more than fivefold increase from the 1930 figure.[15] Homeless workers slept in lumber mills and jail cells, while others moved quickly through town, fully aware of the harbor town residents' reputation for roughly handling "undesirables."[16] Those who remained came together in "hobo jungles" and Hoovervilles, which formed along the riversides in Aberdeen and Hoquiam. One longtime Aberdeen resident recalled the area carved from a "dense growth of wild berry bushes and alders," where three-sided "shanty shelters" with tin roofs and sawdust floors were occupied by those without homes.[17] With few qualms about criminalizing poverty, Aberdeen police officers jailed 451—roughly 15 per day—homeless residents on the dubious charge of "sleeping" during the month of January 1930.[18] One harbor writer captured the circumstances faced by many residents in December 1929: "A breadline a mile long. Hundreds of families in need of the barest necessities of life. Mills and camps closed down. Lumberjacks despondent, full of moonshine and bull."[19] Responding to the brutal treatment meted out toward the poor by lawmen, radical laborer August Jonas predicted that "each cut in wages and each bat of a policeman's club over the head of a hungry worker makes them see red the rest of their lives."[20] In 1934, the Washington State Planning Council observed that "Grays Harbor undoubtedly has the most severe unemployment problem of any county in the state. . . . This is no doubt due to the fact that Aberdeen and Hoquiam are primarily one-industry cities, and that industry—lumbering—has declined greatly in recent years."[21]

With state and private relief groups unable and unwilling to handle the emergency, jobless and underemployed workers turned to creative action, fending off starvation through the bounty available from the woods and beaches. Working people poached deer, elk, and clams. But as the numbers of out-of-work people increased on the harbor, so did the outrage among conservationists at the notion of working people acting for themselves by hunting food for their families. The exact numbers of illegally taken game and clams are unavailable, although the amount of attention given the "problem" by local papers tells much about the scope of these groups' concerns. During the first six months of 1932, the *Daily World* ran several articles attesting to the seriousness of the possibility that poaching was depleting the region's herds of deer and elk. The newspaper also wrote of the urgent need of Aberdeen and Hoquiam authorities to step in and restrict poor families from migrating to the beaches to dig clams.[22]

H. D. McKenney, a former labor spy who became deputy game warden for Grays Harbor County, headed efforts to stop poaching. McKenney applied the same vigor he had used against the IWW more than a decade earlier to halt illegal hunting. During the spring of 1932 he repeatedly brought poachers before the court. One offender was Edwin Scott, who authorities caught in possession of elk meat that he planned to use to feed his thirteen dependents. Many of the poachers received fines of two hundred fifty dollars, an absurd sum, particularly for unemployed persons; the court gave others long jail sentences. Showing his insensitivity toward the plight of those worst hit by the Depression, the county game commissioner called upon "the people of Grays Harbor [who] should frown on these killings and help to preserve one of our greatest out-of-door attractions."[23]

During the early 1930s, most Grays Harbor lumber manufacturing stopped. Those mills that ran operated part-time, thus bringing about the staggering decline from 1.56 billion board feet of lumber cut in Grays Harbor during 1926 to only 232 million board feet six years later.[24] During the especially rough winter of 1931–32, lumber production in Grays

Harbor ran at only 5 percent of its capacity, compared with 24 percent in the Pacific Northwest as a whole.[25] Camps and mills closed; owners that kept operations running did so at reduced levels and with fewer workers. Contributing to the local economic decline was the obsolescence of Grays Harbor sawmill machinery. According to a 1935 US Forest Service study, the harbor's sawmills had been built decades earlier, and running them was not economically feasible.[26] At the Posey Manufacturing plant, a wood-products mill that specialized in producing piano sounding boards made of spruce, owner V. G. Posey's inability to profit during the Depression led him to shut down the mill, throwing approximately one hundred workers "into the heartbreaking labor market of that early year of the depression."[27] Thousands of unemployed lumber workers fought for the few remaining jobs—labor had little to no bargaining power.

As across the country, on the harbor the available relief institutions failed to meet the great and growing need. Those seeking help encountered judgment and religious instruction from those controlling resources. Municipalities blended public funds, granted through the county treasury, with private moneys collected through a series of fund-raisers and not-so-voluntary contributions made by workers. Elites routinely ran local charities, thereby promoting themselves as benevolent rulers while also ensuring that only "deserving" people got help. Two decades earlier, in 1909, banker William Patterson had run the Associated Charities, and he reported that relief got in the way of the "true American spirit of independence" and assured the Aberdeen city council that only "the worthy destitute" could qualify for relief.[28]

During the Depression, municipal funds went to social service organizations with religious affiliations, including the Salvation Army. A welfare association found its leader in Frank Lamb, lumberman and founder of the Port of Grays Harbor. Lamb's thrifty policies allowed Hoquiam's relief bills to be handled through private donations. He insisted that these policies were designed to "be on a more or less temporary basis," to avoid distributing relief to those "people who sought relief who never did any great amount of productive work and never intended to" and to "get rid of the single men," thereby reserving relief payments for local home owners. Even though Lamb and his cohort rejected many desperate people during the association's first year in operation, the agency still provided relief to 7,317 residents of Hoquiam, a tremendous total considering the city's 1930 population was a mere 13,387.[29] The Salvation Army drew fire for its policies, including forcing recipients to pray before receiving relief.[30] One IWW member condemned the "Sally" of Aberdeen for "all such charity organizations as the Salvation Army fatten on the miserable poverty of millions of unorganized wage slaves throughout the world. . . . This in the face of the fact that the crumbs with which it degrades the manhood of honest workers are but a pittance of the wealth stolen from them by the social pirates without whose good-will Sally and others of her kind could not survive."[31]

As the IWW's comments on the Aberdeen Salvation Army illustrate, the Wobblies remained active in the region during the early Depression decade. IWW members played roles as union organizers, picketers, fund-raisers, advocates, and advisors during the lumber and shingle mill strikes of the mid-1920s.[32] In tandem with their culture of solidarity forged around the Wobbly halls, Wobblies helped lead lumber strikes long after their "heyday" had ended.[33]

IWW members were most prominent in the lumber industry, which IWW historian Fred Thompson called the site of the IWW's "greatest triumphs."[34] Wobblies were particularly active during the 1925, 1932, and 1935 lumber strikes; Aberdeen was, in fact, a hub of activity for the IWW's Lumber Workers' Industrial Union (LWIU), a site where radical lumber workers held conventions, organized speakers' series, printed newsletters, and penned strike reports for the single-industry region as its workers experienced horrors of the Depression.[35] On the harbor's docks, the IWW also had a substantial presence. Historian and Sailors' Union of the Pacific activist Ottilie Markholt referred to the Grays Harbor docks as "the Wobbly stronghold" during the "Big Strike" of 1934 that closed the Pacific Coast ports.[36]

A DIFFERENT SHADE OF *RED* HARBOR

The Communist Party entered Grays Harbor in the early 1920s and retained its presence within the local left for more than two decades. Socialists across the globe flocked into the folds of the international communist movement. In the United States, supporters of the Russian Revolution created groups and propaganda to support the nascent communist state. In 1919, which novelist John Dos Pasos called "the springtime of revolution," left-wing socialists rebelled against the moderates within the Socialist Party of America (SPA), defecting toward the Communists. During the 1920s the left wing of the SPA, which had played such a prominent role in US history during the previous two decades, declined in significance. Former socialists formed two factions of American communists: the Communist Party, comprised primarily of eastern European ethnic groups, especially Finns, Russians, and South Slavs, and the Communist Labor Party, which enrolled mostly English-speaking radicals such as journalist John Reed. The two parties merged in May 1921 and formed the Workers' (Communist) Party of America (WCPA) later in the year, and the party adopted the name Communist Party of the USA (CP) in 1929.[37]

Grays Harbor's communist movement linked with national and international bodies, which drew some of their inspiration and direction from Moscow. The WCPA was the American wing of this movement. During the early 1920s, WCPA headquarters was in New York City, before it moved to Chicago in 1923, where it remained until 1927.[38] At party headquarters, officials met, published newspapers, and corresponded with their international counterparts. The Communists divided the country into geographic districts, with each district assigned a headquarters in a large urban area. District Twelve, based in Seattle, represented the Northwest. It was consistently one of the party's smaller regions, containing only a fraction of the members of the New York or Chicago districts.[39] From these humble origins, over the next decade party activists dug roots in critical Northwest industries.

To conduct strikes, District Twelve organizers and "responsible comrades" were sent "from the centre" in succession "to go there and organize or attempt to organize the strikers" in Grays Harbor in 1927, 1930, 1931, 1932, and 1933.[40] At other times, party activists condemned harbor Wobblies' advocacy of "'rank and file' control" over revolutionary organizations because it stood in the way of establishing the "correct Party line."[41]

The largest and most important of the language-based federations of the WCPA was the Finnish-language Federation.[42] And the biggest concentration of Finnish Communists in Washington State lived in southwestern Washington, specifically in Aberdeen, Hoquiam, Raymond, and Ilwaco, towns that contributed 99 of the 212 state members in 1923.[43] Internal records of the WCPA show between twenty and thirty dues-paying members in the Aberdeen local of the Finnish socialist organization in late 1921.[44] Aberdeen's Red Finn hall was the center of Grays Harbor communism. The party and its auxiliaries used the hall to conduct party business and to host dinners, sports events, political speeches, and fund-raisers of many types.[45] Young women and girls were prominent in the movement. They formed and led party organizations like the Young Communist League and Young Pioneers; attended Communist Summer Schools; wrote for party newspapers; and ascended to leadership roles within the party at large.[46] Some Wobblies must have mourned their loss at the vanguard of women's-led unions. One Aberdeen IWW member mocked the party's "sex appeal," critiquing what he saw as the exploitation of a few "bobbed haired girls." But what this Wobbly either ignored or misunderstood was that the "girls" were not only out in front at political rallies, they too were running the party apparatus behind the scenes.[47]

Shortly after the Bolshevik Revolution, Wobblies, like other working-class radicals, gave widespread support to the new state. But optimism faded as early as November 1919, when some IWW members questioned the Russian Communists' actions and policies.[48] Many IWW members believed that Communists were politicians and intellectuals rather than workers. Much like the broader anarchist critique of the Soviet Union, which looked dubiously toward the emerging dictatorship, Wobblies speculated that Communist leaders would be as oppressive as capitalists.[49]

As the two wings of the American left, the IWW and the CP came into recurrent conflict. In the Northwest, some of the earliest conflicts between the Wobblies and the Communists involved the latter group's efforts to control relief operations for the IWW prisoners after the Centralia Tragedy. In Grays Harbor, the Wobblies carried out nearly all defense work between 1919 and 1927. The CP's wedge into that population, and indeed into the entire harbor, came in large part because of work by the International Labor Defense (ILD), an organization founded in 1925 that focused on the release of the class-war prisoners.[50]

Building influence in Grays Harbor, a region thick with IWW sympathies, proved to be difficult for the Reds. Communists established the first Northwest ILD locals in Seattle during 1925–26, but the organization had a limited presence in Grays Harbor until 1927, when the ILD supported striking shingle weavers. During the strike, ILD activists traveled to the harbor, raised donations, and contributed to the strike fund. This marked the first major inroads of the CP into the Northwest lumber industry. The assistance rendered by the ILD to strikers and their families succeeded in ballooning the number of Grays Harbor workers in the organization.[51] By December 1928, three ILD branches operated on the harbor.[52]

Wobblies and Communists also competed for members and influence during strikes. On February 1, 1927, workers at the Schafer shingle mill in Montesano struck to protest wage cuts for both piece-rate shingle sawyers and packers and the hourly mill hands.[53] Within a week the strike had spread across the harbor's shingle industry, shutting down "nearly all plants in [the] county."[54] Most of the 1,500 strikers belonged to no union when the strike began. The main exceptions were the IWW shingle weavers.[55] They reported in the *Industrial Worker* the conditions that sparked the strike and urged workers to "stay away from Aberdeen until strikers win their demands." The strike was significant enough to the IWW for it to send organizer August Radtke to Aberdeen, where he reported the "strikers are unorganized so far as any union influence goes." But, he continued, the "strike is being directed by members of the IWW and may be properly called an IWW strike."[56]

Unlike the Wobblies whose members worked and organized in the harbor's shingle mills, the Communist presence came primarily from outside when Seattle organizer Aaron Fislerman traveled to Grays Harbor and urged the shingle weavers to form a Communist union.[57] Fislerman's actions were characteristic of the CP's relationship with Grays Harbor lumber strikes during the late 1920s. At the time of his arrival, Fislerman had little knowledge of the harbor's history, culture, or strike situation. Fislerman's status as an outsider created difficulties for him, and he complained how difficult it was "to make any connections with the strikers having been a total stranger to them."[58] The organizer's orders from Seattle and party headquarters in Chicago instructed him to keep his party association secret, to "be very careful as to giving away any information as to the role of the Party in this work."[59] Thus, unlike the Wobblies, who lived, worked, and organized openly in Grays Harbor throughout the 1920s and boasted of these facts, Communists often operated in secret and received their orders from party officials far outside the strike zone. To educate Communists about the weavers, the *Daily Worker* ran a lengthy article that expressed that "shingle weaving is not a trade; it is a battle" and explained the dangers of weaving: "Ninety-five per cent of the weavers have lost one or more fingers."[60]

Despite Fislerman's unfamiliarity with the embattled region, he succeeded by building a following among the shingle weavers' leadership. At a strike meeting in Hoquiam on February 20, 1927, Fislerman encouraged the weavers to unionize. According to the Communist, the weavers responded to his call for a union "by a unanimous rising vote . . . [that] decided that shingle weavers union included all workers skilled and unskilled in the union."[61] The workers formed the International Shingle Weavers Union with its headquarters in Aberdeen and four branches on the harbor.[62] Fislerman also recruited O. P. Allison, a popular local weaver, into the party. His fellow unionists elected him as the first president of the new union.[63] The Communist *Daily Worker* reported Allison's impressions of the strike and union movement: "For the first time in my life, and I have followed the game for many years, I am proud of the shingle weavers."[64] Fislerman claimed to be responsible for the union's formation, declaring that "I have been there for some time and succeeded to organize them into a union."[65] The *Daily Worker* asked readers to "have your union vote a monthly contribution at its next meeting" to assist ISWU headquarters in Grays Harbor.[66]

A month into the strike, the balance of forces was clearly on the workers' side. By early March, seven mills conceded to the strikers' demands.[67] Finally, on March 11 the strike ended in victory for the weavers when the Saginaw, Aloha, and Hoquiam shingle companies reopened after acceding to the union's demands.[68] The Grays Harbor weavers were, according to Fislerman, "100 percent organized."[69] Celebrating both the party's organizing achievements and the victory of the striking shingle weavers, Fislerman declared, "We shall not stop there with this single union. But we must proceed with the organization of the rest of the shingle and lumber workers and connect them together."[70]

The unionization of the weavers was a rare success for the Trade Union Educational League (TUEL). From its founding, the TUEL failed to recruit heavily in the Pacific Northwest lumber industry, a casualty in part of the lack of AFL unions in which the "Red" unionists could bore from within, the term for transforming existing unions from the inside as members.[71] What successes the TUEL experienced in lumber involved the shingle weavers. At the 1927 District Twelve convention of the WCPA, nearly the entire written discussion under the "Organize the Unorganized" heading fixed attention on the party's successes among the shingle weavers in Grays Harbor.[72]

The 1927 strike and union drive helped radicalize the weavers, who turned to their union newspaper, the *Shingle Weaver*, to advocate their comrades' interests. Between shifts at the mills, activist weavers contributed to their newspaper, but they also found time to host mass meetings and serve on the executive committee for the Centralia Liberation Committee, a Communist body organized by the ILD.[73] The weavers maintained ties with the party between 1927 and 1929. In October 1929, with a global economic crisis developing, the ISWU and its five locals affiliated with the ILD.[74] The Shingle Weavers' Union, based institutionally in Grays Harbor, affiliated with the Communists—a rarity in the 1920s Pacific Northwest.

COMMUNITY-BASED UNIONISM

Their relationship with the Shingle Weavers' Union gave Communists a wedge into the Northwest's lumber industry. Like the Wobblies, who rooted their unions in local communities, Grays Harbor's communist movement carried its radical program both in the streets of Aberdeen and Hoquiam and at the point of production during the Depression.

The party expanded organizing in lumber during the summer of 1929 with the formation of the National Lumber Workers' Union (NLWU) and Trade Union Unity League (TUUL), the latter founded at the fourth convention of the TUEL, held in Cleveland from August 31 to September 1, 1929.[75] The NLWU itself was an attempt to apply the strategy of dual unionism to the lumber industry where, except for the ISWU, Communists had failed to build a presence. Communists founded the TUUL as a result of the failings of the TUEL, which fell under the heavy fire of red-baiting from both within and outside the AFL. By 1924, Communists had, as historian Fraser M. Ottanelli argues, lost their progressive allies, "and their enemies were quick to take advantage of the situation" by expelling the radicals from AFL unions and denying them from participating in the AFL convention.[76] To ensure that the interests of the Northwest's lumber workforce were represented at the founding of the TUUL, Northwest Communists held a July 1929 planning meeting. The delegates included twenty-four from "heavy industries" such as logging, sawmilling, and shingle manufacturing—including several from Grays Harbor. They "discussed the principal tasks" for the TUUL founding convention later that summer, including fighting wage cuts and speedups, opposition to wars, and defense of the Soviet Union.[77] Communists then traveled "from far off Aberdeen," in the words of the *Daily Worker*, to the Cleveland, Ohio, convention, voicing the lumber workers' plight. "The Loggers' reporter" Delegate Pitkin "demanded a strong industrial union, and told how one strike in Aberdeen was successful only a few months ago. A foundation for the new union was there, he said. All the loggers wanted help and guidance. The men are ready for struggle. In the last months there have been two spontaneous strikes in the saw-mills of Aberdeen." From these seeds grew an important core of loggers, sawmill laborers, and shingle weavers—radical unionists who rebuilt community unionism in the early 1930s.[78]

The militant unionists who organized the mills and camps of Grays Harbor—eventually breaking the open shop wall in lumber—comprised longtime residents, workers who moved to the region during the early Depression, and organizers based outside the region. A new generation of activists emerged in the early and middle 1930s to build—and in many cases lead—the big strikes and found industrial unions. Many of them grew up in Grays Harbor and the wider Pacific Northwest, lived in Grays Harbor, and worked in lumber in the 1930s. Children of the Great Depression, these workers were radicalized by experiencing the horrors of poverty and by involvement in the labor movement and left-wing politics. Their ages and ethnic backgrounds set them apart from the previous generation of the labor-left—made up of mostly immigrant workers, socialists, and Wobblies born before the dawn of the new century. Many Communist activists had years of experience in the lumber industry when they took lead roles rebuilding the Northwest's labor movement in the thirties.

COMMUNISTS IN THE DEPRESSION

An early test of the NLWU and the Communist-affiliated ISWU came in July 1930 at several shingle mills in Aberdeen and in Moclips, Washington, a small community in the northwestern corner of Grays Harbor County.[79] The strike arose as a protest by several hundred workers against a 20 percent wage reduction. Mill owner Paul R. Smith boasted that he "was one of the pioneers in Grays Harbor in reducing wages."[80] Unionists put up a fight in Aberdeen, where the working-class community came together for picket duty and strike relief. Action centered at the large Saginaw shingle mill.[81] Strikers attacked scabs and prevented strikebreakers from entering the mill during late July 1930. Most effective were the strikers' roving pickets where weavers used automobiles to patrol town.[82] To stop the picketing, police and imported gunmen turned to violence. District Twelve CP organizer Sidney Bloomfield informed party leadership in New York that "now the terror of the Lumber Barons has busted out like a shot from the clear sky."[83] NLWU President James Murphy concurred, declaring the "weavers capitulated before terrorism" and shingle manufacturers' "thugs employed tear gas among other forms of brutality" against their striking workers.[84]

The NLWU and other Communists played active roles in the strike. The party had hosted meetings for striking shingle weavers throughout the year.[85] According to James Murphy, after experiencing repression at Moclips, non-Communist union leaders abdicated, only to be replaced by

NLWU organizers who led "these strikers in their fight for a living wage."[86] ILD activists defended the strikers in court, while another CP group put up the bail money.[87] In spite of these relief efforts and the weavers' solidarity, the strike had "petered out" by early September 1930, with ISWU members receiving none of their demands.[88]

Gaining a following among shingle weavers, a group with historic connections to socialism, was one thing; influencing thousands of mill hands and loggers, whose IWW sympathies were well known, was another matter. However, in the aftermath of the 1930 ISWU strike in Grays Harbor, Communists extended their influence from the region's shingle mills into its logging camps and lumber mills.

The Schafer Brothers mills and camps were centers of party activism. Schafer Brothers gained fame and notoriety for their production feats and the speedups that made those feats possible. In 1930, the *Daily Worker* ran the headline "Schafer's—One of the Worst Lumber Speed-Up Outfits," concluding that speedups were the "things the National Lumber Workers' Union is fighting against." The NLWU even established a second Grays Harbor local—at Montesano—near Schafer headquarters.[89]

In fact, the labor press carried several of what could be described as horror stories from Schafer workplaces. Signed by "Lumber Worker," an early 1930 article provided one opinion why the Schafer Brothers company was such a radical hotbed: "Beyond a doubt Schafer Bros. will go even farther in their disregard for the rights of the workers. The workers know this and are organizing into the N.L.W.U."[90] A month later, one "*Worker* correspondent" reported that at a Schafer logging camp, a "bucker worked nine days [and] at the end of that time, after his board and bunk had been deducted he had $2.40 left for his 9 days work." Low wages caused many to complain, but some Schafer logging camp conditions reminded loggers of olden days before strikes had forced employers to improve sanitation: "In the bunk-houses the plumbing is all out of kilter so that it is impossible to get a shower bath or even hot water to wash off the mud and grease after a day's work."[91]

Communists' success hinged on their ability to connect shop-floor struggles to their community-organizing campaigns. Among the most important Depression-era community organizations were the Unemployed

Councils (UCs). Communists established their earliest unemployed organizations in US cities during 1929.[92] On March 6, 1930, the Comintern's International Unemployment Day, marches involving thousands of unemployed workers took place around the globe.[93] That day more than 100,000 men and women gathered to protest in New York and Detroit, while 20,000 or more demonstrated in several US cities.[94] In the Pacific Northwest the largest march occurred in Seattle, where nearly a thousand activists marched through the city's Skid Road district before several of their numbers were arrested and beaten. In Aberdeen, soapboxers from the UC and IWW addressed crowds throughout downtown during the afternoon and evening.[95] Reviving traditions of antiradicalism, city authorities banned demonstrations, informing Communists and Wobblies that their activities would not be tolerated. Aberdeen police broke up speeches by the CP and the IWW, and "all open air meetings" were put to "an end in Aberdeen." Respecting the influence, if not necessarily the politics, of Communist speakers, one Aberdeen Wobbly noted, "The fear of the unemployed demonstrations has probably prompted this action."[96]

A notable feature of Grays Harbor UC activity was its creative use of direct action. Dozens of Reds fought for concessions from city officials, landlords, and bosses. In May 1932, they diverted a water main to provide free water to destitute workers at the Aberdeen CP hall, rallied at the Salvation Army to demand higher-quality relief, and stormed an Aberdeen City Council meeting to demand public relief.[97] Police arrested three CP activists for turning the water on; at their trial a large crowd of workers showed to "back up the accused comrades." In the words of a *Daily Worker* writer, "All of the available police of the city, county, and state was there," and "many of the foreign-born were held for questioning."[98] In November 1932, four hundred activists joined CP gubernatorial candidate Fred Walker in packing the Grays Harbor County Commission meeting in Montesano, demanding unemployment relief. The *Daily Worker* noted the need for ongoing agitation against public officials: "The Commissioners squirmed, but evaded making definite promises for relief. It is plain that still more pressure must be brought against them."[99]

During the late 1920s, Lydia Laukkanen, a second-generation Finnish American worker, became one of the region's most influential Communists. She was one of several young Finnish women who led the Grays Harbor CP—following the path of Wobblies in earlier decades.[100] Before her twentieth birthday, Laukkanen was already one of the best-known Communist organizers in the Northwest. The party showed its faith in Laukkanen by bestowing high-level duties upon her. She was a leader of local unemployed groups and party candidate for city and county office.[101] Laukkanen also served as president and organizer for the Aberdeen Young Communist League.[102]

As the Depression grew worse, UC activities expanded. In 1932 and 1933, UCs held monthly rallies and parades in Aberdeen. In late January 1932, at least two hundred unemployed workers staged a demonstration under the aegis of the UC, carrying banners reading "Fight capitalism."[103] On May Day 1932, approximately one thousand workers attended a rally put on by the local CP.[104] One year later, three hundred workers carrying United Front banners marched through downtown Aberdeen to the welfare commissioner's office, where Laukkanen delivered a speech and the group made demands to the commissioner: minimum wages, cash relief, free medical and dental care, and free milk for children.[105] They also published a shop paper called the *Grays Harbor Worker* during late 1931. The organ mixed strike and election news with opinion and youth sections. Showing that it wasn't the Wobblies alone on the left who had a good sense of humor, the paper also printed a comic featuring "T. Cat" and "I. Promise." The latter represented "all capitalist candidates" who want votes "for the sake of getting office and not for the purpose of solving your problems."[106] During the thirties, local Reds even took to mocking the "Chamber of Comicals" as that group coordinated business on the harbor.[107]

Strikes waged jointly by the Aberdeen UC and rank-and-file workers at sawmills in Aberdeen and Montesano epitomized the connections between workplace and community. Waged in winter 1931–32, UC efforts centered on stopping mill owners from taking advantage of the desperation of unemployed workers, who, following the closures and reopening of their plants, returned to their jobs only to find their former wages cut. At the Schafer Brothers mills in Aberdeen and Montesano, wages proved to be among the lowest: a dollar and fifty cents per day for laborers, after

The Schafer Brothers Logging Company sawmill No. 4 seen from across the Chehalis River in Aberdeen, September 21, 1931. Two ships are docked at the mill, and a log boom floats in the foreground. Schafer-owned mills and logging camps were hotbeds of radical labor activism between the 1910s and 1930s. Polson Museum, Hoquiam, Washington.

a fifty-cent cut took effect in November 1931.[108] "Two young workers," members of the NLWU, reported having "our wages cut five times" during the previous eighteen months. M. J. Oremos, another Communist worker, agreed that "wage-cutting has been the only program the bosses of the lumber industry have been able to give us."[109] Albert Schafer declared as much: "We know the men cannot live on $1.50 a day."[110] With Grays Harbor's lumber production at only 5 percent of its capacity in 1932, mill workers faced dire straits. But radical unionists persisted in pressuring bosses to raise pay.[111]

Party activists hosted mass meetings for Schafer workers and published reports of conditions at the Schafer operations in the party press. In early

1931, a writer named W. B. reported that "a South Slav worker, who had put in 30 days work for the Schafer Bros. of Montesano," after paying his commissary and board fees, had earned only thirteen dollars for the month.[112] To reach a wider audience, the radical unionists distributed flyers proclaiming "Fight or Starve" and "Organize and Fight: Against Wage Cuts! For Decent Conditions!" and "Mill workers, Loggers" to "Join the National Workers Union."[113] In the words of the *Grays Harbor Worker*, it was at the Schafer Brothers mill in Aberdeen where Grays Harbor lumber workers put up the "first definite uprising against their employers" of the Depression era.[114]

On November 3, 1931, the Aberdeen UC, described by the *Daily World* as a "large following of unemployed men," joined employees of Schafer Brothers mill No. 4 outside the plant to protest wage cuts; they declared the revised wage scale to be "too low for livelihood."[115] CP activists blanketed the harbor towns with thousands of Communist handbills and picketed the docks to advertise.[116] Registering his approval with the strike, one Communist organizer informed the party secretariat that "the Lumber Workers are beginning to revolt."[117]

The mass action worked. The strike spread to Schafer Brothers mill No. 1 in Montesano, which like the Aberdeen mill paid only a dollar fifty per day. On November 15, the strikers met and issued their demands: reverse the latest wage cut, a minimum daily wage of two dollars and fifty cents, an eight-hour day, no making up lost time, and no blacklist against unionists. A striker asserted that "these are the demands of the strikers which are not extreme but which will for a time at least better our conditions so that we will not exactly starve on the job."[118] Strikers gained support from the wider community, including small-business owners who depended on worker purchasing power. On November 17, merchants and civic leaders met to support a "solution fair to all sides," while the Hoquiam local of the Four L company union vigorously pushed for a three-dollar minimum at all Grays Harbor lumber mills. In response, both Schafer mills offered a compromise two-dollar minimum wage and an increased wage scale. By November 18 many strikers were back at work.[119]

The militant spirit of the strike, however, had spread. After a brief return to work under the new wage scale, Schafer laborers struck again, demanding a minimum wage of two dollars and fifty cents and an end to mandatory shopping at a company store. The militant stand of these lowly paid mill hands inspired even more support. Approximately two thousand workers listened to a talk by Four L organizer W. D. Smith lambasting "wage slashers" and comparing conditions at the Schafer mills to "that witnessed several years ago in Cosmopolis," a reference to the infamous Grays Harbor Commercial Company. When asked if anyone in the crowd would work for two dollars per day, the crowd "roared out in a negative answer." The workers' militancy and their community support persuaded the Schafers to bargain. When five hundred picketers assembled at their Aberdeen plant—a mill employing only one hundred fifty workers—and prevented cars from crossing the picket line, the Schafers cut a deal. The owners offered strikers a three-dollar minimum—more than the laborers demanded—and agreed to keep the scale "as long as the Schafer company could carry on operations at that figure." Having gained even more confidence, workers demanded and received Thanksgiving Day turkeys from the Schafers.[120]

UNION

The Schafer mills strike provided an effective model of community-based activism for others to follow. Agitation from radicals for a larger, more concentrated labor action on Grays Harbor began in late 1931 and early 1932 when NLWU successes peaked with strike victories at several Aberdeen mills.[121] Entire families took to these picket lines, vivid reminders that strikers were fighting to feed their families during desperate times. Like the strikes two decades earlier, this put entire working-class families—regardless of age and ability to defend themselves—in harm's way. In late 1931, scabs at the Wilson Brothers and Company mill in Aberdeen drove their into a picket line, crashing into a young girl named Marion Hill and an elderly man named O. Tulan.[122] In spite of violence and other obstacles, strikers persisted. In April 1932, an enthusiastic Communist organizer reported, "Some of the achievements we have made in the district" included the addition of a second party unit in Aberdeen and the formation of five CP sections, where "formerly [there were] no sections in the district."[123]

The lumber workers' movement took another step forward in June 1933 when Communist organizers held a District Twelve convention in Aberdeen. At that assembly, the NLWU adopted a broad set of demands that they intended to impose throughout the lumber industry. These demands included a six-hour day and fifty cents per hour minimum wage. Word of these demands spread throughout the region, and within a few short weeks the harbor's lumber workers once again appeared ready to strike.[124]

Falling close on the heels of the District Twelve convention in Aberdeen was the largest Pacific Northwest lumber strike of the early Depression period. The strike coincided with negotiations for the Code of Fair Competition for the Lumber and Timber Products Industry. This code was one of many written for all major US industries under the provisions of the 1933 National Industrial Recovery Act.[125] These codes were supposed to be drawn up by representatives of business, labor, and the public, although in practice industry representatives from the largest corporations had the most influence in their drafting. This was doubly true in the lumber industry, where employers excluded workers and labor organizations from making the provisional codes and then negotiated them with government representatives. Lumber bosses would never have allowed the sole lumber workers' organizations—the IWW's LWIU and CP's NLWU—a say in drafting the lumber code, and the Four Ls (the company union founded by the military whose origins lay in violent coerced membership and collusion with bosses) was hardly a "union." Regulation of the code's rules designed in part to assist workers—such as the maximum hours and minimum wage provisions—suffered from lax enforcement, made more difficult because the lumber industry operated in some of the most isolated parts of the nation. Code inspectors lacked the resources to monitor and enforce the regulations, and many Pacific Northwest employers ignored the codes.[126] Unable to influence the code-planning meetings held in elite circles, lumber workers made their voices heard as two thousand laborers struck at nine Grays Harbor operations in July 1933.

Lumber workers in the Grays Harbor area struck alongside woodworkers across the Pacific Northwest to push negotiations in their favor by proposing their own code. The NLWU issued its "Workers' Code" drawn "from the camps and mills" and submitted it when the "lumber barons and manufacturers" issued their code. Some radicals considered the latter code to be an "insult to every lumber worker" and a "slave code." The National Lumber Workers' Union's demands included a minimum daily wage of three dollars and thirty cents, with a guaranteed cost-of-living increase and a guarantee of full-time employment for no less than thirty-eight weeks per year. They also called for the thirty-hour week, elimination of speed-ups, introduction of bedding provided by logging firms, abolition of company unions and blacklists systems, and an established grievance procedure between workers and employers.[127]

The lumber strike of 1933 began in July when two hundred loggers at a Saginaw Timber Company mill near Aberdeen walked off the job and demanded a minimum wage for bushel workers of three dollars and sixty-five cents per day. They later declared their intention to abolish the bushel system altogether and be paid by the hour.[128] Within a week, loggers at four more camps struck.[129] All told, the strike halted production at five mills and four large camps.[130] The *Daily Worker* proclaimed, "For the first time in ten years the lumber workers of the Northwest, are reviving their old fighting tradition which brought them the reputation among the workers throughout the country of being among the most fearless fighters in the class struggle. Strikes are breaking out in Klamath Falls, Oregon, and Grays Harbor, Washington, in the spirit of 1918 and 1923."[131]

Throughout the strike, Wobblies held large and enthusiastic strike meetings and organized strikes at individual workplaces. On July 23, loggers, including some Wobblies, met at one Grays Harbor Merrill and Ring logging camp and determined by rank-and-file vote to "strike for the six-hour day, 50¢ minimum per hour and no increase in board." The strike was set to begin two days after the vote, but after one particularly active IWW member was fired, "90 per cent of the rigging crew walked out with him, the buckers and fallers followed the next day after getting scaled up."[132]

According to internal CP records, the strike caught the Communists off-guard. It began in mid-July, while NLWU delegates gathered in Seattle. CP officers admitted to being surprised by the loggers' militancy, conceding that they "must re-act fast" and send "more responsible comrades" to build upon the "good sentiment" on the harbor.[133] The conflict quickly mushroomed. CP correspondents reported the scope of the strike: "Industry 'paralyzed' in Grays Harbor," stated one report, as strikers picketed and leafleted at Grays Harbor employment offices, a tactic successful at discouraging unemployed woodsmen from scabbing.[134] Demonstrating the necessity of local control, even while operating with heavy CP support, harbor lumber workers directed the relief drive themselves, soliciting requests from Aberdeen CP headquarters and in the *Voice of Action*.[135]

Strikers formed a union of lumber workers, the direct forerunner of the 1930s industrial unions. In June, AFL organizer C. O. "Dad" Young addressed crowds of lumber workers hopeful of securing union charters. On July 25, one hundred Grays Harbor strikers formed a federal labor union. They elected Oscar Moe as temporary president, raised funds to pay dues and obtain a charter directly from the AFL, and planned to divide the organization into separate locals of loggers, plywood workers, and sawmill laborers. AFL leadership acted quickly; on July 31, the AFL's executive council signed and returned the charter for Aberdeen Local 18345 of the Loggers and Saw Mill Workers Union (LSMWU). At the time, federal labor unions were locals chartered directly with the AFL rather than an international union, often organized as a step toward forming an international union in a previously unorganized industry. During the early 1930s, workers in auto, cement, rubber, and lumber manufacturing formed hundreds of these organizations as steps toward the formation of the United Auto Workers, United Rubber Workers of America, and International Woodworkers of America.[136]

In July 1933, a wave of unionization overtook the lumber industry, with workers across the Northwest forming federal labor unions in lumber. That month, lumber unionists met in Enumclaw, Washington, where they formed the Northwest Council of Sawmill and Timber Workers, the original division of the Sawmill and Timber Workers Union (STWU). Owing to Aberdeen's status as a center of unionism and industry, lumber unionists made it one of the new organization's three headquarters along with Seattle and Portland.[137]

Employers and the state mounted a coordinated response to the strike.

Washington State Governor Clarence Martin dispatched the state patrol to Aberdeen to "back up the local authorities in preserving order." Rather than "preserving order," however, the state police helped local authorities to "intimidate the striking workers to return to work" and round up the "picket line leaders."[138] ILD attorney Irving Goodman represented strikers in court, where he turned accusations of labor's "outside agitators" on its head, contrasting the strike leaders who lived locally with outside state police who assaulted picketers. He explained to the jury the political nature of prosecuting strikers: "You cannot stop the labor movement by convicting these defendants."[139]

While the strikers failed to gain their ambitious demands, their strike paid dividends. According to the *Voice of Action*, each of the struck mills and camps gradually agreed to compromise settlements. On August 8, Schafer Brothers' mill No. 4 resumed a forty-hour-per-week schedule paying forty-two and a half cents per hour, and the *Daily Worker* reported that "some of the mills are now on the six hour basis." At the strike's end, many struck logging camps also went back to work under compromise agreements.[140]

Many of the strikers were Communists, and local party membership grew to 110 members by January 1934.[141] This included Joseph Shenkir, one of the picketers arrested by the state patrol on July 26. Shenkir, who went by the pseudonym L. A. "Red" Johnson, later died fighting fascism during the Spanish Civil War. Johnson first arrived on Grays Harbor before 1930 and appears to have divided his time between urban unemployed agitation and organizing loggers. And he paid dearly for his successes. Forced out of the woods by police harassment and the blacklist, Red found employment as a grocery worker. Still, Johnson's organizational abilities made him a prized target for AFL officials who understood that Communists were among the best organizers. In October 1933, following Red's release from jail during the lumber strike, AFL organizer Art Wilson bribed Johnson with the offer to remove his name from the blacklist—and thus gain the chance at a job in the woods—if he quit the NLWU for the AFL timberworkers' union. "I told him I'd stick with the National Lumber Workers' Union. . . . But I can't help wondering as to just what control the AF of L has over the blacklist," reported Johnson.[142]

The timing of the AFL organizer's offer to Johnson was important. Wilson tried to coopt the radical in October 1933, only three months after the formation of the region's federal labor unions. With lumber workers building unions and striking, and inspired by the passage of federal labor laws and a nationwide union drive, the AFL sought to channel these energies into what its leaders considered a constructive, trade-union-oriented path toward greater union density and strength. Organizers such as Red Johnson who hailed from more radical traditions and movements threatened AFL efforts, particularly in industries such as lumber, where trade unions had a weak history. Between 1933 and 1935, these two wings of the lumber workers' movement collaborated in a marriage of convenience, forming militant woodworkers' unions.

Although dramatic, the 1933 strike, waged during the NRA Lumber Code negotiations, was not the final struggle of 1930s Pacific Northwest labor history. In fact, judging by the silence afforded the conflict, historians have not considered the 1923–33 decade of working-class activism in the lumber industry to be of much significance. Certainly, these sporadic strikes paled in comparison to the 1934 waterfront or 1935 lumber strikes, but it is not only the mass strikes or violent riots that demonstrate working-class consciousness—or that matter in workers' lives. The strikes of the early Depression, a period of mass unemployment and homelessness, likewise revealed the continuities between this and earlier eras as lumber workers resisted capital and forged ties with their community, which turned out in force to support workers in their struggles. In the spring of 1935, these forces united to wage one of the largest labor strikes in Pacific Northwest history, one that drew strength from both the radical and community-centeredness of Wobblies and Communists, as well as the institutional prowess of the Northwest's trade union movement.

10

THE GREAT 1935 LUMBER STRIKE

THE STRUGGLE FOR "ONE UNION IN WOOD"

The decades-long simmering embers of working-class anger in the lumber country burst into flames during the middle years of the 1930s. The Great 1935 Lumber Strike, the largest strike in the Northwest's largest industry, made clear union leaders' capacity to organize and coordinate a disciplined strike force amid militant, often violent, opposition. Few scenes better demonstrated the mass solidarity of Grays Harbor's lumber workers than the picketing and strike parades of July 1935. By the second week of July, thousands of strikers and strike sympathizers took to the streets to protest National Guard occupation of their communities and to reaffirm their commitment to the strike's demands. On July 8, between six thousand and nine thousand people took to the streets to protest the region's military occupation. The *Timber Worker*, the Aberdeen-based newspaper of the Federation of Woodworkers and the International Woodworkers of America, called the scene "perhaps the greatest spontaneous demonstration of union spirit in the history of Western unionism."[1] Workers from Grays Harbor's unions took part in the protest, singing "Solidarity Forever" and waving American flags during the demonstration.[2] Workers marched across bridges and through town, defiantly challenging the troops stationed in their communities—troops who carried guns as they guarded the mills. In the two years between the 1933 Grays Harbor lumber strike and the explosion of solidarity in the Great Strike in 1935 of fifty thousand Northwest mill laborers and loggers, workers developed larger and stronger unions—building upon long-established traditions of solidarity and working-class institutions. The center of the storm were working-class radicals who organized unions, demanded far-reaching

Striking lumber workers and supporters march across the Simpson Avenue Bridge in Hoquiam during the Great 1935 Lumber Strike, when thousands of loggers, sawmill workers, and diverse other wood-product laborers shuttered the Northwest's lumber industry. Jones Photo Historical Collection.

changes in the way the lumber industry operated, and refused to back down to official labor-movement representatives that demanded unionists compromise with employers.

In the aftermath of the 1933 lumber strike, lumber unionists had received some much-needed support from labor officials. On July 25, 1933, Walter Brackinreed, longtime president of the Grays Harbor Central Labor Council (GHCLC), addressed the lumber workers' organizing committee.[3] Three weeks later, Brackinreed presided over the first meeting of the Loggers and Saw Mill Workers' Union (LSMWU) Local 18345. He subsequently attended the union's meetings, gave speeches encouraging further unionization of the industry, and along with GHCLC secretary Gladys Funkhauser, observed the proceedings to help the inexperienced unionists "over the rough spot."[4] The sawmill laborers and loggers welcomed the opportunity to connect with experienced and well-financed unionists. Only four days after its founding in August 1933, LSMWU Local 18345 elected representatives to the GHCLC. The council had more than twenty member unions, its own newspaper—the *Labor Bulletin*—and a long history representing thousands of laborers in diverse trades. The LSMWU adopted the *Labor Bulletin*, a conservative trade union sheet published in Aberdeen, as the official organ of the local.[5]

Many lumber workers considered the AFL and its constituent unions to be important sources of support in an industry where for decades prior, the AFL had offered little. At Local 18345's second meeting, a motion carried to give the GHCLC a vote of gratitude for its assistance in setting up the local.[6] At the November 20, 1934, meeting of Local 18345, unionists "made, seconded, and carried [a motion] to ask William Green, president of the American Federation of Labor, to have Mr. Manard Bright to confine his organizing activities to Grays Harbor for a period of two months."[7]

Lumber workers found close allies among the militant waterfront workers, men who frequently shared the lumber workers' workspaces, culture, political ideas, and a history of rough, dangerous work. Few industries and industrial union histories overlap as much as those of the Pacific Coast's lumber and maritime workers. Historian Bruce Nelson analyzed the connections between maritime and lumber workers, particularly those of migratory loggers and seamen. Similar overlaps existed between longshoremen and sawmill laborers; the two groups regularly interacted with one another on the job.[8] Basic tasks of Grays Harbor longshoremen included stacking and carrying lumber, types of work similar to that demanded of lumber mill hands. Many loggers spent some of each year working on the region's docks, while some sawmill hands had earlier experiences working as longshoremen. August Jonas, a longtime Aberdeen longshoreman who gained prominence for his activism in the early twentieth-century International Longshoremen's Association and Grays Harbor labor council, had by the early 1930s shifted from Grays Harbor's docks to its sawmills. In 1931, he supported the left and took to the *Ab-*

erdeen Daily World to express his contention that the Communist Party of the 1930s received repression similar to that meted out two decades earlier to Grays Harbor AFL maritime unionists, notably William Gohl and the Sailors' Union of the Pacific:

> I recall an injunction suit applied for by employers, against two labor unions here on Grays Harbor in 1906, to which I happened to be a party as a member of one of these unions. In that petition for the injunction we, the members of these unions were branded about the same as the communists are branded today, except that we were murderers. . . . The injunction, as usual in such cases, was granted. We were part of the conservative American Federation of Labor![9]

In May 1934, Pacific Coast longshoremen from Mexico to Canada went on strike in what was to become one of the epic conflagrations in all of US labor history. As Pacific Coast maritime workers shut down coastal shipping during their "Big Strike," lumber unionists raised and delivered prostrike speeches. Support for the maritime strike also appeared in union newspapers and deliberations. At one union meeting, lumber union leader E. E. Wieland "made a motion that we get out some sort of a pamphlet pledging our moral and financial support in the longshoreman strike."[10] Two weeks later, a longshoremen's unionist spoke at a meeting of Local 18345 and "gave us the latest news on the strike. He also asked for any donation we cared to give. This question was put up to the membership to decide what we could give and Brother Walker moved we donate five dollars. . . . carried."[11]

Wieland was critical to the lumber union movement in the 1930s—much as he had been in earlier decades. A longtime sawmill laborer and timber workers' union official, Wieland had served several terms in the 1910s as a socialist member of the Aberdeen City Council. Given his experience as onetime president of the International Union of Timberworkers in the late 1910s, which had thousands of members, it was hardly surprising that his fellow unionists elected Wieland to a series of union leadership positions during the 1930s—including local president during the Great 1935 Lumber Strike. As a union leader, Wieland advocated industrial unionism. In his July 1937 retirement statement, he advised his fellow unionists thus:

> Always remember that to divide is to defeat. So in the interest of our union and the welfare of its members, subordinate all selfish interests for the good of the many, to the end that Local 2639 will always be as in the past, the biggest, strongest, most efficient, and aggressive local union in the lumber industry. Don't allow yourselves or any organization, no matter who they are, to divide you. Stick together. If you have to fight, fight to improve your conditions; and the best way I know of is to remain together in a strong, industrial union, one for all and all for one.[12]

But like J. G. Brown, his old partner in the 1910s union struggles, Wieland's socialism never carried him into the Communist camp; in fact, the former councilmember helped to combat Communists during his tenure as leader of the local union.[13]

Between the formation of Aberdeen Local 18345 of the Loggers and Saw Mill Workers' Union (LSMWU) in July 1933 and the onset of the big maritime strike ten months later, the lumber union persisted with a small membership and limited funds. In March 1934, an official in LSMWU Local 18345 noted that "as soon as possible he will make an attempt to get out in different logging camps and organize the loggers," thus giving a strong indication that the AFL union's early attempts had not met with much success.[14] But in the winter and spring of 1934, harbor lumber unionists struck mills and camps. An old tactic renewed by harbor workers was the "quickie strike," which surprised management unprepared to deal with a sudden absence of labor. In February, ninety Raymond-area loggers won a strike for higher wages and recognition of a worker-run adjustment committee in a National Lumber Workers' Union (NLWU)–led campaign at two Willapa Harbor Lumber Company camps.[15] In early April, a worker correspondent for the radical *Voice of Action* reported that two Raymond-area camps had joined the NLWU. On April 6, NLWU members led a loggers' strike near Aberdeen, one of seven Northwest loggers' strikes happening at that time.[16]

Plywood workers charted a similar path. On April 8, 1934, fifty-two harbor plywood laborers formed a union and sent for their charter from the AFL.[17] Two months after its founding, their union—Federal Labor Union Local 19478—boasted nearly eighty members. The new plywood union got a boost from the federal government's New Deal labor relations authority when, shortly after its founding, Local 19478 brought a wrongful termination claim against the Harbor Plywood Company in Hoquiam. In February 1935, the Seattle-based Regional Labor Board determined that the company had violated the law by terminating the union's officers and recommended that they be reinstated. In May 1935, the federal NLRB upheld the decision. Given the depths of state union-busting up to that point, the fact that a federal government institution had ruled in favor of the harbor's wood-products workers must have seemed remarkable. The decision showed unionists that the NLRB had the potential to be used as a tool to protect union organizing.[18] Bolstered by their NLRB victory, followed by the unionists' successful exposure and subsequent elimination of the local plywood industry's company union, the Federal Labor Union blossomed from little more than a "discussion group" with a handful of members during the latter half of 1934 into one of—if not the—country's largest plywood workers' unions. By 1936, the Grays Harbor plywood union estimated its membership at 1,300.[19]

Union growth and maritime workers' successes inspired the lumber unionists to expand their activities. Unionists discussed flexing their potent political muscles at the ballot box and legislative offices. In January 1935, LSMWU Local 18345 carried a motion to write Congressman Martin Smith letting him know that the union endorsed the Townsend old-age pension plan, a proposal to provide a monthly stipend to all Americans over the age of sixty, "and ask him to use his influence to adopt the plan."[20]

In early 1935, Northwest lumber workers took additional steps to stabilize their unions—a key effort considering that several union locals that had been organized in the previous two decades had disbanded shortly after their formation. On March 12, 1935, LSMWU Local 18345 voted to affiliate with the Washington State Federation of Labor (WSFL).[21] At that same meeting, the local appointed three members to cater to the needs of the delegates of the Northwest Council of Loggers, Sawmill, and Woodworkers Unions, which held its convention in Aberdeen in late March.[22] On March 26, during its first meeting after the Northwest

Council convened in Aberdeen, LSMWU Local 18345—along with the region's other lumber unions—affiliated with the United Brotherhood of Carpenters and Joiners of America (UBCJA), one of the largest unions in the country. For decades, carpenters and other building trades had served as conservative bulwarks. Building trades councils across the country had blocked progressive and socialist initiatives of other unions; locally they had stood in the way of several initiatives driven by Grays Harbor's lumber (and other) workers during the 1910s. Still, many woodworkers greeted the institutional support as members rolled into the newly affiliated union. At that March 26, 1935, meeting, fifty members joined up.[23] During the first week in April, the LSMWU local became Local 2507 of the Sawmill and Timber Workers Union (STWU), an affiliate of the UBCJA. As a sign of the growing popularity of this new local, it inducted between seventy-five and one hundred new members at its first meeting.[24]

With backing of major state and national labor institutions and having witnessed the power of solidarity from their comrades on the Pacific Coast docks, hundreds of lumber workers rushed into unions. By April 19, 1935, the Aberdeen STWU local claimed 1,800 members. By April 21, STWU Local 2507 reportedly represented 90 percent of local millworkers. Union secretary H. A. Murphy claimed that union membership of the town's four largest sawmills would reach 100 percent by April 23 and that large numbers of loggers planned to enter the union that week.[25]

The new local took an aggressive strike footing. It sent delegates to join unionists from throughout the Northwest at a lumber workers' convention in Longview, Washington, at the end of April. The STWU's demands resembled those of the radical National Lumber Workers Union (NLWU) and included a seventy-five-cents-per-hour minimum wage, a thirty-hour workweek, overtime pay, seniority rights, and the closed shop.[26] These terms went beyond the "pork chop" demands of some earlier trade unions and struck at the heart of management's property rights—the sacred rights of employers to run businesses as they saw fit. At the Longview meeting, the region's lumber workers boldly proclaimed to employers: meet these demands or face the greatest strike in the history of the Pacific Northwest.[27]

BUILDING TOWARD THE GREAT STRIKE

By early 1935, labor activists knew that a mass strike, perhaps of historic proportions, lay on the horizon. Across the country, workers struck in numbers not seen since 1919 in the aftermath of World War I. In 1934, the San Francisco General Strike was one of three epic conflagrations—along with the Minnesota Teamsters' Strike and the Toledo (Ohio) Auto-Lite Strike—with left-wing militants leading the way.[28]

Many on the left eagerly awaited the Northwest's lumber workers' strike, sensing in it an opportunity to usher in a new dawn in the lives of the tens of thousands of Pacific Northwest woodworkers and their families. Toward that end, the Communist Party (CP) urged its members to plunge into activity. Through the early 1930s, Communists joined AFL unions, returning to a policy of attempting to radicalize trade unions. Responding to moves being made on the ground by the CP rank and file, on March 16, 1935, the Trade Union Unity League (TUUL) dissolved, making official the turn away from dual unionism. A month later the National Lumber Workers' Union (NLWU) officially disbanded. Communists urged NLWU members to join the AFL and bore from within the union federation.[29] Believing that a great strike lay ahead, CP officials wrote to make sure that no "misleaders" gained control over the strike.[30]

Several Communists emerged as prominent lumber union leaders during 1935 and remained top officials throughout the decade. Communists with years of experience in lumber work, such as Red Johnson, Richard "Dick" Law, and Mickey Orton, organized the early union drives that culminated in the Great 1935 Lumber Strike and subsequent formation of the industrial unions. Well-known Communist and militant unionist Red Johnson served in important roles from the earliest timber union drives of the 1930s, and his comrade Ernest Kozlowski ascended to leadership during the 1935 lumber workers' strike.[31] Orton later served in several leadership positions in the Federation of Woodworkers (FOW) and the International Woodworkers of America (IWA), including as president of the IWA.[32] But the political beliefs of Communist leaders such as Red Johnson antagonized anti-Communist leaders in the state and national labor movement, and cracks within the lumber union movement's solidarity had already begun showing by 1935.

The STWU established May 6 as its strike deadline. Employers unwilling to grant "improved conditions" would be marked "in controversy with the unions" and face a strike.[33] One CP member declared, "The lumber strike will be the biggest thing that ever hit the Northwest. There is not a single city or town in our District that is not connected with the lumber industry and does not have sawmills, woodworking factories, or logging camps in its territory. Lumber is the main industry of the Northwest and now *the entire lumber industry is preparing to go on a general strike*."[34]

Lumber workers also drew inspiration from the introduction and eventual passage of the National Labor Relations Act (NLRA). Known as the Wagner Act, this legislation was the central piece of labor law passed during President Franklin D. Roosevelt's Second New Deal, a period of remarkable transformation that included passage of the Social Security Act. Made possible in part by the massive Democratic majorities in Congress, these landmark pieces of legislation made significant strides toward leveling the playing field between labor and capital.[35] The NLRA's provisions gave workers the right to organize and bargain collectively with employers, defined unfair labor practices, and created the National Labor Relations Board (NLRB), designed to oversee union elections and mediate disputes between organized workers and employers. Introduced on February 21, 1935, by Senator Robert Wagner of New York, the bill became a source of inspiration for the nation's unionists. At a special meeting of the harbor's STWU and the plywood workers' locals in early July 1935, workers got advice from their attorney about the bill and discussed how to best make use of the new law with union members from outside their district.[36] President Roosevelt signed the bill into law on July 5, 1935.[37] When the US Supreme Court declared the law constitutional in April 1937, the *Timber Worker* cheered, "Labor's Magna Charta Sustained" and "Certainly Monday, April 12th, must henceforth be hailed as . . . Labor's Day in Court."[38]

Passage of the Wagner Act spurred unionization. Union membership more than doubled, from slightly less than four million in 1936 to more than eight million in 1938.[39] Although the Democrats maintained control over the federal and Washington State governments from 1933 through the end of the decade, New Dealers weren't the only brand of Democrats operating in the Pacific Northwest. Washington Governor Clarence Martin joined his fellow anti–New Deal Democrats in commanding the balance of power in Olympia. This group often voted with Republicans on matters of old-age pensions, tax policy, and workers' rights. Six months after taking office, Governor Martin had dispatched the Washington State Patrol to help Grays Harbor lumbermen fight the 1933 lumber strike.

The NLRA brought a new dynamic to the Pacific Northwest lumber industry as workers had their first experience with neutral federal entities that provided sets of rules that management, as well as workers, were obliged to follow. Lumber workers made good use of the tools available to them—including the newly won NLRB protections. They brought several cases before the NLRB during its first years, while the board also oversaw contentious lumber union elections throughout the late 1930s.[40]

Others on the left were less sanguine about the impact of the NLRA, which many correctly saw as placing the state at the center of class relations. Whereas the IWW had long favored direct action at the point of production and viewed union contracts as a truce in the class war, the Wagner Act created a bureaucracy to resolve labor conflicts, officiate union elections, and oblige employers to bargain with workers' representatives of their own choosing.[41] In previous decades, workplace struggles and community pressure had determined whether unions would be recognized and contracts would be bargained, but after passage of the Wagner Act, workers looked to the federal government as a mediator—and sometimes as a savior. In September 1938, as a group of Grays Harbor lumber workers voted to unionize with the IWA, unionists showed that they placed a great deal of faith in the NLRB to resolve conflicts. "The workers on Grays Harbor are hoping that the NLRB will soon hand down its decision, based on the hearing held in the first part of July in Aberdeen, in order that we may look forward to the coming fall and winter business with a feeling of confidence," wrote one Aberdeen IWA official.[42]

THE CARPENTERS' COMPROMISE

Woodworker militancy was a well-known fact in Northwest labor relations, and the lumber workers' militant strike footing in 1935 did nothing to change that perception. The carpenters' union, UBCJA, did not want a regional strike, and the thought of a 100,000-strong union led by radicals terrified UBCJA officials. Responsibility for taming the woodworkers fell to Abraham "Abe" Muir, a UBCJA executive board member. Like most AFL union officials, Muir had no experience in lumber, but that did not dampen his confidence. In late April 1935, shortly after being dispatched to control the newly organized Northwest woodworkers' unions, Muir offered employers a compromise forty-hour workweek, a forty-two-and-a-half-cents-per-hour minimum, and union recognition without the protections of a closed shop. Some employers welcomed Muir's intervention, seeing it as a way to head off a costly strike, as well as divide the region's laborers between militants and those who preferred to compromise, rather than challenging the lumbermen. On April 19, amid negotiations between Northwest lumber employers and workers, Muir announced that "there may be spasmodic, widely separated strikes, but I do not believe the entire industry will walk out."[43] In an irony apparently lost on Muir, his announcement coincided with a series of strike votes by STWU locals.[44] As workers voted to strike, AFL officials maneuvered to put on the brakes. C. O. "Dad" Young, a longtime AFL organizer, declared a commitment to securing demands through arbitration rather than striking. In late April, the *Seattle Post-Intelligencer* lent a hand to the antistrike forces, running a headline "Timber Strike Threat Fades" even as the lumber unionists met to discuss the strike.[45]

Not content to wait for the vote or any sort of endorsement from union officials, loggers and mill workers struck in advance of the May 6 strike date. On April 20, 518 Oregon loggers went on strike.[46] In Bellingham, 2,000 mill workers struck during the last week in April, while the town's longshoremen walked off the docks in a sympathy strike. By May Day, lumber workers across Washington and Oregon took to the picket lines. Handbills—most likely circulated by local Communists—urged Grays Harbor lumber workers to follow the example of these strikers.[47]

On May 6, with operators unwilling to concede to labor's demands, thousands of lumber workers across Washington and Oregon struck. On the harbor, most mills and camps remained in operation in the hopes that the passing deadline would bring an agreement. But the next day, with all hope of employers meeting their demands dashed, the entire lumber workforce in Grays Harbor, one of the world's largest concentrations of lumber workers, struck. A headline of the *Aberdeen Daily World* read, "5,000 Workers Out in Lumber Plants and Woods Camps." Two days later, 800 plywood workers, organized under a charter separate from the sawmill and timber workers, joined the strike, taking to the picket lines alongside their fellow unionists. On May 9, 1935, 30,000 lumber workers were on strike.[48] On May 14, Grays Harbor Veneer Company laborers joined the strike, their numbers adding to the ballooning conflict. With the men and women who worked in plywood and veneer mills joining loggers and sawmill laborers on the picket lines, Northwest lumber workers had carried out a general tie-up of the region's primary industry.

Meanwhile, Muir persisted in his efforts to secure a settlement to employers' satisfaction. On May 10, Longview workers refused a deal negotiated between Muir and the town's largest employers, one that Muir and other AFL officials planned to apply throughout the region.[49] On May 27, journalists reported Muir's announcement of an impending end to the strike; the UBCJA official hoped the strikers would agree to the operator-friendly terms in the bargain, including a fifty-cents-per-hour minimum wage, adoption of the union as collective bargaining agent but without the closed shop, and a forty-hour workweek. On the harbor, local sawmill union president Harry Semples followed Muir's lead by offering to negotiate with employers, individually or collectively.[50] Opponents of the deal labeled Muir's compromise a "sell-out."[51]

NORTHWEST JOINT STRIKE COMMITTEE

On June 5, 1935, 240 union delegates to the strike committee met at Aberdeen to "wrest control" of the strike from Muir and his supporters. Even before the strike's onset, the Northwest CP urged its members and supporters to form strike committees "in every locality to be in control of the strike and to elect delegates to the general strike committee. The strike must not be left in the hands of a few officials."[52] The CP reported, "In Aberdeen some comrades hold some important positions on strike committees."[53] The local committees inspired the formation of a larger body to lead the strike in a more militant direction, to keep leadership in the hands of elected lumber workers' union officials, and to coordinate the strikers' activities across the Northwest. Communists influenced the meeting and the organization of the committee. On May 16, delegates from the Aberdeen and Everett STWU locals met and proposed to form a Northwest Joint Lumber Strike Committee. The CP used its members' positions within the strikers' ranks to advocate for a conference of Northwest strikers to "set up a Northwest Joint Strike Committee as the sole authority in the field to run the strike and to negotiate."[54]

As home to one of the largest concentrations of strikers, Grays Harbor served as a logical site for the meeting. CP organizers proposed "that the Aberdeen strike committee issue the call and that the Conference should be held in Aberdeen."[55] Harbor Communists provided leadership roles in planning the meeting and gained election to key leadership posts within the new organization.[56] Delegates rejected Muir's compromise settlement and formed their own Northwest Joint Strike Committee (NJSC) to negotiate for the strikers' original demands. The meeting achieved many of its planners' main goals, including rank-and-file control over strike decisions. Delegates named a committee to renew the campaign for original strike demands: seventy-five cents an hour minimum, a six-hour day, a thirty-hour workweek, and union recognition. Militant unionists emphasized that the real purpose of the meeting was to establish "a representative body of a size that will cast the mountainous shadow of the Northwest's 40,000 lumber strikers over the waning glow of Muir's one-man attempt at strike control."[57]

Militants resented Muir's control over the strike, particularly his advocacy of compromise—what appeared to many unionists to be efforts to secure a business-friendly deal. Muir and others in UBCJA leadership further inflamed workers when Muir ordered Grays Harbor left-wing strike leaders Red Johnson, Ernest Kozlowski, William Rayburn, and

J. W. Wenzel expelled from the union. In the expulsion telegram, Muir wrote, "They have been interfering with orderly procedure and spreading dissention among our local unions." Walter Brackinreed, a vice president in the WSFL and leader of the GHCLC, joined in the accusations, condemning the militants for "breaking the harmony of the union."[58] Rank-and-file workers exploded with indignation at the expulsion. The Grays Harbor plywood workers' union demanded the removal of Muir from office, as did a mass meeting of lumber unionists. Adding a stamp of official sanction to the protests, a committee of union activists representing each of the striking mills met on June 3 and demanded the reinstatement of the expelled leftists. A day later, the local plywood union voted to have no further dealings with Muir and banned the bureaucrat from their hall.[59]

One of the first actions of the NJSC was to reinstate the four expelled radical unionists from Grays Harbor back into the STWU. Driven by the rank and file, this action from the NJSC showed the lumber workers' potential power without being ruled by the UBCJA. At a meeting of 2,500 STWU members at the Aberdeen American Legion hall, members reinstated the four ousted union militants and gave Red Johnson "an ovation that shook the town and must have been heard by half the town," according to the *Voice of Action*. As a final insult to the UBCJA, the NJSC also elected Johnson as one of the committee's executive board members. The committee then renounced the compromise deal offered by Muir and restated the union's original demands. In bold letters, the *Voice of Action* celebrated that "Muir is no longer at the head of the strike" and "Strike Remains Solid; 240 Delegates from Every Important STWU Local at Aberdeen Parley; Muir Swept Aside."[60]

A great deal of rank-and-file support unified the NJSC. According to *One Union in Wood*, forty locals affiliated with the Northwest Joint Strike Committee by July 1 with overwhelming support for the NJSC by many locals. Despite accusations from Muir and employers that the Northwest Joint Strike Committee was run by the CP, a majority of strikers supported the committee.[61]

STRIKEBREAKING

Mill and logging camp owners used imported strikebreakers, armed guards, and scabs to break the strike, but state officials took center stage in the effort to drive strikers back on the job.[62] Aberdeen unionist and future IWA president Mickey Orton summarized the terror the unionists faced in those harried days of mid-1935: "Professional strikebreakers were imported into many localities and the State Highway Patrol and the State Militia were placed at the disposal of the operators and local law enforcement agencies, at their request, by the definitely hostile anti-labor state administration[s] of Washington and Oregon. Practically in every instance where the State Highway Patrol and the National Guard were brought into the picture, violence became rampant. Peaceful, striking workers were gassed, beaten, maimed, and injured."[63] Governor Clarence Martin took an active role in breaking the strike. Using "right to work" rhetoric, as early as June 7 the governor ordered the state patrol to "protect workers" in Malone, a small town in eastern Grays Harbor County, where employers had complained of "interference from outsiders by picketing and threats" against scabs. On June 8, a detachment of patrolmen went to Longview to break a picket line that blockaded automobile and pedestrian traffic from entering the city's large Long-Bell and Weyerhaeuser mills. To justify his use of state forces to protect scabs, Martin resorted to red-baiting:

> Investigation has revealed such interference and threats come primarily from agitators, including some professional communists who are taking advantage of the situation to foment discontent and violence. These forces are determined to promote industrial trouble even to the extent of undermining our institutions and government. Now, as governor, I serve notice such communistic activities, professional agitation, coercion and intimidation must not be tolerated in Washington . . . and I direct the Washington state patrol to cooperate fully with local authorities for the prompt arrest of the leaders and members of any groups which resort to threats and intimidation to prevent men from working and to prevent the resumption of operations in the lumber industry in Washington.[64]

On June 24, Governor Martin sent the National Guard to Tacoma to protect scabs as lumber operators fought to forcibly reopen the mills. Guardsmen set up a machine gun and attacked picketing workers with tear gas. Brigadier General Carlos A. Pennington of the National Guard banned picketing in Tacoma. The troops made arrests, interning the strikers at the local armory.[65]

Organized labor united in denouncing the governor. Max Barnett, financial secretary of the Northwest Joint Strike Committee, responded by criticizing the governor for "prostituting his high office to the Committee of 500 and ask our brothers and friends to take the same action." The GHCLC issued a resolution protesting Martin's strikebreaking. Representing the rank-and-file militants on strike, the *Voice of Action* condemned the "state-wielded terror by Governor Clarence D. Martin of Washington and Governor Charles Martin of Oregon." On July 11, at its convention in Port Angeles, Washington, the WSFL condemned the "action of Gov. Clarence D. Martin in calling on armed forces to subdue a purely imaginative labor insurrection."[66]

Pressure from labor did not sway the governor's opinions and actions. At the request of the mayors of Aberdeen and Hoquiam, the governor ordered the National Guard to Grays Harbor on July 7 to back up the state troopers already dispatched to the county. Three hundred members of the Second Battalion, 161st Regiment of the Washington National Guard, descended on the harbor. A day into their occupation, one hundred fifty armed members of the National Guard confronted three thousand pickets at the Bay City mill, informing the strikers that they were banned from picketing the mills and prodding them with rifle butts.[67] On July 20, guardsmen charged at strikers with fixed bayonets, assaulting and eventually dispersing the strikers.[68] Members of the National Guard tossed tear gas bombs to disperse picketers at several mills. In addition to its use of bayonets and gas, the National Guard also employed tools more typical of professional strikebreakers and vigilantes to curb the actions of strikers. In mid-July, men wearing National Guard uniforms seized striking shingle weaver A. W. Huntley, forced him into their car, drove him outside of Hoquiam, and beat him until Huntley escaped into the woods.[69] The violent acts previously committed by vigilante businessmen

Armed National Guard troops surround striking workers in Aberdeen during the Great 1935 Lumber Strike. Strikers and their supporters accused the National Guard of serving as a strikebreaking tool during the conflict. Jones Photo Historical Collection.

or the American Legion were—during the Great 1935 Lumber Strike—accomplished by official military forces.

Supplementing force was a sophisticated public relations plan akin to the Mohawk Valley Formula made famous during the thirties. Employers joined sympathetic politicians and journalists in portraying rank-and-file strike activists as Communists and outside agitators; blaming the strike for tossing workers, already impoverished by years of economic depression, onto the unemployment lines; and claiming a minority of unionists forced the strike on an unwilling majority of workers. "Red Baiting was raised here in 1935 to such an extent that headlines appeared in London papers branding our Parades here as Red Marches," noted a union bulletin published after the strike.[70] Employers feigned sympathy for the loss of income faced by the strikers and those affected by the strike: "The industry may face a long shutdown and the people of the West Coast should prepare themselves for a more serious immediate loss in income than that which occurred from 1929 to 1932."[71]

If the federal government provided a rulebook that occasionally evened the playing field between workers and employers, the latter group retained its hold on many of the local institutions of power—notably municipal governments and the mainstream press. Union leader Mickey Orton explained media's relationship with labor: "The Grays Harbor press has been especially anti-labor in character and expression. They have editorially attempted to smear our Union and its militant leadership." Orton believed the local press, like the business-controlled media of old, incited violence: "The inflammatory character of the Grays Harbor press has encouraged violence. It has played down, or suppressed, comment on the actual situation as regards law enforcement. It is, and always has been, pro-employer and anti-union. It has failed to criticize in one single instance the failure of law enforcement agencies to carry out their duties in a responsible manner."[72]

From the onset of the strike, employers recruited scabs for the struck mills, both on Grays Harbor and in the wider Pacific Northwest. On May 14, a car driven by scabs ran through a picket line at the Aberdeen Plywood factory, seriously injuring one picketer.[73] On July 24, a Hoquiam scab whose house was being picketed by strikers and strike sympathizers fired a shotgun into the picket line, spraying birdshot onto the crowd. The scab wounded four men and a boy with the flurry.[74]

Working-class women led the battle to dissuade scabs from crossing picket lines. The *Voice of Action* reported that women picketed the homes of Grays Harbor–area scabs in July.[75] As in earlier strikes, women's militancy on the harbor caught widespread attention. Women's auxiliaries performed much of the work to connect the new labor movement to the community. Auxiliaries were thus the leading agents in broadening the appeal of the labor movement on the harbor and beyond during the 1930s. Auxiliaries, both official organizations of the labor movement and informal groupings of working-class women that usually formed during strikes, had long histories on the harbor. Union supporters had set up card and label leagues during the first decade of the twentieth century and operated soup kitchens during strikes in 1912 and 1935.[76] Opening and operating these kitchens required coordination among strike officials. They also showed the level of community acceptance for worker-run welfare groups: unlike during earlier IWW strikes, when workers ran soup kitchens that eventually were destroyed by police and vigilantes, those operated during the 1935 conflict remained relatively unmolested by anti-union forces. Union auxiliaries also complemented local card and label leagues, long a feature of regional labor activism, in supporting working-class goals such as purchasing union-made goods. In June 1937, the Aberdeen card and label league carried out a Card and Label Week designed to educate consumers on the importance of buying "fair" and boycotting "unfair" goods.[77]

Grays Harbor's auxiliaries also had a history of militancy. In August 1934, a Finnish American women's committee angrily condemned the actions of the Aberdeen municipal government for its "Fascist actions in refusing to give the workers' elected water committee the right to speak in behalf of their demand at the City Council meeting of August 23rd."[78] In McCleary, a company town in eastern Grays Harbor, an auxiliary formed out of a card and label league during a millworkers' strike. The McCleary auxiliary activists inspired their fellow workers throughout the region, and shortly after the group's formation, working-class women spread the auxiliary movement across the Northwest.[79]

Grays Harbor youth also joined the protests. High-school students announced in July 1935 that they intended to refuse to play on athletic teams alongside any fellow student who scabbed during the strike; young people on the community sports clubs made a similar proclamation. Strikers and strike supporters also barred scabs and National Guardsmen from visiting dance halls and other amusement places in the Aberdeen area.[80]

The harbor's ugly tradition of vigilantism reemerged during the Great Strike of 1935 as strikebreakers joined far-right organizations in their attacks on the union and supporters. On the night of July 1, 1935, assailants dynamited the home of the strikers' attorney, Frank L. Morgan, president of the Grays Harbor Bar Association. The blast tore through the first floor but did not harm Morgan or the attorney's two daughters who slept inside. The blast went off only a day before Morgan's appearance in court to defend Communist striker Ernest Kozlowski on charges of disorderly conduct and interference with the free passage of a car.[81] The *Industrial Worker* reported from Aberdeen, "Quite a number of private gunmen are in our fair city driving around town. They make their headquarters in Cosmopolis and are a tough-looking aggregation to say the least. All of them have permits from Sheriff Bartell to carry 'rods' but no power of arrest. In other words they can bump you off but they can't arrest you."[82]

The picketing of mills and logging camps in Grays Harbor demonstrated the union leaders' capacity to organize and coordinate a disciplined strike force amid militant, often violent, opposition. The thousands of workers who turned out for picket duty and strike parades in July 1935 provided vivid illustrations of the strikers' solidarity and community support. Two thousand workers took to the picket lines on July 1 to block the entrance to Harbor Plywood Corporation. By the second week of July, thousands of harbor strikers and strike sympathizers joined the protests against National Guard occupation of their communities and to reaffirm their commitment to the strike's original demands.[83]

Disturbed by the size, length, and violence of the strike, Secretary of Labor Frances Perkins named a board of elite Northwesterners to a mediation board to conclude the dispute. After taking power in 1933, New Deal Democrats had intervened in several labor conflicts—at times favoring management, at times siding with workers. But in a move largely characteristic of New Deal actions, the Democrats prioritized ending the strikes, articulating that they sided with "the public good." But with eyes toward their history of doing as they liked in labor relations, lumber employers bristled when Secretary Perkins interceded in the strike. They protested to federal officials and claimed "there is nothing to mediate." Expanding the critique further, one lumberman contended that Perkins and the labor department were "biased in its handling of labor matters."[84]

By the end of July, the strike had collapsed in most Pacific Northwest lumber centers. On August 3, 1935, Tacoma strikers voted to accept the employers' deal and end the strike.[85] Only in Grays Harbor, Raymond, and a few smaller lumber-producing areas did workers remain out on strike. Eight hundred strike supporters demonstrated in Aberdeen on August 12, a protest in the face of employers and state officials determined to bring the strike to an end.[86] But intending to deal the death blow to the last holdouts, Governor Martin again sent Brigadier General Pennington to the harbor to mediate an end to the strike. With employers and much of the state apparatus aligned against them, strikers recognized defeat. Thirteen weeks into the strike, members of the Grays Harbor STWU accepted a deal nearly identical to the one offered by Muir's sell-out negotiated months earlier.[87]

While the strike succeeded at meeting only some of the workers' demands, at least some unionists saw the conflict as part of a larger struggle to unite the region's working class in common cause. Near the end of the strike, the Grays Harbor strike bulletin envisioned the solidarity of the future labor movement that beckoned:

> As we see the strike situation as it stands today, an honorable and just settlement is not impossible in the very near future. We must say the members have carried on this fight in a way it would make many of the old union men look like amateurs carrying on a strike. We came out May 6th but partly organized. It was seen immediately that an organizing campaign was needed. The proper committees were elected and put in the field. This was done. For the first time in the history of the lumber industry we had an organization composed nearly 100 percent of the lumber workers of the industry of Grays Harbor. And over three months later with but a few in exception we remain the same, as when we came out, one solid body joined together fighting for a common cause. We are surely making history in the labor movement. The majority of our members never belonged to an organization before, but they carry on as veterans. But let us not forget when we return to our jobs we still belong to the union, we still have much work to do. Don't forget your dues, and also the many business people and others to have given us their moral and financial support as well. As we go forward it is our duty to see that they go on also. Remember, we claim and really have one of the largest locals on the Coast if not the entire United States. May it always remain one local, one union composed of a solid rank and file organization carried on in a manner to be as an example for others to follow.[88]

By autumn 1935, workers in the Northwest's primary industry had united to launch an industry-wide strike that crippled its largest industry for more than two months. The strike brought gains for the timber workers and their families, including higher wages, shorter hours, and better working conditions. It also led to a ballooning of the region's timber unions, which by the end of 1935 counted 35,000 members, with thousands more joining each month.[89] To carry on the struggle, in September 1935 Grays Harbor lumber unionists launched the *Timber Worker*, a weekly sheet based in Aberdeen that grew into the official organ of the Federation of Woodworkers and the International Woodworkers of America.[90] A greater sense of hope and solidarity likewise came with the strike. By August 1935, lumber workers had a better idea of what they could accomplish when united. In the years ahead, organizers and activists worked to institutionalize the collective activity seen during the Great 1935 Lumber Strike.

CONCLUSION

Lumber unions experienced years of growth after the Great Strike of 1935—but it was not all smooth sailing for the new unions. In September 1936, hundreds of union delegates from across the lumber industry met in Portland to create the Federation of Woodworkers (FOW). With labor militant and Communist Harold Pritchett elected as president, the new federation boasted of 72,000 members, the largest union on the Pacific Coast.[1] The FOW then turned to the newly formed Committee on Industrial Organization (CIO), precursor to the Congress of Industrial Organizations within the American Federation of Labor (AFL), for aid. After initially rebuffing the lumber workers, CIO leaders by early 1937 showed a willingness to enroll the new union in their ranks. On August 4, 1936, the AFL had suspended the unions affiliated with the CIO; early in 1937, AFL leadership expelled those unions. With successful organizing campaigns and strikes across auto, steel, and a host of other industries, the CIO had by 1937 emerged as a rival to the decades-old AFL. The dramatic growth of the CIO inspired confidence among its leaders. These men, including John L. Lewis, showed a new willingness to expand their ranks in new areas and to raid AFL unions. Meanwhile, woodworkers' unions continued to make entreaties to the CIO and to condemn AFL union leaders.[2] On June 26, 1937, Lewis wrote to the secretary of the FOW that they "will be glad to have affiliation of Wood-Workers on same basis as any other international or national union now affiliated with CIO. Stop. Will be glad to meet with committee of your Board in advance of your convention as you suggest."[3]

At a July 1937 convention in Tacoma, delegates representing more than 75,000 woodworkers debated the issue of CIO affiliation for four and a half days before voting 363 to 75 in favor of joining the new labor organization. All fifty-seven delegates from the Grays–Willapa Harbor Council voted yes on the question of joining the CIO. The Aberdeen auxiliary of the FOW took a similar position. The convention settled on the International Woodworkers of America (IWA) as the name for the new union.[4] Aberdeen's local received another new name, becoming Sawmill and Timber Workers Union, Local 3-2, IWA.[5] In December 1937, the IWA held its first regular convention, boasting a dues-paying membership of 45,000.[6] Unionists waged internal struggles over issues including the place of Communists in the union. After the IWA's formation and connection to the CIO, the carpenters persisted in efforts to control the woodworkers—and retained control over thousands of lumber workers within United Brotherhood of Carpenters and Joiners of America locals—within the folds of the AFL.

On Grays Harbor, one of the major differences between life before and after the Great Strike of 1935 was the unprecedented level of militancy shown by lumber workers in the years following. Whereas before the strike workers had been forced to deal with employer power unrestrained by the state or collective power of workers, unionized lumber workers met employer opposition over workplace issues by striking, placing companies on unfair lists, and petitioning the National Labor Relations Board (NLRB). The shift toward a more confrontational collective bargaining by strike method of labor relations was made possible both by the actions of local activists and by wider circumstances. Creation of the NLRB gave workers a legal path to unionization and a federal body to facilitate and oversee the unionization process. Feeling that they had some degree of legal protection and inspired by the solidarity of 1935, Grays Harbor lumber workers struck in impressive numbers. Lumber unionists joined those in auto, steel, coal, and other major industries in waging wildcat strikes. Through the winter of 1936–37, loggers struck the large Polson Logging Company in Grays Harbor for union recognition, reemployment of all strikers, and improved camp conditions. Polson loggers won the strike after more than four months, a victory greeted by a front-page headline in the *Timber Worker*: "Polson Crew Wins Strike Victory."[7]

More than two years after the big 1935 lumber strike, the *Timber Worker*, then-official newspaper for the FOW, moved from its founding headquarters in Aberdeen to Seattle, the Northwest's largest city, which was on the cusp of experiencing a World War II and Cold War boom in population and prominence.[8] The newspaper's move to the big city symbolized many of the changes remaking the world of labor and politics in the 1930s. When it left Grays Harbor, the *Timber Worker* was the official voice for an organization with the potential to serve as the long-sought "one union in wood."

Although pejoratives like "Big Labor" and "labor boss" are widely understood as code used by businesses and their allies to attack labor, it's also clear that the terms are more suitable for the post-1935 era than before. Spurred by militant union organizers building industrial unions and the possibilities for the New Deal state to provide neutral, sometimes prounion, state involvement, the labor movement brought in millions of new members during the 1930s and 1940s as union density peaked during the 1950s. In the years since President Franklin D. Roosevelt's first election, unions became increasingly involved in national and international affairs—tied to the Democratic Party as solid foundations of the New Deal Coalition—and in World War II, part of the "Arsenal of Democracy," providing war materials for the Allies.

It's partly for these reasons that I end this book's narrative in 1935, a moment of woodworker solidarity and a period of transition from an era when lumber unions were mostly small and unstable, organized and led by radicals, to an era of bureaucratic large urban institutions connected to—even embedded within—elite institutions. Indeed, 1935 served as a bridge between the community-based worker mobilization of the early twentieth century and mass industrial unions. The large industrial unions were far bigger, more stable, and more embedded within powerful institutions like the Democratic Party than the working-class organizations detailed in this book. The new era was different enough that any single chapter covering such an epic period of working-class organization would seem insufficient to record those struggles and workers'—and employers'—lives that made those struggles possible.

A community study can provide valuable insights to most any place in any era, but as labor unions grew during the 1930s and 1940s, their relationships with communities changed. Local unions—small trade unions, the radical IWW, and the emergent industrial unions of lumber—all had close connections to, and often deep roots within, their local communities. Although national and international conditions influenced local labor struggles—through, for example, vast strikebreaking operations and immigration restrictions—community-based studies provide, in historian Alan Dawley's words, apt lenses "to trace . . . the twisting paths that led from the factory to the cultural values, political opinions, and the organizational activities" of workers and employers.[9] A local study focusing on Grays Harbor proved especially fruitful in yielding insights about the IWW. In Grays Harbor, the Wobblies crafted a community-based form of unionism, one responsive to the needs of the local population and that was led, joined, and supported by long-term Grays Harborites. Thousands of people—men, women, children, and families—supported the IWW. The radicals gained support from a cross section of the community and used that support to remain a significant part of the local labor movement for two decades. Wobblies came together in their halls and on picket lines; their actions were reminders to elites that they had failed to excise the IWW from their community.

A main goal of this book is to look at the work and social lives of everyday people and their connections to their local community. Class was a primary animating force in the lives of early twentieth-century Northwesterners, a fact that was evinced by the multitude and variety of class struggles covered in this book. Moreover, this book shows that class formation is a process, one resulting from the interaction between classes over time. Grays Harbor workers and employers engaged in a variety of struggles during the first four decades of the twentieth century. Workers and bosses learned from their struggles and reshaped their actions accordingly. To maintain workplace power and to maximize profits, lumbermen and their allies employed deportations, blacklists, and hall closures to contest community-based radical movements; used injunctions and mass arrests to deal with aggressive picketers; and formed employers' organizations to coordinate their efforts once local unions proved too powerful for individual employers to defeat on their own. Employers' actions likewise helped to shape those of working people. Low wages, dangerous work, gross inequality, and other conditions common to the early twentieth-century lumber industry inspired workers to determine that theirs was not a cooperative relationship with the boss but, instead, one based on exploitation. Harbor workers responded to scabs and gunmen with militant, sometimes violent forms of direct action and formed class-based workers' organizations once trade unions failed to effectively represent the local working class as a whole or consistently deliver bread-and-butter gains for their members. Grays Harbor workers also carried out mass cultural celebrations to bring working people's struggles from the shop floor to the street corner, hall, and parade route.

In 1935, the great strike in lumber country united striking loggers with their urban counterparts to battle against their collective class enemies—much as they had repeatedly done earlier in the century, notably in 1912, 1917, 1923, and 1933. And it was the collective struggle—the power exerted—by the rural loggers and the urban mill workers, longshoremen, and their allies in the community that *forced* management to ultimately recognize the authority of labor unions in their industries. Of course, the 1935 lumber strike was not the last labor conflict in the Northwest's timber empire. But the Great 1935 Lumber Strike and subsequent organizing and strikes forced lumber and shipping operators to, for the first time, deal with organized workers at the bargaining table. When the burning embers of class antagonism finally burst into the flames of mass unionism and strikes, the thousands of working people who had been politicized on the picket line, shop floor, and radical halls of the 1910s, 1920s, and early 1930s were present to provide guidance to their fellow workers.

Workers built larger and increasingly powerful and stable industrial unions in lumber during the late 1930s. But that's not to say that lumbermen ceased their fight against labor. Instead, Grays Harbor employers remained a potent and oft-unified group—and frequently continued to lead Northwest employers' movements—in their efforts to stamp out radical unionism. Those unions, notably the International Woodworkers of America and International Longshoremen's and Warehouse Union with leftist leaderships and policies, ran into the monster's maw of American business repression. Both ILWU president Harry Bridges and IWA president Harold Pritchett were immigrants who felt the weight directly as the federal government conspired with business and conservative unionists to remove the elected union leaders. In Pritchett's case, the repression worked; the US Immigration Service denied him entry to the country in 1940. Unable to work in the United States, Pritchett, one of the most successful union-builders in Pacific Coast history, resigned his post as IWA president in late 1940.[10] The legal and political repression experienced by unions across the country—the shift from "blackjacks to briefcases," in the words of historian Robert Michael Smith, did change the tools of anti-union efforts, as employers looked for state and federal assistance in their crusade.[11] But on Grays Harbor, blackjacks—or, rather, axe handles—remained popular tools. Vigilantes and police aimed their weapons leftward while the local media either incited the violence or looked the other way. Following his 1939 visit to Washington, DC, Dan McGillicuddy, a leading local employer, told a business crowd, "Grays Harbor is known as the Little Soviet of the US. . . . We have that reputation and we must get rid of it." To "get rid of it," employers and their allies organized into reactionary organizations such as citizens' committees, the Ku Klux Klan, and Grays Harbor Business Builders (an antiradical group formed on the harbor that many locals blamed for the era's vigilantism).[12]

The employer terrorism of the post-1935 strike era in Grays Harbor took its toll on the labor-left and the wider population. On December 1, 1939, vigilantes raided, looted, and destroyed the Aberdeen Red Finn hall, which had served as the main meeting place of the labor-left since 1906. With the closure of the Finnish IWW hall at the end of the 1930s and destruction of the Aberdeen Red Finn hall in December 1939, the harbor's Finnish radicals confronted the reality of their marginalization from the community. For years, their halls had been raided, their fellow workers and comrades had been jailed, and their activities had been spied upon. But these militant workers had always boasted impressive halls—homes where they could unite and discuss shared conditions.

A month after the hall's raid, Laura Luoma Law, wife of local Communist and union leader Dick Law and daughter of IWW supporters Sally and Nestor Luoma, was murdered in her Aberdeen home while Dick attended a union meeting.[13] The weeks-long terror against the harbor's labor-left made national news, with an estimated seven thousand workers attending

Laura Law's funeral, and leftist luminaries such as Richard Wright and Carey McWilliams organizing groups to halt the antilabor attacks.[14]

Although the Laura Law case remains officially unsolved, the Laws had received threats from employers and their allies prior to the murder, indicating a strong likelihood that she was yet another casualty of Grays Harbor's several-decades-long class war. Police and prosecutors' responses to the weeks of terror against the harbor's labor-left were vivid reminders of capital's continued influence over state decisions on the harbor. Perhaps unsurprisingly, the Aberdeen Police Department failed to intervene to stop the attack on the Red hall. Weeks later, those same police joined county, state, and federal authorities in focusing their murder investigations on Dick Law, rather than the anti-union employers or their allies who had spied on, harassed, and threatened the Law family.

Caught in the wider arena of anti-Communist activity, some Grays Harborites joined state and national politicians in their assaults on progressives and leftists. The attention focused on Grays Harbor, a longtime center of radicalism, could not have been surprising. More than five thousand people signed a petition asking Martin Dies of the House Un-American Activities Committee to investigate un-American activities in Grays Harbor.[15] Both the House Un-American Activities Committee and the state-level anti-Communist Canwell Committee hearings in Olympia fixed their gaze on the harbor towns, an area labeled the "Little Soviet of Washington. Western Capital of Communism" in an AFL periodical.[16] In 1940, Aberdeen mayor Herbert Horrocks thanked the American Legion, by then a mass organization, for helping to "whip certain subversive elements here."[17] For the mayor's years of union-busting, the Grays Harbor Communist Party distributed a 1940 election flyer labeling him "Gas Bomb Horrocks."[18]

To survive in the New Deal order, unions worked with institutions and actors far beyond their local communities. Although Grays Harbor labor remained a vital and powerful group of unions, they were also, in part, cogs in a machine whose engines lay in Washington, DC, Seattle, and Olympia. In the years ahead, Grays Harbor workers would need new tools and new spaces to act collectively against an aggressive, often-united employing class—one that had the resources and organization to enact antilabor policies through careful, long-term planning. Although today we might scoff at the notion that big lumber companies, which are so infamous for reckless destruction of the environment, would be long-term planners, it's worth reflecting on the ultimate fate of, for example, the Weyerhaeuser Corporation, which remains one of the Northwest's celebrated iconic companies; its corporate leaders and Weyerhaeuser family members remain wealthy beyond belief and their charitable contributions guarantee that the "W" will never fade from Northwesterners' minds. Contrast that with the fate of the tens of thousands of working-class families in lumber country devastated by Weyerhaueser's—and other companies'—shutdowns. Even the once-powerful IWA, the "one union in wood," declined and ultimately evaporated before the end of the twentieth century; its membership joining the International Association of Machinists and Aerospace Workers as the Woodworking Department.

Despite the business attacks on labor—of both the blackjacks and briefcases varieties—Grays Harbor remained fertile (if not Red) union territory throughout much of the twentieth century, as workers affiliated with the IWA, ILWU, Association of Western Pulp and Paper Workers, and several other unions won relatively humane wages and benefits from their employers.[19] In fact, before the permanent recession hit lumber country during the 1980s (turning lumber country into a green and gray rust belt outpost), unionists could turn thousands of people out for a Labor Day parade or solidarity rally for striking workers. It was little wonder that Harry Bridges, a Communist, founder of the ILWU, and onetime Wobbly, liked to say, "Aberdeen feels like home to me."[20]

ACKNOWLEDGMENTS

This book has been a part of my life for a long time. It began as my doctoral work at Simon Fraser University, where I benefited from the guidance and camaraderie of a group of labor-left scholars whose good works could fill the bed of a medium-sized 1990s pickup truck. It took me well over a decade to weave the dissertation into this final form, and I've racked up a load of debts along the way. Since finishing my doctorate, I was hired as a history professor, earned tenure, was elected department chair, helped form a faculty union (destroyed by bosses), and was then purged for my workplace and political activism. I want to thank all my former coworkers for struggling to secure faculty governance and workers' rights in the face of united managerial opposition.

But the biggest delay in finishing this book has been my need to include the voices of Finnish American workers who made up such a large part of the Pacific Northwest's labor-left during the early twentieth century—but whose words, bizarrely, remain missing from nearly all studies on the subject. To begin filling this massive hole, my family and I twice moved to Finland to locate and translate the sources necessary to better understand the Pacific Northwest's labor and working-class history. As such, I owe some of my biggest debts to the Finland Fulbright Commission and the Department of History and Ethnology at the University of Jyväskylä, who hosted me for a year as a Fulbright Scholar at their impressive research institution. Thanks as well to the Institute of Advanced Social Research at Finland's University of Tampere, where I worked as a senior researcher for two years. The coworkers, peers, and friends I met in Finland are as responsible as anyone for this book's completion. It is no stretch to say that this book would have never been completed without the help of my Finnish colleagues—especially the brilliant historian Matti Roitto.

I wish to thank the staffs of the following archival institutions: The University of Washington's Labor Archives; the Walter Reuther Library at Wayne State University; the Washington State Archives in Olympia and the Southwest Regional Branch of the Washington State Archives in Olympia; John Larson and Scott Lucas of the Polson Museum in Hoquiam; the Finnish American Historical Archive in Hancock, Michigan; the Migration Institute of Finland and the Department of European and World History at the University of Turku, Finland; the Butte–Silver Bow Public Archives in Montana; the Jones Photo Historical Collection in Aberdeen; and the Washington State Library in Olympia. These institutions hold tremendous collections of materials, and the staffs at all of them are first-rate. And a bittersweet note of gratitude to the Aberdeen Museum of History, where I conducted some of the primary research for this book before it tragically burned to the ground in 2018; fortunately, I photographed hundreds of working-class history documents before the fire robbed them from posterity.

It's difficult to express just how much of a big deal it is for me to work with an institution as impressive as the University of Washington Press. The thrill of it all has only increased the past few years as UW Press workers unionized with SEIU Local 925 and won their first contract, allowing me to publish a labor history book with a labor union publisher. It's unfortunate that there are so few unionized academic presses in the United States, but up in the country's far northwest corner UW Press is providing a shining illustration of what's possible in unionized academic publishing. Much gratitude goes to everyone at that fine institution. I need to single out Mike Baccam, the editor who guided me through this lengthy, hurdle-filled process and whose solid support kept me moving forward in the face of some difficult conditions. And a big thank-you to Andrew Berzanskis for guiding me through my previous book and to Catherine Cocks, who first contacted me about working with UW Press.

I've amassed some debts these past decades, and many of the manuscript's improvements came from the good advice of other scholars. Thanks especially to Roger Snider, Brian Barnes, Jerry Lembcke, Helena

Hirvonen, Keri Graham, Heather Mayer, Pertti Ahonen, Todd Goings, Erika Naficy, Aaron Jesch, Betsy Pingree, Sarah Fox, Rex Casillas, David H. Price, Yunchen Tian, Peter Cole, Jeremy Milloy, Gary Kaunonen, Brandon Anderson, Cal Winslow, Laurie Mercier, Jeffrey St. Clair, Chris Henry, Amanda Swarr, Jess Bever, Heather Grob, and John Hughes. Many on this list advised me on drafts of the manuscript, edited portions of it, helped me locate resources, and otherwise inspired my work. I owe a special debt of gratitude to my graduate advisors Karen Blair, Betsy Jameson, and Mark Leier, for their years of generosity, kindness, and intellectual guidance. My work has benefited tremendously from historians—notably Rosemary Feurer and Chad Pearson—whose studies of bosses and employers' organizations have helped to invigorate the study of American social relations and class conflict. To Lauren Love, granddaughter of incomparable Jennie "the real rebel girl" Sipo, thank you for sharing your family's history.

Thank you as well to my new coworkers at Peninsula College who have welcomed me with open arms. I'm fortunate to be in our union.

This book is for my wonderful family. They have supported me at every step along the way. To my aunts and uncles, brothers and cousins, in-laws and nephews—thank you for your sweetness, generosity, and good humor. And the biggest thank-you goes to Jessica Sheinbaum, who has been the best part of these past twenty years.

NOTES

COLLECTIONS

AHM	Aberdeen Historical Museum, Aberdeen, Washington
	Aberdeen History Collection
	Pacific Northwest History Collection
	RGHL-IWA—Records of the Grays Harbor Locals of the International Woodworkers of America
ATL	Aberdeen Timberland Library Special Collections, Aberdeen, Washington
	Aberdeen: Before 1920
	Aberdeen Historical Records
	City of Cosmopolis Papers
NARA	National Archives and Records Administration, Pacific Alaska Region, Seattle, Washington
RTsKhIDNI	Russian Center for the Preservation and Study of Documents of Recent History, Tamiment Library, New York University, New York
USBC	United States Bureau of the Census
UW	University of Washington Libraries Special Collections, Seattle
	Bob Reed Papers
	EGA Papers—Edwin Gardner Ames Papers
	IWW Papers—Industrial Workers of the World Papers
	John Caughlan Papers
	Merrill and Ring Papers: Merrill and Ring Lumber Company Papers
	WSFL Records—Washington State Federation of Labor Records
WDGSR	War Department General Staff Records, Military Intelligence Division, Plant Protection, Portland District
WSA	Washington State Archives, Olympia, Washington, http://digitalarchives.wa.gov.

Gov. Lister, State Secret Service—Governor Ernest Lister, State Secret Service, Correspondence Files, 1917–21

Governor Ernest Lister Papers

Governor Roland Hartley Papers

SRB-WSA—Southwest Regional Branch, Washington State Archives, Olympia, Washington

Laura Law Records

Washington State Governor's Papers

WSU Walter Reuther Library, Wayne State University, Detroit, Michigan

IWW Collection—Industrial Workers of the World Collection

INTRODUCTION

1. Fred Lockley, "Grays Harbor: The Largest Lumber-Shipping Port in the World," *Pacific Monthly* 17, no. 6 (June 1907): 721. The "lumber capital of the world" slogan had its roots in a chamber of commerce publicity campaign, with local business marketing the region's achievement as the first port to ship a billion board feet of lumber. See *Washingtonian*, December 27, 1924. The *Washingtonian* newspaper, published in Hoquiam for several decades, changed the first part of its name on several occasions while always retaining *Washingtonian*. Filed in 1907, articles of incorporation for the "Grays Harbor Washingtonian" relate to the company that published the *Washingtonian*, though the paper changed its name from *Hoquiam Washingtonian* to *Grays Harbor Washingtonian* to *Daily Washingtonian*. To avoid confusion, I refer to this newspaper exclusively by *Washingtonian* throughout this book. See Articles of Incorporation of the Grays Harbor Washingtonian, March 25, 1907, Grays Harbor County Auditor, Articles of Incorporation, box 5, acc. 99-SW-245, file 402, Southwest Regional Branch, Washington State Archives, Olympia (hereafter SRB-WSA).

2. Contrast the destruction of so much labor history with the celebration of elites whose names grace public schools, parks, and streets. Employers' history—or at least their names—it seems, are what should be remembered: more than a dozen local employers many of them having committed or supported horrific acts of violence, are immortalized on signs across Grays Harbor.

3. Bryan Palmer, *A Culture in Conflict: Skilled Workers and Industrial Capitalism in Hamilton, Ontario, 1860–1914* (Montreal: McGill-Queen's University Press, 1979), xvi. See also Palmer, *Working-Class Experience: Rethinking the History of Canadian Labour, 1800–1991* (Toronto: McClelland and Stewart, 1992).

4. The seminal study of everyday forms of working-class consciousness and activism is E. P. Thompson's *The Making of the English Working Class* (New York: Vintage Books, 1966).

5. *Industrial Worker*, October 4, 1919; Ralph Chaplin, *Wobbly: The Rough-and-Tumble Story of an American Radical* (Chicago: University of Chicago Press, 1948), 291.

6. "Financial Statement of the General Defense Committee for the Month of December 1923," *General Office Bulletin for the Month of January 1923* 23, Industrial Workers of the World Collection, box 31, folder 8, Walter Reuther Library, Wayne State University, Detroit, Michigan (hereafter IWW Collection, WSU); "Financial Statement of the General Defense Committee for the Month of December, 1924," *General Office Bulletin* 25, IWW Collection, box 31, folder 31, WSU; "Financial Statement of the General Defense Committee for the Month of December, 1923," *General Office Bulletin* 19, IWW Collection, box 31, folder 19, WSU. Notably, Fred Hendricks, a resident of Aberdeen, donated $225 to the General Defense Committee on December 18, 1923. See "Financial Statement of the General Defense Committee for the Month of December, 1923," *General Office Bulletin* 19, IWW Collection, box 31, folder 19, WSU; Receipts, Publicity, Defense, and Jail Relief Records, 6, 14, 22, 46, 52, 58, 118, 134, 136, 186, 198, 200, 201, 206, 220, 242, 250, 264, IWW Collection, box 134, WSU; *Industrialisti*, November 10, 1919.

7. *Solidarity* (Chicago), July 31, 1915.

8. Charter, Aberdeen Branch of Industrial Union 460, Industrial Workers of the World Papers, October 26, 1923, box 17, folder 4, IWW Collection, WSU.

9. *Industrial Worker*, June 24, 1922.

10. Lauren Love, "Jennie Sipo Heikkila Timeline" (unpublished manuscript, n.d.), typescript, in author's possession. Robert Benson and Jennie Sipo, Certificate of Marriage, November 3, 1924, Clark County Auditor, Marriage Records, 1843–Present, Washington State Archives, Digital Archives, http://digitalarchives.wa.gov, accessed January 22, 2024; United States Bureau of the Census, *Fifteenth Census of the United States Taken in the Year 1930*, Washington State, Chehalis County, Aberdeen; Aaron Goings, Brian Barnes, and Roger Snider, *The Red Coast: Radicalism and Anti-Radicalism in Southwest Washington* (Corvallis: Oregon State University Press, 2019), 131–45.

11. The main standout exception is the excellent work of Heather Mayer, *Beyond the Rebel Girl: Women and the Industrial Workers of the World in the Pacific Northwest, 1905–1924* (Corvallis: Oregon State University Press, 2018).

12. Elizabeth Jameson, *All That Glitters: Class, Conflict, and Community in Cripple Creek* (Urbana: University of Illinois Press, 1998).

13. *Seattle Post-Intelligencer*, January 1, 1890.

14. *Grays Harbor Post*, September 5, 1908; *R. L. Polk and Company's Grays Harbor Cities Directory*, 1912, 523–24.

15. United States Forest Service, Pacific Northwest Region, *Draft Environmental Statement, Satsop Block Planning Unit Land Management Plan* (Portland, OR: US Forest Service, 1978), 1.

16. Erik Loomis, *Empire of Timber: Labor Unions and the Pacific Northwest Forests* (Cambridge, UK: Cambridge University Press, 2016); Jerry Lembcke and William M. Tattam, *One Union in Wood: A Political History of the International Woodworkers of America* (New York: International Publishers, 1984).

17. Robin D. G. Kelley, *Hammer and Hoe: Alabama Communists During the Great Depression* (Chapel Hill: University of North Carolina Press, 1990), 1.

18. For similar analyses, see Jameson, *All that Glitters*; Kim Moody, *Tramps and Trade Union Travelers: Internal Migration and Organized Labor in Gilded Age America, 1870–1900* (Chicago: Haymarket Books, 2019).

19. This book follow historian Chad Pearson's *Capital's Terrorists: Klansmen, Lawmen, and Employers in the Long Nineteenth Century* (Chapel Hill: University of North Carolina Press, 2022), which in his words "explores the relationships between management and repression, highlighting the ways that numerous powerful individuals and employers . . . used violence against ordinary people to achieve their managerial and societal goals" (p. 2).

20. Cited in Nell Irvin Painter, *The History of White People* (New York: W. W. Norton, 2010), 304.

21. Eric Hobsbawm, *The Age of Capital, 1848–1875* (London: Weidenfield and Nicolson, 1975), 255–56, 288–91.

22. Cited in Robert E. Ficken, *Washington State: The Inaugural Decade, 1889–1899* (Pullman: Washington State University Press, 2007), 171.

23. Rosemary Feurer, *Radical Unionism in the Midwest, 1900–1950* (Urbana: University of Illinois Press, 2006), xiii.

24. Studies on Finns in the Northwest include Paul George Hummasti, *Finnish Radicals in Astoria, Oregon: A Study in Immigrant Socialism, 1904–1940* (New York: Arno Press, 1979); and Peter T. Alter's article "The Creation of a Multi-Ethnic Peoplehood: The Wilkeson, Washington Experience," *Journal of American Ethnic History* 15, no. 3 (Spring 1996): 3–21.

25. Joyce L. Kornbluh, ed., "Preamble of the Industrial Workers of the World," in *Rebel Voices: An IWW Anthology*, new and expanded ed. (Chicago: Charles H. Kerr Publishing Co., 1998), 12–13.

26. On the syndicalism of the IWW, see Salvatore Salerno, *Red November, Black November: Culture and Community in the Industrial Workers of the World* (Albany: State University of New York Press, 1989); Peter Cole, David Struthers, and Kenyon Zimmer, eds., *Wobblies of the World: A Global History of the IWW* (London: Pluto Press, 2017); Mark Leier, *Where the Fraser River Flows: The IWW in British Columbia* (Vancouver, BC: New Star Books, 1990).

27. Daniel Rosenberg, "The IWW and Organization of Asian Workers in Early Twentieth Century America," *Labor History* 36, no. 1 (1995): 77–78.

28. Robert Conlin, "Introduction," in *At the Point of Production: The Local History of the IWW*, edited by Joseph Robert Conlin (Westport, CT: Greenwood Press, 1981), 24. For a useful analysis of the cultural and ideological diversity within the IWW, see Salerno, *Red November, Black November*.

29. Two fine exceptions are Kornel Chang's book *Pacific Connections: The Making of the U.S.-Canadian Borderlands* (Berkeley: University of California Press, 2012); and Maia Ramnath, *Haj to Utopia: How the Ghadar Movement Charted Global Radicalism and Attempted to Overthrow the British Empire* (Berkeley: University of California Press, 2011). See also Tariq Khan, "Living Social Dynamite: Early Twentieth-Century IWW–South Asian Connections," in *Wobblies of the World*, edited by Cole, Struthers, and Zimmer, 59–73.

30. Cole, Struthers, and Zimmer, *Wobblies of the World*, 1.

31. On the primary role of repression in IWW history, see Ahmed White, *Under the Iron Heel: The Wobblies and the Capitalist War on Radical Workers* (Berkeley: University of California Press, 2022).

32. Chaplin, *Wobbly*, 298.

33. Auvo Kostiainen, "For or Against Americanization? The Case of the Finnish Immigrant Radicals," in *American Labor and Immigration History: 1877–1920s: Recent European Research*, edited by Dirk Hoerder, 259–75 (Urbana: University of Illinois Press, 1983). See also Fraser M. Ottanelli, *The Communist Party of the United States* (New Brunswick, NJ: Rutgers University Press, 1991), 23–55; James Barrett, *William Z. Foster and the Tragedy of American Radicalism* (Urbana: University of Illinois Press, 1999), 167–71.

1 LUMBER EMPIRE

1. It's unclear when Brown first arrived in Grays Harbor, but by January 1902 he had already moved to Aberdeen and taken up a leadership position in that city's shingle weavers' union. *Shingle Weaver*, January 1902, March 1904; US Commission on Industrial Relations, *Industrial Relations, Final Report and Testimony, submitted to Congress by the Commission on Industrial Relations, created by the Act of August 23, 1912* (Washington, DC: Government Printing Office, 1916), 4272.

2. *Aberdeen Herald*, December 10, 1903.

3. *Shingle Weaver*, June, August 1907; US Commission on Industrial Relations, *Industrial Relations: Final Report*, 4207.

4. *Shingle Weaver*, February 1904; "How a Western City Grows: Hoquiam, Washington," *The Coast* 5, no. 6 (June 1903), 213. In 1904, the Hoquiam Lumber and Shingle Company cut 150 million shingles, approximately twice as many as the next largest shingle operation on the harbor. *Hoquiam Sawyer*, December 31, 1904; *Grays Harbor*

Post, May 13, 1911; *Washingtonian*, December 20, 1914; William Farrand Prosser, *A History of the Puget Sound Country: Its Resources, Its Commerce and Its People*, vol. 2 (New York: Lewis Publishing Co., 1903), 429; Edwin Van Syckle, *They Tried to Cut It All: Grays Harbor . . . Turbulent Years of Greed and Greatness* (Seattle: Pacific Search Press, 1980), 120–21, 264; John D. "Bus" Fairbairn, "Fairbairn's Guide to History of Logging in Chehalis-Grays Harbor County Since 1882," Pacific Northwest History Collection, Aberdeen Historical Museum, Aberdeen, Wash. (hereafter AHM), 35; Articles of Incorporation of the Lytle Logging and Mercantile Company, April 21, 1899, box 2, acc. 99-SW-245, file 146, SRB-WSA.

5. *Pacific Lumber Trade Journal*, January 1907, 61; *Grays Harbor Post*, May 26, 1906; "In Southwestern Washington: Where Lumbering and Agriculture Go Hand-in-Hand," *The Coast* 12, no. 1 (July 1906): 18–26.

6. Erik Loomis, *Empire of Timber: Labor Unions and the Pacific Northwest Forests* (Cambridge, UK: Cambridge University Press, 2016).

7. Michael Goldfield, *The Southern Key: Class, Race, and Radicalism in the 1930s and 1940s* (Oxford: Oxford University Press, 2020), 180–84.

8. Ronald L. Olson, "The Quinault Indians," *University of Washington Publications in Anthropology* 6 (November 1936): 66–86; Jacqueline M. Storm and Pauline K. Capoeman, *Land of the Quinault* (Taholah, WA: Quinault Indian Nation, 1990).

9. James Swan, *The Northwest Coast; Or, Three Years' Residence in Washington Territory* (New York: Harper and Brothers Publishers, 1857), 397.

10. As quoted in Chang, *Pacific Connections*, 21.

11. *Washington Standard* (Olympia), August 19, 1865; Edwin Van Syckle, *The River Pioneers: Early Days on Grays Harbor* (Seattle: Pacific Search Press, 1982), 84, 88, 98.

12. Jacilee Wray, ed., *Native Peoples of the Olympic Peninsula* (Norman: University of Oklahoma Press, 2002), 108.

13. Cited in Alexandra Harmon, *Reclaiming the Reservation: Histories of Indian Sovereignty Suppressed and Renewed* (Seattle: University of Washington Press, 2019), 77.

14. *Washington Standard* (Olympia), August 19, 1865.

15. *Pioneer and Democrat* (Olympia), December 7, 1860.

16. United States Bureau of the Census (hereafter USBC), 1860 Census, Chehalis County, Territory of Washington; Thomas W. Prosch, "The United States Army in Washington Territory," *Washington Historical Quarterly* 2, no. 1 (1907): 31.

17. W. P. Bonney, "Captain Maloney at Fort Chehalis," *Washington Historical Quarterly* 20, no. 3 (1929): 190–91.

18. "How a Western City Grows," 210.

19. Storm and Capoeman, *Land of the Quinault*; Andrew Parnaby, *Citizen Docker: Making a New Deal on the Vancouver Waterfront, 1919–1939* (Toronto: University of Toronto Press, 2008), 75–99.

20. Port Gamble S'Klallam Tribe, *The Strong People: A History of the Port Gamble S'Klallam Tribe* (Port Gamble: Port Gamble S'Klallam Tribe, 2012), 79; Elizabeth Pingree, "The Footloose Labor System: Work and Migration in the Pacific Northwest, 1850–1940." (PhD diss., Boston College, 2023), 19–33.

21. Harmon, *Reclaiming the Reservation*, 77.

22. Peter J. Replinger, *The Schafer Brothers: Pioneer Loggers of the Satsop Valley* (Centralia, WA: Gorham Printing, 2018), 1.

23. *Washington Standard* (Olympia), January 18, 1862.

24. Robert E. Ficken, *The Forested Land: A History of Lumbering in Western Washington* (Seattle: University of Washington Press, 1987), 58.

25. Thomas R. Cox, *Mills and Markets: A History of the Pacific Coast Lumber Industry to 1900* (Seattle: University of Washington Press, 1974), 191–92; Cloice R. Howd, "Industrial Relations in the West Coast Lumber Industry," *Bulletin of the United States Bureau of Labor Statistics*, no. 349 (Washington, DC: Government Printing Office, 1924), 15.

26. Howd, "Industrial Relations," 14–16; Chang, *Pacific Connections*, 20–21.

27. Howd, "Industrial Relations," 14–16; Chang, *Pacific Connections*, 20–21; Henry Gannett, *Census Bulletin, Manufactures: The Lumber Industry*, no. 203 (Washington, DC: n.p., 1902), 66. See also Ficken, *Forested Land.*

28. Cited in Cox, *Mills and Markets*, 164.

29. Ficken, *Forested Land*; Cox, *Mills and Markets*, 191–92.

30. Ficken, *Forested Land*, 57–58.

31. Edwin Gardner Jones, ed., *The Oregonian's Handbook of the Pacific Northwest* (Portland: Oregonian Publishing Co., 1894), 326.

32. Robert Weinstein, *Grays Harbor, 1885–1913* (New York: Penguin Books, 1978), 22; cited in Jennifer Ott, "Samuel and Martha Benn Trade Their Homestead for Reuben Redman's Land at the Mouth of the Wishkah River, Future Site of Aberdeen, on March 13, 1868," https://www.historylink.org/File/9261, accessed June 11, 2024.

33. Van Syckle, *They Tried to Cut It All*, 220.

34. Van Syckle, *They Tried to Cut It All*, 219–20.

35. Van Syckle, *River Pioneers*, 24.

36. "How a Western City Grows," 24; Van Syckle, *They Tried to Cut It All*, 26; Herbert Hunt and F. C. Kaylor, *Washington, West of the Cascades: Historical and Descriptive; the Explorers, the Indians, the Pioneers, the Modern* (Seattle: S. J. Clarke Publishing Co., 1917), 92.

37. Van Syckle, *River Pioneers*, 368; Van Syckle, *They Tried to Cut It All*, 23–24.

38. Weinstein, *Grays Harbor, 1885–1913*, 23; *Aberdeen Herald*, December 23, 1890.

39. *Aberdeen Herald*, October 23, 30, 1890; "Aberdeen! On Grays Harbor: The Duluth of Washington," Aberdeen: Before 1920, Aberdeen Timberland Library Special Collections, Aberdeen, Wash. (hereafter ATL).

40. "How a Western City Grows," 24;

41. Ficken, *Forested Land*, 100.

42. *Washingtonian*, January 1, 8, May 28, June 18, 25, July 23, 1891; Weinstein, *Grays Harbor, 1885–1913*, 18–19. The *Washingtonian* newspaper changed its name on several occasions, always retaining "*Washingtonian*": established as the *Hoquiam Washingtonian* in 1907, the paper changed its name to *Grays Harbor Washingtonian*, then *Daily Washingtonian*. To avoid confusion, I refer to this newspaper exclusively by the name "*Washingtonian*" throughout this book.

43. Weinstein, *Grays Harbor: 1885–1913*, 18.

44. Van Syckle, *River Pioneers*, 250–62; *Washingtonian*, January 25, 1927.

45. US Bureau of Labor Statistics, *Bulletin of the U.S. Bureau of Labor Statistics, No. 550: Cargo Handling and Longshore Labor Conditions* (Washington, DC: US Bureau of Labor Statistics, 1932), 48.

46. Bruce Nelson, *Workers on the Waterfront: Seamen, Longshoremen, and Unionism in the 1930s* (Urbana: University of Illinois Press, 1990), 62.

47. *Aberdeen Daily Bulletin*, June 9, 1906.

48. *Seattle Post-Intelligencer*, April 24, 1896; Articles of Incorporation of the North Western Lumber Company, January 29, 1902, box 3, acc. 99-SW-245, file 197, SRB-WSA.

49. "How a Western City Grows"; Wallace J. Miller, *South-western Washington, Its Topography, Climate, Resources, Productions, Manufacturing Advantages, Wealth, and Growth, with Illustrated Reviews of the Principal Cities and Towns, and Pen Sketches of their Representative Business Men* (Olympia: Pacific Publishing Co., 1890), 185–98; *Washingtonian*, January 25, 1927, 6; George Emerson, "Lumbering on Grays Harbor," *Grays Harbor Post*, October 5, 1907.

50. W. F. Allen, *The Official Northern Pacific Railway Guide* (St. Paul, MN: W. C. Riley, 1899), 388–89; Van Syckle, *River Pioneers*, 207–8; Weinstein, *Grays Harbor*, 24.

51. Van Syckle, *River Pioneers*, 209–10.

52. Weinstein, *Grays Harbor, 1885–1913*, 24.

53. Cited in Stewart Holbrook, *A Narrative of Schafer Bros. Logging Company's Half Century in the Timber* (Seattle: Dogwood Press, 1945), 30. For similar quotations, see "A Typical Lumbering City: Aberdeen, Washington," *The Coast* 6, no. 1 (July 1903): 6.

54. "Managers' report to the Directors of the North Western Lumber Company," 1902, Emerson Letterbooks, University of Washington Libraries Special Collections, Seattle (hereafter UW).

55. *Grays Harbor News*, April 19, 1884.

56. *Aberdeen Daily Bulletin*, January 9, 1906.

57. Weinstein, *Grays Harbor, 1885–1913*, 20; Van Syckle, *They Tried to Cut It All*, 45–47.

58. Weinstein, *Grays Harbor, 1885–1913*, 20; Van Syckle, *They Tried to Cut It All*, 45–47.

59. J. A. Robertson, "Cosmopolis in 1908," City of Cosmopolis Papers, ATL; *Grays Harbor Post*, July 24, 1909; *Grays Harbor Post*, January 14, 1905.

60. *Grays Harbor Post*, May 6, 1905.

61. *Grays Harbor Post*, November 10, 1906.

62. *Grays Harbor Post*, August 13, 1904; "Death Summons C. F. White, One of Pacific Coast's Great Lumbermen," *West Coast Lumbermen*, May 1, 1917, 26.

63. *Grays Harbor Post*, July 16, 1904; April 21, 1906; May 20, 1909.

64. *Shingle Weaver*, April 21, 1917; Robertson, "Cosmopolis in 1908," City of Cosmopolis Papers, ATL.

65. Van Syckle, *They Tried to Cut It All*, n.p.; US Commission on Industrial Relations, *Industrial Relations: Final Report . . . 1912*, 4278.

66. *Washingtonian*, May 28, June 18, 25, July 23, 1891; *Aberdeen Herald*, October 23, 1890.

67. Hunt and Kaylor, *Washington, West of the Cascades*, vol. 3, 334; US Commission on Industrial Relations, *Industrial Relations: Final Report . . . 1912*, 4272.

68. *Seattle Post-Intelligencer*, May 8, 1891.

69. Weinstein, *Grays Harbor, 1885–1913*, 20; Van Syckle, *They Tried to Cut It All*, 45–47.

70. Ficken, *Forested Land*, 122.

71. *Aberdeen Herald*, January 27, 1908.

72. Emily M. Wilson, *From Boats to Board Feet: The Wilson Family of the Pacific Coast* (Seattle: Wilson Brothers Family Foundation, 2007), 118–19, 134, 146; *Aberdeen Herald*, October 29, 1906; August 30, 1909.

73. US Commission on Industrial Relations, *Industrial Relations: Final Report . . . 1912*, 4284.

74. Stephen H. Norwood, "The Student as Strikebreaker: College Youth and the Crisis of Masculinity in the Early Twentieth Century," *Journal of Social History* 28, no. 2 (Winter 1994): 332, 336.

75. Cited in Ficken, *The Forested Land*, 80. Emerson's hostility toward working people can be seen in Ficken's book, which includes several of Emerson's quotations.

76. Ficken, *The Forested Land*, 135. Ficken's wording was "moved with alacrity to 'destroy,' as George Emerson put it, 'the caterpillars before they breed.'"

77. Richard Rajala, *Clearcutting the Rainforest: Production, Science, and Regulation* (Vancouver: University of British Columbia Press, 1998), 7–30; Loomis, *Empire of Timber*, 20–22.

78. USBC, *Thirteenth Census of the United States Taken in the Year 1910* (hereafter *Thirteenth Census . . . 1910*), Washington State, Chehalis County, City of Aberdeen.

79. Replinger, *Schafer Brothers*. For simplicity, throughout the book, I refer to the Schafer family enterprises as Schafer Brothers Logging Company or simply Schafer Brothers.

80. Richard Rajala, "The Forest as Factory: Technological Change and Worker Control in the West Coast Logging Industry, 1880–1930," *Labour/Le Travail* 32, 73–104.

81. These figures were drawn from Fairbairn, "Fairbairn's Guide to History of Logging in Chehalis-Grays Harbor County." The actual number of logging firms founded during the 1890s is no doubt greater than that reported by Fairbairn because few sources are available for that decade.

82. "Population Statistics of the Pacific Coast," *Whitakers Review and Handbook of the Pacific Coast* 3, no. 1 (November 1912): 37.

83. Michael A. Bellesiles, *1877: America's Year of Living Violently* (New York: New Press, 2010), 114.

84. Frank Tobias Higbie, *Indispensable Outcasts: Hobo Workers and Community in the American Midwest, 1880–1930* (Urbana: University of Illinois Press, 2003).

85. Stephen H. Norwood, *Strikebreaking and Intimidation: Mercenaries and Masculinity in Twentieth-Century America* (Chapel Hill: University of North Carolina Press, 2001), 8.

86. Bellesiles, *1877*, 111.

87. Washington Territorial Legislative Assembly, *Laws of the Territory of Washington, Enacted by the Legislative Assembly in the Year A.D. 1875* (Olympia, WA: C. B. Bagley, Public Printer, 1875), 89–90. The territorial vagrancy law remained in force during Washington's statehood. See Richard Achilles Ballinger, *Ballinger's Annotated Codes and Statutes of Washington* (Seattle: Bancroft-Whitney Co., 1897), 1863.

88. *Aberdeen Daily Bulletin*, April 13, 1906.

89. *Aberdeen Daily Bulletin*, April 11, 1906.

90. City of Hoquiam, Police Record, 1905–1915, SRB-WSA. Hoquiam's main newspaper, the *Washingtonian*, reported an even greater number of vagrancy arrests for the year 1913. It reported that "out of 786 arrests 501 of them were vagrants of the inoffensive type who were taken from the streets late at night and given a place of shelter from the inclement fall and winter weather." *Washingtonian*, January 7, 1914.

91. *Washingtonian*, March 7, 1914.

92. J. A. Robertson, "Cosmopolis in 1908," City of Cosmopolis Papers, ATL. Robertson, a printer living in Aberdeen, estimated in "Cosmopolis in 1908" that 4,380 men had been shipped to Cosmopolis in 1907. That doesn't consider those who traveled into Aberdeen or Hoquiam first.

93. *Aberdeen Herald*, March 25, May 20, 1907.

94. *Aberdeen Herald*, January 23, 1913,

95. *Grays Harbor Post*, December 10, 1904; May 25, 1907.

96. Elma Brandt, Report for the Polson Museum Nationality Study, Grays Harbor Immigrant Archives, Polson Museum, Hoquiam, Wash.

97. Don F. Smith, "Poland," in *Chehalis County Nationality Survey, 1848–1915*, edited by Joe Randich and Dorothea Parker (Olympia: Washington Commission for the

Humanities, 1984); *Grays Harbor Post*, February 6, 1909; *Aberdeen Herald*, April 9, 1908; *Aberdeen Daily World*, August 8, 1912. See also John Bukowczyk, *And My Children Did Not Know Me: A History of the Polish Americans* (Bloomington: Indiana University Press, 1987).

98. On the Arciezewski family, see Certificate of Marriage, Charles Arciezewski and Paulina Kuklinski, November 13, 1913, Grays Harbor County Auditor, Marriage Records, 1871–Present, Washington State Archives, Digital Archives, http://digital archives.wa.gov, accessed June 8, 2024; USBC, Census for the Year, 1920, Aberdeen, Grays Harbor County, State of Washington; International Woodworkers of America, membership cards for Charlie and Edmont Archie, in author's possession. These are among the thousands of records I photographed at the Aberdeen History Museum before it burned down.

99. Pingree, "Footloose Labor System," 74.

100. Egbert S. Oliver, "Sawmilling on Grays Harbor: A Personal Reminiscence," *Pacific Northwest Quarterly* 69, no. 1 (January 1978): 1–18.

101. State of Washington, Bureau of Labor, *Fourth Biennial Report of the Bureau of Labor of the State of Washington, 1903–1904* (Olympia, WA: Blankenship Satterlee Co., 1904), 251; US Commission on Industrial Relations, *Industrial Relations: Final Report, 1912*, 4753–56.

102. *Grays Harbor Post*, August 13, 27, 1904.

103. Philip S. Foner, *The History of the Labor Movement in the United States*, vol. 4, *The Industrial Workers of the World, 1905–1917* (1965; reprint, New York: International Publishers, 1978), 178.

104. Cal Winslow, *Radical Seattle: The General Strike of 1919* (New York: Monthly Review Press, 2020), 79–81; Heather Mayer, *Beyond the Rebel Girl: Women and the Industrial Workers of the World in the Pacific Northwest, 1905–1924* (Corvallis: Oregon State University Press, 2018).

105. State of Washington, Bureau of Labor, *Fourth Biennial Report . . . 1903–1904*, 217–42.

106. *Aberdeen Daily World*, March 13, 1909.

107. "Population Statistics of the Pacific Coast," *Whitakers Review and Handbook of the Pacific Coast* 3, no. 1 (November 1912): 37.

108. USBC, *Thirteenth Census . . . 1910*; Department of Commerce and Labor, Bureau of the Census, *Population by Counties and Minor Civil Divisions, 1890, 1900, 1910* (Washington, DC: Government Printing Office, 1912), 546; Supplement for Washington State, 603–4.

109. Grays Harbor County Territorial Auditor, *Grays Harbor County Census, 1889*, Washington State Archives, Digital Archives, http://digitalarchives.wa.gov, accessed April 3, 2021.

110. Grays Harbor County Auditor, *Grays Harbor County Census, 1894*, Washington State Archives, Digital Archives, http://digitalarchives.wa.gov, accessed April 3, 2021.

111. Ella Johansson, "Men Without Bosses: Encounters with Modernity in the Logging Camps of Northern Sweden, 1860–1940," in *Sustainability, the Challenge: Power, People, and the Environment*, edited by L. Anders Sandberg and Sverker Sorlin (Montreal: Black Rose Books, 1998), 141. Johansson estimates that there were between 150,000 and 200,000 loggers in Sweden each year during the 1910s.

112. *Aberdeen Herald*, November 23, 1893; March 22, 1894.

113. *Aberdeen Herald*, June 26, 1905.

114. *Grays Harbor Post*, May 27, 1905; April 14, 1906; *Aberdeen Daily Bulletin*, June 17, 1905.

115. USBC, *Thirteenth Census . . . 1910*, Junction City; State of Washington, Bureau of Labor, *Ninth Biennial Report of the Bureau of Labor Statistics and Factory Inspection, 1913–1914* (Olympia: Public Printer, 1914), 272.

116. *Aberdeen Herald*, August 26, 1909. In his book *Pacific Connections*, Kornel Chang details a similar conflict when South Asian workers refused to work for a Finnish foreman and later "struck the Finnish foreman with a piece of lumber." Police arrested the assailants (p. 115).

117. *Washingtonian*, April 6, 1912.

118. *Aberdeen Herald*, May 26, 1892.

119. *Aberdeen Herald*, November 1, 1900.

120. *Aberdeen Daily World*, July 5, 1924.

121. *Aberdeen Herald*, February 26, 1891.

122. *Aberdeen World*, January 21, 1909.

123. Chang, *Pacific Connections*, 20–21.

124. *Seattle Post-Intelligencer*, May 13, 1892.

125. Grays Harbor County Territorial Auditor, *Grays Harbor County Census, 1889*.

126. J. S. Carlson, "The Asians," in *Chehalis County Nationality Survey, 1848–1915*, edited by Joe Randich and Dorothea Parker (Olympia: Washington Commission for the Humanities, 1984).

127. On the Seattle and Tacoma expulsions, see John C. Putman, *Class and Gender Politics in Progressive-Era Seattle* (Reno: University of Nevada Press, 2008), 19–20; Carlos Schwantes, *Radical Heritage: Labor, Socialism, and Reform in Washington and British Columbia, 1885–1917* (1979; reprint, Moscow: University of Idaho Press, 1994), 24–26. For a history of the Aberdeen expulsion, see Aaron Goings, Brian Barnes, and Roger Snider, *The Red Coast: Radicalism and Anti-Radicalism in Southwest Washington* (Corvallis: Oregon State University Press, 2019), 25–33; *Aberdeen Herald*, October 12, 1903.

128. Van Syckle, *River Pioneers*, 379; *Daily Morning Astorian*, September 18, 1890; *Seattle Post-Intelligencer*, September 18, 21, 25, November 12, 1890.

129. *Aberdeen Herald*, October 30, November 13, 27, 1890.

130. *Aberdeen Herald*, November 13, 1890; December 19, 1902; October 12, 1903; May 12, 1904; October 4, 1909.

131. *Seattle Post-Intelligencer*, August 16, 1891.

132. *Aberdeen Herald*, October 12, 1903.

133. *Aberdeen Herald*, May 24, 1910.

134. USBC, *Thirteenth Census . . . 1910*.

135. *Aberdeen Herald*, March 26, 1893, November 19, 1894.

136. *Aberdeen Herald*, March 23, 1893.

137. Carlson, "The Asians"; USBC, *Thirteenth Census . . . 1910*.

2 THE "HOUSE OF LABOR"

1. Philip S. Foner, *The History of the Labor Movement in the United States*, vol. 3, *The Policies and Practices of the American Federation of Labor, 1900–1909* (New York: International Printers, 4th printing, 1981), 32–54.

2. See Michael Kazin and Stephen J. Ross, "America's Labor Day: The Dilemma of a Workers' Celebration," *Journal of American History* 78, no. 4 (March 1992): 1294–1323.

3. *Shingle Weaver* (Ballard, Wash.), October 1906.

4. Washington State Federation of Labor (hereafter WSFL), *Proceedings of the Fourth Annual Convention of the Washington State Federation of Labor, 1906*, Aberdeen, WA; *Aberdeen Herald*, January 8, 1906.

5. *Spokane Press*, January 10, 1906.

6. David Montgomery, *The Fall of the House of Labor: The Workplace, the State, and American Labor Activism, 1865–1925* (New Haven, CT: Yale University Press, 1987), 5.

7. WSFL, *Proceedings of the Third Annual Convention of the Washington State Federation of Labor, 1905*, Everett, Wash., 12, 27; *Aberdeen Herald*, July 18, September 5, October 24, 1901; May 12, 19, August 25, 1902.

8. *Grays Harbor Post*, May 3, 1905; January 20, September 15, 1906; May 4, 1907, March 21, August 22, 1908.

9. *Grays Harbor Post*, May 4, 1905; June 15, 1907; *Aberdeen Daily Bulletin*, March 19, 1904.

10. In April 1904, Hoquiam had 782 union members in good standing. *Grays Harbor Post*, April 2, 1904; May 27, 1905. See "Aberdeen, Washington," *The Coast* 13, no. 5 (May 1907): 298.

11. WSFL, *Proceedings of the Third Annual Convention*, 27.

12. *Grays Harbor Post*, May 29, 1909.

13. *Shingle Weaver*, October 1905.

14. State of Washington, Bureau of Labor, *Seventh Biennial Report of the Bureau*

of Labor Statistics and Factory Inspection, 1909–1910 (Olympia: C. W. Gorham, Public Printer, 1908), 80.

15. Elwood R. Maunder and Harold M. Stilson, *Western Red Cedar: The Shingle Weaver's Story: An Interview with Harold M. Stilson Sr.* (Santa Cruz, CA: Forest History Society, 1975), 10.

16. Bruce Rogers, "The War of Gray's [*sic*] Harbor," *International Socialist Review* 12 (May 1912): 749–53.

17. James Rowan, *The IWW in the Lumber Industry* (Seattle: Lumber Workers Industrial Union No. 500, 1919), 3.

18. Eric Hobsbawm, *Workers: Worlds of Labor* (London: Pantheon Books, 1984), 214–26; Mark Leier, *Red Flags and Red Tape: The Making of a Labor Bureaucracy* (Toronto: University of Toronto Press, 1995), 102–8.

19. Jonathan Dembo, *Unions and Politics in Washington State, 1885–1935* (New York: Garland Press, 1982), 625.

20. John Higham, *Strangers in the Land: Patterns of American Nativism, 1860–1925* (New Brunswick, NJ: Rutgers University Press, 1955), 163–66; Dana Frank, *Purchasing Power: Consumer Organizing, Gender, and the Seattle Labor Movement, 1919–1945* (Cambridge, UK: Cambridge University Press, 1994), 8–10, 20, 30–32.

21. See Shirley Tillotson, "'We May All Soon Be First-Class Men': Gender and Skill in Canada's Early Twentieth Century Urban Telegraph Industry," *Labour/Le Travail* 27 (Spring 1991): 97–125.

22. Leier, *Red Flags and Red Tape*, 132–33; Anne Phillips and Barbara Taylor, "Sex and Skill: Notes toward a Feminist Economics," *Feminist Review* 6 (1980): 79–88; James Green, *The World of the Worker: Labor in Twentieth-Century America* (1980; reprint, Urbana: University of Illinois Press, 1998), 67–99; Ella Johansson, "Men Without Bosses: Encounters with Modernity in the Logging Camps of Northern Sweden, 1860–1940," in *Sustainability, the Challenge: Power, People, and the Environment*, edited by L. Anders Sandberg and Sverker Sorlin, 141 (Montreal: Black Rose Books, 1998).

23. *Aberdeen Herald*, January 5, March 2, 1893.

24. Carlos A. Schwantes, *Radical Heritage: Labor, Socialism, and Reform in Washington and British Columbia, 1885–1917* (1979; reprint, Moscow: University of Idaho Press, 1994), 23–26; Art Chin, *Golden Tassels: A History of the Chinese in Washington State, 1857–1977* (Seattle: self-pub., 1977), 58.

25. Nell Irvin Painter, *Standing at Armageddon: The United States, 1885–1917* (New York: W. W. Norton, 1987), 95.

26. Jonathan Garlock, *Guide to the Local Assemblies of the Knights of Labor* (Westport, CT: Greenwood Press, 1982), 528.

27. *Aberdeen Herald*, December 29, 1892.

28. *Aberdeen Herald*, January 5, 1893.

29. *Aberdeen Herald*, February 23, 1893.

30. *Weekly Recorder* (Aberdeen, Wash.), June 1, 1894.

31. Cited in Robert E. Ficken, *Washington State: The Inaugural Decade, 1889–1899* (Pullman: Washington State University Press, 2007), 171.

32. *Weekly Recorder*, June 8, 1894.

33. See Cloice R. Howd, "Industrial Relations in the West Coast Lumber Industry," *Bulletin of the United States Bureau of Labor Statistics*, no. 349 (Washington, DC: Government Printing Office, 1924), 57; Vernon Jensen, *Lumber and Labor* (New York: Arno Press, 1971; first published 1945 by J. J. Little and Ives Co., New York), 119.

34. *Grays Harbor Post*, April 24, May 14, 1904.

35. *Grays Harbor Post*, July 23, 1904.

36. Norman S. Hayner, "Taming the Lumberjacks," *American Sociological Review* 10, no. 2 (April 1945): 217–25.

37. *Grays Harbor Post*, May 7, 14, 1904.

38. *Grays Harbor Post*, May 14, July 23, 1904.

39. *Grays Harbor Post*, May 14, 1904.

40. US Commission on Industrial Relations, *Industrial Relations: Final Report and Testimony, submitted to Congress by the Commission on Industrial Relations, created by the Act of August 23, 1912* (Washington, D C: Government Printing Office, 1916), 4220.

41. *Shingle Weaver*, June 1905; Foner, *History of the Labor Movement*, vol. 4, *The Industrial Workers of the World, 1905–1917* (1965; reprint, New York: International Publishers, 1978), 218; Murray Morgan, *The Last Wilderness* (Seattle: University of Washington Press, 1955), 140–41; Charlotte Todes, *Lumber and Labor* (New York: International Publishers, 1931), 152–61; Jensen, *Lumber and Labor*, 117–19; *Four L Bulletin* (January 1922): 21. For background on Northwest shingle weavers, see Aaron Goings, Brian Barnes, and Roger Snider, *The Red Coast: Radicalism and Anti-Radicalism in Southwest Washington* (Corvallis: Oregon State University Press, 2019), ch. 11.

42. *Shingle Weaver*, January 1903.

43. Jensen, *Lumber and Labor*, 122; Norman Clark, *Mill Town: A Social History of Everett, Washington, from Its Earliest Beginnings on the Shores of Puget Sound to the Tragic and Infamous Event Known as the Everett Massacre* (Seattle: University of Washington Press, 1970; 5th printing 1990), 91.

44. Clark, *Mill Town*, 91–93.

45. *Shingle Weaver*, October 1904.

46. This poem, entitled "Why the Shingle Weavers Struck," by J. E. Elliot, was originally printed in the *Shingle Weaver* and reprinted in the *Grays Harbor Post* August 11, 1906.

47. *Hoquiam Sawyer*, April 8, 22, 1905.

48. *Washingtonian*, February 6, 1902; July 14, 1904; *Shingle Weaver*, February, March,

April, May, July 1904; July, October 1905; June, July, August, September 1906; *Grays Harbor Post*, April 16, 1905; February 3, 17, 1906; *Aberdeen Daily Bulletin*, February 5, 1906. See also Aaron Goings, "Hoquiam Shingle Weavers," Essay 8629, *History Link*, October 21, 2008, http://www.historylink.org/index.cfm?DisplayPage=output.cfm &file_id=8629.

49. On this strike see State of Washington, Bureau of Labor, *Fifth Biennial Report of the Bureau of Labor Statistics and Factory Inspection*, 1905–1906 (Olympia: C. W. Gorham, Public Printer, 1906), 177; *Hoquiam Sawyer*, April 15, 1905; *Aberdeen Daily Bulletin*, April 11, 1905; *Grays Harbor Post*, April 15, 29, 1905; *Shingle Weaver*, April, May, June 1905.

50. *Shingle Weaver*, May 1905.

51. *Grays Harbor Post*, 3, 17 February 1906; *Shingle Weaver*, May 1905.

52. *Shingle Weaver*, June 1905; *Grays Harbor Post*, April 29, 1905.

53. Richard William Judd, *Socialist Cities: Municipal Politics and the Grass Roots of American Socialism* (Albany: State University of New York Press, 1989), 57.

54. "A Remarkable Growth," *Appeal to Reason*, November 16, 1901.

55. Jeffrey Johnson, *They Are All Red Out Here* (Norman: University of Oklahoma Press, 2014), 51–52.

56. The platform of the Socialist Party of Washington, 1912, can be found in Jeffrey Johnson, *They Are All Red*, 171–74.

57. *Grays Harbor Post*, December 1, 8, 1906. The Hoquiam Working Men's League did endorse two victorious candidates, L. C. Houser for city treasurer and Z. T. Wilson for city clerk.

58. *Shingle Weaver*, April 1907.

59. *Shingle Weaver*, March 1904.

60. President Taft earned zero votes from the Raymond weavers. See *Shingle Weaver*, October 26, 1912.

61. *Aberdeen Daily World*, March 7, 1913.

62. An excellent analysis of the attitudes of the AFL toward organizing women can be found in Alice Kessler Harris, *Out to Work: A History of Wage-Earning Women in the United States* (Oxford, UK: Oxford University Press, 1982), 152–71. See also Philip S. Foner, *Women and the American Labor Movement: From the First Trade Unions to the Present* (New York: Free Press, 1979), 98–119.

63. *Shingle Weaver*, February 1903, January 1904, December 1906.

64. *Shingle Weaver*, April 1904.

65. *Shingle Weaver*, December 1907.

66. *Shingle Weaver*, August 1904. On trade union leaders' anti-immigrant views, see also *Grays Harbor Post*, February 8, 15, 1908; January 8, 15, 1910.

67. *Shingle Weaver*, May 1904.

68. *Grays Harbor Post*, September 7, 1907.

69. For a fine study of diverse forms of working-class masculinity, see Stephen Meyer, *Manhood on the Line: Working-Class Masculinities in the American Heartland* (Urbana: University of Illinois Press, 2016), 2.

70. *Shingle Weaver*, September 1907; *Grays Harbor Post*, May 9, 30, 1908.

71. US Commission on Industrial Relations, *Industrial Relations: Final Report . . . 1912*, 4214.

72. *Aberdeen Herald*, January 23, 1902.

73. *Aberdeen Herald*, December 6, 1906; May 4, 1908; August 19, 1909; March 9, August 17, 1911; *The Lumber World*, October 15, 1907, 16.

74. For discussions of Ingram's work and management of the shingle industry, see *Shingle Weaver*, August 1907; *Aberdeen Herald*, November 17, 1904; July 27, 1905; February 15, 1908; February 13, 1909; July 4, 1910; USBC, *Thirteenth Census of the United States Taken in the Year 1910*, Washington State, Chehalis County, Cities of Aberdeen and Hoquiam.

75. According to the 1910 US Census, forty-four out of the eighty-one Hoquiam shingle weavers were married. USBC, *Thirteenth Census . . . 1910*, City of Hoquiam.

76. Brown was listed as an elected union official in the first shingle weavers' local in Aberdeen during January 1902. *Shingle Weaver*, November 1905.

77. USBC, *Thirteenth Census . . . 1910*, City of Hoquiam; *R. L. Polk and Company's Grays Harbor Cities Directory*, 1907; *Shingle Weaver*, January, April 1903; January, February, May, August, September 1904; March, June, July, August, November 1905; March, April, May, June, August, September, October, November 1906. According to the 1910 census for the city of Hoquiam, eighty-two men listed "shingle weaver" as their occupation or "shingle mill" as their industry.

78. *Shingle Weaver*, November 1906.

79. Nate Holdren, *Injury Impoverished: Workplace Accidents, Capitalism, and Law in the Progressive Era*, (Cambridge, UK: Cambridge University Press, 2020), 1.

80. J. Tripp, "An Instance of Labor and Business Cooperation: Workmen's Compensation in Washington State (1911)," *Labor History* (1976): 531–50.

81. US Commission on Industrial Relations, *Industrial Relations: Final Report . . . 1912*, 4211.

82. Tripp, "An Instance of Labor and Business Cooperation."

83. Maxwell Wilson, interview by Donald L. Myers, November 26, 1975, Washington State Oral/Aural History Project, Washington State Division of Archives and Records Management, Olympia, 22.

84. A detailed list of labor laws for the State of Washington can be found in State of Washington, Bureau of Labor, *Labor Laws of the State of Washington* (Olympia: Public Printer, 1907).

85. Historian Alan Derickson lists the number of American workers killed in industrial accidents between 1930 and 1970 as 1,578,176 in "Down Solid: The Origins and Development of the Black Lung Insurgency," *Journal of Public Health Policy* 4, no. 1 (March 1983): 26. See also Stephen H. Norwood, *Strikebreaking and Intimidation: Mercenaries and Masculinity in Twentieth-Century America* (Chapel Hill: University of North Carolina Press, 2001); Louis Adamic, *Dynamite! A Century of Class Violence in America, 1830–1930* (London: Rebel Press, 1984); Richard O. Boyer and Herbert M. Morais, *Labor's Untold Story: The Adventure Story of the Battles, Betrayals, and Victories of American Working Men and Women*, 3rd ed. (New York: United Electrical, Radio, and Machine Workers of America, 1979).

86. US Commission on Industrial Relations, *Industrial Relations: Final Report . . . 1912*, 4218.

87. Cited in the *Grays Harbor Post*, November 3, 1906.

88. *Grays Harbor Post*, November 3, 1906. See also *Grays Harbor Post*, August 17, 31, October 5, 1907; July 24, August 7, October 2, 1909.

89. Andrew M. Prouty, *"More Deadly Than War!" Pacific Coast Logging, 1827–1981* (Seattle: University of Washington Press, 1985), xvii-xix, 143, 190–95; Todes, *Lumber and Labor*, 137. The statistic for five times as many deaths comes from Robert E. Ficken, *The Forested Land: A History of Lumbering in Western Washington* (Seattle: University of Washington Press, 1987), 132.

90. *Aberdeen Daily World*, December 19, 1904.

91. Todes, *Labor and Lumber*, 135.

92. *Washingtonian*, April 3, 1913.

93. *Washingtonian*, March 1, 1914.

94. *Industrial Worker*, September 2, 1916.

95. Prouty, *"More Deadly Than War!"* 143, 190–95; *Aberdeen Daily Bulletin*, September 16, 1905.

96. Cited in Erik Loomis, *Empire of Timber: Labor Unions and the Pacific Northwest Forests* (Cambridge, UK: Cambridge University Press, 2015), 10–11.

97. On cedar asthma, see Loomis, *Empire of Timber*, 138–47; Morgan, *Last Wilderness*, 140; Todes, *Labor and Lumber*, 137–138; State of Washington, Bureau of Labor, *Eleventh Biennial Report of the Bureau of Labor Statistics and Factory Inspection, 1917–1918* (Olympia: Public Printer, 1918), 50–54.

98. *Daily Worker*, March 18, 1927.

99. *Shingle Weaver*, July, August 1907.

100. State of Washington, Bureau of Labor, *Eleventh Biennial Report . . . 1917–1918* , 51–54.

101. Archie Green, *Wobblies, Pile Butts, and Other Heroes: Laborlore Explorations*

(Urbana: University of Illinois Press, 1993); Sean Burns, *Archie Green: The Making of a Working-Class Hero* (Urbana: University of Illinois Press, 2011).

102. Walker Smith, *The Everett Massacre* (Chicago: Industrial Workers of the World, 1917), 27; *Shingle Weaver*, August 25, 1917.

103. *Shingle Weaver*, October 13, 1917.

104. *Shingle Weaver*, April 21, 1917. See also International Union of Timberworkers, *Proceedings of the Third Annual Convention of the International Union of Timberworkers* (Spokane, WA: Trade Printery, 1920).

105. *American Lumberman*, May 28, 1904, 52.

106. *Shingle Weaver*, June 16, 1917.

107. *Shingle Weaver*, June 16, September 29, 1917.

108. Norwood, *Strikebreaking and Intimidation*, 99, 171, 175.

109. For local examples of violent treatment against scabs, see *Aberdeen Herald*, October 24, 1901; in the Justice's Court City of Aberdeen Precinct, August 30, 1906, *State of Washington v. William Gohl*, no. 6499, SRB-WSA; *Aberdeen Daily Bulletin*, July 12, August 25, 1906.

110. *Aberdeen Herald*, October 31, 1901; *Aberdeen Daily Bulletin*, August 22, September 18, 19, 1906.

111. *Shingle Weaver*, August 1906; September 21, November 9, 1912.

112. *Shingle Weaver*, September, October 1906.

113. *Shingle Weaver*, September 29, 1917.

114. *Shingle Weaver*, March 17, April 14, September 15, 22, October 13, 1917.

115. *Shingle Weaver*, April 14, 28, May 19, June 16, 23, 30, July 7, 1917; "Si Gotchy," *BoxRec*, https://boxrec.com/en/box-pro/146555, accessed May 29, 2024.

116. Ralph Warren Andrews, *This Was Sawmilling* (Seattle: Superior Publishing Co., 1957), 134; *Washingtonian*, July 2, 4, 1916.

117. *Shingle Weaver*, September 22, 1917.

118. *Shingle Weaver*, April 7, 14, 1917.

119. *Shingle Weaver*, July 15, 1916.

120. *Shingle Weaver*, October 26, 1912.

121. Although *Grays Harbor Post* started as a union periodical, Clarke's politics and priorities shifted so that by the 1910s the weekly paper resembled mainstream newspapers.

122. *Labor Journal*, June 12, 1914.

123. US Commission on Industrial Relations, *Industrial Relations: Final Report . . . 1912*, 4378–79.

124. *Grays Harbor Post*, December 10, 1904. In an irony apparently lost on its editor, the masthead for the *Post* included the words "no discrimination."

125. *Grays Harbor Post*, December 10, 1904.

126. *Aberdeen Daily World*, April 5, 1915; May 4, 1933; Articles of Incorporation for the Croatian Workingman's Company, March 4, 1910, Grays Harbor County Auditor, Articles of Incorporation, box 7, acc. 99-SW-245, file 561, SRB-WSA; Joe Randich and Dorothea Parker, eds., *Chehalis County Nationality Survey, 1848–1915* (Olympia: Washington Commission for the Humanities, 1984); *Aberdeen Herald*, August 4, 1910; October 12, 1911; July 7, 1914; July 4, 1915.

127. *Grays Harbor Post*, December 10, 1904.

128. Peggy Pascoe, "Race, Gender, and Intercultural Relations: The Case of Interracial Marriage," *Frontiers: A Journal of Women's Studies* 12 (1991): 5–17; Paul C. P. Siu, *The Chinese Laundryman: A Study of Social Isolation* (New York: New York University Press, 1987).

129. *Aberdeen Herald*, September 21, 1908.

130. *Grays Harbor Post*, December 10, 1904.

131. *Grays Harbor Post*, December 10, 1904.

132. *Grays Harbor Post*, May 25, 1907.

133. *Shingle Weaver*, June 1904.

134. *Grays Harbor Post*, April 16, 1904; *Shingle Weaver*, June, July, September, November 1904; Elizabeth Jameson, *All that Glitters: Class, Conflict, and Community in Cripple Creek* (Urbana: University of Illinois Press, 1998); Mark Wyman, *Hard Rock Epic: Western Miners and the Industrial Revolution* (Berkeley: University of California Press, 1989).

135. *Shingle Weaver*, May 1904.

136. *Shingle Weaver*, April 1904.

137. *Shingle Weaver*, March 1904, June 1905.

138. *Shingle Weaver*, June 1905.

139. *Shingle Weaver*, April, June, July, September 1905. Brown's opponents referred to him as a "n——" for his advocacy of industrial unionism.

140. *Shingle Weaver*, June 1905.

141. See Alexander Saxton, *The Rise and Fall of the Great White Republic* (London: Verso Press, 1990), 312–16.

142. *Shingle Weaver*, September 1906.

143. For a close study of the 1906 maritime strike, see Aaron Goings, *The Port of Missing Men: Billy Gohl, Labor, and Brutal Times in the Pacific Northwest* (Seattle: University of Washington Press, 2020), 77–94.

144. *Shingle Weaver*, October 1905; July, September 1907; February, April 1908.

145. *Shingle Weaver*, May 1905.

146. *Shingle Weaver*, October 1906.

3 "AS ONE MAN"

1. *Grays Harbor Post*, May 7, August 20, September 3, 1904; May 3, 1905; January 20, August 4, 11, 18, 25, 1906; August 31, 1907; March 21, September 5, 1908. WSFL, *Proceedings of the Third Annual Convention of the Washington State Federation of Labor, 1905* (Everett, Wash.), 12, 27; *Proceedings of the Fourth Annual Convention of the Washington State Federation of Labor*, 1906 (Aberdeen, Wash.), 12.

2. Vilja Hulden, *The Bosses' Union: How Employers Organized to Fight Labor Before the New Deal* (Urbana: University of Illinois Press, 2023).

3. US Commission on Industrial Relations, *Industrial Relations: Final Report and Testimony, submitted to Congress by the Commission on Industrial Relations, created by the Act of August 23, 1912* (Washington, DC: Government Printing Office, 1916), 4221.

4. *Aberdeen Herald*, September 1, 1902.

5. *Grays Harbor Post*, December 2, 1905.

6. Rosemary Feurer and Chad Pearson, eds., *Against Labor: How U.S. Employers Organized to Defeat Union Activism* (Urbana: University of Illinois Press, 2017), 6–7.

7. Chad E. Pearson, *Capital's Terrorists: Klansmen, Lawmen, and Employers in the Long Nineteenth Century* (Chapel Hill: University of North Carolina Press, 2022), 18.

8. On "cut-throat struggle," see Charlotte Todes, *Lumber and Labor* (New York: International Publishers, 1931), 31; Robert E. Ficken, *Lumber and Politics: The Career of Mark E. Reed* (Seattle: University of Washington Press, 1980). On "cutthroat competition," see Cloice R. Howd, "Industrial Relations in the West Coast Lumber Industry," *Bulletin of the United States Bureau of Labor Statistics*, no. 349 (Washington, DC: Government Printing Office, 1924), 27.

9. *Grays Harbor Post*, April 6, 1907.

10. Robert E. Ficken, *The Forested Land: A History of Lumbering in Western Washington* (Seattle: University of Washington Press, 1987), 85.

11. *Aberdeen Herald*, October 11, 1894; March 7, June 6, 1895.

12. *Aberdeen Herald*, February, 18, 1892.

13. *Seattle Post-Intelligencer*, October 8, 1896.

14. *Aberdeen Herald*, March 17, 31, April 14, 1892; January 4, 11, June 21, December 27, 1894.

15. Articles of Incorporation for the Grays Harbor Loggers' Association, February 29, 1904, Grays Harbor County Auditor, Articles of Incorporation, box 4, acc. 99-SW-245, no. 272, SRB-WSA; *Aberdeen Daily Bulletin*, March 26, 1904; Interstate Red Cedar Shingle Association: *Aberdeen Daily Bulletin*, January 16, 1904; May 14, 1906. Quote from *Aberdeen Daily Bulletin*, March 26, 1904; June 14, 1905; Charles Pierce Lewarne, "The Aberdeen, Washington, Free Speech Fight," *Pacific Northwest Quarterly* 66 (January 1975): 9; W. W. Sheppard to Mr. Louis Titus, December 15, 1923, Edwin Garner

Ames Papers, acc. no. 3820, box 120, folder 15, UW; Pacific Coast Lumber Manufacturers' Association, *Annual Reports of President and Secretary of the Pacific Coast Lumber Manufacturers' Association at the Annual Meeting at Seattle, Wash., December 8, 1903* (Seattle: Office of Secretary, Lumber Exchange, 1903), 3–7.

16. For example, see Articles of Incorporation for the Grays Harbor Loggers' Association; Articles of Incorporation of the American Mill Company, December 17, 1898, Grays Harbor Auditor, Articles of Incorporation, box 2, acc. 99-SW-245, no. 142, SRB-WSA; *Washingtonian*, March 7, 1895.

17. *Aberdeen Daily Bulletin*, May 9, 1904; May 9, 1906; *Grays Harbor Post*, December 2, 1905; *Washingtonian*, July 4, 1906.

18. *Aberdeen Herald*, January 4, 1904.

19. Thorpe Babcock, "Cooney: Ship's Carpenter to Millionaire," *Aberdeen Daily World*, December 17, 1970.

20. Edwin Van Syckle, *They Tried to Cut It All: Grays Harbor . . . Turbulent Years of Greed and Greatness* (Seattle: Pacific Search Press, 1980), 30, 47; Robert Weinstein, *Grays Harbor, 1885–1913* (New York: Penguin Books, 1978), 23–24; *Aberdeen Daily World*, January 14, February 2, 14, 1909; March 9, 10, 1910; *R. L. Polk and Company's Grays Harbor Cities and Chehalis County Directory*, 1908, 69; *Grays Harbor Post*, September 3, 10, 1906; *Pacific Lumber Trade Journal*, January 1907, 61; James H. DeVeuve to Everett G. Griggs, September 11, 1918, Record Group 165, box 4, file 721a, War Department General Staff Records, Military Intelligence Division, Plant Protection, Portland District (hereafter WDGSR), National Archives and Records Administration, Pacific Alaska Region, Seattle, Wash. (hereafter NARA); *American Lumberman*, April 28, 1906.

21. Herbert Hunt and F. C. Kaylor, *Washington, West of the Cascades: Historical and Descriptive; the Explorers, the Indians, the Pioneers, the Modern* (Seattle: S. J. Clarke Publishing Co., 1917), 63–65; Richard Sterling, *Aloha Lumber Company, Aloha, Wash., 1906–2006* (Olympia: Aloha Lumber Corp., Publishers, 2007), 37.

22. *Grays Harbor Post*, June 16, 1906; John C. Hughes and Ryan Teague Beckwith, eds., *On the Harbor: From Black Friday to Nirvana* (Aberdeen, WA: Daily World, 2001), 77.

23. Lewarne, "Aberdeen, Washington Free Speech Fight," 8. See also Hughes and Beckwith, eds., *On the Harbor*, 10.

24. See Mary Ann Clawson, *Constructing Brotherhood: Class, Gender, and Fraternalism* (Princeton, NJ: Princeton University Press, 1989).

25. *Aberdeen Daily World*, June 30, 1908; Van Syckle, *They Tried to Cut It All*, 225–26.

26. *Aberdeen Daily Bulletin*, March 26, 1904; Articles of Incorporation of the Grays Harbor Loggers' Association, February 29, 1904, Grays Harbor County Auditor, Articles of Incorporation, box 4, no. 272, SWA; Frank H. Lamb, *Rotary: A Businessman's Interpretation* (Hoquiam, WA: Rotary Club of Hoquiam, 1927), 79. See also Frank H.

Lamb, *Fifty Years in Hoquiam: Memoirs of Frank H. Lamb* (n.p., 1948); Hunt and Kaylor, *Washington, West of the Cascades*, 151.

27. Farrar Newberry, "The Concatenated Order of Hoo Hoo," *Arkansas Historical Quarterly* 22, no. 4 (Winter 1963): 305.

28. "Harmony Conspicuous in Twenty-First Anniversary of Hoo-Hoo Order," *Pacific Lumber Trade Journal* 18, no. 9 (January 1913): 47; Newberry, "Concatenated Order," 303.

29. *Grays Harbor Post*, August 29, 1908; May 29, 1909; *Aberdeen Daily World*, April 17, 25, 1913.

30. *Aberdeen Herald*, April 25, 1913; *Washingtonian*, April 26, 1913.

31. *Aberdeen Herald*, July 20, 1905; *Aberdeen Daily Bulletin*, July 24, 1905; *Aberdeen Daily World*, June 1, 1909; November 25, 1911.

32. US Commission on Industrial Relations, *Industrial Relations: Final Report . . . 1912*, 4276.

33. US Commission on Industrial Relations, *Industrial Relations: Final Report . . . 1912*, 4278.

34. Cited in Todes, *Labor and Lumber*, 34–35.

35. US Commission on Industrial Relations, *Industrial Relations: Final Report . . . 1912*, 4292.

36. US Commission on Industrial Relations, *Industrial Relations: Final Report . . . 1912*, 4294.

37. Elwood R. Maunder, *A Forester's Log: Fifty Years in the Pacific Northwest*, an interview with George L. Drake in four sessions, 1958, 1961, 1967, 1968 (Durham, NC: Forest History Society, 2004), https://foresthistory.org/wp-content/uploads/2016/12/Drake-George.pdf, 10.

38. Cited in Ficken, *Forested Land*, 133.

39. *Shingle Weaver*, May 1905.

40. *Aberdeen Herald*, April 13, 1905; *Aberdeen Daily World*, July 22, 1908; *Grays Harbor Post*, March 4, 1905; *Aberdeen Daily Bulletin*, September 24, 1904; February 28, 1905; *Aberdeen Daily World*, October 13, 1911.

41. The *Aberdeen Herald*, June 8, 1893, referred to a group of "forty or fifty dagos" working in the area.

42. State of Washington, Bureau of Labor, *Ninth Biennial Report of the Bureau of Labor Statistics and Factory Inspection, 1913–1914* (Olympia: Public Printer, 1914), 50.

43. State of Washington, Bureau of Labor, *Third Biennial Report of the Bureau of Labor Statistics and Factory Inspection, 1901–1902* (Olympia: Blankenship Saterlee Co., 1904), 71.

44. State of Washington, Bureau of Labor, *Ninth Biennial Report . . . 1913–1914*, 34–35.

45. Robert Higgs, "Race, Skills, and Earnings: American Immigrants in 1909," *Journal of Economic History* 31, no. 2 (June 1971): 420–25.

46. *Hoquiam Sawyer*, May 12, 1905.

47. Philip J. Dreyfus, "Timber Workers, Unionism and Syndicalism in the Pacific Northwest, 1900–1917" (PhD diss., Graduate School of the City University of New York, 1993), 128–42.

48. *Seattle Times*, March 30, 1912. See also *Aberdeen Herald*, March 18, April 1, 1912.

49. *Pacific Lumber Trade Journal*, April 1912, 24.

50. Cited in Ficken, *Forested Land*, 136.

51. Craig Scharlin and Lilia Villanueva, *Philip Vera Cruz: A Personal History of Filipino Immigrants and the Farmworkers Movement* (Seattle: University of Washington Press, 2011), 64.

52. Peter J. Replinger, *The Schafer Brothers: Pioneer Loggers of the Satsop Valley* (Centralia, WA: Gorham Printing, 2018), 176.

53. Replinger, *Schafer Brothers*, 169.

54. *Grays Harbor Post*, December 2, 1905.

55. *Hoquiam Sawyer*, May 12, 1905; *Grays Harbor Post*, December 17, 1904.

56. *Grays Harbor Post*, February 15, 1908.

57. *Aberdeen Herald*, October 28, 1912.

58. Sterling, *Aloha Lumber Company*, 192–93.

59. Babcock, "Cooney."

60. Article from *Puget Sound Lumberman* reprinted in *Aberdeen Herald*, March 1, 1894.

61. Weinstein, *Grays Harbor, 1885–1913*, 19.

62. *Grays Harbor Post*, October 5, 1907; *Shingle Weaver*, April 21, 1917.

63. *Shingle Weaver*, November 1905.

64. *Grays Harbor Post*, April 7, 1906; US Commission on Industrial Relations, 4278.

65. *Grays Harbor Post*, August 13, 1904; November 10, 1906. On C. F. White, see "Death Summons C. F. White, One of Pacific Coast's Great Lumbermen," *West Coast Lumbermen*, May 1, 1917, 26.

66. Melvyn Dubofsky, *We Shall Be All: A History of the Industrial Workers of the World* (Chicago: Quadrangle Books, 1969, 1973), 128–30; Philip S. Foner, *The History of the Labor Movement in the United States*, vol. 4 (1965; reprint, New York: International Publishers, 1978), 219–27; "The IWW and the Limits of Inter-Ethnic Organizing: Reds, Whites, and Greeks in Grays Harbor, Washington, 1912," *Labor History* 38 (Fall 1997): 450–71.

67. *Grays Harbor Post*, April 14, 1906.

68. Rosemary Feurer, *Radical Unionism in the Midwest, 1900–1950* (Urbana: University of Illinois Press, 2006), 1.

69. *Grays Harbor Post*, May 29, 1909; "A. L. Paine Accepts Presidency," *West Coast Lumberman*, February 1917, 21.

70. Hughes and Beckwith, eds., *On the Harbor*, 77.

71. Edwin Van Syckle, *The River Pioneers: Early Days on Grays Harbor* (Seattle: Pacific Search Press, 1982), 293; Hughes and Beckwith, *On the Harbor*, 76–77.

72. Articles of Incorporation for the Aberdeen Savings and Loan Association, box 5, acc. 99-SW-245, file 423, SRB-WSA; *R. L. Polk and Company's Grays Harbor Cities Directory, 1913*, 118; Hunt and Kaylor, *Washington, West of the Cascades*, 69–70; *Grays Harbor Post*, June 17, 1911. "Mr. Aberdeen" comes from Ben K. Weatherwax, "Hometown Scrapbook—No. 71—The Wobblies," radio script for KBKW, Aberdeen, recorded October 27, 1953, Aberdeen Historical Records, ATL.

73. Chad Pearson, "'Free Shops for Free Men?' The Challenges of Strikebreaking and Union-Busting in the Progressive Era," in *Against Labor: How U.S. Employers Organized to Defeat Union Activism*, edited by Rosemary Feurer and Chad Pearson, 51–77 (Urbana: University of Illinois Press, 2017). On citizens' alliances, see Pearson, *Capital's Terrorists*, 9–11, 144–83.

74. Aaron Goings, *The Port of Missing Men: Billy Gohl, Labor, and Brutal Times in the Pacific Northwest* (Seattle: University of Washington Press, 2020).

75. *Aberdeen Daily World*, February 5, 1909; *Grays Harbor Post*, March 26, 1910; *Aberdeen Herald*, May 3, 1910.

76. *Grays Harbor Post*, May 13, 1911; *Washingtonian*, December 20, 1914.

77. William Farrand Prosser, *A History of the Puget Sound Country: Its Resources, Its Commerce and Its People*, vol. 2 (New York: Lewis Publishing Co., 1903), 429; *Shingle Weaver*, November 1905; Van Syckle, *They Tried to Cut It All*, 120–21, 264; John D. "Bus" Fairbairn, "Fairbairn's Guide to History of Logging in Chehalis–Grays Harbor County Since 1882," Pacific Northwest History Collection, AHM, 35; Articles of Incorporation of the Lytle Logging and Mercantile Company, April 21, 1899, box 2, acc. 99-SW-245, file 146, SRB-WSA; "How a Western City Grows: Hoquiam, Washington," *The Coast* 5, no. 6 (June 1903): 206–19.

78. *Pacific Lumber Trade Journal*, January 1907, 61; *Grays Harbor Post*, May 26, 1906; "In Southwestern Washington: Where Lumbering and Agriculture Go Hand-in-Hand," *The Coast* 12, no. 1 (July 1906): 18–26.

79. *Shingle Weaver*, March 1906; *Grays Harbor Post*, February 3, 17, 1906. This strike closely followed one waged by piecework packers and knot sawyers at the Hoquiam Lumber and Shingle Company. In October 1905, these laborers struck to protest the poor quality of lumber being used by the mill. The Hoquiam branch of the ISWUA

demanded either an increased wage scale to compensate for the discrepancy or a blanket $3.50 daily wage. See State of Washington, Bureau of Labor, *Fifth Biennial Report of the Bureau of Labor Statistics and Factory Inspection, 1905–1906* (Olympia: C. W. Gorham, Public Printer, 1906), 194; *Hoquiam Sawyer*, October 13, 1905.

80. *Grays Harbor Post*, February 3, 17, 1906; *Aberdeen Daily Bulletin*, February 5, 1906. According to the State of Washington, Bureau of Labor, *Fifth Biennial Report . . . 1905–1906*, Hoquiam Local 21 engaged in three strikes between January 1, 1905, and August 1, 1906.

81. *Washingtonian*, August 2, 1906.

82. *Washingtonian*, February 1, 1906; John H. Cox, "Trade Associations in the Lumber Industry of the Pacific Northwest," *Pacific Northwest Quarterly* 41, no. 4 (October 1950): 288–89.

83. *Pacific Lumber Trade Journal*, September 1910, 21; Cox, "Trade Associations," 288; *Washingtonian*, February 1, 1906; *The Timberman* 11, no. 11 (September 1910): 38; *Industrial Worker*, December 14, 1911; *Shingle Weaver*, September 1906.

84. William Millikan, *A Union Against Unions: The Minneapolis Citizens Alliance and Its Fight Against Organized Labor, 1903–1947* (St. Paul: Minnesota Historical Society Press, 2001).

85. *Aberdeen Herald*, May 14, August 20, October 11, December 17, 1906.

86. *Seattle Union Record*, June 23, 1906; *Ballard News*, June 22, 1906; *Grays Harbor Post*, August 11, 1906.

87. *Seattle Union Record*, June 16, 1906. Cited in Dreyfus, "Timber Workers," 97.

88. *Seattle Times*, June 18, 1906.

89. Dreyfus, "Timber Workers," 94–98.

90. Howd, "Industrial Relations," 56; Dreyfus, "Timber Workers," 102; *Seattle Times*, July 18, 20, 1906.

91. *Shingle Weaver*, June 1906; *Ballard News*, June 22, July 27, 1906; Stephen H. Norwood, *Strikebreaking and Intimidation: Mercenaries and Masculinity in Twentieth-Century America* (Chapel Hill: University of North Carolina Press, 2001).

92. *Ballard News*, June 22, July 20, 27, 1906; *Seattle Times*, June 11, 18, 19, July 18, 20, 1906.

93. As of July 24, forty-two mills, representing about 6 percent of the state's output of shingles, had signed the shingle weavers' union agreement. Four of these mills, which were all small firms, were in Grays Harbor County. *Washingtonian*, July 24, 1906.

94. *Aberdeen Daily Bulletin*, August 21, 1906.

95. On July 11, 1906, Grays Harbor shingle mill owners met in Elma and declared that once operations at their mills resumed, "it will be under the policy of the open shop." *Grays Harbor Post*, September 8, 1906; *Aberdeen Daily Bulletin*, July 12, September 5, 1906.

96. Dreyfus, "Timber Workers," 104; *Ballard News*, July 20, 1906; *Shingle Weaver*, July 1907.

97. *Washingtonian*, August 2, 1906.

98. *Grays Harbor Post*, September 8, 1906.

99. See Goings, *The Port of Missing Men*.

100. *Aberdeen Herald*, April 1, 4, May 20, 1912; *Grays Harbor Post*, June 22, November 16, 1912; *Industrial Worker*, February 1, 1912; *Aberdeen Daily World*, March 21, May 17, 18, 1912.

101. On the power exerted by lumbermen in the Washington State Legislature, see *Aberdeen Daily Bulletin*, November 14, 1904; Ficken, *Lumber and Politics*. See Hunt and Kaylor, *Washington, West of the Cascades*, 130–31, 393–95, 476.

4 *TOVERI* AND *TOVERITAR*

1. *Aberdeen Daily Bulletin*, July 18, 19, 20, 22, 1905; *Aberdeen Herald*, July 22, 1905; *Hoquiam Sawyer*, July 21, 1905; *Raivaaja*, July 3, 1905, trans. Matti Roitto; State of Washington, Bureau of Labor, *Fifth Biennial Report of the Bureau of Labor Statistics and Factory Inspection, 1905–1906* (Olympia: C. W. Gorham, Public Printer, 1906), 239; State of Washington, Bureau of Labor, *Eighth Biennial Report of the Bureau of Labor Statistics and Factory Inspection, 1911–1912* (Olympia: E. L. Boardman, Public Printer, 1912), 112; In the Matter of the Increase of the Capital Stock of the West and Slade Mill Company, Articles of Incorporation of the West and Slade Lumber Company, July 7, 1902, Grays Harbor Auditor, Articles of Incorporation, box 3, acc. 99-SW-245, no. 220, SRB-WSA. A. J. West, co-owner of the West and Slade mill, sold his interest in the mill in May 1905. However, the name "West and Slade" remained in popular use until well after the sale. See *Aberdeen Herald*, June 1, 1905; *Aberdeen Daily Bulletin*, May 27, 1905.

2. *Raivaaja*, July 3, 1905, trans. Matti Roitto.

3. *Raivaaja*, July 3, 1905, trans. Matti Roitto. See Aleksi Huhta, "Toward a Red Melting Pot: The Racial Thinking of Finnish-American Radicals, 1900–1938" (PhD diss., University of Turku, Finland, 2017), 172.

4. *Aberdeen Herald*, July 24, 1905. Employers also sometimes refused to hire married men, preferring single men and firing any man who admitted to being married. See *Grays Harbor Post*, February 13, 1909.

5. *Aberdeen Herald*, July 24, 1905; *Aberdeen Daily Bulletin*, July 22, 24, 1905.

6. *R. L. Polk and Company's Grays Harbor Cities Directory, 1910*. The city directory shows many men with Finnish surnames working at the Slade mill for years after the strike.

7. On Minnesota's radical Finnish mine workers, see Gary Kaunonen, *Flames of*

Discontent: The 1916 Minnesota Iron Ore Strike (Minneapolis: University of Minnesota Press, 2001).

8. *Washingtonian,* March 15, 1912.

9. *Toveri,* March 31, 1912, trans. Matti Roitto.

10. *Aberdeen Daily Bulletin,* March 3, April 19, August 9, 1904; July 18, 22, 24, 1905; *Washingtonian,* August 11, 18, 1904; *Aberdeen Herald,* July 20, 24, 1905; May 15, 1910; *Grays Harbor Post,* May 29, July 3, 1909; *Aberdeen Daily World,* May 31, June 1, 2, 3, 1909; May 18, 1910; Philip J. Dreyfus, "The IWW and the Limits of Inter-Ethnic Organizing: Reds, Whites, and Greeks in Grays Harbor, Washington, 1912," *Labor History* 38 (Fall 1997): 450–71.

11. Michael M. Passi, "Introduction: Finnish Immigrants and the Radical Response to Industrial America," in *For the Common Good: Finnish Immigrants and the Radical Response to Industrial America,* edited by Michael G. Karni and Douglas J. Ollila Jr. (Superior, WI: Työmies Society, 1977), 12; Paul George Hummasti, "'The Working Man's Daily Bread': Finnish-American Working Class Newspapers, 1900–1921," in *For the Common Good,* edited by Karni and Ollila Jr., 167–97.

12. David Roediger and James Barrett, "Inbetween Peoples: Race, Nationality, and the 'New Immigrant" Working Class," in *Colored White: Transcending the Racial Past,* edited by David R. Roediger (Berkeley: University of California Press, 2002), 138–68.

13. For background on Finnish-American history, see the works of Auvo Kostiainen, including Auvo Kostiainen, ed., *Finns in the United States: A History of Settlement, Dissent, and Integration* (East Lansing: Michigan State University Press, 2014).

14. These lists appeared at the end of each year in the special holiday issue of *Työmies, Toveri,* the IWW's Finnish-language paper *Industrialisti,* and other periodicals.

15. Reino Hannula, *An Album of Finnish Halls* (San Luis Obispo, CA: Finn Heritage, 1991).

16. Riitta Stjärnstedt, "Finnish Women in the North American Labour Movement," in *Finnish Diaspora II: The United States,* edited by Michael G. Karni (Toronto: Multicultural History Society of Ontario, 1981), 260; Irma Sulkunen, "The Mobilization of Women and the Birth of Civil Society," in *The Lady with the Bow,* edited by Merja Manninen and Päivi Setälä, translated by Michael Wynne-Ellis (Helsinki: Otava Publishing Co., 1990), 49–53.

17. USBC, *Thirteenth Census of the United States Taken in the Year 1910,* Washington State, Chehalis County, Grays Harbor County Clerk, Declarations of Intention, 1884–1980, Office of the Secretary of State, Washington State Archives, Digital Archives, http://digitalarchives.wa.gov, accessed June 20, 2014.

18. Michael Karni and Douglas J. Ollila Jr., *For the Common Good: Finnish Immigrants and the Radical Response to Industrial America* (Superior, WI: Työmies Society,

1977); Paul George Hummasti, *Finnish Radicals in Astoria, Oregon, 1904–1940: A Study in Immigrant Socialism* (New York: Arno Press, 1979); Auvo Kostiainen, *The Forging of Finnish-American Communism, 1917–1924: A Study in Ethnic Radicalism* (Turku, Finland: Turin Yliopisto, 1978); Gary Kaunonen, *Challenge Accepted: A Finnish Immigrant Response to Industrial America in Michigan's Copper Country* (East Lansing: Michigan State University Press, 2010).

19. Auvo Kostiainen, "For or Against Americanization? The Case of the Finnish Immigrant Radicals," in *American Labor and Immigration History: 1877–1920s: Recent European Research*, edited by Dirk Hoerder (Urbana: University of Illinois Press, 1983), 259–75; Robert Higgs, "Race, Skills, and Earnings: American Immigrants in 1909," *Journal of Economic History* 31, no. 2 (June 1971): 424.

20. There are multiple examples from the Pacific Coast correspondents to Finnish socialist papers. In 1905, the primary Aberdeen *Raivaaja* agent and writer was Gustave Kinnunen.

21. *Toveri*, April 12, 1912.

22. *Toveri*, May 30, 1910.

23. *Toveri*, May 30, 1910. Previously called the West and Slade Mill Company, the mill became known as the S. E. Slade Lumber Company following co-owner A. J. West's sale of his interest in the company in 1905.

24. Stephen H. Norwood, *Strikebreaking and Intimidation: Mercenaries and Masculinity in Twentieth-Century America* (Chapel Hill: University of North Carolina Press, 2001), 15–33.

25. *Shingle Weaver*, March 1904; February 17, August 18, September 22, 1917.

26. *Grays Harbor Post*, January 18, 1908.

27. *Raivaaja*, July 3, 1905.

28. *Toveri*, April 5, 8, 9, 1912.

29. Reino Kero, "Migration Traditions from Finland to North America," in *A Century of European Migrations, 1830–1930*, edited by Rudolph J. Vecoli and Suzanne M. Sinke (Urbana: University of Illinois Press, 1991), 111–33; Hummasti, *Finnish Radicals*, 15–16.

30. Auvo Kostiainen, "A Dissenting Voice of Finnish Radicals in America: The Formative Years of *Sosialisti-Industrialisti* in the 1910s," *American Studies in Scandinavia* 23 (1991): 83–94; Kaunonen, *Flames of Discontent*.

31. Julianna Niemim Tipton, "Bits and Pieces of My Childhoods," *East Aberdeen Finns: Grays Harbor County, Washington* (published by Finnish-American Historical Society of the West) 25, no. 1 (December 1998): 29; USBC, *Thirteenth Census . . . 1910*; Ina Kari Smits, Sylvia Niemi Fisher, and Paul Kari, "The Finns in Hoquiam," in *Chehalis County Nationality Survey, 1848–1915*, edited by Joe Randich and Dorothea Parker (Olympia: Washington Commission for the Humanities, 1984); Aaron Goings,

"Hall Syndicalism: Radical Finns and Wobbly Culture in Grays Harbor, Washington," *Journal of Finnish Studies* 14, no. 1 (Summer 2010): 25.

32. Leslie Woodcock Tentler, *Wage-Earning Women: Industrial Work and Family Life in the United States, 1900–1930* (Oxford, UK: Oxford University Press, 1979), 140–41, 170–71.

33. Smits et al., "Finns in Hoquiam."

34. Juha Niemala, "Hiski Salomaa (1891–1957)," in *The American Midwest: An Interpretive Encyclopedia*, edited by Richard Sission, Christian K. Zacher, and Andrew Robert Lee Cayon (Columbus: Ohio State University Press, 2007), 396.

35. Joyce L. Kornbluh, ed., *Rebel Voices: An IWW Anthology*, new and expanded ed. (Chicago: Charles H. Kerr Publishing Co., 1998), 29–30.

36. Smits et al., "Finns in Hoquiam"; Financial Records, 1917–1919, Aberdeen, Wash., IWW Collection, box 36, folder 1, Walter Reuther Library, Wayne State University, Detroit, Michigan (hereafter WSU). W. H. Abel was so opposed to the IWW that he refused to serve as Wobbly Frederick Meischke's attorney in 1917, stating that "there was not sufficient money to hire him to defend such a case." *Aberdeen Daily World*, July 12, 1917.

37. USBC, *Thirteenth Census . . . 1910*, City of Aberdeen, First Ward.

38. Aku Rissanen, *Suomalaisten Sosialistiosastojen ja Työväenyhdistysten viidennen: Pöytäkirja, 1–5, 7–10 p. kesäkuuta, 1912* (Fitchburg, MA: Suomalainen Sosialisti Kustannus Yhtiö, 1912), 51–52.

39. USBC, *Thirteenth Census . . . 1910*, Cities of Hoquiam and Aberdeen.

40. State of Washington, Bureau of Labor, *Sixth Biennial Report of the Bureau of Labor Statistics and Factory Inspection, 1907–1908* (Olympia: C. W. Gorham, Public Printer, 1908), 42.

41. *Aberdeen Daily Bulletin*, July 18, 1905; *Aberdeen Herald*, July 22, 1905; *Grays Harbor Post*, May 29, 1909; State of Washington, Bureau of Labor, *Seventh Biennial Report of the Bureau of Labor Statistics and Factory Inspection, 1909–1910* (Olympia: C. W. Gorham, Public Printer, 1910), 47, 55, 72.

42. *Aberdeen Daily World*, March 15, 1912.

43. *Grays Harbor Post*, May 29, 1909.

44. Jessica Wilkerson, *To Live Here, You Have to Fight* (Urbana: University of Illinois Press, 2019), 5.

45. For useful background, see Samira Saramo, "Capitalism as Death: Loss of Life and the Finnish," *Journal of Social History* 55, no. 3 (2022): 668–94.

46. USBC, *Fifteenth Census of the United States Taken in the Year 1930*, Washington State, Chehalis County, Aberdeen; Merle A. Reinikka, "Death Certificates of Finns in Chehalis [Grays Harbor] County, 1907–1947," Aberdeen History Collection, AHM.

47. *Industrial Worker*, April 18, 1912; *Aberdeen Daily World*, April 2, 1912; *Aberdeen Herald*, April 1, 1912.

48. On Carrie Walker, see *Aberdeen Herald*, April 1, 1912; *Oregonian*, April 2, 1912; USBC, *Thirteenth Census . . . 1910*, City of Aberdeen; Bruce Rogers, "The War of Gray's [*sic*] Harbor," *International Socialist Review* 12, no. 11 (May 1912): 753.

49. *Industrialisti*, December 14, 1935; USBC, *Fifteenth Census . . . 1930*, Grays Harbor.

50. Elizabeth Jameson, *All that Glitters: Class, Conflict, and Community in Cripple Creek* (Urbana: University of Illinois Press, 1998), 38–39, 117.

51. USBC, *Thirteenth Census . . . 1910*, City of Aberdeen.

52. *Työmies mies-Eteenpain, 1903–1973: Seventieth Anniversary Souvenir Journal* (Superior, WI: Työmies Society, n.d.,), 10.

53. USBC, *Thirteenth Census . . . 1910*, City of Aberdeen.

54. Elis Sulkanen, ed., *Amerikan Suomalaisen Työväenliikkeen Historia* (Fitchburg, MA: Amerikan Suomalainen Kansanvallen Liitto ja Raivaaja Publishing Co., 1951), 467. This work by Elis Sulkanen includes several local histories of Red Finnish strongholds in the United States, including for Aberdeen and Hoquiam, Washington. *Toveri*, June 3, 1910; November 3, 1911; July 8, 1912.

55. Articles of Incorporation of the Finnish Socialist Sick and Funeral Benefit Association of America, March 21, 1910, Grays Harbor Auditor, Articles of Incorporation, box 7, acc. 99-SW-245, no. 568, SRB-WSA; *Toveri*, January 5, 1912.

56. Articles of Incorporation of Hoquiam Finnish Workingman's Association Ahjola, April 21, 1909, Grays Harbor Auditor, Articles of Incorporation, box 6, acc. 99-SW-245, no. 516, SRB-WSA; Articles of Incorporation of the Finnish Socialist Sick and Funeral Society of Washington, March 21, 1910, Grays Harbor Auditor, Articles of Incorporation, box 7, no. 568, SRB-WSA; Articles of Incorporation of the Finnish Socialist Sick and Funeral Society of Washington, October 9, 1910, Grays Harbor Auditor, Articles of Incorporation, box 7, acc. 99-SW-245, no. 642, SRB-WSA; Articles of Incorporation of Finnish Socialist Club of Aberdeen, February 2, 1911, Grays Harbor Auditor, Articles of Incorporation, box 7, acc. 99-SW-245, no. 618, SRB-WSA.

57. Thomas Laqueur, "Bodies, Death, and Pauper Funerals," *Representations* 1 (February 1983): 112; Saramo, "Capitalism as Death," 668–94.

58. Aaron Goings, Brian Barnes, and Roger Snider, *The Red Coast: Radicalism and Anti-Radicalism in Southwest Washington* (Corvallis: Oregon State University Press, 2019), 111–18.

59. *Aberdeen Daily World*, April 30, 1913.

60. Cited in *Aberdeen Daily Bulletin*, May 4, July 5, 1906; February 4, 1913.

61. *Aberdeen Daily Bulletin*, July 6, 1906.

62. David Roediger, *Working Toward Whiteness: How America's Immigrants Became White, the Strange Journey from Ellis Island to the Suburbs* (New York: Basic Books, 2005), 64.

63. F. W. Rudler and G. G. Chisholm, *Europe* (London: Edward Stanford, 55 Charing

Cross SW, 1885), 576; Augustus Henry Keane, *Ethnology* (London: C. J. Clay and Sons, 1901), 295, 301, 308.

64. Cited in Wayne Gudmundson and Suzanne Winckler, *Testaments in Wood: Finnish Log Structures at Embarrass, Minnesota* (Minneapolis: Minnesota Historical Society Press, 1991), 22.

65. Peter Kivisto, "The Decline of the Finnish American Left, 1925–1945," *International Migration Review* 17, no. 1 (Spring 1983): 68.

66. Kivisto, "Decline of the Finnish American Left," 68.

67. Roediger, *Working Toward Whiteness*, 63.

68. *Aberdeen Daily Bulletin*, May 3, 4, 1906.

69. "Finns of Hoquiam and Aberdeen, Grays Harbor County, Washington," *Finnish-American Historical Society of the West* 15, no. 1 (October 1987): 18.

70. Rissanen, *Suomalaisten Sosialistiosastojen ja Työväenyhdistysten viidennen*, 51–52; *Grays Harbor Post*, April 6, 1912.

71. *Aberdeen Daily World*, April 17, 1912.

72. *Grays Harbor Post*, April 6, 1912.

73. Gary Kaunonen, *Finns in Michigan* (East Lansing: Michigan State University Press, 2009); Karni, "The Founding of the Finnish Socialist Federation and the Minnesota Strike of 1907," in *For the Common Good*, edited by Karni and Ollila Jr. (Superior, WI: Työmies Society, 1977), 65–86; Hummasti, *Finnish Radicals.*

74. Sulkanen, ed., *Amerikan Suomalaisen Työväenliikkeen Historia*, 466–69, trans. Matti Roitto.

75. Karni, "Founding of the Finnish Socialist Federation," 66.

76. Sulkanen, ed., *Amerikan Suomalaisen Työväenliikkeen Historia*, 486, 493; Rissanen, *Suomalaisten Sosialistiosastojen ja Työväenyhdistysten viidennen*, 51–52.

77. Sulkanen, ed., *Amerikan Suomalaisen Työväenliikkeen Historia*, 466–69; Betty Charette, "The Finns in Aberdeen before 1915," in *Chehalis County Nationality Survey, 1848–1915*, edited by Joe Randich and Dorothea Parker (Olympia: Washington Commission for the Humanities, 1984); Smits et al., "Finns in Hoquiam."

78. Passi, "Introduction," 12.

79. *Amerikan S. S. Jarjeston Lansipiirin ensimmaisen piirikokouksen Poytakrja, Pidety Astoriassa, OR, huhtik, 21–23, 1911*, 4, 20–25, 34–35, Finnish American Historical Archives, Finlandia University, Hancock, Mich.; Rissanen, *Suomalaisten Sosialistiosastojen ja Työväenyhdistysten viidennen*, 51–52.

80. Sulkanen, *Amerikan Suomalaisen Työväenliikkeen Historia*, 170.

81. *Aberdeen Daily World*, April 17, 1912.

82. *Työmies Kymmenvuotias, 1903–1913* (Hancock, MI: Työmies Kustannusyhtio, 1913), 147. Hoquiam's English Socialist Party of America local formed in 1900–1901. See *Grays Harbor Post*, February 25, 1905; Sulkanen, *Amerikan Suomalaisen Työväen-*

liik Historia, 466–69; *Grays Harbor Post*, May 29, 1909; October 29, 1910; *Industrial Worker*, November 26, 1911; *Washingtonian*, July 7, 11, 1911; *Aberdeen Daily World*, May 24, 1911.

83. *Grays Harbor Post*, May 29, 1909.

84. *Toveri*, January 30, 1912.

85. Picture postcard in author's possession.

86. Ira Kipnis, *The American Socialist Movement*, rev. ed. (Chicago: Haymarket Books, 2004), 262; Mari Jo Buhle, *Women and American Socialism, 1870–1920* (Urbana: University of Illinois Press, 1981), 160.

87. Stjärnstedt, "Finnish Women," 25; Reino Kero, *Migration from Finland to North America in the years between the United States Civil War and the First World War* (Turku, Finland: Institute of Migration, 1974), 91–94.

88. *Köyhälistön Nuija* (Hancock, MI: Työmiehen Kustannusyhtiön Kustannuksella, 1906), n.p.; Rissanen, *Suomalaisten Sosialistiosastojen ja Työväenyhdistysten viidennen*, 51–52.

89. Buhle, *Women and American Socialism*, 303–4; Hilja Karvonen, "Three Proponents of Women's Rights," in *Women Who Dared: The History of Finnish-American Women*, edited by Carl Ross and K. Marianne Wargelin Brown (St. Paul, MN: Immigration History Research Center, 1986), 126–28; *Toveritar* (Astoria, OR), February 15, 22, March 21, April 25, May 23, 30, July 18, August 1, September 12, 26, 1916, June 24, August 26, 1930.

90. Buhle, *Women and American Socialism*, 303–4; Hilja Karvonen, "Three Proponents of Women's Rights," in *Women Who Dared: The History of Finnish-American Women*, edited by Carl Ross and K. Marianne Wargelin Brown (St. Paul: Immigration History Research Center, University of Minnesota, 1986), 126–28.

91. Sulkanen, *Amerikan Suomalaisen Työväenliikkeen Historia*, 170; photograph of Aberdeen, Washington, Finnish Socialist Club members, Finnish American Socialist Photograph Collection, Finnish American Historical Archives, Finlandia University, Hancock, Michigan.

92. Kostianen, *Forging of Finnish American Communism*, 171, 186.

93. *Toveri*, October 26, 1912, trans. Matti Roitto.

94. David R. Roediger and Elizabeth D. Esch, *The Production of Difference: Race and the Management of Labor in US History* (Oxford, UK: Oxford University Press, 2012), 154.

95. *Grays Harbor Post*, May 25, 1907; *Washingtonian*, December 26, 1914.

96. *Evening Standard* (Walla Walla, Wash.), February 7, 1908. The word "Pacific" was not italicized in the original.

97. *Toveri*, April 12, 1912, trans. Matti Roitto.

98. Johanna Ogden, "Ghadar, Historical Silences and Notions of Belonging: Early

1900s Punjabis of the Columbia River," *Oregon Historical Quarterly* (Summer 2012): 164–97.

99. *Industrial Union Bulletin* (Chicago), September 28, 1907.

100. *Timber Worker*, April 12, 1913.

101. Evidence for this argument comes from my analysis of the surnames of Slade workers collected from the *R. L. Polk and Company's Grays Harbor Cities Directory*, 1910, which listed 347 employees of the S. E. Slade Lumber Company mill in Aberdeen, many of whom had Finnish surnames. Although sometimes called the "West and Slade mill," after owner A. J. West sold his interests in the mill, the mill was officially the S. E. Slade Lumber Company by 1906.

102. *Hoquiam Sawyer*, May 12, 1905; *Aberdeen Herald*, July 20, 24, 1905; May 15, 1910; *Grays Harbor Post*, May 29, July 3, 1909; *Aberdeen Daily World*, May 18, 1910.

103. Wilson, *From Boats to Board Feet*, 160–61; *Grays Harbor Post*, May 29, June 5, 1909; *Aberdeen Daily World*, June 1, 4, 1909.

104. *Grays Harbor Post*, May 29, June 5, 1909; *Aberdeen Daily World*, May 31, June 1, 2, 3, 4, 5, 6, 7, 8, 10, 1909.

105. *Grays Harbor Post*, June 5, 1909; *Aberdeen Daily World*, June 1, 1909.

106. *Grays Harbor Post*, May 29, June 5, 1909.

107. *Aberdeen Herald*, June 24, 1909.

108. *Aberdeen Daily World*, June 6, 1909; *Grays Harbor Post*, June 12, 1909.

109. *Aberdeen Daily World*, June 4, 1909.

110. *Aberdeen Daily World*, June 10, 1909.

111. *Aberdeen Daily World*, June 4, 1909; *Grays Harbor Post*, June 5, 1909; *Aberdeen Herald*, February 8, 1912; Joe Randich, "Austria-Hungary," in *Chehalis County Nationality Survey, 1848–1915*, edited by Joe Randich and Dorothea Parker (Olympia: Washington Commission for the Humanities, 1984).

112. *Aberdeen Daily World*, April 5, 1915; Articles of Incorporation for the Croatian Workingman's Company, March 4, 1910, Grays Harbor County Auditor, Articles of Incorporation, box 7, acc. 99-SW-245, file 561, SRB-WSA; Randich, "Austria-Hungary."

113. *Grays Harbor Post*, May 29, 1909; April 6, 1912; Articles of Incorporation for the Croatian Workingman's Company, SRB-WSA; *Aberdeen Daily World*, May 31, June 1, 2, 1909; April 5, 1915.

114. *Aberdeen Herald*, May 16, 19, 1910.

115. *Aberdeen Daily World*, May 18, 1910.

116. *Industrial Worker*, June 4, 1910.

117. *Aberdeen Daily World*, May 19, 20, 23, 1910.

118. *Industrial Worker*, March 28, 1912.

119. Rogers, "War of Gray's [*sic*] Harbor," 749–53.

5 BUILDING THE "W" CITY

1. *Industrial Worker*, April 4, 1912.

2. Bruce Rogers, "The War of Gray's [*sic*] Harbor," *International Socialist Review* 12, no. 11 (May 1912): 752; *Industrial Worker*, April 4, 1912, referenced "Another Parade" led by the Finnish brass band, playing "revolutionary music."

3. *Industrial Worker*, April 4, 25, 1912.

4. *Washingtonian*, March 15, 1912.

5. *Grays Harbor Post*, April 6, 1912; Rogers, "War of Gray's [*sic*] Harbor"; *Industrial Worker*, February 29, 1912.

6. *Oregonian*, April 2, 1912; *Industrial Worker*, April 25, 1912.

7. *Industrial Worker*, April 18, 1912.

8. *Industrial Worker*, April 4, 1912; W. S. Seavey to E. G. Ames, July 29, 1912, Edwin Gardner Ames Papers, acc. no. 3820, box 93, folder 29, University of Washington Libraries Special Collections, Seattle (hereafter EGA Papers, UW). Even at an early point in the strike, the IWW claimed that in Hoquiam there were four hundred IWW members with "many others coming." *Industrial Worker*, March 28, 1912.

9. Philip S. Foner, *The History of the Labor Movement in the United States*, vol. 4, *The Industrial Workers of the World, 1905–1917* (1965; reprint, New York: International Publishers, 1978), 220–24; Philip J. Dreyfus, "Timber Workers, Unionism and Syndicalism in the Pacific Northwest, 1900–1917" (PhD diss., Graduate School of the City University of New York, 1993), 113–73; Fred Thompson, *The IWW—Its First Fifty Years* (Chicago: Industrial Workers of the World, 1955), 68; *Aberdeen Daily World*, March 14, 18, 20, 1912; *Industrial Worker*, April 4, 25, 1912; *Aberdeen Herald*, March 21, 1912; *Oregonian*, March 29, 1912.

10. *Aberdeen Daily World*, March 19, 20, 22, 23, 1912; *Aberdeen Herald*, March 28, 1912; *Industrial Worker*, April 4, 1912.

11. *Tacoma Times*, April 11, 1912; *Aberdeen Herald*, June 3, 1912.

12. Erik Loomis, *Empire of Timber: Labor Unions and the Pacific Northwest Forests* (Cambridge, UK: Cambridge University Press, 2015), 52.

13. Foner, *History of the Labor Movement*, vol. 4, 219–20.

14. *Timber Worker* (Seattle), March 1, 1913.

15. *Industrial Worker*, March 13, 1913.

16. The composition of the trade union movement in Grays Harbor is analyzed in chapters 2–4.

17. The Greek Strike of 1912 is covered in detail in Philip J. Dreyfus, "The IWW and the Limits of Inter-Ethnic Organizing: Reds, Whites, and Greeks in Grays Harbor, Washington, 1912," *Labor History* 38 (Fall 1997): 450–71.

18. *Aberdeen Daily World*, November 25, 1911.

19. *Industrial Worker*, February 1, 1912.

20. Don Mitchell, *The Right to the City: Social Justice and the Fight for Public Space* (New York: Guilford Press, 2003), 56.

21. Heather Mayer, *Beyond the Rebel Girl: Women and the Industrial Workers of the World in the Pacific Northwest, 1905–1924* (Corvallis: Oregon State University Press, 2018), 25–50.

22. John C. Hughes and Ryan Teague Beckwith, eds., *On the Harbor: From Black Friday to Nirvana* (Aberdeen, WA: Daily World, 2001), 36; *Aberdeen Daily World*, November 22, 1911.

23. *Aberdeen Daily World*, November 24, 25, 26, 1911; Charles Pierce LeWarne, "The Aberdeen, Washington, Free Speech Fight," *Pacific Northwest Quarterly* 66 (January 1975): 4–5; *Industrial Worker*, January 21, 1911.

24. *Industrial Worker*, February 1, 1912; *Seattle Star*, April 13, 1912; *Oregonian*, March 21, April 1, 1912.

25. Philip S. Foner argued that the Aberdeen Citizens' Committee represented a new and dedicated unity among western employers to eradicate the IWW menace, at any cost. See Foner, ed., *Fellow Workers and Friends: IWW Free Speech Fight as Told by Participants* (Westport, CT: Greenwood Press, 1981), 123–24; *Industrial Worker*, February 1, 1912; November 24, 1917; April 13, 1918; September 4, 1921; June 10, 1922; *Solidarity*, December 23, 1911; April 13, 1912; *Grays Harbor Post*, April 6, 1912; *Aberdeen Daily World*, November 25, 26, 1911; April 3, 4, 1912; September 16, 1917; November 12, 1919; August 5, 1921; *Grays Harbor Post*, November 4, 1922; *Industrial Worker*, June 17, 24, 1922.

26. Cited in John McClelland, *Wobbly War: The Centralia Story* (Tacoma: Washington State Historical Society, 1987), 60.

27. *Aberdeen Daily World*, November 24, 1911.

28. *Industrial Worker*, February 1, 1912; Ben K. Weatherwax, "Hometown Scrapbook—No. 71–The Wobblies," radio script for KBKW, Aberdeen, recorded October 27, 1953, Aberdeen Historical Records, ATL.

29. *Industrial Worker*, January 21, 1911; February 1, 1912; LeWarne, "Aberdeen, Washington, Free Speech Fight," 4–5; *Aberdeen Daily World*, November 25, 26, 1911; *Washingtonian*, November 25, 1911.

30. *Aberdeen Daily World*, August 1, 29, 1912.

31. *Industrial Worker*, November 20, 1911; January 4, 1912; *Solidarity*, December 23, 1911; March 2, 1912.

32. *Industrial Worker*, January 11, 1912.

33. *Aberdeen Herald*, January 11, 1912; *Grays Harbor Post*, January 20, 1912; *Aberdeen Daily World*, November 24, 25, 1911; *Washingtonian*, November 25, 1911.

34. *Industrial Worker*, January 4, 1912.

35. Ed Gilbert to Honorable Marion E. Hay, December 18, 1911, Washington State

Governor's Papers, Governor Marion E. Hay, Judiciary, 1911-Labor Conflicts/IWW, box 2G-2-19, Labor Conflicts-Aberdeen, Raymond, Spokane, 1910–1912, Washington State Archives, Olympia (hereafter WSA); *Industrial Worker*, November 30, December 7, 14, 21, 1911; January 11, 18, 1912; Henry E. McGuckin, *Memoirs of A Wobbly* (Chicago: Charles H. Kerr Publishing Co., 1987), 36–38.

36. McGuckin, *Memoirs of A Wobbly*, 36-38; *Seattle Star*, April 16, 1912.

37. *Industrial Worker*, February 1, 1912.

38. *Industrial Worker*, January 25, February 1, March 14, 1912; Lewarne, "Aberdeen, Washington, Free Speech Fight," 11.

39. *Aberdeen Herald*, January 11, 1912; *Grays Harbor Post*, January 20, 1912.

40. *Industrial Worker*, February 29, 1912.

41. *Agitator*, December 15, 1911.

42. *Industrial Worker*, January 11, 18, March 14, 1912; Rogers, "War of Gray's [*sic*] Harbor," 749–53.

43. *Industrial Worker*, April 28, 1912; Howard Kimeldorf, *Reds or Rackets: The Making of Radical and Conservative Unions on the Waterfront* (Berkeley: University of California Press, 1992), 27–29.

44. *Industrial Worker*, April 18, 1912; Thompson, *The IWW*, 69.

45. *Washingtonian*, March 15, 1912.

46. *Il Lavoratore Industriale* (San Francisco). The first issue of the Italian-language IWW newspaper published in San Francisco beginning on May 1, 1912, carried strike reports, as did several Finnish socialist newspapers. *Il Lavoratore Industriale* ran front-page lumber-strike news. The cover states that the Branch Latino IWW published the newspaper.

47. *Toveri*, April 24, 1912, trans. Matti Roitto.

48. *Industrial Worker*, April 4, 18, 1912. Cited in *Aberdeen Herald*, March 28, 1912; *Agitator*, December 15, 1911; January 15, February 1, 1912.

49. *Aberdeen Daily World*, April 2, 1912; *Industrial Worker*, April 18, 1912; *Oregonian*, April 2, 1912; *Solidarity*, April 13, 1912.

50. A copy of the leaflet appeared in Agnes C. Laut, "Revolution Yawns!" *Technical World Magazine*, October 1912, 143.

51. *Industrial Worker*, April 4, 1912.

52. *Oregonian*, April 1, 1912.

53. *Voice of Action* (Seattle), November 2, 1934.

54. *Aberdeen Daily World*, April 10, 1912; *Seattle Star*, April 8, 10, 13, 1912; *Tacoma Times*, April 13, 1912.

55. *Industrial Worker*, April 18, 1912.

56. See *Vappu*, May Day 1913, 130; Rogers, "War of Gray's [*sic*] Harbor."

57. *Strike Bulletin*, April 9, 1912.

58. *Toveri*, April 11, 1912, trans. Matti Roitto.

59. *Seattle Star*, April 1, 2, 1912; *Aberdeen Daily World*, April 11, 1912.

60. *Aberdeen Daily World*, April 11, 1912.

61. *Seattle Star*, April 13, 1912.

62. *Aberdeen Daily World*, March 15, 1912.

63. Dreyfus, "IWW and the Limits of Inter-Ethnic Organizing," 462.

64. *Oregonian*, March 16, 1912; *Aberdeen Herald*, April 1, 1912; *Aberdeen Daily World*, March 15, 22, 23, April 6, 1912.

65. *Washingtonian*, April 6, 1912; *Aberdeen Herald*, April 11, 1912.

66. *Industrial Worker*, April 18, May 23, 1912.

67. *Washingtonian*, July 18, 30, August 1, 2, 1911.

68. *Pacific Lumber Trade Journal*, April 1912, 24.

69. *Tacoma Times*, April 11, 1912.

70. *Toveri*, April 24, 1912, trans. Matti Roitto.

71. *Pacific Lumber Trade Journal*, June 1912, 33.

72. *Aberdeen Herald*, June 3, 1912.

73. *Oregonian*, March 21, 1912; *Aberdeen Daily World*, August 1, September 5, 1912.

74. Dreyfus, "Timber Workers," 152.

75. *Aberdeen Daily World*, March 23, 1912.

76. *Timber Worker* (Aberdeen), Labor Day ed., September 7, 1936.

77. *Shingle Weaver*, June, July, September 1905; February 1, 1913; Cloice R. Howd, "Industrial Relations in the West Coast Lumber Industry," *Bulletin of the United States Bureau of Labor Statistics*, no. 349 (Washington, DC: Government Printing Office, 1924), 57–58.

78. For useful background on Jay Fox and the anarchist and syndicalist influences on the timber workers' unions, see Greg Hall, *Writing Labor's Emancipation: The Anarchist Life and Times of Jay Fox* (Seattle: University of Washington Press, 2022).

79. *Labor Journal*, July 11, 1913.

80. *The Syndicalist* (Chicago), April 15, September 1–15, 1913.

81. *Timber Worker* (Seattle), September 6, 1913.

82. *Aberdeen Daily World*, January 13, 1914; Howd, "Industrial Relations," 57–60.

83. Howd, "Industrial Relations," 57–60; Hall, *Writing Labor's Emancipation*.

84. *Timber Worker*, March 1, 1913; Paul George Hummasti, *Finnish Radicals in Astoria, Oregon, 1904–1940: A Study in Immigrant Socialism* (New York: Arno Press, 1979), 99–101.

85. *Shingle Weaver*, February 1, 1913.

86. *Timber Worker*, September 27, 1913.

87. *Timber Worker*, March 1, 1913.

88. *Agitator*, June 1, 1912.

89. James R. Barrett, *William Z. Foster and the Tragedy of American Radicalism* (Urbana: University of Illinois Press, 1999), 53–65; *Timber Worker*, April 4, 18, 1914.

90. William Z. Foster, *From Bryan to Stalin* (New York: International Publishers, 1937), 6.

91. *The Syndicalist* (Chicago), March 1, 1913.

92. *Timber Worker*, January 31, April 18, 1914.

93. Alexander Saxton, *The Rise and Fall of the Great White Republic* (London: Verso Press, 1990), 312–16.

94. *Shingle Weaver*, February 1, 1913.

95. Hummasti, *Finnish Radicals*, 99–101.

96. *Shingle Weaver*, February 1, 1913. See Peter Cole, *Ben Fletcher: The Life and Times of a Black Wobbly*, rev. 2nd ed. (Oakland, CA: PM Press, 2021) for an analysis of the IWW's antiracism.

97. *Aberdeen Daily World*, May 2, 1913.

98. W. L. Brackinreed, Secretary, Central Labor Council, Aberdeen, Washington, to President Woodrow Wilson, December 1, 1916, Department of Justice Investigative Files, Part I: Industrial Workers of the World, folder 002366-001-0000; January 1, 1910–December 31, 1916, microfilm. This file also contains letters from the Aberdeen branch of the International Brotherhood of Electrical Workers and the Aberdeen-Hoquiam Building Trades Council.

99. *Solidarity*, March 2, 1912.

100. W. S. Seavey to E. G. Ames, July 29, 1912, EGA Papers, acc. no. 3820, box 93, folder 29, UW.

101. William D. Haywood, "The Fighting IWW," *International Socialist Review* 8, no. 3 (September 1912): 247.

102. *Industrial Worker*, August 29, December 26, 1912.

103. Foner, *History of the Labor Movement in the United States*, vol. 4, 150.

104. *Aberdeen Daily World*, August 24, 1912.

105. Elis Sulkanen, ed., *Amerikan Suomalaisen Työväenliikkeen historia* (Fitchburg, MA: Amerikan Suomalainen Kansanvallen Liitto ja Raivaaja Publishing Co., 1951), 466–69; Aku Rissanen, *Suomalaisten Sosialistiosastojen ja Työväenyhdistysten: Pöytäkirja, 1–5, 7–10 p. kesäkuuta, 1912* (Fitchburg, MA: Suomalainen Sosialisti Kustannus Yhtiö, 1912), 51–52.

106. Auvo Kostiainen, "A Dissenting Voice of Finnish Radicals in America: The Formative Years of *Sosialisti-Industrialisti* in the 1910s," *American Studies in Scandinavia* 23 (1991): 83–94; Hummasti, *Finnish Radicals*, 98–101.

107. *Sosialisti* (Duluth, Minn.), January 8, November 25, December 21, 1916.

108. For general information about the 1913–1915 recession, see Foner, *History of the Labor Movement*, vol. 4, 435–36.

109. Howd, "Industrial Relations," 24.

110. State of Washington, Bureau of Labor, *Ninth Biennial Report of the Bureau of Labor Statistics and Factory Inspection, 1913–1914* (Olympia: Public Printer, 1914), 51.

111. Howd, "Industrial Relations," 18–19; *Aberdeen Daily World*, April 16, May 1, 1914.

112. Howd, "Industrial Relations," 59–60; *Timber Worker*, February 1, 1915.

113. W. S. Seavey to E. G. Ames, July 29 and September 17, 1912, EGA Papers, acc. no. 3820, box 93, folder 30, UW. Logging corporations utilized blacklists as early as February 1912. There is no reason to believe that its use was discontinued during or shortly after the 1912 IWW lumber strike. *Industrial Worker*, January 4, 1912.

114. State of Washington, Bureau of Labor, *Eleventh Biennial Report of the Bureau of Labor Statistics and Factory Inspection, 1917–1918* (Olympia: C. H. Younger, Public Printer, 1918), 122.

115. State of Washington, Bureau of Labor, *Eleventh Biennial Report . . . 1917–1918*, 76.

116. State of Washington, Bureau of Labor, *Eleventh Biennial Report . . . 1917–1918*, 78.

117. *Aberdeen Herald*, April 4, 1912.

118. *Grays Harbor Post*, April 4, 1912; April 7, 1917. See also *Grays Harbor Post*, April 12, 1919.

119. "Resolution Adopted by Aberdeen Central Labor Council Friday, February 12, without any dissenting vote," *Grays Harbor Post*, March 6, 1915.

120. "Judge James Phillips, Washington's First Native American Judge," *Washington Courts*, September 23, 2008, https://www.courts.wa.gov/newsinfo/?fa=newsinfo.pressdetail&newsid=1196; *Grays Harbor Post*, June 22, 1907; *Quarterly Journal of Society of American Indians* 3, no. 3 (September 30, 1915): 235; *Sunset: The Pacific Monthly*, November 1915, 955.

121. *Southwest Washington Labor Press* (Hoquiam, WA), March 5, 1915.

122. Jeffrey Johnson, *They Are All Red Out Here* (Norman: University of Oklahoma Press, 2014).

123. *Southwest Washington Labor Press*, March 5, 1915; *Labor News*, July 11, 1919; *Timber Worker*, May 3, 1913; *Seattle Star*, January 23, 1915; *Washington Standard*, January 17, 1919; *Labor Journal*, January 28, 1916; December 7, 1917; July 18, 1919; *Labor Journal*, July 18, 1919.

124. *Northwest Worker*, February 15, 1917.

125. *Northwest Worker*, April 26, 1917.

126. Cited in Joyce L. Kornbluh, ed., *Rebel Voices: An IWW Anthology*, new and expanded ed. (Chicago: Charles H. Kerr Publishing Co., 1998), 316.

127. Melvyn Dubofsky, *We Shall Be All: A History of the Industrial Workers of the World* (Chicago: Quadrangle Books, 1969, 1973), 354.

128. H. D. McKenney to F. B. Stansbury, May 5, 1918, WDGSR, Record Group 165, box 2, file 563, NARA. *Industrial Worker*, June 16, 1917.

129. *Industrial Worker*, October 7, 1916; November 24, 1917; *Aberdeen Daily World*, September 6, 1917.

130. J. F. Rhodes and W. H. Margason to George F. Vanderveer, November 15, 1917, box 99, file 1, *United States v. Haywood, et al.*, IWW Collection, box 110, folder 3, 5713, WSU.

131. *Industrial Worker*, May 13, June 3, August 5, October 14, 1916; Foner, *History of the Labor Movement in the United States*, vol. 4, 520–21.

132. *Industrial Worker*, September 16, 1916; *Solidarity*, July 15, 1916. See also "The Lumber Workers' Conference," *International Socialist Review* 17, no. 2 (August 1916): 119; C. E. Payne, "The Spring Drive of the Lumber Jacks," *International Socialist Review* 17, no. 12 (June 1917): 729–30.

133. Foner, *History of the Labor Movement in the United States*, vol. 4, 220; *Industrial Worker*, July 1, 15, 29, 1916; James Rowan, *The IWW in the Lumber Industry* (Seattle: Lumber Workers Industrial Union No. 500, 1919), 30.

134. *Industrial Worker*, October 7, 14, 1916.

135. *Industrial Worker*, November 25, 1916.

136. Staughton Lynd, ed., *"We Are All Leaders": The Alternative Unionism of the Early 1930s* (Urbana: University of Illinois Press, 1996), 7.

137. Walker Smith, *The Everett Massacre* (Chicago: Industrial Workers of the World, 1917), 84–109; Norman H. Clark, *Mill Town: A Social History of Everett, Washington, from Its Earliest Beginnings on the Shores of Puget Sound to the Tragic and Infamous Event Known as the Everett Massacre* (Seattle: University of Washington Press, 1970), 205–9; Dubofsky, *We Shall Be All*, 339–43.

138. *Industrialisti*, May 15, 1917, trans. Matti Roitto.

139. *Everett Prisoners' Defense Fund*, Industrial Workers of the World Papers, acc. no. 544, box 3, folder 9, University of Washington Libraries Special Collections, Seattle (hereafter IWW Papers, UW); Walker Smith, *Everett Massacre*, 289–96; *Industrial Worker*, August 19, 1916; May 12, 1917; *Industrialisti*, May 15, 1917; Elizabeth Gurley Flynn, *The Rebel Girl: An Autobiography, My First Life (1906–1926)*, new ed. (New York: International Publishers, 3rd printing, 1973), 224; Charlotte Todes, *Labor and Lumber* (New York: International Publishers, 1931), 163; Foner, *History of the Labor Movement in the United States*, vol. 4, 539–48; Heather Mayer, *Beyond the Rebel Girl: Women and the Industrial Workers of the World in the Pacific Northwest, 1905–1924* (Corvallis: Oregon State University Press, 2018), 139.

140. Robert L. Tyler, "The Everett Free Speech Fight," *Pacific Historical Review* 23, no. 1 (February 1954): 30.

141. On the circulation of Finnish American Communist periodicals, see Auvo

Kostiainen, *The Forging of Finnish-American Communism, 1917–1924: A Study in Ethnic Radicalism* (Turku, Finland: Turin Yliopisto, 1978), 144.

142. Hummasti, *Finnish Radicals*, 183–84; Archibald E. Stevenson, *Revolutionary Radicalism: Its History, Purpose and Tactics, with an Exposition and Discussion of the Steps Being Taken to and Required to Curb It, being the Report of the Joint Legislative Committee Investigating Seditious Activities, Filed April 24, 1920, in the Senate of the State of New York* (New York: J. B. Lyon, 1920), 865–66, 2006; Kostiainen, *Forging of Finnish American Communism*, 91.

143. *Industrialisti*, May 15, July 3, 1917; January 7, 28, 1920; January 29, 1921; January 14, 20, 24, 1931.

144. *Industrialisti*, May 15, 1917; January 17, 19, February 3, 1920.

145. The number of "Greetings" issued to Grays Harbor workers by the *Industrialisti* remained steady from its first Christmas Greetings issue in 1917 to 1935. See, for instance, *Industrialisti*, December 14, 1935.

146. *Industrialisti*, July 3, 1917; February 3, 1920; January 20, 1931; December 3, 1935.

147. *Industrialisti*, January 20, 1931.

148. Kostiainen, "A Dissenting Voice." The *Industrial Worker* was published as a daily briefly during September 1923.

149. The "Young People's Section" was a daily feature of the *Industrialisti*. Attacks on scabs were made in *Industrialisti*, April 5, May 21, June 8, December 14, 1935. Violet Nurmi of Aberdeen was contacted in the January 29, 1931, edition of this section.

150. *Industrialisti* began publication in March 1917. See Hummasti, *Finnish Radicals*, 183; *Industrialisti*, July 7, 1917.

151. US Bureau of Aircraft Production, *Report of the United States Bureau of Aircraft Production* (Washington, DC: US Government Printing Office, 1918), 7.

152. US House of Representatives, *Hearings before the Select Committee on Expenditures in the War Department*, Sixty-Sixth Congress, First Session on War Expenditures, Serial 1—Part 9 (Washington, DC: Government Printing Office, 1919), 1680; Robert E. Ficken, *The Forested Land: A History of Lumbering in Western Washington* (Seattle: University of Washington Press, 1987), 138–39.

153. Howd, "Industrial Relations," 104.

154. Robert L. Tyler, *Rebels of the Woods: The IWW in the Pacific Northwest* (Eugene: University of Oregon Books, 1967), 92–93; Dubofsky, *We Shall Be All*, 361.

155. US Bureau of Labor Statistics, "Report of President's Mediation Commission," *Monthly Review of the U.S. Bureau of Labor Statistics* 6, no. 3 (March 1918): 57.

156. The IWW was frequently referred to as "one big union," a nickname stemming from its efforts to organize all workers into one big union of all workers.

157. *Industrial Worker*, June 9, 1917.

158. *Industrial Worker*, May 5, June 9, 23, 30, July 7, 1917; *Everett Prisoners' Defense*

Fund; Aberdeen, Wash., IWW Collection, box 36, folder 1, WSU; *Industrialisti*, July 3, 1917.

159. *Industrial Worker*, July 7, 1917; *Aberdeen Daily World*, July 3, 1917; Cal Winslow, *Radical Seattle: The General Strike of 1919* (New York: Monthly Review Press, 2020), 118–19.

160. *Industrial Worker*, July 7, 1917.

161. *Industrial Worker*, October 20, 1917.

162. *Shingle Weaver*, September 15, 1917; *Industrial Worker*, June 2, 1917.

163. *Industrial Worker*, July 7, 1917.

164. *Industrial Worker*, May 12, 1917.

165. Frank Waterhouse and Company, *Pacific Ports*, vol. 5 (Seattle: Pacific Ports, 1919), 403; Hughes and Beckwith, *On the Harbor*, 68–72.

166. Sandy Polishuk, ed., *Sticking to the Union: An Oral History of the Life and Times of Julia Ruutila* (New York: Palgrave MacMillan, 2003), 31; *Grays Harbor Post*, August 4, 1917; *Aberdeen Daily World*, July 13, 1917.

167. Reports by Agent 31, Aberdeen, Wash., November 15, 20, 1917, Governor Ernest Lister, State Secret Service, Correspondence Files, 1917–1921, acc. no. AR2-H-5, WSA (hereafter Gov. Lister, State Secret Service, WSA); *Industrialisti*, June 16, July 3, 23, 1917; *New Unionist*, January 14, 1928.

168. Report by Agent 31, Aberdeen, Wash., November 20, 1917, Gov. Lister, State Secret Service, WSA.

169. *Aberdeen Daily World*, July 13, 14, 1917; *Industrial Worker*, July 21, 1917.

170. *Industrial Worker*, July 21, 1917; *Washingtonian*, July 14, 1917; *Aberdeen Daily World*, July 14, 1917.

171. *Industrial Worker*, July 21, 1917; *New York Times*, July 13, 1917; *Chicago Tribune*, July 13, 1917.

172. Testimony of Charles R. Griffin, *United States v. Haywood, et al.*, IWW Collection, box 110, folder 3, 5625, WSU.

173. *Aberdeen Daily World*, July 16, 17, 1917.

174. *Industrial Worker*, July 21, 28, 1917

6. PERSISTENT WOBBLIES

1. W. S. Seavey to E. G. Ames, July 29, 1912, EGA Papers, acc. no. 3820, box 93, folder 29, UW; "Reports by Agent 31, Aberdeen, Wash., Nov. 15, 20, 1917," Gov. Lister, State Secret Service, acc. no. AR2-H-5, WSA; *Industrialisti*, June 16, July 3, 23, 1917; *New Unionist* (Los Angeles), January 14, 1928; *Industrial Worker*, May 5, 1923; *Industrialisti*, December 14, 1935.

2. *Industrialisti*, May 15, 1917, trans. Matti Roitto.

3. Cited in Melvyn Dubofsky, *We Shall Be All: A History of the Industrial Workers of the World*, abridged ed. (Urbana: University of Illinois Press, 2000), 224–25.

4. Dubofsky, *We Shall Be All*, abridged ed., 200–14.

5. Cal Winslow, *Radical Seattle: The General Strike of 1919* (New York: Monthly Review Press, 2020), 32.

6. Robert E. Ficken, "The Wobbly Horrors: Pacific Northwest Lumbermen and the Industrial Workers of the World, 1917–1918," *Labor History* 24, no. 3 (Summer 1983): 329.

7. Vernon Jensen, *Lumber and Labor* (New York: Arno Press, 1971; first published 1945 by J. J. Little and Ives Co., New York), 125–26; Robert E. Ficken, "Wobbly Horrors," 329; Cloice R. Howd, "Industrial Relations in the West Coast Lumber Industry," *Bulletin of the United States Bureau of Labor Statistics*, no. 349 (Washington, DC: Government Printing Office, 1924), 72–73; *Industrial Worker*, July 21, 28, 1917; *Washingtonian*, July 17, 1917.

8. *Industrial Worker*, July 21, 1917.

9. *Grays Harbor Post*, July 21, 1917.

10. Jonathon Dembo, *Unions and Politics in Washington State, 1885–1935* (New York: Garland Press, 1982), 625; WSFL, Local Organization's Report, Washington State Federation of Labor Records, acc. 301, box 70, ledger 7, 4–83, UW.

11. *Grays Harbor Post*, September 1, 1917; State of Washington, Bureau of Labor, *Eleventh Biennial Report of the Bureau of Labor Statistics and Factory Inspection, 1917–1918* (Olympia: C. H. Younger, Public Printer, 1918), 80–83.

12. *Labor Press*, November 1, 1918.

13. Much of the coverage in the *Shingle Weaver* throughout summer 1917 concerned the eight-hour day.

14. *Seattle Union Record*, July 21, 1917.

15. *Shingle Weaver*, September 8, 29, 1917.

16. *American Timberworker* (Aberdeen, Wash.), February 24, 1917; *Labor Journal* (Everett, Wash.), March 2, 1917. IUT news regularly appeared as a column titled "Timberworkers Bulletin" in the *Labor Journal*; Howd, "Industrial Relations," 59.

17. The *Labor Journal* of Everett wrote on February 9, 1917, they "have received the third number of the American Timberworker."

18. *Shingle Weaver*, August 4, 1917.

19. *Labor Journal*, July 23, 1920; *Washington Standard* (Olympia, Wash.), March 15, 1918.

20. *Labor Journal*, July 18, 1919; May 21, 1921; Howd, "Industrial Relations," 97–101.

21. WSFL, Local Organization's Report, Washington State Federation of Labor Records, acc. 301, box 70, ledger 9, 17–20, UW; *Labor Journal*, March 29, 1918.

22. Howd, "Industrial Relations," 99.

23. *Labor Journal*, November 23, 1917; July 18, 1919.

24. *American Timberworker*, February 24, 1917.

25. *American Timberworker*, February 24, 1917.

26. *Shingle Weaver*, August 4, 1917.

27. *Shingle Weaver*, August 4, 1917; *Seattle Union Record*, July 21, 1917.

28. *Aberdeen Herald*, April 7, 1916.

29. *Labor Journal*, October 29, 1920; WSFL, *Official Year Book and Who's Who in Organized Labor* (Olympia: Washington State Federation of Labor, 1927), 13.

30. *Aberdeen Herald*, May 15, 1917.

31. *Labor Journal*, March 8, 1918.

32. Cited in Robert Walter Bruere, *Following the Trail of the IWW: A First-Hand Investigation into Labor Troubles in the West—A Trip into the Copper and the Lumber Camps of the Inland Empire with the Views of the Men on the Job* (New York: New York Evening Post, 1918), 20.

33. *Grays Harbor Post*, July 21, 1917.

34. Testimony of W. E. Hall, *United States v. Haywood, et al.*, IWW Collection, box 114, folder 1, 8812, WSU.

35. *Industrial Worker*, July 17, 1917.

36. "Report by Agent 31, Aberdeen, Wash., Nov. 16, 1917," Gov. Lister, State Secret Service, WSA; *Aberdeen Daily World*, August 31, 1917.

37. *Washingtonian*, May 18, 1918.

38. *Washingtonian*, August 23, 1917; *Chicago News* article reprinted in the *Defense News Bulletin* (Chicago), November 24, 1917. The *Industrial Worker* recorded that the name of the terrorist group was the "Black Gown." *Industrial Worker*, November 24, 1917.

39. *Aberdeen Daily World*, July 23, 1917; Philip S. Foner, *History of the Labor Movement in the United States*, vol. 7, *Labor and World War I, 1914–1918* (New York: International Publishers, 1987) , 253; Philip J. Dreyfus, "Timber Workers, Unionism and Syndicalism in the Pacific Northwest, 1900–1917" (PhD diss., Graduate School of the City University of New York, 1993), 200; *Grays Harbor Lumber Company v. Industrial Workers of the World, et al.*, No. 14,101, Superior Court of the State of Washington, for Chehalis County (1917), SRB-WSA; *Aberdeen Daily World*, July 23, 1917; Chehalis (Grays Harbor) County Jail Record: Civil/Criminal, 1913–1922, acc. no. 86-1-9, SWA; *Washingtonian*, August 1, 3, 12, 1917.

40. Chehalis County Jail Record: Civil/Criminal, 1913–1922, SWA; *Washingtonian*, July 13, 15, 17, 20, August 1, 3, 7, 9, 11, 12, 15, 1917; *Aberdeen Daily World*, April 2, July 12, August 12, 14, 17, 1917; *Washingtonian*, July 13, 1917; City of Aberdeen, Police Department, Daily Report Journals, 1917–1919, SWA; Gerald E. Shenk, *"Work or Fight!" Race, Gender, and the Draft in World War One* (New York: Palgrave Macmillan, 2005).

41. *Washingtonian*, May 22, 1918.

42. James Rowan, *The IWW in the Lumber Industry* (Seattle: Lumber Workers Industrial Union No. 500, 1919), ch. 5; Howd, "Industrial Relations," 70.

43. *Washingtonian*, August 18, 1917; *R. L. Polk and Company's Grays Harbor Cities Directory*, 1910, 412.

44. *Washingtonian*, August 21, 1917.

45. Philip J. Dreyfus, "Nature, Militancy, and the Western Worker: Socialist Shingles, Syndicalist Spruce," *Labor: Studies in Working-Class History of the Americas* 1, no. 3 (Fall 2004): 86; Testimony of John A. McBride, *United States v. Haywood, et al.*, IWW Collection, box 110, file 3, 5719, WSU, 3778, 3795, 3806–3806; Dubofsky, *We Shall Be All*, 364; Jensen, *Lumber and Labor*, 127; F. B. Stansbury to Colonel Bryce P. Disque, November 22, 1917, WDGSR, Record Group 165, box 9, file 1065, NARA; *Washingtonian*, August 12, 1917.

46. *Washingtonian*, June 14, 1918; *Aberdeen Daily World*, June 11, 12, 1918.

47. *Washingtonian*, August 11, 12, 1917; *Aberdeen Daily World*, July 14, 1917; Chehalis (Grays Harbor) County Jail Record: Civil/Criminal, 1913–1922, acc. no. 86-1-9, SWA; John McClelland, *Wobbly War: The Centralia Story* (Tacoma: Washington State Historical Society, 1987), 55; Testimony of Walter Horace Margason, *United States v. Haywood, et al.*, IWW Collection, box 110, file 3, 5719, WSU; Patrick Renshaw, "The IWW and the Red Scare, 1917–1924," *Journal of Contemporary History* (October 1968): 68; Lowell Stillwell Hawley and Ralph Bushnell Potts, *Counsel for the Damned: A Biography of George Francis Vanderveer* (Philadelphia: J. B. Lippincott Co., 1953); J. F. Rhodes and W. H. Margason to George F. Vanderveer, November 15, 1917, box 99, file 1, *United States v. Haywood, et al.*, IWW Collection, box 110, folder 3, 5713, WSU.

48. Governor Ernest Lister to S. V. Stewart, Governor of Montana, April 22, 1918, Gov. Lister, State Secret Service, WSA; Dreyfus, "Timber Workers," 200; Ficken, "Wobbly Horrors," 329; Robert E. Ficken, *The Forested Land: A History of Lumbering in Western Washington* (Seattle: University of Washington Press, 1987), 135; City of Aberdeen, Police Department, Daily Report Journals, 1917–1919, SWA; F. B. Stansbury to Edmund Leigh, August 26, 1918, WDGSR, Record Group 165, box 4, file 721, NARA; Testimony of Walter Horace Margason, *United States v. Haywood, et al.*, IWW Collection, box 110, folder 3, 5761, WSU; *Industrial Worker*, November 24, 1917; February 2, 1918; F. B. Stansbury to Edmund Leigh, December 27, 1917, WDGSR, Record Group 165, box 2, file No. 540B, NARA.

49. *Washingtonian*, November 26, 1918.

50. Rowan, *IWW in the Lumber Industry*, 48; Fred Thompson, "The IWW Tells Its Own Story," *Industrial Worker*, March 22, 1932.

51. See *Industrial Worker*, September 26, 29, October 3, November 3, 10, 17, December 15, 1917; Howd, "Industrial Relations," 102; Report of Agent 63, Hoquiam, Decem-

ber 1, 1917, WDGSR, Record Group 165, box 9, file 1095, NARA; A. C. Hughes to C. H. Younger, February 15, 1918, Gov. Lister, State Secret Service, acc. no. AR2-H-5, WSA; *Lumberjack Bulletin*, March 16, 1918.

52. William Preston Jr., *Aliens and Dissenters: Federal Suppression of Radicals, 1903–1933*, (Cambridge, MA: Harvard University Press, 1963), 106–8; *Washingtonian*, July 20, 1917.

53. *Washingtonian*, July 20, 1917; July 21, 1917.

54. Dreyfus, "Timber Workers," 215.

55. Office of Military Intelligence, Seattle, Washington, to Intelligence Officer, Western Dept. US Army, San Francisco, Calif., December 14, 1918, War Department, Intelligence Office, US Army, Seattle, Wash., folder 101114-009-0001, Jan 01, 1918–Dec 31, 1918, Department of Justice Investigative Files, Part III: The Use of Military Force by the Federal Government in Domestic Disturbances, 1900–1938, "History Vault Collection," *Proquest Digital Collections*, https://www.proquest.com.

56. *Aberdeen Daily World*, September 5, 6, 1917; *Industrial Worker*, September 19, 1917. J. F. Rhodes and W. H. Margason to George F. Vanderveer, November 15, 1917, IWW Collection, box 99, folder 1, WSU; Joyce L. Kornbluh, ed., *Rebel Voices: An IWW Anthology*, new and expanded ed. (Chicago: Charles H. Kerr Publishing Co., 1998), 318.

57. Dubofsky, *We Shall Be All*, abridged ed., 237.

58. Ficken, "Wobbly Horrors," 334–36.

59. Howd, "Industrial Relations," 98.

60. Howd, "Industrial Relations," 82.

61. A list of the "objects which the Four L sought to accomplish" appears in Howd, "Industrial Relations," 87.

62. *Washingtonian*, May 25, 1918.

63. *Washingtonian*, May 2, 1918.

64. *Washingtonian*, April 7, 1918.

65. *Industrial Worker*, January 5, 1918.

66. "Four Hells" derives from an article written in the *Industrial Worker*, January 5, 1918. See also Testimony of Frank Milward, *United States v. Haywood, et al.*, IWW Collection, box 108, folder 2, 4405–8, WSU; Ralph Chaplin, *The Centralia Conspiracy* (Chicago: Industrial Workers of the World, 1924), 48; *Industrial Worker*, July 16, 1921; Howd, "Industrial Relations," 81–84; Rowan, *IWW in the Lumber Industry*, 53; Harrison George, *The IWW Trial: Story of the Greatest Trial in Labor's History by One of Its Defendants*, reprint (New York: Arno Press, 1969), 54–56; Testimony of Walter Horace Margason, *United States v. Haywood, et al.*, IWW Collection, box 110, folder 3, 5713, WSU.

67. *Industrial Worker*, January 19, 1918.

68. *Industrial Worker*, July 16, 1921.

69. Chaplin, *Centralia Conspiracy*, 48.

70. See, for example, *Washingtonian*, May 29, 1918.

71. *Washingtonian*, July 18, 19, 1918.

72. For background on welfare capitalism in the United States, see David Brody, *Steelworkers in America: The Nonunion Era* (Cambridge, MA: Harvard University Press, 1960), 89.

73. As historian Richard Rajala shows, several Northwest lumber companies instituted welfare capitalist programs to "the theme of mutual obligation and partnership" between worker and employer. Managers intended for these plans to incentivize loyalty and stability from a lumber workforce with a reputation for frequently leaving jobs. See Rajala, "Bill and the Boss: Labor Protest, Technological Change and the Transformation of the West Coast Logging Camp, 1890–1930," *Journal of Forest History* 33 (October 1989): 175.

74. *Poseygram* (Hoquiam, WA), December 1935.

75. An extensive collection of the *Poseygram* is available in the Posey Manufacturing Company Records at the Polson Historical Museum in Hoquiam, Wash.

76. *Aberdeen Daily World*, January 23, 1919.

77. *Aberdeen Daily World*, December 1, 1917.

78. *Aberdeen Daily World*, December 5, 6, 13, 1917; F. B. Stansbury to Edmund Leigh, December 27, 1917, Military Intelligence Division, Plant Protection, WDGSR, box 2, file 540-B, Portland District, NARA; *Aberdeen Daily World*, April 5, 1924.

79. *Industrial Worker*, October 18, 1919.

80. *Aberdeen Daily World*, December 1, 1917; "Documentary Report on the Logging Camps of the Pacific North West with Recommendations by Worth M. Tippy," IWW Collection, box 159, folder D, WSU.

81. On criminal syndicalism laws as a tool to attack the IWW, see especially Ahmed White, *Under the Iron Heel: The Wobblies and the Capitalist War on Radical Workers* (Berkeley: University of California Press, 2022).

82. Aaron Goings, Brian Barnes, and Roger Snider, *The Red Coast: Radicalism and Anti-Radicalism in Southwest Washington* (Corvallis: Oregon State University Press, 2019), 87–100.

83. Governor's Secret Service, Statement of Expenses from August 13th 1917 to November 1st 1918, Gov. Lister, State Secret Service, WSA; Albert F. Gunns, *Civil Liberties in Crisis: The Pacific Northwest, 1917–1940* (New York: Garland Publishing, 1983), 17; Ernest Lister to Honorable S. V. Stewart, Governor of Montana, April 22, 1918, Gov. Lister, State Secret Service, WSA; Howard P. Wright, Special Agent in Charge, Department of Justice, Bureau of Investigation, to Honorable Clay Allen, United States Attorney, October 22, 1917, Gov. Lister, State Secret Service, WSA; John I. O'Phelan to Hon. Ernest Lister, Governor, February 25, 1918, Gov. Lister, State Secret Service, WSA.

84. C. B. Reed to Governor Ernest Lister, December 30, 1918, Gov. Lister, State Secret Service, WSA. This letter provides a full documentation of all investigations un-

dertaken by the secret service between August 13, 1917, and December 30, 1918; Ernest Lister to Honorable S. V. Stewart, Governor of Montana, April 22, 1918, Gov. Lister, State Secret Service, WSA.

85. Report of Agent 31, December 20, 1917, Gov. Lister, State Secret Service, WSA.

86. Governor's Secret Service, Statement of Expenses from August 13, 1917, to November 1, 1918, Gov. Lister, State Secret Service, WSA; C. B. Reed to Governor Ernest Lister, December 30, 1918, Gov. Lister, State Secret Service, WSA; Report of Agent 31, December 20, 1917, Gov. Lister, State Secret Service, WSA; WDGSR, Record Group 165, box 9, file 1095, NARA. Each report cited from box 9, file 1095 was included as part of a general report sent from Bryce P. Disque to F. B. Stansbury, January 24, 1919; Report of Agent 31, November 26–27, 1917, Gov. Lister, State Secret Service, WSA; Report of Agent 31, January 2, 1918; Gov. Lister, State Secret Service, WSA; Report of S-7, February 7–8, 1918, Gov. Lister, State Secret Service, WSA; Report of E. B., January 30, 1918, Gov. Lister, State Secret Service, WSA.

87. Report of Agent 31, November 20, 1917, Gov. Lister, State Secret Service, WSA.

88. F. B. Stansbury to Captain George Gund, USNA, in Charge Military Intelligence, WDGSR, Record Group 165, box 2, file 570, NARA.

89. Report of Agent 11, December 31, 1917, WDGSR, Record Group 165, box 9, file 1095, NARA; Testimony of Walter Horace Margason, *United States v. Haywood, et al.*, IWW Collection, box 110, folder 3, 5708, WSU.

90. *Industrial Worker,* April 8, 1918; Robert L. Tyler, *Rebels of the Woods: The IWW in the Pacific Northwest* (Eugene: University of Oregon Books, 1967), 129; Tom Copeland, *The Centralia Tragedy of 1919: Elmer Smith and the Wobblies* (Seattle: University of Washington Press, 1993), 31; *Washingtonian*, April 7, 1918.

91. *Industrial Worker*, April 8, 1918; *Aberdeen Daily World*, April 8, 10, 1918; Report of H. D. McKenney to F. B. Stansbury, April 11, 1918, Military Intelligence Division, Plant Protection, Portland District, WDGSR, Record Group 165, box 1, file 508, NARA.

92. *Aberdeen Daily World*, April 11, 1918. Frank Little was lynched in Butte, Montana, on August 1, 1917. See Kornbluh, *Rebel Voices*, 295.

93. *Washingtonian*, April 18, September 22, 1918.

94. *Industrial Worker*, April 14, 1918; *Aberdeen Daily World*, April 11, 1918.

95. See Aaron Goings, *The Port of Missing Men: Billy Gohl, Labor, and Brutal Times in the Pacific Northwest* (Seattle: University of Washington Press, 2020).

96. *Aberdeen Daily World*, April 11, 1918.

97. *Washingtonian*, April 10, 1918.

98. *Washingtonian*, April 11, 1918.

99. *Aberdeen Daily World*, September 5, 6, 1917; *Industrial Worker*, September 19, November 24, 1917; April 8, 1918; Tyler, *Rebels of the Woods*, 129; Copeland, *Centralia Tragedy of 1919*, 31.

100. *Literary Digest for November 22, 1919*, 15. *Industrial Worker*, December 13, 1919, reprinted this article.

101. The most recent, accessible, and cogent history of the Seattle General Strike is Winslow, *Radical Seattle*.

102. Victoria L. Johnson, *How Many Machine Guns Does It Take to Cook One Meal? The Seattle and San Francisco General Strikes* (Seattle: University of Washington Press, 2015), 49–55; Dana Frank, *Purchasing Power: Consumer Organizing, Gender, and the Seattle Labor Movement, 1919–1945* (Cambridge, UK: Cambridge University Press, 1994), 34–35.

103. *Aberdeen Daily World*, January 17, 1919; *Washingtonian*, January 17, 1919.

104. Anna Louise Strong, *Seattle General Strike* (Seattle: Seattle Union Record Publishing Co., 1919), 28; Winslow, *Radical Seattle*.

105. *Washingtonian*, February 6, 1919; Winslow, *Radical Seattle*.

106. *Washingtonian*, January 23, 1919.

107. *Washingtonian*, January 28, February 7, 1919.

108. Anna Louise Strong, *I Change Worlds* (Seattle: Seal Press, 1979; first published 1935 by Holt, Rinehart, and Winston, New York), 78; "On Thursday at 10 A.M.," *Seattle Union Record*.

109. *Washingtonian*, February 7, 1919.

110. Frank, *Purchasing Power*, 39.

111. Winslow, *Radical Seattle*; Strong, *Seattle General Strike*, 63; Frank, *Purchasing Power*, 39.

112. Robert E. Ficken, *Lumber and Politics: The Career of Mark E. Reed* (Seattle: University of Washington Press, 1980), 40; Alex Polson to Mr. Irvin W. Ziegans, Secretary to Governor, March 12, 1917, Governor Ernest Lister Papers, box 2H-2-112, 1917–1919, WSA.

113. N. J. Blagen to Hon. Earnest Lister, Governor of State of Washington, March 14, 1917, Governor Ernest Lister Papers, Industrial Workers of the World—Judiciary Files, box no. 2H-2-112, 1917–1919, WSA.

114. Gunns, *Civil Liberties in Crisis*, 37; Ficken, *Lumber and Politics*, 40; Alex Polson to Mr. Irvin W. Ziegans, Secretary to Governor, March 12, 1917, Governor Ernest Lister Papers, box no. 2H-2-112, 1917–1919, WSA; see Governor Ernest Lister Papers, Industrial Workers of the World—Judiciary Files, box no. 2H-2-112, 1917–1919, WSA; Alex Polson to Mr. Irvin W. Ziegans, Secretary to Governor, March 12, 1917, Gov. Lister, State Secret Service, WSA; Dubofsky, *We Shall Be All*, 381; N. J. Blagen to Hon. Earnest Lister, Governor of State of Washington, March 14, 1917, Governor Ernest Lister Papers, Industrial Workers of the World—Judiciary Files, box no. 2H-2-112, 1917–1919, WSA; *Senate Journal of the Fifteenth Legislature of the State of Washington, Begun and Held at Olympia, the State Capital, January 8, 1917* (Olympia: Frank M. Lamborn, Public Printer, 1917), 390; Copeland, *Centralia Tragedy of 1919*, 90.

115. Meeting Minutes, July 2, 1918, Anacortes City Council, Minutes, 1891–2005, Washington State Archives, Digital Archives, http://digitalarchives.wa.gov, accessed November 22, 2020; Meeting Minutes, January 27, 1919, Sedro-Woolley City Council, Minutes, 1892–2009, Washington State Archives, Digital Archives, http://digitalarchives.wa.gov, accessed April 21, 2020; *Washingtonian*, April 18, 1918.

116. *Washingtonian*, April 27, 1918.

117. Chehalis County Jail Record: Civil/Criminal, 1913–1922, SWA. According to this record, police arrested and held in county jail twenty-three IWW members between July 14 and August 23. This number does not include those arrested and held in local jails or those IWW members merely harassed by local, state, and federal law enforcement agents. *Washingtonian*, May 15, 16, 1918.

118. Gunns, *Civil Liberties in Crisis*, 37; *Aberdeen Daily World*, January 14, 1919; Copeland, *Centralia Tragedy of 1919*, 90.

119. *Aberdeen Daily Bulletin*, March 30, 1904; Jensen, *Lumber and Labor*, 116.

120. *Aberdeen Daily World*, January 14, 1919; Copeland, *Centralia Tragedy of 1919*, 23–24; Dubofsky, *We Shall Be All*, 455; Tyler, *Rebels of the Woods*, 155–84; Patrick Renshaw, *The Wobblies: The Story of Syndicalism in the United States* (New York: Anchor Books, 1967), 163–67; Adamic, *Dynamite*, 167–73.

121. *Four L Bulletin*, December 1919.

122. White, *Under the Iron Heel*, 2.

123. *Senate Journal of the Sixteenth Legislature of the State of Washington* (Olympia: Public Printer, 1919), 518–19. This law passed the Senate on March 3, 1919, passed the House of Representatives on March 11, 1919, and was approved by the governor on March 19, 1919.

124. *Aberdeen Daily World*, November 12, 1919.

125. Chehalis/Grays Harbor County Jail Record: Civil/Criminal, Jail Record, 1913–22, SWA; *Aberdeen Daily World*, November 15, 17, 1919.

126. *Industrial Worker*, October 21, 28, 1922; Chehalis/Grays Harbor County Jail Record: Civil/Criminal, Jail Record, 1913–22, SWA; *Aberdeen Daily World*, November 12, 13, 15, 17, 1919; February 10, 1920.

127. Jack London, *The Iron Heel* (Girard, KS: Appeal to Reason, 1908).

128. On the IWW resilience during and after the Red Scare crackdowns, see Fred Thompson, "They Didn't Suppress the Wobblies," *Radical America* 1, no. 2 (September-October 1967): 3–5.

7. ALBERT JOHNSON'S GRAYS HARBOR

1. See Aaron Goings, "Johnson, Albert (1869–1957)," Essay 8721, *History Link*, September 3, 2008, http://www.historylink.org/index.cfm?DisplayPage=output.cfm&file

_id=8721; Alfred J. Hillier, "Albert Johnson, Congressman," *Pacific Northwest Quarterly* 36 (1945): 193–211.

2. David A. Reed, "America of the Melting Pot Comes to End," *New York Times*, April 27, 1924; "Applaud Alien Bill in D.A.R. Convention," *New York Times*, April 19, 1924.

3. Adam Hochschild, *American Midnight: The Great War, a Violent Peace, and Democracy's Forgotten Crisis* (New York: Harper Collins, 2023), 350.

4. *Aberdeen Daily World*, July 5, 1924.

5. *Aberdeen Daily World*, December 12, 1923.

6. *Aberdeen Daily World*, July 5, 1924.

7. *Seattle Star*, May 26, 1924.

8. *Washington Times*, May 27, 1924.

9. *Wisconsin Kourier*, December 12, 1924.

10. Edith Terry Bremer, "Immigration: A Look Ahead," *The Survey* 52, no. 4 (May 15, 1924): 210.

11. *Home Defender* (Hoquiam, Wash.), May 15, 1912. On Johnson's politics as part of mainstream American views, see Kristopher Allerfeldt, "'And We Got Here First': Albert Johnson, National Origins, and Self-Interest in the Immigration Debate of the 1920s," *Journal of Contemporary History* 45, no. 1 (January 2010): 7–26.

12. Dana Frank, *Purchasing Power: Consumer Organizing, Gender, and the Seattle Labor Movement, 1919–1945* (Cambridge, UK: Cambridge University Press, 1994), 66.

13. *Southwest Washington Labor Press*, September 3, 1926.

14. US Bureau of the Census, *Fourteenth Census of the United States Taken in the Year 1920*, Washington, Grays Harbor County.

15. USBC, *Fifteenth Census of the United States Taken in the Year 1930*, Washington State, Grays Harbor County, Aberdeen.

16. *Grays Harbor Post*, December 13, 1924. The city's 1920 population was 15,337, and its 1930 population was 21,723. The city had 5,969 registered voters in 1924, according to the *Grays Harbor Post*.

17. See, for example, Eric Foner, "Why Is There No Socialism in the United States?" *History Workshop* (Spring 1984): 57–80. For an exaggerated view of the absence of class consciousness in the United States, see Michael Kazin, "Struggling with Class Struggle: Marxism and the Search for a Synthesis of U.S. Labor History," *Labor History* (Fall 1987): 297–514.

18. Charlotte Todes, *Lumber and Labor* (New York: International Publishers, 1931), 87–89; Anna M. Lind, "Women in Early Logging Camps: A Personal Reminiscence," *Journal of Forest History* 19, no. 3 (July 1975): 128–30.

19. Charter, Aberdeen Branch of Industrial Union 460, IWW Collection, October 26, 1923, box 17, folder 4, WSU; USBC, *Fourteenth Census . . . 1920*.

20. Edwin Van Syckle, *They Tried to Cut It All: Grays Harbor . . . Turbulent Years of Greed and Greatness* (Seattle: Pacific Search Press, 1980), 201; Robert M. Cour, *The Plywood Age: A History of the Fir Plywood Industry's First Fifty Years* (Portland: Douglas Fir Plywood Assoc., 1955), 65; Manufacturers' Association of Washington (MAW), *Directory of Washington Manufacturers and List of Products Manufactured by Them*, 9th ed. (Seattle: Manufacturers' Association of Washington, 1931), 59.

21. MAW, *Directory of Washington Manufacturers and List of Products Manufactured by Them*, 7th ed. (Seattle: Manufacturers' Association of Washington, 1923), 109; MAW, *Directory of Washington Manufacturers and List of Products Manufactured by Them*, 8th ed. (Seattle: Manufacturers' Association of Washington, 1924) 56.

22. MAW, *Directory of Washington Manufacturers*, 8th ed.; MAW, *Directory of Washington Manufacturers*, 9th ed.

23. USBC, *Fifteenth Census . . . 1930*.

24. "Aberdeen, Washington, Plywood Local No. 2521," *Timber Worker*, Labor Day ed., September 7, 1936.

25. *Daily Worker*, May 30, 1929.

26. See Annelise Orleck, *Common Sense and a Little Fire: Women and Working-Class Politics in the United States, 1900–1965* (Chapel Hill: University of North Carolina Press, 2000), 72.

27. This quotation is often mistaken as "the business of America is business."

28. Van Syckle, *They Tried to Cut It All*, 112–14; The Timberman, *Directory of the Lumber Industry (Pacific Coast)* (Portland: The Timberman, 1926), 165.

29. *Washingtonian*, June 19, 1918; Testimony of Albert and John Schafer, *United States v. Haywood et al.*, IWW Collection, box 110, folder 3, 5713, WSU.

30. Van Syckle, *They Tried to Cut It All*, 114.

31. Stewart Holbrook, *A Narrative of Schafer Bros. Logging Company's Half Century in the Timber* (Seattle: Dogwood Press, 1945).

32. The Merrill and Ring Papers at the University of Washington Libraries Special Collections contains several instances of managers from different firms sharing information about wage and conditions. See W. J. Chisholm to Robert Polson, February 6, 1924, Merrill and Ring Lumber Company Papers, acc. no. 726, box 51, folder 1, UW.

33. A report from the Fourth Annual Red Cedar Shingle Congress appeared in *The Timberman*, December 1920, 48D; The Timberman, *Directory of the Lumber Industry (Pacific Coast)*, 1926 ed., 283.

34. "Highly individualistic" appears in Robert E. Ficken and Charles P. LeWarne, *Washington: A Centennial History* (Seattle: University of Washington Press, 1989), 47.

35. *Timberman*, December 1925, 234.

36. *Aberdeen Daily World*, October 23, 1925; *Washingtonian*, March 3, 1927; *Voice of Action*, October 23, November 13, 1933.

37. Richard A. Rajala, "A Dandy Bunch of Wobblies: Pacific Northwest Loggers and the Industrial Workers of the World, 1900–1930," *Labor History* 37, no. 2 (Spring 1996): 231–32; *Industrial Worker*, January 4, 1912.

38. *Washingtonian*, March 3, 1927.

39. *Daily Worker*, September 4, 1929.

40. Andrew Parnaby, *Citizen Docker: Making a New Deal on the Vancouver Waterfront, 1919–1939* (Toronto: University of Toronto Press, 2008), 27–28.

41. See Rajala, "A Dandy Bunch of Wobblies," 231–32.

42. Loggers Information Association to Members, January 3, 1918, Merrill and Ring Papers, acc. no. 726, box 10, folder 2, UW.

43. *Appendix to the Annual Report of the Attorney General of the United States for the Fiscal Year 1922* (Washington, DC: Government Printing Office, 1924), 668–69. This report included a letter from E. B. Benn to Attorney General, Washington, DC, August 21, 1922.

44. *Timberman*, September 1921, 129.

45. State of Washington, Department of Labor and Industries, *Bulletin, Department of Labor and Industries, State of Washington* (April 1923): 4.

46. The Timberman, *Directory of the Logging Industry (Pacific Coast)*, 1922 ed., 161–62.

47. *American Lumberman* (Chicago), July 14, 1923, 77.

48. *American Lumberman*, December 1, 1923, 77.

49. Robert E. Ficken, *The Forested Land: A History of Lumbering in Western Washington* (Seattle: University of Washington Press, 1987), 162.

50. *Timberman*, January 1924, 117; February 1924, 116. The paper also declared, "The recent catastrophe has brought about an unprecedented animation in the lumber market."

51. *American Lumberman*, September 15, 1923, 73.

52. F. L. Moravets, "Lumber Production in Oregon and Washington, 1869–1948," *US Forest Service, Pacific Northwest Forest and Range Experimentation Station Forest Survey, 1949*, Forest Survey Report 100 (Portland: USFS, 1948); John C. Hughes and Ryan Teague Beckwith, eds., *On the Harbor: From Black Friday to Nirvana* (Aberdeen, WA: Daily World, 2001), 72.

53. *Timberman*, January 1927, 118.

54. For studies of on-the-job violence, see Jeremy Milloy, *Blood, Sweat, and Fear: Violence and Work in the North American Auto Industry, 1960–1980* (Vancouver: University of British Columbia Press, 2017); Nate Holdren, *Injury Impoverished: Workplace Accidents, Capitalism, and Law in the Progressive Era* (Cambridge, UK: Cambridge University Press, 2020).

55. *Industrial Worker*, May 28, 1924; Merle A. Reinikka, "Death Certificates of Finns

in Chehalis (Grays Harbor] County, 1907–1947," Aberdeen History Collection, AHM.

56. Van Syckle, *They Tried to Cut It All*, 65.

57. *History of Aberdeen USKB&S Lodge No. 9*, 6, United Finnish Kaleva Brothers and Sisters Lodge 9 Collection, AHM.

58. Todes, *Labor and Lumber*, 130–40.

59. Andrew M. Prouty, *"More Deadly Than War!" Pacific Coast Logging, 1827–1981* (Seattle: University of Washington Press, 1985), 186.

60. Reinikka, "Death Certificates of Finns."

61. *Shingle Weaver*, August 25, 1917.

62. *Aberdeen Daily World*, November 20, 1924.

63. *Aberdeen Daily World*, January 11, 1924. This article closely resembled one that the *World* ran six years earlier under the headline "Aberdeen Still Healthiest City," January 12, 1917.

64. *Washingtonian*, February 12, 1924. The state's Bureau of Labor was the forerunner of the Department of Labor and Industries. The latter began operating in 1921 following its creation by the Washington State Legislature.

65. *Industrial Worker*, September 2, 1916.

66. *Lumberjack Bulletin* (Seattle), March 16, 1918. The term "Fellow Worker" was and is a term of endearment and solidarity among IWWs. Wobbly writings routinely include the term "Fellow Worker" in place of a first name such as "Fellow Worker Holmes" in this article.

67. Prouty, *"More Deadly Than War!"* 205.

68. *Industrial Worker*, June 9, 1917; May 31, 1924.

69. David Montgomery, *The Fall of the House of Labor: The Workplace, the State, and American Labor Activism, 1865–1925* (New Haven, CT: Yale University Press, 1987); Jonathan Dembo, *Unions and Politics in Washington State, 1885–1935* (New York: Garland Press, 1982), 271; Frank, *Purchasing Power*, 244.

70. Washington State Federation of Labor Ledger Books 10 and 13, box 71, WSFL Records, UW.

71. *Southwest Washington Labor Press*, August 28, September 5, 12, 1925.

72. According to historian Jonathan Dembo, Washington State unemployment reached more than 11 percent in 1921. Dembo, *Unions and Politics*, 623.

73. Cloice R. Howd, "Industrial Relations in the West Coast Lumber Industry," *Bulletin of the United States Bureau of Labor Statistics*, no. 349 (Washington, DC: Government Printing Office, 1924), 101; Washington State Federation of Labor Ledger Book 12, box 71, WSFL Records, UW.

74. Grays Harbor lumber workers struck on several occasions during the 1920s. Many of these were small, short-lived strikes while others spread across the harbor's

lumber industry. See, for example, *Aberdeen Daily World*, October 2, 1925, February 4, 1927; *Industrial Unionist*, October 14, 1925; *Washingtonian*, February 5, 1927; *Montesano Vidette*, February 4, 1927.

75. *Four L Bulletin*, December 1919, 34. During the 1920s, the registration card system became an increasingly prominent part of labor relations methods that spread well beyond the lumber industry. See Parnaby, *Citizen Docker*, 27–28.

76. *Timberman*, January 1921, 33; July 1921, 62; Howd, "Industrial Relations," 88; Vernon Jensen, *Lumber and Labor* (New York: Arno Press, 1971; first published 1945 by J. J. Little and Ives Co., New York), 151.

77. *Four L Bulletin*, November 1922, 32.

78. Howd, "Industrial Relations," 90.

79. Washington State Federation of Labor Ledger Book 12, box 71, WSFL Records, UW; *Southwest Washington Labor Press*, April 22, 1927; September 4, 1925; February 26, 1926.

80. *Southwest Washington Labor Press*, May 25, October 12, 19, 1923; January 2, 1925. See *Southwest Washington Labor Press*, March 5, 1915. There are almost no remaining copies of early issues of the *Southwest Washington Labor Press*, although fortunately many of its 1920s issues have been digitized and are available through the Library of Congress.

81. *Grays Harbor Press*, November 29, 1929.

82. *Southwest Washington Labor Press*, August 29, 1924.

83. *Southwest Washington Labor Press*, April 11, 1924.

84. *Southwest Washington Labor Press*, September 3, 1926.

85. *Poseygram* (Hoquiam, WA), April 1924. The Four Ls supported restricting lumber jobs to native-born Americans. See *Timberman*, November 1920, 31, 68.

86. The Hoquiam labor council placed the owner of a local "colored" barber shop on the "unfair list" and declared a boycott against his shop—as well as white-owned barber shops. *Southwest Washington Labor Press*, April 10, 1925.

87. Frank, *Purchasing Power*, 28.

88. *Southwest Washington Labor Press*, February 2, 1922.

89. *Southwest Washington Labor Press*, October 2, 1925.

90. *Southwest Washington Labor Press*, January 26, 1923.

91. *Southwest Washington Labor Press*, September 3, 1926.

92. *Southwest Washington Labor Press*, January 29, September 3, 1926.

93. *Congressional Record*, 1918, 8529.

94. This *Washingtonian* article appeared under the headline "Congressman Albert Johnson Advises Mob Violence," in *Industrial Worker*, April 27, 1918.

95. Cited in Tom Copeland, *The Centralia Tragedy of 1919: Elmer Smith and the Wobblies* (Seattle: University of Washington Press, 1993), 42.

96. On the Second Ku Klux Klan, see Linda Gordon, *The Second Coming of the KKK: The Ku Klux Klan of the 1920s and the American Political Tradition* (New York: Liveright Publishing, 2017), 3; Daniel Okrent, *The Guarded Gate: Bigotry, Eugenics, and the Law That Kept Two Generations of Jews, Italians, and Other European Immigrants Out of America* (New York: Scribner, 2019).

97. Trevor Griffey, "KKK Super Rallies in Washington State, 1923–24," *Seattle Civil Rights and Labor History Project*, 2007, https://depts.washington.edu/civilr/kkk_rallies.htm.

98. *Watcher on the Tower* (Seattle), August 25, 1923.

99. Cited in Trevor Griffey, "Citizen Klan: Electoral Politics and the KKK in WA," *Seattle Civil Rights and Labor History Project*, 2007, https://depts.washington.edu/civilr/kkk_politicians.htm.

100. Gordon, *Second Coming of the KKK*, 6.

101. *Watcher on the Tower*, Klan Directory, University of Washington Photo and Document Repository, http://depts.washington.edu/labpics/zenPhoto/KKK/Watcher-on-the-Tower-15-full-issues-1923, accessed February 16, 2025.

102. *Washingtonian*, August 7, 1921; *Tacoma Daily Ledger*, August 8, 1921; *Lynden Tribune*, December 29, 1921.

103. *Industrial Worker*, August 20, 1921.

104. *Industrial Worker*, July 30, 1921.

105. Nancy MacLean, *Beyond the Mask of Chivalry: The Making of the Second Ku Klux Klan* (New York: Oxford University Press, 1994), 53–54.

106. *Industrial Worker*, July 30, 1921.

107. *Oregon Daily Journal* (Portland), December 11, 1921.

108. On the Klan and temperance, see Gordon, *Second Coming of the KKK*, 28–29, 95–96.

109. MacLean, *Beyond the Mask of Chivalry*, 116.

110. USBC, *Fourteenth Census . . . 1920*, Washington State, Grays Harbor County, Satsop; *Washington Farmer*, July 25, 1918; *Third Biennial Report of the Department of Agriculture of the State of Washington* (Olympia, WA: Frank M. Lamborn, Public Printer, 1918), 43; *Grays Harbor Post*, March 16, 1940; Washington State Grange, *Journal of Proceedings, Thirty-Second Annual Session of the Washington State Grange* (Aberdeen, WA: Washington State Grange, 1920), 136.

111. *Aberdeen Herald*, August 14, September 8, November 6, 10, 1914.

112. *Automotive Daily News*, 1950, vol. 26, 32; *Motor West and California Motor*, December 15, 1927, 53.

113. *Aberdeen Daily World*, July 27, 1923.

114. Photograph of Ku Klux Klan parade in downtown Hoquiam, July 4, 1925, Photographs Collection, Polson Museum, Hoquiam, Wash.

115. Ku Klux Klan, *Principles and Purposes of the Knights of the Ku Klux Klan*,

Outlined by an Exalted Cyclops of the Order, 1920, p, 3, Paul W. Bean Civil War Papers, University of Maine Special Collections, Orono, https://digitalcommons.library.umaine.edu/cgi/viewcontent.cgi?article=1071&context=paul_bean_papers, accessed April 10, 2024.

116. Alex Polson to Mr. Timothy Jerome, July 23, 1917, Merrill and Ring Papers, acc. no. 726, box 7, folder 21, UW.

117. Reports to Council, 1921–1962, Aberdeen Police Department, Aberdeen Municipal Government, acc. no. SW351-2-0-3, SRB-WSA.

118. Aberdeen Police Department, Daily Report for June 24, 1924, City of Aberdeen, Police Department, Daily Report Journals, Chronological, box 4, 1921–1924, acc. no. SW20060210-03, SRB-WSA.

119. USBC, *Fourteenth Census . . . 1920*; Dorothy B. Fujita Rony, *American Workers, Colonial Power: Philippine Seattle and the Transpacific West* (Berkeley: University of California Press, 2003), 108–14.

120. Clara Weatherwax, *Marching! Marching!* (New York: John Day Co., 1935). Clara Weatherwax was the granddaughter of the mill owner J. M. Weatherwax, one of the harbor's earliest elites.

121. Fujita Rony, 110–11.

122. *Aberdeen Daily World*, July 7, 1924.

123. *Aberdeen Daily World*, December 3, 1924.

124. *Southwest Washington Labor Press*, August 29, 1924; *Directory of the Lumber Industry (Pacific Coast)*, 1926 ed., 132.

125. *Congressional Record: Proceedings and Debates of the 71st Cong., 2nd Sess.* (1930), 1859.

126. *Congressional Record, 71st Cong., 2nd Sess.*, S1884.

127. USBC, *Thirteenth Census . . . 1910*, Aberdeen; *Aberdeen Herald*, November 19, 1903; November 16, 1905; December 7, 1908; *Grays Harbor Post*, December 9, 1905; *Seattle Times*, January 11, 1924; April 7, September 15, 1925; *Bellingham Herald*, April 6, 8, 1925; *Tacoma Daily Ledger*, January 4, April 9, 1925.

128. *Washingtonian*, December 9, 1922; *Timberman*, September 1924, 30.

129. *Aberdeen Daily World*, November 24, 1923; July 16, 1924. Grays Harbor court records are filled with arrests made by Hopkins, for liquor violations and other offenses. See, for example, In the Justice Court of the State of Washington, County of Grays Harbor, Aberdeen Precinct, Criminal Docket, Book 6, June 26, 1924–October 8, 1925, SRB-WSA.

130. *Seattle Times*, November 4, 1923. The alleged moonshiner was Bailey's tenant rather than the mayor, but the dramatic raid on the mayor's home caught headlines.

131. *Seattle Times*, January 11, 1924.

132. *Grays Harbor Post*, November 8, December 13, 1924.

133. See Gordon, *The Second Coming.*

134. *Aberdeen Daily World*, November 10, 1924. *Tacoma Daily Ledger*, April 9, 1925.

135. Gordon, *Second Coming of the KKK.*

136. *Seattle Star*, April 8, 1925.

137. *Seattle Star*, April 6, 1925.

138. *Seattle Star*, April 8, 9, 1925; *Tacoma Daily Ledger*, April 9, 1925. Aberdeen City Council Minutes, January 7, 1925, City of Aberdeen, Clerk, Minutes, Inclusive Dates, 1923–1926, acc. no. 983W287, box 10, SRB-WSA.

139. *Southwest Washington Labor Press*, March 18, 1925.

140. *Aberdeen Daily World*, March 17, 1925.

141. *Seattle Star*, April 6, 8, 1925.

142. *Grays Harbor Post*, May 31, 1924.

143. The quotation from *Watcher in the Tower* appeared in the *Grays Harbor Post*, May 31, 1924.

144. *Grays Harbor Post*, May 31, 1924.

145. *Grays Harbor Post*, May 31, November 8, 15, December 13, 1924.

146. *Grays Harbor Post*, December 13, 1924.

147. *Seattle Star*, April 6, 1925.

148. USBC, *Fifteenth Census . . . 1930*, Grays Harbor County, Aberdeen.

149. *Seattle Daily Times*, March 27, 1936.

150. On the Better Housing Program Committee, see *Local Chairmen of Better Housing Program Committees* (Washington, DC: Federal Housing Administration, 1934), 43; *Senate Journal of the Twenty-Ninth Legislature of the State of Washington at Olympia, the State Capital, Convened January 8, 1945, Adjourned Sine Die March 8, 1945* (Olympia: State Printing Plant, 1945); 44; Ransom Minkler, Oath of Office, Grays Harbor Junior College, State Government Oaths of Office, 1854–2022, Office of the Secretary of State, Washington State Archives, Digital Archives, http://digitalarchives.wa.gov, accessed November 4, 2022.

151. *Washington Farmer*, July 25, 1918; *Third Biennial Report of the Department of Agriculture of the State of Washington* (Olympia, WA: Frank M. Lamborn, Public Printer, 1918), 43; *Grays Harbor Post*, March 16, 1940.

8 HALL RADICALISM

1. *Industrialisti*, October 16, 1923, trans. Matti Roitto; Articles of Incorporation of Aberdeen Finnish Workers' Association, 1923, Grays Harbor Auditor, Articles of Incorporation, box 6, acc. 99-SW-245, no. 516, SRB-WSA.

2. *Industrialisti*, October 16, 1923; November 12, 1924; *Grays Harbor Post*, March 29, April 5, 1924; *Aberdeen Daily World*, March 27, October 24, 1924.

3. Antti Maki, "Puolesta Joukon Miljoonaisen," *Tie Vapauteen* (November 1925): 7–8, trans. Jenni Salmi.

4. See Melvyn Dubofsky, *We Shall Be All: A History of the Industrial Workers of the World* (Chicago: Quadrangle Books, 1969, 1973), 464–66; Robert L. Tyler, *Rebels of the Woods: The IWW in the Pacific Northwest* (Eugene: University of Oregon Books, 1967), 153–55; Joseph Robert Conlin, *Bread and Roses Too: Studies of the Wobblies* (Westport, CT: Greenwood Publishing Corp., 1969), 140–46; Joseph Robert Conlin, "Industrial Unionist," in *American Radical Press, 1880–1960*, vol. 1, edited by Joseph Robert Conlin (Westport, CT: Greenwood Press, 1974), 128–30.

5. Peter J. Campbell, "The Cult of Spontaneity: Finnish-Canadian Bushworkers and the Industrial Workers of the World in Northern Ontario, 1919–1934," *Labour/Le Travail* 41 (Spring 1998): 117–46.

6. See, especially, Ahmed White, *Under the Iron Heel: The Wobblies and the Capitalist War on Radical Workers* (Berkeley: University of California Press, 2022).

7. Dubofsky, *We Shall Be All*, 466; Industrial Workers of the World, *Twenty-Five Years of Industrial Unionism* (Chicago: Industrial Workers of the World, 1930); *Industrial Worker*, September 8, 12, 13, 15, 22, 1923.

8. John S. Gambs, *The Decline of the IWW* (New York: Columbia University Press, 1932), 123; *Industrial Unionist*, April 18, July 4, 1925; Charter, Aberdeen Branch of Industrial Union 460, October 26, 1923, IWW Collection, box 17, folder 4, WSU.

9. *Industrialisti*, May 22, 1929; January 21, 1931; November 18, 1939.

10. *Industrialisti*, October 1, 4, 6, 7, 8, 18, 21, 27, 1925.

11. Egbert S. Oliver, "Sawmilling on Grays Harbor: A Personal Reminiscence." *Pacific Northwest Quarterly* 69, no. 1 (January 1978): 14.

12. Sidney Bloomfield to Org. Dept. R. Baker, March 11, 1931, Russian Center for the Preservation and Study of Documents of Recent History, Tamiment Library, New York University, New York (hereafter RTsKhIDNI), f. 515, op. 1, d. 2318; M. Raport to the Pol Buro, August 2, 1935, RTsKhIDNI, f. 515, op. 1, d. 3873.

13. Gordon "Brick" Moir, interview by Gary Murrell, audio recording, Hoquiam, Wash., March 27, 2000, in author's possession.

14. *Industriali*, May 15, 1918.

15. *Industrial Worker*, July 16, August 30, 1924.

16. *Industrial Worker*, January 12, 1924; Auvo Kostiainen, "Finnish-American Workmen's Associations," in *Old Friends—Strong Ties: The Finnish Contribution to the Growth of the USA*, edited by Vilho Niitemaa et al. (Turku, Finland: Institute of Migration, 1976), 205–34. On *Tie Vapauteen*, see *Minutes of the Convention of the Industrial Workers of the World, Held at Phoenix Hall, Chicago, Ill., May 9–27, 1921* (Chicago: IWW Workers Industrial Union No. 450, 1921), 22, IWW Papers, box 1, UW; *Industrialisti*, June 15, 1929.

17. Conlin, "Industrial Unionist," 1933; Conlin, *Bread and Roses Too*, 140–41; Dubofsky, *We Shall Be All*; Robert E. Ficken, "The Wobbly Horrors Pacific Northwest Lumbermen and the Industrial Workers of the World, 1917–1918," *Labor History* 24, no. 3 (Summer 1983): 329; Tom Copeland, *The Centralia Tragedy of 1919: Elmer Smith and the Wobblies* (Seattle: University of Washington Press, 1993), 76.

18. Fred Thompson, "They Didn't Suppress the Wobblies," *Radical America* 1, no. 2 (September-October 1967): 3–5. See Greg Hall, *Harvest Wobblies: The Industrial Workers of the World and Agricultural Laborers in the American West, 1905–1930* (Corvallis: Oregon State University Press, 2001); Peter Cole, *Wobblies on the Waterfront: Interracial Unionism in Progressive-Era Philadelphia* (Urbana: University of Illinois Press, 2007); Nigel Sellars, *Oil, Wheat, and Wobblies: The Industrial Workers of the World in Oklahoma, 1905–1930* (Norman: University of Oklahoma Press, 1998); Elizabeth Gurley Flynn, *The Rebel Girl: An Autobiography, My First Life (1906–1926)*, new ed. (New York: International Publishers, 3rd printing, 1973), 76–77; Paul Brissenden, *The IWW: A Study of American Syndicalism* (1919; reprint, 2nd ed., New York: Russell and Russell, 1957), 110; Conlin, *Bread and Roses Too*, 41; Cloice R. Howd, "Industrial Relations in the West Coast Lumber Industry," *Bulletin of the United States Bureau of Labor Statistics*, no. 349 (Washington, DC: Government Printing Office, 1924), 102; Gambs, *Decline of the IWW*, 173; *Lumberjack Bulletin* (Seattle), March 16, 1918; *Industrial Worker*, January 12, 1918; August 16, 1919; *Industrialisti*, June 16, July 3, 23, 1917; *New Unionist*, January 14, 1928; Report of Agent 31, November 20, 1917, Gov. Lister, State Secret Service, Correspondence Files, 1917–1921, acc. no. AR2-H-5, WSA.

19. *Industrial Worker*, October 9, 16, 1920; May 1, 14, June 11, 1921.

20. Hall, *Harvest Wobblies*. On the postwar strength of the AWIU and LWIU, see Hall, 205, 209–10; David R. Roediger, ed., *Fellow Worker: The Life of Fred Thompson* (Chicago: Charles H. Kerr Publishing Co., 1993), 59–60; *Industrial Worker*, October 9, 16, 1920; May 27, June 14, 17, October 14, 1922; April 28, July 24, September 15, October 27, 1923; August 30, 1924; Chehalis/Grays Harbor County Jail Record: Civil/Criminal, 1913–1922, acc. no. 86-1-19, box 245D, SRB-WSA; Records, 1923–1925, Publicity, Defense, and Jail Records (IWW), IWW Collection, box 134, folder 1, WSU.

21. Oiva Carl Wirkalla, interviewed by Donald L. Myers, September 22, 1976, Washington State Oral/Aural History Project, Washington State Division of Archives and Records Management, 4.

22. *Industrial Worker*, September 15, 1923; *Industrialisti*, March 24, 1921. See Stephen Martin Kohn, *American Political Prisoners: Prosecutions Under the Espionage and Sedition Acts* (Westport, CT: Praeger Publishers, 1994), 91; Ralph Chaplin, *Wobbly: The Rough-and-Tumble Story of an American Radical* (Chicago: University of Chicago Press, 1948), 322–24; *Aberdeen Daily World*, August 5, 1921; *Industrial Worker*, September 23, 1922.

23. William Preston Jr., "Shall This Be All? *U.S. Historians Versus William D. Haywood, et al.*" *Labor History* 12, no. 3 (Summer 1971): 435–53.

24. Auvo Kostiainen, *The Forging of Finnish-American Communism, 1917–1924: A Study in Ethnic Radicalism* (Turku, Finland: Turin Yliopisto, 1978), 144–45.

25. *Industrial Worker*, May 27, October 14, 1922; May 12, July 24, 1923; August 30, 1924; Chehalis/Grays Harbor County Jail Record: Civil/Criminal, 1913–1922, acc. no. 86-1-19, box 245D, SRB-WSA; *Industrial Solidarity*, March 10, 1926; *The Contrast*, Resolution adopted by the membership of the Aberdeen Branch of LWIU No. 120, IWW, n.d., IWW Collection, box 158, WSU; Names for Charter and Seal, Aberdeen, 120, IWW Collection, box 17, folder 8, WSU; Minutes of the Central Branch Conference of Grays Harbor District, April 15, 1923, 3, IWW Collection, box 46, folder 12, WSU; *Industrial Unionist*, April 18, May 2, 9, 23, July 4, September 16, November 11, December 30, 1925; January 27, February 17, March 10, 24, 31, April 7, 1926; Convention Minutes, Lumberworkers I.U. No. 120 of the IWW, IWW Papers, acc. no. 544, box 1, folder 12, UW.

26. Records, 1923–1925, Publicity, Defense, and Jail Records (IWW), IWW Collection, box 134, folder 1, WSU.

27. US Bureau of the Census, *Fifteenth Census of the United States Taken in the Year 1930*, Washington State, Grays Harbor County, Aberdeen; *Bulletin No. 1: Lumber Workers' Industrial Union No. 120 of the IWW* (Aberdeen, Wash.), 1933, IWW Collection, box 46, folder 9, WSU; *Industrial Worker*, December 5, 1933.

28. Cited in John C. Hughes and Ryan Teague Beckwith, eds., *On the Harbor: From Black Friday to Nirvana* (Aberdeen, WA: Daily World, 2001), 72.

29. *Industrial Worker*, November 2, 30, December 7, 14, 21, 1929; *Marine Worker* (New York), June 1, 1925; May 1, 1926; June 1, 1928; February 15, 1929; July 1, 1936; Marine Transport Workers Industrial Union No. 510 of the IWW, Financial Statement for the Months of May, June, July, August and October, 1929, IWW Collection, box 28, folder 13, WSU.

30. Jeff Jewell, "History of Grays Harbor Longshoremen," International Longshoremen's and Warehouse Union Local 24 Archives, Aberdeen, Wash.

31. Harry Bridges, interviewed by Howard Kimeldorf, February 25, 1984, University of Washington Libraries Special Collections, Oral History Collection, Digital Collections, http://digitalcollections.lib.washington.edu/cdm/singleitem/collection/ohc/id/1316/rec/31, accessed March 10, 2018; Ottilie Markholt, *Maritime Solidarity: Pacific Coast Unionism, 1929–1938* (Tacoma, WA: Pacific Coast Maritime History Committee, 1998), 195.

32. *Aberdeen Daily World*, June 9, 1938; Markholt, *Maritime Solidarity*, 333, 381–82; Ottilie Markholt, "Against the Current: A Social Memoir" (unpublished MS, 2001, University of Washington Libraries Special Collections, Digital Archives, http://digital

collections.lib.washington.edu/cdm/ref/collection/pnwhm/id/837, accessed June 8, 2023), ch. 7, pp. 7–8; Maritime Federation of the Pacific Coast, *Proceedings of the Fourth Annual Convention* (June 6–25, 1938, San Francisco, Calif.), 68–77, 102–103.

33. The number of paid and unpaid women Wobblies does not equal the total because my count of the total number of adult women IWW members includes those for whom no occupational data could be gathered from the US Census or city directories. For a detailed study on women and the Wobblies in the Pacific Northwest before 1924, see Heather Mayer, *Beyond the Rebel Girl: Women and the Industrial Workers of the World in the Pacific Northwest, 1905–1924* (Corvallis: Oregon State University Press, 2018).

34. Charter, Aberdeen Branch of Industrial Union 460, IWW, October 26, 1923, IWW Collection, box 17, folder 4, WSU; Aberdeen Women's Union Records, IWW Collection, box 36, file 1, WSU.

35. *Industrialisti*, December 14, 1935.

36. Lauren Love, "Biographical Statement on Jennie Mathilda Heikkila (Sipo)" (unpublished MS in author's possession). Jennie Sipo's granddaughter Lauren Love conducted a great deal of family research and produced several materials that assisted with the writing of this book.

37. Charter, Aberdeen Branch of Industrial Union 460, October 26, 1923, IWW Collection, box 17, folder 4, WSU; USBC, *Fourteenth Census . . . 1920*, Washington State, Chehalis County, Aberdeen.

38. Chehalis/Grays Harbor County Jail Record: Civil/Criminal, 1913–1922, acc. no. 86-1-19, box 245D, SRB-WSA. Two other IWW members, loggers William Newman and Henry McCoy, joined their fellow workers in jail on criminal syndicalism charges in August 1922. See also *Grays Harbor Post*, November 4, 1922; *Industrial Worker*, October 21, 28, 1922.

39. *Industrial Worker*, June 10, 1922.

40. *Industrial Worker*, June 24, 1922.

41. Biographical Info and Testament to Emily Kaiyala, by Brother Garnet and Sister-in-Law Marguerite Kaiyala, Butte/Silver Bow Archives, Butte, Mont.; Lauren Love, "Biographical Statement on Emily Kaiyala" (unpublished MS in author's possession).

42. *Industrialisti*, May 14, 1918; November 10, 1919; *Industrial Worker*, July 21, 1923; "Financial Statement of the General Defense Committee for the Month of December 1923," *General Office Bulletin for the Month of January 1923*, 23, IWW Collection, box 31, folder 8, WSU; "Financial Statement of the General Defense Committee for the Month of December 1924," *General Office Bulletin*, 25, IWW Collection, box 31, folder 31, WSU; "Financial Statement of the General Defense Committee for the Month of December 1923," 19, IWW Collection, box 31, folder 19, WSU. Notably, Fred Hendricks, a resident of Aberdeen, donated $225 to the General Defense Committee on December

18, 1923. See "Financial Statement of the General Defense Committee for the Month of December 1923," 19, IWW Collection, box 31, folder 19, WSU; Receipts, Publicity, Defense, and Jail Relief Records, 6, 14, 22, 46, 52, 58, 118, 134, 136, 186, 198, 200, 201, 206, 220, 242, 250, 264, IWW Collection, box 134, WSU.

43. *Industrialisti*, January 5, 1920; June 15, 1929. Grays Harbor Wobblies occasionally led the nation in subscription receipts to the *Industrialisti* during the 1920s and 1930s. See *Industrialisti*, February 15, 1920; November 21, 1928.

44. *Industrialisti*, March 16, 1935. See also *Industrialisti*, May 13, August 9, 1935. Throughout the 1920s and 1930s, Niemi was one of the country's top *Industrialisti* subscription hustlers, and seeing Niemi leading the country in subscription sales was not unusual. See *Industrialisti*, April 12, 1934.

45. For example, see *Industrialisti*, December 15, 1920; December 14, 1921; December 15, 1926; December 15, 1927; December 15, 1928; April 14, December 15, 1935.

46. The Junior Wobblies Union also published the *Young Recruit* from Chicago during the 1930s. See *Industrial Worker*, December 5, 1933; *Young Recruit*, June 1, 1930.

47. *Industrial Worker*, April 11, 18, 25, 1912; June 30, November 10, 1923; January 12, August 30, December 13, 1924. See also Mayer, *Beyond the Rebel Girl*.

48. Richard Ellington, "Fellow Worker Guy Askew," in *Songs About Work: Essays in Occupational Culture, For Richard A. Reuss*, edited by Archie Green (Bloomington: Folklore Institute, Indiana University Bloomington, 1993), 312. See also Betty Charette, "The Finns in Aberdeen before 1915," in *Chehalis County Nationality Survey, 1848–1915*, edited by Joe Randich and Dorothea Parker (Olympia: Washington Commission for the Humanities, 1984).

49. Saku Pinta, "Educate, Organize, Emancipate! The Work People's College and the Industrial Workers of the World," in *Anarchist Pedagogies: Collective Actions, Theories, and Critical Reflections on Education*, edited by Robert H. Haworth (Oakland, CA: PM Press, 2012), 58.

50. *Industrialisti*, August 30, 1928. The youth department page in the *Industrialisti* was called "Nuorten Osasto." To reach as big an audience as possible among Finnish American children, material for this page appeared in both English and Finnish.

51. *Industrialisti*, December 15, 1928. On the Work People's College, see Pinta, "Educate, Organize, Emancipate," 47–68; Auvo Kostiainen, "Work People's College: An American Immigrant Institution," *Scandinavian Journal of History* 54 (1980): 295–309.

52. *Industrialisti*, July 26, 1928.

53. Ralph Chaplin, *The Centralia Conspiracy* (Chicago: Industrial Workers of the World, 1924), 11; Dubofsky, *We Shall Be All*, 128–30.

54. Auvo Kostiainen, ed., *Finns in the United States: A History of Settlement, Dissent, and Integration* (East Lansing: Michigan State University Press, 2014); Gary Kaunonen and Aaron Goings, *Community in Conflict: A Working-class History of the 1913–14*

Michigan Copper Strike and the Italian Hall Tragedy (East Lansing: Michigan State University Press, 2013).

55. *Industrialisti*, December 19, 1917; December 14, 1921; December 17, 1924; December 15, 1927; December 15, 1928; December 14, 1935.

56. The shortcomings are especially clear in studies of the IWW in the Upper Midwest, northern Rockies, and Pacific Coast, where Finns made up much of local Wobbly movements.

57. The 1920 Census for Grays Harbor County listed more than 2,200 Finnish Americans. USBC, *Fourteenth Census . . . 1920*, Washington State, Grays Harbor County.

58. *Industrialisti*, October 16, 1923.

59. I compiled this information through a thorough search of *Industrialisti* issues from 1928.

60. The Finnish IWW hall hosted a traveling Finnish opera group on January 25, 1931. See *Industrialisti*, January 17, 1931. See also *History of Aberdeen USKB&S Lodge No. 9*, 6, United Finnish Kaleva Brothers and Sisters Lodge 9 Collection, AHM; *Industrialisti*, October 26, 1928; November 13, 1928; September 4, 1929; December 14, 1935; Felix Hyrske scrapbook, Hyrske-Jaskar family personal collection, Tacoma Wash.

61. *Industrial Worker*, January 9, 12, April 5, 23, May 7, 28, 31, June 3, July 6, August 6, November 19, December 13, 1924; Chaplin, *Wobbly*, 291.

62. Pam Sporn, *Against Itself: The Federal Theater and Writers' Projects in the Midwest* (Detroit: Wayne State University Press, 1995), 94–103; *Industrialisti*, October 2, 1925; September 1, November 20, 1928; September 15, 1929.

63. Reino Hannula, *Blueberry God: The Education of a Finnish-American* (San Luis Obispo, CA: Quality Hill Books, 1981), 191.

64. *Industrialisti*, March 14, 1935.

65. *Industrial Worker*, June 30, 1923.

66. *Industrialisti*, January 17, 1931; Charette, "Finns in Aberdeen." Further analysis of the importance of the IWW's Finn hall in Aberdeen can be found in Goings, "Hall Syndicalism: Radical Finns and Wobbly Culture in Grays Harbor, Washington," *Journal of Finnish Studies* 14, no. 1 (Summer 2010): 18–28. A comprehensive analysis of the significance of radical working-class theater in Finnish American communities can be found in Sporn, *Against Itself*; Timo Riippa, "The Finnish Immigrant Theatre in the United States," in *Finnish Diaspora II: United States*, edited by Michael G. Karni (Toronto: Multicultural History Society of Ontario, 1981), 277–89; Hannula, *Blueberry God*, 191–95.

67. *Industrialisti*, August 30, December 11, 1924.

68. *Industrialisti*, September 26, November 6, 1928.

69. *Industrialisti*, October 16, 1928.

70. *Industrialisti*, September 4, 1929.

71. Thos. A Randall, "Report," Polson Museum Nationality Study Survey Documentation for *Chehalis County Nationality Survey, 1848–1915*, edited by Joe Randich and Dorothea Parker (Olympia: Washington Commission for the Humanities, 1984), Polson Museum, Hoquiam, Wash.

72. *Industrialisti*, November 28, 1939; Felix Hyrske scrapbook, Hyrske-Jaskar family personal collection, Olympia, Wash.; Sporn, *Against Itself*, 102.

73. Bryan Palmer, "The *New* New Poor Law: A Chapter in the Current Class War Waged from Above," *Labour/Le Travail* 84 (Fall 2019): 57.

74. Clemens P. Work, *Darkest Before Dawn: Sedition and Free Speech in the American West* (Albuquerque: University of New Mexico Press, 2006), 31.

75. Len Decaux, *Labor Radical: From the Wobblies to the CIO* (Boston: Beacon Press, 1970), 88; Conlin, *Bread and Roses Too*, 141; Dubofsky, *We Shall Be All*, 465.

76. *Industrial Worker*, April 28, May 2, 12, 16, 1923. One of the only books to mention 1920s free-speech fights is Gambs, *Decline of the IWW*, 169, 172.

77. *Industrial Worker*, June 17, 1922.

78. *Industrial Worker*, May 27, October 21, 28, 1922; *Grays Harbor Post*, November 4, 1922; Chehalis/Grays Harbor County Jail Record: Civil/Criminal, 1913–1922, acc. no. 86-1-19, box 245D, SRB-WSA.

79. *Industrial Worker*, May 27, June 24, August 5, 1922.

80. *Industrial Worker*, September 16, October 21, 28, 1922.

81. William Haywood, "The General Strike," in *Rebel Voices: An IWW Anthology*, new and expanded ed., edited by Joyce Kornbluh (Chicago: Charles H. Kerr Publishing Co., 1998), 49–50.

82. Minutes of the Central Branch Conference of Grays Harbor District, April 15, 1923, 2, IWW Collection, box 46, folder 12, WSU; Gambs, *Decline of the IWW*, 70–71.

83. *Industrial Worker*, April 25, 1923.

84. *The Strike Call for April 25, 1923*, IWW Collection, box 46, folder 28, WSU; *Industrial Worker*, April 25, May 2, 5, 1923; *General Strike Bulletin*, Seattle District, May 7, 1923, IWW Collection, box 162, folder 1, WSU.

85. *Industrial Worker*, May 5, 1923; *Seattle Union Record*, May 3, 1923; *Aberdeen Daily World*, April 26, 1923.

86. Douglas Fir Company Business, May 2, 1923, EGA Papers, acc. no. 3826, box 120, folder 8, UW; *Industrial Worker*, July 28, 1923; *Aberdeen Daily World*, May 3, 8, 1923.

87. *General Strike Bulletin*, Seattle District, May 7, 1923, IWW Collection, box 162, folder 1, WSU; *Industrial Worker*, May 16, July 28, 1923; *Southwest Washington Labor Press*, May 11, 1923; Coroner's Inquest into the Death of William McKay, Aberdeen, Wash., May 4, 1923, Grays Harbor County Papers, SRB-WSA.

88. *Industrial Solidarity*, May 12, 19, 1923; *Seattle Post-Intelligencer*, May 4, 1923; *In-*

dustrial Worker, May 16, 1923; Aaron Goings, Brian Barnes, and Roger Snider, *The Red Coast: Radicalism and Anti-Radicalism in Southwest Washington* (Corvallis: Oregon State University Press, 2019), 111–18.

89. *Seattle Union Record*, May 7, 1923.

90. Hughes and Beckwith, eds., *On the Harbor*, 42; *Industrial Worker*, May 16, 1923.

91. Photographs from the funeral featuring working-class families have appeared in several different publications, including Elis Sulkanen, ed., *Amerikan Suomalaisen Työväenliikkeen Historia* (Fitchburg, MA: Amerikan Suomalainen Kansanvallen Liitto ja Raivaaja Publishing Co., 1951), 205; Hughes and Beckwith, *On the Harbor*, 42. Wobblies also reproduced these images on picture postcards, one of which is in the author's possession. Pictures of McKay's funeral also appeared in the IWW's *Industrial Pioneer*, June 1923, 5.

92. Cited in Fred Thompson, *The IWW—Its First Fifty Years* (Chicago: Industrial Workers of the World, 1955), 155. On the IWW dehorn movement, see Stewart H. Holbrook, "Wobbly Talk," *American Mercury* 7, no. 15 (January 1926): 62; Testimony of Walter Horace Margason, *United States v. Haywood, et al.*, 5719, IWW Collection, box 110, file 3, WSU.

93. *Industrial Worker*, October 31, 1923.

94. Ellington, "Fellow Worker Guy Askew," 310.

95. Norman Clark, *The Dry Years: Prohibition and Social Change in Washington*, revised ed. (Seattle: University of Washington Press, 1988), 108–27, 129, 134.

96. Merle A. Reinikka, "Death Certificates of Finns in Chehalis [Grays Harbor] County, 1907–1947," Aberdeen History Collection, AHM.

97. *Industrial Worker*, June 27, September 19, October 10, 20, 31, 1923; October 25, 1924.

98. *Industrial Worker*, July 4, 1923.

99. John McClelland, *Wobbly War: The Centralia Story* (Tacoma: Washington State Historical Society, 1987), 48–49.

100. Testimony of Walter Horace Margason, *United States v. Haywood, et al.*, 5715–19, 5737, 5743–47, IWW Collection, box 110, folder 3, WSU; *Industrial Worker*, July 11, 14, 1923; April 8, 1924; Fred Thompson, *The IWW*, 147–48; *Industrial Worker*, January 12, 1924.

101. Nelson, *Break Their Haughty Power*, 181; Tyler, *Rebels of the Woods*, 204. While *Break Their Haughty Power* is a work of historical fiction, the actions of the fictional Aberdeen dehorn gang conforms closely to the activities of IWW members recorded in the *Industrial Worker*.

102. *Industrial Worker*, May 5, 1923. These events appear in the novel by Eugene Nelson, *Break Their Haughty Power: Joe Murphy in the Heyday of the Wobblies* (San Francisco: ISM Press, 1996), 181.

103. *Industrial Worker*, December 28, 1929.

104. *Industrial Worker*, May 9, 1923.

105. *Aberdeen Daily World*, September 22, 1923.

106. Fred Thompson, "They Didn't Suppress the Wobblies," *Radical America* 1, no. 2 (September-October 1967): 1–5.

107. Industrial Workers of the World, *Eight Men Buried Alive: The Centralia Case Calls Every Decent Man and Woman in the State of Washington to Act Quickly* (Chicago: General Defense Committee, 1924), 1–32; Copeland, *Centralia Tragedy of 1919*, 185.

108. Gambs, *Decline of the IWW*, 56–57; Dubofsky, *We Shall Be All*, 428–29; Chaplin, *Centralia Conspiracy*; Copeland, *Centralia Tragedy of 1919*, 113, 147.

109. *Industrial Worker*, September 23, 1922; July 21, 1923; December 13, 1924; "Financial Statement of the General Defense Committee for the Month of December 1923," *General Office Bulletin for the Month of January 1923*, 23, IWW Collection, box 31, folder 8, WSU; "Financial Statement of the General Defense Committee for the Month of December, 1924," *General Office Bulletin*, 25, IWW Collection, box 31, folder 31, WSU; "Financial Statement of the General Defense Committee for the Month of December 1923," *General Office Bulletin*, 19, IWW Collection, box 31, folder 19, WSU.

110. *Industrial Worker*, November 23, 1923. Joe Hill, the famed Swedish-born IWW activist and musician, was executed in 1915 by the State of Utah after being convicted for a murder that many Wobblies and historians argue he did not commit.

111. *Industrialisti*, December 26, 1923; December 11, 1924.

112. *Industrialisti*, November 18, 1928.

113. *Industrial Worker*, August 6, 1924. In this article, the Wobbly writer thanked the "business men of Aberdeen [who] donated $19 to the Centralia Publicity Committee."

114. *Industrial Worker*, May 17, November 19, 1924; September 19, 1933; Tyler, *Rebels of the Woods*, 223–24; Hall, *Harvest Wobblies*, 231.

115. *Aberdeen Daily World*, March 22, 1932; Copeland, *Centralia Tragedy of 1919*, 125, 168, 173, 175, 185.

116. Smith's speaking tours are covered extensively in Copeland, *Centralia Tragedy of 1919*, 104, 142–43.

117. Copeland, *Centralia Tragedy of 1919*, 164.

118. Edwin Patrick Coll, "Open Letter to Members of American Legion on Centralia Case," October 1, 1928, IWW Collection, box 167, WSU. See also Copeland, *Centralia Tragedy of 1919*, 164–66.

119. Copeland, *Centralia Tragedy of 1919*, 160–70.

120. *Industrialisti*, October 20, 1928, trans. Matti Roitto.

121. Copeland, *Centralia Tragedy of 1919*, 166.

122. *Aberdeen Daily World*, May 3, 4, 1923.

123. Alex Polson to R. D. Merrill, September 13, 1922, Merrill and Ring Papers, acc. no. 726, box 39, folder 10, UW.

124. *Southwest Washington Labor Press*, December 29, 1922; January 5, 1923; The Register of Reverend Aaron Allen Heist Papers, 1910–1964, MSS 088, Southern California Library, Los Angeles.

125. Harry F. Ward, *News Letter No. 2*, February 20, 1923, Reverend Aaron Alan Heist Papers, Southern California Library, Los Angeles. This collection of Heist's papers includes references to his work in Grays Harbor as he helped to reshape public opinion around the Wobblies.

9 ORGANIZE!

1. *Washingtonian*, July 26, 1933; *Aberdeen Daily World*, July 26, 1933.

2. *Voice of Action*, August 7, 1933.

3. Jerry Lembcke and William M. Tattam, *One Union in Wood: A Political History of the International Woodworkers of America* (New York: International Publishers, 1984), 30–31; Paul William Parks, "Labor Relations in the Grays Harbor Lumber Industry" (master's thesis, University of Washington, 1948), 28.

4. On early Depression organizing before the New Deal, see Michael Goldfield, *The Southern Key: Class, Race, and Radicalism in the 1930s and 1940s* (Oxford, UK: Oxford University Press, 2020).

5. "Organize and Fight: Against Wage Cuts! For Decent Conditions!" flyer issued by the National Lumber Workers Union, Local 2–Grays Harbor; "Fight or Starve" flyer issued by the National Lumber Workers' Union, Aberdeen, Washington, RTsKhIDNI, f. 515, op. 1, d. 2180. Neither of these flyers have dates, but they were filed alongside other CP documents from 1930.

6. On working-class conservatism, see John Bodnar, *Workers' World: Kinship, Community, and Protest in and Industrialized Society* (Baltimore: Johns Hopkins University Press, 1983).

7. *Aberdeen Daily World*, January 29, 1932.

8. Staughton Lynd, ed., *"We Are All Leaders": The Alternative Unionism of the Early 1930s* (Urbana: University of Illinois Press, 1996), 4; Len DeCaux, *The Living Spirit of the Wobblies* (New York: International Publishers, 1978); Archie Green, *Wobblies, Pile Butts, and Other Heroes: Laborlore Explorations* (Urbana: University of Illinois Press, 1993), 422. See also Rosemary Feurer, *Radical Unionism in the Midwest, 1900–1950* (Urbana: University of Illinois Press, 2006), 23–47.

9. "Activity Questionnaire from September 1st to December 31st [1928]," RTsKhIDNI, f. 515, op. 1, d.1433; *Industrial Worker*, March 22, April 26, 1930; August 8, 15, 1933; *Voice of Action*, August 7, 1933; *Aberdeen Daily World*, July 25, 28, 30, 1930; November

4, 5 13, 16, 1931; “Fight or Starve” flyer issued by the National Lumber Workers’ Union, Aberdeen, Washington, RTsKhIDNI, f. 515, op. 1, d. 2180.

10. Minutes of the District Buro Meeting Held on July 25th, 1933, Seattle, Washington, RTsKhIDNI, f. 515, op. 1, d. 3289, Il. 8; Resolution of District 12 Convention, September 30–October 1, 1932, 2, RTsKhIDNI, f. 515, op. 1, d. 2907.

11. Lembcke and Tattam, *One Union in Wood*, 17–18; Jensen, *Lumber and Labor* (New York: Arno Press, 1971; first published 1945 by J. J. Little and Ives Co., New York), 151–52; William Robbins, *Hard Times in Paradise Coos Bay, Oregon, 1850–1986* (Seattle: University of Washington Press, 1988).

12. *Industrial Worker*, January 12, 1924.

13. Affidavit of O. M. Micky Orton, 1940, John Caughlan Papers, box 7, folders 8–9, acc. no. 704, University of Washington Libraries Special Collections, Seattle.

14. Parks, “Labor Relations,” 17.

15. John Howell Harris, *Bloodless Victories: The Rise and Fall of the Open Ship in the Philadelphia Metal Trades, 1890–1940* (Cambridge, UK: Cambridge University Press, 2000), 369; William G. Robbins, “The Social Context of Forestry: The Pacific Northwest in the Twentieth Century,” *Western Historical Quarterly* 16, no. 4 (October 1985): 418.

16. *Industrial Worker*, January 11, February 8, 1930.

17. Laila Walli Silva, “The Pockets of East Aberdeen,” *East Aberdeen Finns: Grays Harbor County, Washington* (Finnish-American Historical Society of the West) 25, no. 1 (December 1998): 3; on “Hoovervilles,” see Gordon “Brick” Moir, interview by Gary Murrell, audio recording, Hoquiam, Wash., March 27, 2000, in author’s possession.

18. Prison Record for the City of Aberdeen, Washington, 1928–34, SRB-WSA; *Industrial Worker*, March 15, 1930.

19. *Industrial Worker*, December 21, 1929.

20. *Aberdeen Daily World*, February 11, 1931.

21. Alice Kessler Harris, *Gendering Labor History* (Urbana: University of Illinois Press, 2007), 369.

22. *Aberdeen Daily World*, January 22, 23, 29, February 2, 5, June 7, 1932; *Industrial Worker*, March 15, 1930.

23. *Aberdeen Daily World*, January 22, 29, June 7, 1932.

24. F. L. Moravets, “Lumber Production in Oregon and Washington, 1869–1948,” *US Forest Service, Pacific Northwest Forest and Range Experimentation Station Forest Survey, 1949*, Forest Survey Report 100 (Portland: USFS, 1948).

25. *Aberdeen Daily World*, April 4, 8, 1932; Parks, “Labor Relations,” 19.

26. Robbins, “Social Context of Forestry,” 418.

27. Edwin Van Syckle, *They Tried to Cut It All: Grays Harbor . . . Turbulent Years of Greed and Greatness* (Seattle: Pacific Search Press, 1980), 210; J. V. G. Posey, “From Our Friend and Former Owner,” *Poseygram* (Hoquiam, Wash.), December 1935, 5;

"By the Staff," *Poseygram*, December 1935, 22; *Grays Harbor Post*, February 13, 1932.

28. *Grays Harbor Post*, February 6, 1909.

29. *Aberdeen Daily World*, September 15, 24, 26, December 4, 1931; April 12, 1932; Lamb, *Fifty Years in Hoquiam: Memoirs of Frank H. Lamb* (n.p., 1948), 295–97; US Bureau of Census, *Fifteenth Census of the United States Taken in the Year 1930*, City of Hoquiam, http://www2.census.gov/prod2/decennial/documents/10612982v3p2ch10.pdf, 1221, accessed March 24, 2011.

30. *Industrial Worker*, February 1, 1929.

31. *Industrial Worker*, February 15, 1930.

32. Fred Thompson, *The IWW—Its First Fifty Years* (Chicago: Industrial Workers of the World, 1955), 173; *Industrial Unionist*, May 2, October 7, 21, 1925; March 24, 1926; *Industrial Worker*, May 10, 14, 17, 1924; February 12, 19, 1927.

33. *Industrial Worker*, August 8, 15, December 5, 1933; *New Unionist*, May 18, 1929; *Bulletin No. 1: Lumber Workers' Industrial Union No. 120 of the IWW* (Aberdeen, Wash.), 1933, IWW Collection, box 46, folder 9, WSU.

34. Fred Thompson, *The IWW*, 173; *Industrial Unionist*, May 2, October 7, 21, 1925; March 24, 1926; *Industrial Worker*, May 10, 14, 17, 1924; February 12, 19, 1927.

35. Fred Thompson, *The IWW*, 173; *Industrial Unionist*, May 2, October 7, 21, 1925; J. J. Dunning, "The Lumber Industry: Will Its Workers Awaken?" *Industrial Pioneer* 3, no. 10 (February 1926): 6–7; *Industrial Worker*, July 25, August 8, 15, December 5, 1933; *New Unionist*, May 18, 1929; *Bulletin No. 1: Lumber Workers' Industrial Union No. 120 of the IWW* (Aberdeen, Wash.), 1933, IWW Collection, box 46, folder 9, WSU.

36. Ottilie Markholt, *Maritime Solidarity: Pacific Coast Unionism, 1929–1938* (Tacoma, WA: Pacific Coast Maritime History Committee, 1998), 189.

37. Fraser M. Ottanelli, *The Communist Party of the United States* (New Brunswick, NJ: Rutgers University Press, 1991), 10; Theodore Draper, *The Roots of American Communism*, Transaction ed. (New Brunswick, NJ: Transaction Publishers, 2003), 176–96; *Grays Harbor Post*, January 4, April 12, 1919.

38. Randi Storch, *Red Chicago: American Communism and Its Grassroots, 1928–1935* (Urbana: University of Illinois Press, 2007), 23.

39. Draper, *Roots of American Communism*, 391.

40. Report of District Organizer, Aaron Fislerman to the District Convention Held Sunday, August 21, 1927, RTsKhIDNI, f. 515, op. 1, d. 1166; Minutes of the District Buro Meeting of the C.P. August 10, 1933, Seattle, Wash., 254/3288; "from the centre" comes from Sidney Bloomfield to Org. Dept. R. Baker, March 11, 1931, RTsKhIDNI, f. 515, op. 1, d. 2318.

41. M. Rupert to Central Committee, June 7, 1934, RTsKhIDNI, f. 515, op. 1, d. 3605.

42. Auvo Kostianinen, *The Forging of Finnish-American Communism, 1917–1924:*

A Study in Ethnic Radicalism (Turku, Finland: Turin Yliopisto, 1978), 126, 137–38.

43. Kostianinen, *The Forging*, 220; *Työmies* (Superior, Wisc.), December 20, 1922; December 16, 1923.

44. Finnish Federation Dues for November 1921, RTsKhIDNI, f. 515, op. 1, d. 75; Finnish Federation Dues—December 1921, RTsKhIDNI, f. 515, op. 1, d. 75.

45. "Contributors to Christmas Campaign of ILD," *Labor Defender* (March 1929): 62; *Labor Defender* (October 1928); Resolution to Governor Roland Hartley on behalf of Centralia Prisoners, Jugo Slav Branch ILD No. 332, Aberdeen, Wash., Governor Roland Hartley Papers, acc. no. 2K-1-28, Insurance Commission–IWW, 1929, WSA; Resolution to Governor Roland Hartley on behalf of Centralia Prisoners, April 15, 1932, Young Communist League, Aberdeen, Wash., Governor Roland Hartley Papers, acc. no. 2K-1-28, Insurance Commission–IWW, 1929, WSA; Report of Central Commission on the Miners Relief Case to the Polcom, 4–7 December 1928, 1–4, RTsKhIDNI, f. 515, op. 1, d. 1433; Resolution of District 12, Convention, September 30–October 1, 1932, 2–3, RTsKhIDNI, f. 515, op. 1, d. 2907; Sidney Bloomfield to Org. Dept., 18 May 1931, RTsKhIDNI, f. 515, op. 1, d. 2318; Betty Charette, "The Finns in Aberdeen before 1915," in *Chehalis County Nationality Survey, 1848–1915*, edited by Joe Randich and Dorothea Parker (Olympia: Washington Commission for the Humanities, 1984), 9–10.

46. Resolution to Governor Roland Hartley on behalf of Centralia Prisoners, April 15, 1932, Young Communist League, Aberdeen, Wash., Governor Roland Hartley Papers, acc. no. 2K-1-28, Insurance Commission–IWW, 1929, WSA; Resolution Calling upon the Governor and the Parole Board to Release the Eight Centralia Victims, Unanimously Adopted, December 2, 1928, Governor Roland Hartley Papers, acc. no. 2K-1-28, Insurance Commission–IWW, folder "IWW (Centralia Massacre) 1927–1928," WSA; *Young Pioneer* (New York), December 1930; *Young Comrade* (Chicago), January 1925; *Voice of Action*, August 31, 1934.

47. *Industrial Worker*, January 11, 1930.

48. *Industrial Worker*, November 8, 1919; Greg Hall, *Harvest Wobblies: The Industrial Workers of the World and Agricultural Laborers in the American West, 1905–1930* (Corvallis: Oregon State University Press, 2001), 178.

49. *Industrial Worker*, December 31, 1921; March 4, 1922.

50. Bryan Palmer, *James P. Cannon and the Origins of the American Revolutionary Left, 1890–1928* (Urbana: University of Illinois Press, 2007), 252–84.

51. *Labor Defender*, August 1925; March, October 1926; November 1927; "The Labor Defender on the Pacific Coast," *Labor Defender* (July 1928): 158; Charlotte Todes, *Labor and Lumber* (New York: International Publishers, 1931), 182.

52. "Contributors to Christmas Campaign of ILD," *Labor Defender* (March 1929): 62; "Building the I.L.D.," *Labor Defender* (October 1928); Resolution to Governor

Roland Hartley on behalf of Centralia Prisoners, Jugo Slav Branch ILD No. 332, Aberdeen, Wash., Governor Roland Hartley Papers, acc. no. 2K-1-28, Insurance Commission–IWW, 1929, WSA; *Industrial Worker*, November 30, 1929.

53. *Washingtonian*, February 5, 1927; *Montesano Vidette*, February 4, 1927.

54. Solon DeLeon and Nathan Fine, eds., *The American Labor Yearbook* (New York: Rand School of Social Science, 1929), 135; *Aberdeen Daily World*, February 4, 1927.

55. Cloice R. Howd, "Industrial Relations in the West Coast Lumber Industry," *Bulletin of the United States Bureau of Labor Statistics*, no. 349 (Washington, DC: Government Printing Office, 1924), 101.

56. *Industrial Worker*, February 12, 19, 1927.

57. Workers' Party of America, District 12, Polcom Session of February 14, 1927, RTsKhIDNI, f. 515, op. 1, d. 1166.

58. Workers' Party of America, District 12, Polcom Session of February 21, 1927, RTsKhIDNI, f. 515, op. 1, d. 1166.

59. Acting General Secretary to A. Fislerman, May 18, 1927, RTsKhIDNI, f. 515, op. 1, d. 1042.

60. *Daily Worker*, March 18, 1927.

61. Workers' Party of America, District 12, Polcom Session of February 21, 1927, RTsKhIDNI, f. 515, op. 1, d. 1166; *Washingtonian*, March 12, 1927.

62. *Washingtonian*, March 3, 1927; *Aberdeen Daily World*, March 3, 1927; Workers' (Communist) Party of America, District 12, Report of District Organizer, Aaron Fislerman to the District Convention held Sunday, August 21, 1927, RTsKhIDNI, f. 515, op. 1, d. 1166.

63. Aaron Fislerman to C. E. Ruthenberg, General Secretary, February 25, 1927, RTsKhIDNI, f. 515, op. 1, d. 1042; Workers' Party of America, District 12, Polcom Session of February 21, 1927, RTsKhIDNI, f. 515, op. 1, d. 1166.

64. *Daily Worker*, March 10, 1927.

65. Aaron Fislerman to C. E. Ruthenberg, General Secretary, February 25, 1927, RTsKhIDNI, f. 515, op. 1, d. 1042; "Minutes of Meeting, Workers Party of America, District 12, Seattle Wash., February 21, 1927," RTsKhIDNI, f. 515, op. 1, d. 1166.

66. *Daily Worker*, March 18, 1927.

67. Aaron Fislerman to C. E. Ruthenberg, February 25, 1927, RTsKhIDNI, f. 515, op. 1, d. 1042; Workers' Party of America, District 12, Polcom Session of March 14, 1927, RTsKhIDNI, f. 515, op. 1, d. 1166.

68. *Washingtonian*, March 11, 12, 1927; *Aberdeen Daily World*, March 12, 1927.

69. Workers (Communist) Party of America, District 12, Report of District Organizer, Aaron Fislerman, to the District Convention held Sunday, August 21, 1927, RTsKhIDNI, f. 515, op. 1, d. 1166.

70. Workers' Party of America, District 12, Polcom Session of 21 February 1927,

RTsKhIDNI, f. 515, op. 1, d. 1166; "Trade Union Educational League National Conference," December 3, 1927, RTsKhIDNI, f. 515, op. 1, d. 1192.

71. Ottanelli, *Communist Party of the United States*, 12–14; Lembcke and Tattam, *One Union in Wood*, 20.

72. Workers (Communist) Party of America, District 12, Report of District Organizer, Aaron Fislerman to the District Convention held, Sunday, August 21, 1927, RTsKhIDNI, f. 515, op. 1, d. 1166.

73. Resolution Calling upon the Governor and the Parole Board to Release the Eight Centralia Victims, Unanimously Adopted, December 2, 1928, Governor Roland Hartley Papers, acc. no. 2K-1-28, Insurance Commission–IWW, Folder "IWW (Centralia Massacre) 1927–1928," WSA.

74. *Daily Worker*, October 21, 1929. Activities of the TUEL, District 12, 1929, RTsKhIDNI, f. 515, op. 1, d. 1790; *Industrial Worker*, December 28, 1929.

75. Todes, *Labor and Lumber*, 188; Ottanelli, *Communist Party of the United States*, 21–23; Philip S. Foner, *The History of the Labor Movement*, vol. 10, *The TUEL, 1925–1929* (New York: International Publishers, 1991), 270; Storch, *Red Chicago*, 136–37.

76. Ottanelli, *Communist Party of the United States*, 13, 21.

77. *Daily Worker*, July 30, 1929.

78. *Daily Worker*, September 4, 1929.

79. On Moclips, see Edwin Van Syckle, *The River Pioneers: Early Days on Grays Harbor* (Seattle: Pacific Search Press, 1982), 212, 216.

80. "Red Cedar Shingle and Shakes: The Labor Story, Interviews with Elwood R. Maunder," *Journal of Forest History* 19, no. 3 (July 1975): 125.

81. *Aberdeen Daily World*, July 25, 1930; *Industrial Worker*, April 26, 1930.

82. *Aberdeen Daily World*, July 28, 1930.

83. Letter from Sidney Bloomfield to the Secretariat, September 16, 1930, RTsKhIDNI, f. 515, op. 1, d. 1958.

84. James Murphy, "History of the National Lumber Workers Union," *Voice of Action*, July 6, 1934.

85. "Organize and Fight: Against Wage Cuts! For Decent Conditions!" flyer issued by the National Lumber Workers Union, Local 2–Grays Harbor, RTsKhIDNI, f. 515, op. 1, d. 2180; "Fight or Starve," flyer issued by the National Lumber Workers' Union, Aberdeen, Wash., RTsKhIDNI, f. 515, op. 1, d. 2180.

86. *Voice of Action*, July 6, 1934.

87. Todes, *Labor and Lumber*, 183; *Vanguard*, July-August 1930.

88. Letter from Sidney Bloomfield to the Secretariat, September 11, 1930, RTsKhIDNI, f. 515, op. 1, d.1958.

89. *Daily Worker*, February 27, 1930.

90. *Daily Worker*, February 7, 1930.

91. *Daily Worker*, March 4, 1930. The original spelled "kilter" as "kelter."

92. Franklin Folsom, *Impatient Armies of the Poor: The Story of Collective Action of the Unemployed* (Boulder: University Press of Colorado, 1991), 261.

93. Storch, *Red Chicago*, 104–5; T. H. Watkins, *The Hungry Years: A Narrative History of the Great Depression* (New York: MacMillan, 2000), 118–22; Folsom, *Inpatient Armies of the Poor*, 244–60.

94. Folsom, *Inpatient Armies of the Poor*, 255.

95. *Aberdeen Daily World*, March 6, 7, 1930.

96. *Industrial Worker*, March 29, 1930.

97. *Grays Harbor Post*, March 12, May 7, November 5, 1932; *Aberdeen Daily World*, May 5, 1932; Ed Leavitt to Org. Dept., C.C., May 13, 1932, RTsKhIDNI, f. 515, op. 1, d. 2908; D. O. to the Secretariat, C.C. CPUSA, August 16, 1932, RTsKhIDNI, f. 515, op. 1, d. 2908.

98. *Daily Worker*, May 13, 1932.

99. *Daily Worker*, November 3, 1932.

100. USBC, *Fifteenth Census . . . 1930*, Washington State, Chehalis County, Aberdeen; Merle A. Reinikka, "Death Certificates of Finns in Chehalis [Grays Harbor] County, 1907–1947," Aberdeen History Collection, AHM.

101. Report of Central Commission on the Miners Relief Case to the Polcom, December 4–7, 1928, 1–4, RTsKhIDNI, f. 515, op. 1, d. 1433; Resolution Calling upon the Governor and the Parole Board to Release the Eight Centralia Victims, Unanimously Adopted, December 2, 1928, Governor Roland Hartley Papers, acc. no. 2K-1-28, Insurance Commission–IWW, Folder "I.W.W. (Centralia Massacre) 1927–1928," WSA; "Congressional Election Platform of the Communist Party," issued by the Grays Harbor Section Committee Communist Party, RTsKhIDNI, f. 515, op. 1, d. 3605.

102. Resolution Calling upon the Governor and the Parole Board to Release the Eight Centralia Victims, Unanimously Adopted, December 2, 1928, Governor Roland Hartley Papers, acc. no. 2K-1-28, Insurance Commission–IWW, Folder "IWW (Centralia Massacre) 1927–1928," WSA.

103. *Aberdeen Daily World*, January 29, 1932.

104. Ed Levitt to Org. Dept., C.C., April 25, 1932, RTsKhIDNI, f. 515, op. 1, d. 2908; Ed Leavvitt to Org. Dept., C.C., May 13, 1932, RTsKhIDNI, f. 515, op. 1, d. 2908.

105. *Voice of Action*, April 17, 24, May 8, June 28, 1933; *Grays Harbor Post*, November 5, 1932; Aberdeen Report, RTsKhIDNI, f. 515, op. 1, d. 2908.

106. Alex Noral to Wn Weiner, December 21, 1931, RTsKhIDNI, f. 515, op. 1, d. 2318; *Grays Harbor Worker*, November 13, 1931. The only known copy of this newspaper is found in RTsKhIDNI, f. 515, op. 1, d. 2494; *Daily Worker*, November 23, 1931

107. *Daily Worker*, May 13, 1932.

108. *Grays Harbor Post*, November 7, 1931.

109. *Grays Harbor Worker*, November 13, 1931; *Daily Worker*, November 21, 1931.

110. *Aberdeen Daily World*, November 4, 1931.

111. *Aberdeen Daily World*, April 4, 8, 1932.

112. *Daily Worker*, February 5, 1931.

113. Three flyers from the 1930 lumber strike in Grays Harbor are included in RTsKhIDNI, f. 515, op. 1, d. 2280. Their headlines read "Fight the Wage Cut: Spread the Strike!" "Fight or Starve," and "Organize and Fight: Against Wage Cuts! For Decent Conditions!" The "Organize and Fight" flyer is dated January 5, 1930.

114. *Grays Harbor Post*, November 7, 1931; *Grays Harbor Worker*, November 13, 1931.

115. *Aberdeen Daily World*, November 4, 1931.

116. *Aberdeen Daily World*, November 4, 5, 13, 1931.

117. D. O., District 12 to the Secretariat, December 8, 1931, RTsKhIDNI, f. 515, op. 1, d. 2281.

118. *Daily Worker*, November 21, 1931.

119. *Aberdeen Daily World*, November 4, 5, 13, 16, 18, 19, 23, 1931; *Daily Worker*, November 21, 1931.

120. *Aberdeen Daily World*, November 21, 23, 25, 31, 1931.

121. Aberdeen Report, RTsKhIDNI, f. 515, op. 1, d. 2909, il. 1–3. *Aberdeen Daily World* wrote extensively of the 1932 Wilson Brothers mill strike. See *Aberdeen Daily World*, January 30, February 1, 2, 3, 1932; A. N. [Alex Noral] to the Secretariat, C.P.USA, February 9, 1932, RTsKhIDNI, f. 515, op. 1, d. 2908.

122. *Aberdeen Daily World*, February 1, 1932.

123. D. O. District 12 to Organization Dept. CPUSA, April 23, 1932, RTsKhIDNI, f. 515, op. 1, d. 2908.

124. Minutes of the District Buro Meeting Held on July 25th, 1933, RTsKhIDNI, f. 515, op. 1, d. 3289, Il. 8.

125. National Recovery Administration, *Code of Fair Competition for the Lumber and Timber Products Industry, as approved on August 19, 1933, by President Roosevelt* (Washington, DC: Government Printing Office, 1934), 1.

126. Lembcke and Tattam, *One Union in Wood*, 30–31; William G. Robbins, *Lumberjacks and Legislators: Political Economy of the US Lumber Industry* (College Station: Texas A & M Press, 1982), 174–81; Jensen, *Lumber and Labor*, 145.

127. *Voice of Action*, August 7, 28, 1933.

128. *Industrial Worker*, July 25, 1933.

129. *Voice of Action*, July 19, 26 1933. In logging, the bushel system was a form of piecework, better known as "gyppo" logging.

130. *Aberdeen Daily World*, July 24, 25, 1933.

131. *Daily Worker*, July 29, 1933. Published in the East, it's possible that the *Daily Worker* here was confused about the big WWI–era lumber strike of 1917.

132. *Industrial Worker*, August 8, 15, 1933; *Voice of Action*, August 7, 1933.

133. Minutes of the District Buro Meeting held on July 25th, 1933, Seattle, Wash., RTsKhIDNI, f. 515, op. 1, d. 3289, il. 10. The *Daily Worker* announced the conference in its July 12, 1933, issue.

134. *Voice of Action*, July 26, 1933; Minutes of the District Buro Meeting Held on July 25th, 1933, Seattle, Wash., RTsKhIDNI, f. 515, op. 1, d. 3289; Minutes of the District Buro Meeting of the C.P., August 10, 1933, Seattle, Wash., RTsKhIDNI, f. 515, op. 1, d. 3288.

135. *Voice of Action*, August 7, 1933; *Aberdeen Daily World*, July 29, 1933.

136. American Federation of Labor, Certificate of Affiliation for the Loggers and Saw Mill Workers Union No. 18345, Aberdeen, Wash., July 31, 1933, Records of the Grays Harbor Locals of the International Woodworkers of America; *Washington State Labor News*, July 7, 1933; *Aberdeen Daily World*, July 26, 1933; Dembo, *Unions and Politics in Washington State, 1885–1935* (New York: Garland Press, 1982), 612; Estelle May Stewart, *Handbook of American Trade-Unions*, 1936 ed. (Washington, DC, US Department of Labor, 1936), 9; *Timber Worker*, Labor Day ed., September 7, 1936.

137. Lembcke and Tattam, *One Union in Wood*, 31; Jensen, *Lumber and Labor*, 159–60; *Washington State Labor News*, July 28, 1933; Dembo, *Unions and Politics*, 590–91; Irving Bernstein, *The Turbulent Years: A History of the American Worker, 1933–1941* (Boston: Houghton-Mifflin, 1979), 624; *Voice of Action*, August 7, 1933. Chartered in 1933, lumber industry union locals such as Aberdeen's LSMWU Local 18345 retained their name for two years before affiliating with the United Brotherhood of Carpenters and Joiners.

138. *Aberdeen Daily World*, July 25, 26, 1933.

139. *Daily Worker*, August 16, 1933.

140. *Aberdeen Daily World*, August 8, 9, 1933; *Voice of Action*, August 7, 21, November 13, 1933; *Daily Worker*, August 16, 1933.

141. Organizational Bulletin, Communist Party of the U.S.A., District 12, February 10, 1934, 2, RTsKhIDNI, f. 515, op. 1, d. 3606.

142. Brick Moir to Jeremy, October 21, 1985, Bob Reed Papers, box 2, Chapin, Wilred folder, acc. no. 3512-7, UW; *Timber Worker*, October 9, 1937; *R. L. Polk and Company's Grays Harbor Cities Directory*, 1935; *Voice of Action*, October 23, 1933.

10 THE GREAT 1935 LUMBER STRIKE

1. "We Object!" *Timber Worker*, Labor Day ed., September 7, 1936.

2. *Voice of Action*, July 12, 19, 1935; Todd Goings, "Battles on the Harbor: Inter-Labor Conflict, Anti-Communism, Women's Auxiliaries, and the Murder of Laura Law" (master's thesis, Central Washington University, 2014), 37; John C. Hughes and Ryan

Teague Beckwith, eds., *On the Harbor: From Black Friday to Nirvana* (Aberdeen, WA: Daily World, 2001), 81.

3. *Aberdeen Daily World*, July 26, 1933. On Brackinreed, see Harry W. Call, *History of the Washington State Federation of Labor, 1902–1954: Fifty-Two Years of Legislative, Organizational, and Educational Effort on Behalf of the Wage Earners* (Seattle: Washington State Federation of Labor, 1954), 49.

4. Minutes of the Loggers and Saw Mill Workers Union (LSMWU) Local 18345, August 18, 22, 1933, Records of the Grays Harbor Locals of the International Woodworkers of America (hereafter RGHL-IWA), AHM; *R. L. Polk and Company's Grays Harbor Cities Directory*, 1933, 665.

5. Minutes of the LSMWU Local 18345, August 22, 1933, RGHL-IWA, AHM; *R. L. Polk and Company's Grays Harbor County Directory*, 1933, 665; *Labor Bulletin* was the Aberdeen-based voice of Grays Harbor trade unions in the 1930s–1940s.

6. Minutes of the LSMWU Local 18345, August 22, 1933, RGHL-IWA, AHM.

7. Minutes of the LSMWU Local 18345, November 20, 1934, RGHL-IWA, AHM. The spelling of the organizer's name is unclear; "Mr. Manard Bright" is the closest approximation I could make.

8. Bruce Nelson, *Workers on the Waterfront: Seamen, Longshoremen, and Unionism in the 1930s* (Urbana: University of Illinois Press, 1990), 62–64.

9. *Aberdeen Daily World*, February 11, 1931. Born in Germany in the 1870s, August (A. C.) Jonas resided in Grays Harbor for several decades where he worked in the lumber and maritime industries.

10. Minutes of LSMWU Local 18345 Meeting, May 13, 1934, RGHL-IWA, AHM; Jerry Lembcke and William M. Tattam, *One Union in Wood: A Political History of the International Woodworkers of America* (New York: International Publishers, 1984), 28–30.

11. Minutes of LSMWU Local 18345 Meeting, May 25, 1934, RGHL-IWA, AHM.

12. *Timber Worker*, July 2, 1937; Ray Nouska, "History of Local 2369," *Timber Worker*, Labor Day ed., September 7, 1936.

13. "Attention!" Laura Law Collection, box 10, folder 10-4, SRB-WSA; "A Call to the Members of Local No. 2," Laura Law Collection, box 9, folder 9-4, SRB-WSA.

14. Minutes of LSMWU Local 18345 Meeting, March 26, 1934, RGHL-IWA, AHM.

15. *Voice of Action*, February 12, 20, 1934; Minutes of the District Buro Meeting for February 17, 1934, 1, RTsKhIDNI, f. 515, op. 1, d. 3603; Minutes of LSMWU Local 18345 Meeting, March 26, 1934, RGHL-IWA, AHM. An excellent study of the Willapa Harbor (Raymond-area) labor movement in the lumber industry is Jeremy Egolf, "Labor Control in Crisis: The 4L and the Bedaux System in the U.S. Northwest Lumber Industry, 1931–1935" (master's thesis, University of British Columbia, Canada, 1980).

16. *Voice of Action*, April 3, 10, 1934.

17. Minutes of LSMWU Local 18345 Meeting, April 8, 1934, RGHL-IWA, AHM.

18. In the Matter of Harbor Plywood Corporation and Federal Labor Union No. 19478, Case No. 379—Decision, May 4, 1935, in *Decisions of the National Labor Relations Board*, vol. 1–2 (Washington, DC: Government Printing Office, 1935), 456–57.

19. "Aberdeen, Washington, Plywood Local No. 2521," *Timber Worker*, Labor Day ed., September 7, 1936.

20. Minutes of LSMWU Local 18345 Meeting, January 29, 1935, RGHL-IWA, AHM; *Voice of Action*, March 22, 1935.

21. Minutes of LSMWU Local 18345 Meeting, March 12, 1935, RGHL-IWA, AHM; Jonathan Dembo, *Unions and Politics in Washington State, 1885–1935* (New York: Garland Press, 1982), 625.

22. Minutes of LSMWU Local 18345 Meeting, March 12, 1935, RGHL-IWA, AHM. The Northwest Council is referred to by several different names in the sources, including as the "Northwest District Council of Loggers and Sawmill Workers" in Nouska, "History of Local 2369," while the union minutes call it the "Northwest Council of Loggers, Sawmill, and Woodworkers Unions," which I use in the main text.

23. Minutes of LSMWU Local 18345 Meeting, March 26, 1935, RGHL-IWA, AHM; Minutes of LSWU Local 2507, April 2, 9, 1935, RGHL-IWA, AHM.

24. Minutes of LSMWU Local 2507 Meeting, April 9, 1935, RGHL-IWA, AHM. An outline of this history appears in Nouska, "History of Local 2369."

25. *Aberdeen Daily World*, April 19, 21, 1935.

26. Lembcke and Tattam, *One Union in Wood*, 32; *Voice of Action*, May 3, 1935.

27. Minutes of LSMWU Local 2507 Meeting, April 23, 1935, RGHL-IWA, AHM.

28. Historians have produced several useful studies on the 1934 strikes. See, especially, Bryan D. Palmer, *Revolutionary Teamsters: The Minneapolis Truckers' Strike of 1934* (Chicago: Haymarket, 2014); Bruce Nelson, *Workers on the Waterfront*; Elizabeth Faue, *Community of Suffering and Struggle: Women, Men, and the Labor Movement in Minneapolis, 1915–1945* (Chapel Hill: University of North Carolina Press, 1991).

29. Fraser M. Ottanelli, *The Communist Party of the United States* (New Brunswick, NJ: Rutgers University Press, 1991), 51–53; Lembcke and Tattam, *One Union in Wood*, 36; *Voice of Action*, February 23, 1935.

30. N. S. to All Sections, April 19, 1935, 1, RTsKhIDNI, f. 515, op. 1, d. 3872.

31. *Aberdeen Daily World*, May 9, 1935.

32. Vernon Jensen, *Lumber and Labor* (New York: Arno Press, 1971; first published 1945 by J. J. Little and Ives Co., New York), 239–40, 263–68.

33. *Seattle Post-Intelligencer*, April 29, 1935.

34. N. S. to All Sections, April 19, 1935, 1, RTsKhIDNI, f. 515, op. 1, d. 3872.

35. Irving Bernstein, *The Turbulent Years: A History of the American Worker, 1933–1941* (Boston: Houghton-Mifflin, 1979), 323.

36. Special Meeting of Sawmill and Timber Workers' Union 2507 and the Plywood

Workers' Union, n.d. (appears in the minutes book directly after the meeting held on July 2, 1935), RGHL-IWA, AHM.

37. *Aberdeen Daily World*, May 16, 1935; Bernstein, *Turbulent Years*, 323–48; Melvyn Dubofsky, *The State and Labor in Modern America* (Chapel Hill: University of North Carolina Press, 1994), 128; Dembo, *Unions and Politics in Washington State*, 587.

38. *Timber Worker*, April 16, 1937.

39. Gerald Mayer, *Union Membership Trends in the United States* (Washington, DC: Congressional Research Service, 2004), 23.

40. *Timber Worker*, February 5, 12, September 17, 1938; *Hearings before the Committee on Education and Labor, United States Senate, 76th Congress, First Session*, part 7 (Washington, DC: Government Printing Office, 1939): 1251–62; *Hearings before the Special Committee to Investigate National Labor Relations Board, House of Representatives, 76th Congress, Third Session*, vol. 7 (Washington, DC: Government Printing Office, 1940), 1830–50.

41. Melvyn Dubofsky, *We Shall Be All: A History of the Industrial Workers of the World*, abridged ed. (Urbana: University of Illinois Press, 2000), 268; Nigel Sellars, *Oil, Wheat, and Wobblies: The Industrial Workers of the World in Oklahoma, 1905–1930* (Norman: University of Oklahoma Press, 1998), 191; Ottanelli, *Communist Party of the United States*, 75.

42. *Timber Worker*, September 17, 1938.

43. *Voice of Action*, April 26, 1935; Lembcke and Tattam, *One Union in Wood*, 32; *Tacoma News Tribune*, April 19, 1935; *Aberdeen Daily World*, April 18, 19, 1935.

44. *Aberdeen Daily World*, April 20, 27, 1935.

45. *Seattle Post-Intelligencer*, April 28, 29, 1935.

46. *Tacoma News Tribune*, April 20, 1935.

47. *Aberdeen Daily World*, April 27, 30, 1935; *Seattle Post-Intelligencer*, May 2, 1935.

48. *Aberdeen Daily World*, May 6, 7, 9, 1935; Lembcke and Tattam, *One Union in Wood*, 32.

49. Lembcke and Tattam, *One Union in Wood*, 35.

50. *Aberdeen Daily World*, May 27, 1935.

51. Lembcke and Tattam, *One Union in Wood*, 35; Paul William Parks, "Labor Relations in the Grays Harbor Lumber Industry" (master's thesis, University of Washington, 1948), 30.

52. N. S. to All Sections, April 19, 1935, 2, RTsKhIDNI, f. 515, op. 1, 3872.

53. No name to Comrade Stachel, May 13, 1935, 2, RTsKhIDNI, f. 515, op. 1, 3873.

54. *Voice of Action*, May 17, 1935; N. S. to Comrade Stachel, May 21, 1935, RTsKhIDNI, f. 515, op. 1, d. 3973.

55. N. S. to Comrade Stachel, May 21, 1935, RTsKhIDNI, f. 515, op. 1, d. 3973.

56. *Aberdeen Daily World*, June 4, 1935.

57. *Voice of Action*, June 7, 1935.

58. *Voice of Action*, June 7, 1935; Nouska, "History of Local No. 2639."

59. *Aberdeen Daily World*, June 3, 4, 1935.

60. *Aberdeen Daily World*, June 5, 6, 14, 1935; *Voice of Action*, June 7, 14, 1935.

61. Lembcke and Tattam, *One Union in Wood*, 35–38.

62. Parks, "Labor Relations," 33.

63. Affidavit of O. M. Micky Orton, *State v. Richard Law*, 1940, John Caughlan Papers, box 7, folders 8–9, acc. no. 704, UW.

64. *Aberdeen Daily World*, June 7, 8, 1935.

65. *Tacoma News Tribune*, June 24, 1935; *Seattle Post-Intelligencer*, June 24, 26, 1935.

66. *Voice of Action*, June 14, 1935; *Seattle Post-Intelligencer*, July 12, 1935.

67. Hughes and Beckwith, *On the Harbor*, 84–85.

68. *Tacoma News Tribune*, July 20, 1935.

69. *Voice of Action*, July 19, 1935; Nouska, "History of Local No. 2639."

70. "Red Baiting," bulletin of the Publicity Committee, IWA Local No. 2, Laura Law Records, box 9, folder 9–7, SRB-WSA.

71. *Seattle Post-Intelligencer*, May 13, 1935.

72. Affidavit of O. M. Micky Orton, *State v. Richard Law*, 1940, John Caughlan Papers, box 7, folders 8–9, acc. no. 704, UW.

73. *Aberdeen Daily World*, May 14, 1935.

74. *Seattle Post-Intelligencer*, July 25, 1935; *Tacoma News Tribune*, July 25, 1935.

75. *Voice of Action*, July 19, 1935.

76. *Aberdeen Daily World*, May 14, 21, 1935.

77. *Timber Worker*, October 16, 1936; June 18, November 27, 1937.

78. "Halt to Fascist Actions," Letter from Mary Lee, Chairman of Naisjaosto, to the members of the Aberdeen City Council and City Mayor, August 23, 1934, Laura Law Records, box 12, 1, SRB-WSA.

79. *Timber Worker*, January 8, 29, September 4, December 4, 1937.

80. *Voice of Action*, July 19, 1935.

81. *Seattle Post-Intelligencer*, July 3, 1935.

82. *Industrial Worker*, July 13, 1935.

83. *Voice of Action*, July 12, 19, 1935; Todd Goings, "Battles on the Harbor," 37; Hughes and Beckwith, *On the Harbor*, 81.

84. Jensen, *Lumber and Labor*, 182–84; *Seattle Post-Intelligencer*, June 27, 1935.

85. *Tacoma Labor Advocate*, August 9, 1935.

86. Selden C. Menefee, "How the Lumber Strike Was Broken," *The Nation*, September 4, 1935, 275–76.

87. This account of the 1935 strike is drawn from Hughes and Beckwith, *On the Harbor*, 80–85; and Lembcke and Tattam, *One Union in Wood*, 39–41.

88. *Official Strike Bulletin, Sawmill and Timber Workers, Local 2639, Affiliated with A.F. of L.*, August 13, 1935, Laura Law Records, box 11, folder 11-2cc, SRB-WSA.

89. Lembcke and Tattam, *One Union in Wood*, 41. Any study of the IWA should begin with *One Union in Wood*, the clearest and most complete study of the post-1935 era in lumber worker history. According to an official STWU history written and published in the *Timber Worker* in 1936, Muir announced shortly after the strike that approximately 50,000 members had joined 180 lumber unions. See Nouska, "History of Local 2369."

90. Nouska, "History of Local 2369."

CONCLUSION

1. Jerry Lembcke and William M. Tattam, *One Union in Wood: A Political History of the International Woodworkers of America* (New York: International Publishers, 1984), 43; Irving Bernstein, *The Turbulent Years: A History of the American Worker, 1933–1941* (Boston: Houghton-Mifflin, 1979), 626–27.

2. Lembcke and Tattam, *One Union in Wood*, 45; Bernstein, *Turbulent Years*, 626–27, 682–86.

3. *Timber Worker*, July 2, 1937.

4. *Timber Worker*, July 2, 16, 23, 1937; Lembcke and Tattam, *One Union in Wood*, 54.

5. Minutes of Sawmill and Timber Workers Union Local 3-2, August 7, 1937, International Association of Machinists and Aerospace Workers, W2 Collection, International Association of Machinists and Aerospace Workers, W2 Hall, Aberdeen, Wash. (hereafter Minutes, STWU Local 3-2).

6. Walter Galenson, *The United Brotherhood of Carpenters: The First Hundred Years* (Cambridge: Harvard University Press, 1983), 19, 263.

7. *Timber Worker*, January 8, February 12, 19, 1937.

8. Vernon Jensen, *Lumber and Labor* (New York: Arno Press, 1971; first published 1945 by J. J. Little and Ives Co., New York), 306.

9. Alan Dawley, *Class and Community: The Industrial Revolution in Lynn* (Cambridge: Harvard University Press), 7.

10. *Timber Worker*, November 30, December 7, 1940; Lembcke and Tattam, *One Union in Wood*, 75–102.

11. Robert Michael Smith, *From Blackjacks to Briefcases: A History of Commercialized Strikebreaking and Unionbusting in the United States* (Athens: Ohio University Press, 2003).

12. "Harbor Termed 'Little Soviet,'" clipping from unknown periodical, March 20, 1939, Laura Law Records, box 26, folder 8, SRB-WSA.

13. Robert Saltvig, "The Tragic Legend of Laura Law," *Pacific Northwest Quarterly*

78, no. 3 (April 1987): 91–99, 100–123; *Industrialisti*, December 14, 1921. Laura Luoma's name appeared alongside her parents in the 1921 *Industrialisti* "Greetings" list.

14. Herbert Lundy, "The Laura Law Murder," *The Nation*, March 23, 1940, 383–85; Todd Goings, "Battles on the Harbor: Inter-Labor Conflict, Anti-Communism, Women's Auxiliaries, and the Murder of Laura Law" (master's thesis, Central Washington University, 2014), 121; Lembcke and Tattam, *One Union in Wood*, 73.

15. John C. Hughes and Ryan Teague Beckwith, eds., *On the Harbor: From Black Friday to Nirvana* (Aberdeen, WA: Daily World, 2000), 114.

16. "Woodworkers of Grays Harbor," flyer issued by Oregon-Washington Council of Lumber and Sawmill Workers, American Federation of Labor, Laura Law Records, box 9, folder 7, SRB-WSA.

17. Cited in Hughes and Beckwith, *On the Harbor*, 114.

18. "Defeat 'Gas Bomb' Horrocks," Laura Law Records, box 10, folder 10-4B, SRB-WSA.

19. On the International Woodworkers of America, see Lembcke and Tattam, *One Union in Wood*. The best history of the Association of Western Pulp and Paper Workers can be found in John McClelland III, "Union Rebels," *Cowlitz Historical Quarterly* 44, no. 3 (September 2002): 3–39.

20. Cited in Hughes and Beckwith, *On the Harbor*, 85. Bridges made this remark to journalist and historian John Hughes at an International Longshoremen's and Warehouse Union (ILWU) event in Grays Harbor. John Hughes, interviewed by author, March 15, 2018; notes in author's possession.

SELECTED READING

This list includes the most important works consulted in *Red Harbor* along with several significant studies in labor, left, and Pacific Northwest history that will help readers to understand and contextualize the topics covered this book. The notes section includes comprehensive documentation of the sources used in *Red Harbor*.

Alter, Thomas, II. *Toward a Cooperative Commonwealth: The Transplanted Roots of Farmer-Labor Radicalism in Texas*. Urbana: University of Illinois Press, 2022.

Asaka, Megan. *Seattle from the Margins: Exclusion, Erasure, and the Making of a Pacific Coast City*. Seattle: University of Washington Press, 2022.

Barrett, James R. *William Z. Foster and the Tragedy of American Radicalism*. Urbana: University of Illinois Press, 1999.

———. *Work and Community in the Jungle: Chicago's Packinghouse Workers, 1894–1922*. Urbana: University of Illinois Press, 1990.

Bernstein, Irving. *The Lean Years: A History of the American Worker, 1920–1933*. Boston: Houghton-Mifflin, 1960.

———. *The Turbulent Years: A History of the American Worker, 1933–1941*. Boston: Houghton-Mifflin, 1979.

Bhatt, Amy, and Nalini Iyer. *Roots and Reflections: South Asians in the Pacific Northwest*. Seattle: University of Washington Press, 2013.

Bird, Stewart, Dan Georgakas, and Deborah Shaffer. *Solidarity Forever: An Oral History of the IWW*. Chicago: Lake View Press, 1985.

Bodnar, John. *The Transplanted: A History of Immigrants in Urban America*. Bloomington: Indiana University Press, 1985.

Brissenden, Paul. *The IWW: A Study of American Syndicalism*. 1919. Reprint, 2nd ed. New York: Russell and Russell, 1957.

Brody, David. *Steelworkers in America: The Nonunion Era*. Cambridge, MA: Harvard University Press, 1960.

Buhle, Mari Jo. *Women and American Socialism, 1870–1920*. Urbana: University of Illinois Press, 1981.

Buhle, Paul, and Nicole Schulman, eds. *Wobblies! A Graphic History of the Industrial Workers of the World*. London: Verso Press, 2005.

Butler, Anne M. *Daughters of Joy, Sisters of Misery: Prostitutes in the American West, 1865–90*. Urbana: University of Illinois Press, 1985.

Chang, Kornel. *Pacific Connections: The Making of the U.S.-Canadian Borderlands*. Berkeley: University of California Press, 2012.

Chaplin, Ralph. *Wobbly: The Rough-and-Tumble Story of an American Radical*. Chicago: University of Chicago Press, 1948.

Cherny, Robert. *Harry Bridges: Labor Radical, Labor Legend*. Urbana: University of Illinois Press, 2024.

Clark, Norman H. *Mill Town: A Social History of Everett, Washington, from Its Earliest Beginnings on the Shores of Puget Sound to the Tragic and Infamous Event Known as the Everett Massacre*. Seattle: University of Washington Press, 1970.

Cole, Peter. *Ben Fletcher: The Life and Times of a Black Wobbly*. Rev. 2nd ed. Oakland, CA: PM Press, 2021.

———. *Dockworker Power: Race and Activism in Durban and the San Francisco Bay Area*. Urbana: University of Illinois Press, 2018.

———. *Wobblies on the Waterfront: Interracial Unionism in Progressive-Era Philadelphia*. Urbana: University of Illinois Press, 2007.

Cole, Peter, David Struthers, and Kenyon Zimmer, eds. *Wobblies of the World: A Global History of the IWW*. London: Pluto Press, 2017.

Conlin, Joseph Robert. *Big Bill Haywood and the Radical Union Movement*. Syracuse, NY: Syracuse University Press, 1969.

———. *Bread and Roses Too: Studies of the Wobblies*. Westport, CT: Greenwood Publishing Corp., 1969.

Copeland, Tom. *The Centralia Tragedy of 1919: Elmer Smith and the Wobblies*. Seattle: University of Washington Press, 1993.

Cox, Thomas R. *Mills and Markets: A History of the Pacific Coast Lumber Industry to 1900*. Seattle: University of Washington Press, 1974.

Davis, Mike. *Prisoners of the American Dream: Politics and Economy of the U.S. Working Class*. London: Verso Press, 1986.

Dawley, Alan. *Class and Community: The Industrial Revolution in Lynn*. Cambridge, MA: Harvard University Press, 1976.

Dembo, Jonathan. *Unions and Politics in Washington State, 1885–1935*. New York: Garland Press, 1982.

Draper, Theodore. *American Communism and Soviet Russia*. New ed. New Brunswick, NJ: Transaction Publishers, 2003. First published 1957 by Viking Press (New York).

Dreyfus, Philip J. "Timber Workers, Unionism and Syndicalism in the Pacific Northwest, 1900–1917." PhD diss., Graduate School of the City University of New York, 1993.

Dubofsky, Melvyn. *The State and Labor in Modern America*. Chapel Hill: University of North Carolina Press, 1994.

———. *We Shall Be All: A History of the Industrial Workers of the World*. Chicago: Quadrangle Books, 1969, 1973. Abridged ed. Urbana: University of Illinois Press, 2000.

Ealham, Chris. *Anarchism and the City: Revolution and Counter-Revolution in Barcelona, 1898–1937*. Oakland, CA: AK Press, 2010.

Faue, Elizabeth. *Community of Suffering and Struggle: Women, Men, and the Labor Movement in Minneapolis, 1915–1945*. Chapel Hill: University of North Carolina Press, 1991.

Feurer, Rosemary. *Radical Unionism in the Midwest, 1900–1950*. Urbana: University of Illinois Press, 2006.

Feurer, Rosemary, and Chad Pearson, eds. *Against Labor: How U.S. Employers Organized to Defeat Union Activism*. Urbana: University of Illinois Press, 2017.

Ficken, Robert E. *Lumber and Politics: The Career of Mark E. Reed*. Seattle: University of Washington Press, 1980.

———. "The Wobbly Horrors: Pacific Northwest Lumbermen and the Industrial Workers of the World, 1917–1918." *Labor History* 24, no. 3 (Summer 1983): 325–41.

Ficken, Robert E., and Charles Pierce Lewarne. "The Aberdeen, Washington, Free Speech Fight of 1911–1912." *Pacific Northwest Quarterly* 66 (January 1975): 1–15.

Flynn, Elizabeth Gurley. *The Rebel Girl: An Autobiography, My First Life (1906–1926)*. New ed. New York: International Publishers, 3rd printing, 1973.

Folsom, Franklin. *Inpatient Armies of the Poor: The Story of Collective Action of the Unemployed*. Boulder: University Press of Colorado, 1991.

Foner, Philip S., ed. *Fellow Workers and Friends: IWW Free Speech Fight as Told by Participants*. Westport, CT: Greenwood Press, 1981.

———. *The History of the Labor Movement in the United States*. Vol. 2, *From the AF of L to the Emergence of American Imperialism*. New York: International Publishers, 1964.

———. *The History of the Labor Movement in the United States*. Vol. 3, *The Policies and Practices of the American Federation of Labor, 1900–1909*. New York: International Publishers, 4th printing, 1981.

———. *The History of the Labor Movement in the United States*. Vol. 4, *The Industrial Workers of the World, 1905–1917*. 1965. Reprint. New York: International Publishers, 1978.

———. *Women and the American Labor Movement: From the First Trade Unions to the Present*. New York: Free Press, 1979.

Frank, Dana. *Purchasing Power: Consumer Organizing, Gender, and the Seattle Labor Movement, 1919–1945*. Cambridge, UK: Cambridge University Press, 1994.

Friday, Chris. *Organizing Asian-American Labor: The Pacific Coast Canned-Salmon Industry, 1870–1942*. Philadelphia: Temple University Press, 1994.

Fujita Rony, Dorothy B. *American Workers, Colonial Power: Philippine Seattle and the Transpacific West*. Berkeley: University of California Press, 2003.

Galenson, Walter. *The United Brotherhood of Carpenters: The First Hundred Years*. Cambridge, MA: Harvard University Press, 1983.

Gambs, John S. *The Decline of the IWW*. New York: Columbia University Press, 1932.

Goldfield, Michael. *The Southern Key: Class, Race, and Radicalism in the 1930s and 1940s*. Oxford: Oxford University Press, 2020.

Gordon, Linda. *The Second Coming of the KKK: The Ku Klux Klan of the 1920s and the American Political Tradition*. New York: Liveright Publishing, 2017.

Green, Archie. *Wobblies, Pile Butts, and Other Heroes: Laborlore Explorations*. Urbana: University of Illinois Press, 1993.

Green, James R. *Grass-Roots Socialism: Radical Movements in the Southwest, 1895–1943*. Baton Rouge: Louisiana State University Press, 1978.

Greene, Julie. *Pure and Simple Politics: The American Federation of Labor and Political Activism, 1881–1917*. Cambridge, UK: Cambridge University Press, 1999.

Greenwald, Maurine Weiner. "Working-Class Feminism and the Family Wage Ideal: The Seattle Debate on Married Women's Right to Work, 1914–1920." In *Women in Pacific Northwest History*, rev. ed., edited by Karen Blair, 94–134. Seattle: University of Washington Press, 2001.

Gunns, Albert F. *Civil Liberties in Crisis: The Pacific Northwest, 1917–1940*. New York: Garland Publishing, 1983.

Gutman, Herbert G. *Work, Culture, and Society in Industrializing America*. New York: Alfred A. Knopf, 1976.

Hall, Greg. *Harvest Wobblies: The Industrial Workers of the World and Agricultural Laborers in the American West, 1905–1930*. Corvallis: Oregon State University Press, 2001.

———. *Writing Labor's Emancipation: The Anarchist Life and Times of Jay Fox*. Seattle: University of Washington Press, 2022.

Harmon, Alexandra. *Reclaiming the Reservation: Histories of Indian Sovereignty Suppressed and Renewed*. Seattle: University of Washington Press, 2019.

Harris, Alice Kessler. *Gendering Labor History*. Urbana: University of Illinois Press, 2007.

Harris, John Howell. *Bloodless Victories: The Rise and Fall of the Open Shop in the Philadelphia Metal Trades, 1890–1940*. Cambridge, UK: Cambridge University Press, 2000.

Higbie, Frank Tobias. *Indispensable Outcasts: Hobo Workers and Community in the American Midwest, 1880–1930*. Urbana: University of Illinois Press, 2003.

Hobsbawm, Eric. *The Age of Capital, 1848–1875*. London: Weidenfield and Nicolson, 1975.

———. *Workers: Worlds of Labor*. London: Pantheon Books, 1984.

Hochschild, Adam. *American Midnight: The Great War, a Violent Peace, and Democracy's Forgotten Crisis*. New York: Harper Collins, 2023.

Holdren, Nate. *Injury Impoverished: Workplace Accidents, Capitalism, and Law in the Progressive Era*. Cambridge, UK: Cambridge University Press, 2020.

Hughes, John C., and Ryan Teague Beckwith, eds. *On the Harbor: From Black Friday to Nirvana*. Aberdeen, WA: Daily World, 2001.

Hulden, Vilja. *The Bosses Union: How Employers Organized to Fight Labor Before the New Deal*. Urbana: University of Illinois Press, 2023.

Hummasti, Paul George. "Fighting for Temperance Ideas." In *Finns in the United States: A History of Settlement, Dissent, and Integration*, edited by Auvo Kostiainen, 91–106. East Lansing: Michigan State University Press, 2014.

———. *Finnish Radicals in Astoria, Oregon, 1904–1940: A Study in Immigrant Socialism*. New York: Arno Press, 1979.

Jacobson, Matthew Frye. *Whiteness of a Different Color: European Immigrants and the Alchemy of Race*. Cambridge, MA: Harvard University Press, 1998.

Jameson, Elizabeth. *All That Glitters: Class, Conflict, and Community in Cripple Creek*. Urbana: University of Illinois Press, 1998.

Jensen, Vernon. *Lumber and Labor*. New York: Arno Press, 1971. First published 1945 by J. J. Little and Ives Co. (New York).

Jesch, Aaron. "The Industrial Workers of the World and the Performance of Protest." PhD diss., Washington State University, Pullman, 2023.

Johnson, Jeffrey. *They Are All Red Out Here*. Norman: University of Oklahoma Press, 2014.

Johnson, Victoria. *How Many Machine Guns Does It Take to Cook One Meal? The Seattle and San Francisco General Strikes*. Seattle: University of Washington Press, 2015.

Karni, Michael G., and Douglas J. Ollila Jr. *For the Common Good: Finnish Immigrants and the Radical Response to Industrial America*. Superior, WI: Työmies Society, 1977.

Kaunonen, Gary. *Challenge Accepted: A Finnish Immigrant Response to Industrial America in Michigan's Copper Country*. East Lansing: Michigan State University Press, 2010.

———. *Flames of Discontent: The 1916 Minnesota Iron Ore Strike*. Minneapolis: University of Minnesota Press, 2001.

Kealey, Gregory S. *Toronto Workers Respond to Industrial Capitalism, 1867–1892*. Toronto: University of Toronto Press, 1980.

Kelley, Robin D. G. *Hammer and Hoe: Alabama Communists During the Great Depression*. Chapel Hill: University of North Carolina Press, 1990.

Kelly, Brian. *Race, Class, and Power in the Alabama Coalfields, 1908–1921*. Urbana: University of Illinois Press, 2001.

Kelly, Kim. *Fight Like Hell: The Untold History of American Labor*. New York: Simon and Schuster, 2022.

Kimeldorf, Howard. *Battling for American Labor: Wobblies, Craft Workers, and the Making of the Union Movement*. Berkeley: University of California Press, 1999.

Kivisto, Peter. "The Decline of the Finnish American Left, 1925–1945." *International Migration Review* 17, no. 1 (Spring 1983): 65–94.

Klug, Thomas. "Employers' Strategies in the Detroit Labor Market, 1900–1929." In *On the Line: Essays in the History of Auto Work*, edited by Nelson Lichtenstein and Stephen Meyer, 42–72. Urbana: University of Illinois Press, 1989.

Kornbluh, Joyce L., ed. *Rebel Voices: An IWW Anthology.* New and expanded ed. Chicago: Charles H. Kerr Publishing Co., 1998.

Kostiainen, Auvo. "A Dissenting Voice of Finnish Radicals in America: The Formative Years of *Sosialisti-Industrialisti* in the 1910s." *American Studies in Scandinavia* 23 (1991): 83- 94.

———, ed. *Finns in the United States: A History of Settlement, Dissent, and Integration.* East Lansing: Michigan State University Press, 2014.

———. *The Forging of Finnish-American Communism, 1917–1924: A Study in Ethnic Radicalism*. Turku, Finland: Turin Yliopisto, 1978.

Lause, Mark. *The Great Cowboy Strike: Bullets, Ballots, and Class Conflicts in the American West*. London: Verso Press, 2018.

Leier, Mark. *Red Flags and Red Tape: The Making of a Labor Bureaucracy*. Toronto: University of Toronto Press, 1995.

———. *Where the Fraser River Flows: The Industrial Workers of the World in British Columbia.* Vancouver, BC: New Star Books, 1990.

Lembcke, Jerry, and William M. Tattam. *One Union in Wood: A Political History of the International Woodworkers of America*. New York: International Publishers, 1984.

Loomis, Erik. *Empire of Timber: Labor Unions and the Pacific Northwest Forests*. Cambridge, UK: Cambridge University Press, 2016.

Lynd, Staughton, ed. *"We Are All Leaders": The Alternative Unionism of the Early 1930s*. Urbana: University of Illinois Press, 1996.

MacLean, Nancy. *Beyond the Mask of Chivalry: The Making of the Second Ku Klux Klan*. New York: Oxford University Press, 1994.

Markholt, Ottilie. *Maritime Solidarity: Pacific Coast Unionism, 1929–1938*. Tacoma, WA: Pacific Coast Maritime History Committee, 1998.

Mayer, Heather. *Beyond the Rebel Girl: Women and the Industrial Workers of the World in the Pacific Northwest, 1905–1924*. Corvallis: Oregon State University Press, 2018.

Mercier, Laurie. *Anaconda: Labor, Community, and Culture in Anaconda's Smelter City*. Urbana: University of Illinois Press, 2001.

Merritt, Keri Leigh. *Masterless Men: Poor Whites and Slavery in the Antebellum South.* Cambridge, UK: Cambridge University Press, 2017.

Meyer, Stephen. *Manhood on the Line: Working-Class Masculinities in the American Heartland.* Urbana: University of Illinois Press, 2016.

Milkman, Ruth. *On Gender, Labor, and Inequality.* Urbana: University of Illinois Press, 2016.

Millikan, William. *A Union Against Unions: The Minneapolis Citizens Alliance and Its Fight Against Organized Labor, 1903–1947.* St. Paul: Minnesota Historical Society Press, 2001.

Milloy, Jeremy. *Blood, Sweat, and Fear: Violence and Work in the North American Auto Industry, 1960–1980.* Vancouver: University of British Columbia Press, 2017.

Mitchell, Don. *The Right to the City: Social Justice and the Fight for Public Space.* New York: Guilford Press, 2003.

Mitrani, Sam. *The Rise of the Chicago Police Department: Class and Conflict, 1850–1894.* Urbana: University of Illinois Press, 2013.

Montgomery, David. *The Fall of the House of Labor: The Workplace, the State, and American Labor Activism, 1865–1925.* New Haven, CT: Yale University Press, 1987.

———. *Workers' Control in America: Studies in the History of Work, Technology, and Labor Struggles.* Cambridge, UK: Cambridge University Press, 1979.

Moody, Kim. *Tramps and Trade Union Travelers: Internal Migration and Organized Labor in Gilded Age America, 1870–1900.* Chicago: Haymarket Books, 2019.

Murphy, Mary. *Mining Cultures: Men, Women, and Leisure in Butte, 1914–1941.* Urbana: University of Illinois Press, 1987.

Nelson, Bruce. *Workers on the Waterfront: Seamen, Longshoremen, and Unionism in the 1930s.* Urbana: University of Illinois Press, 1990.

Nelson, Eugene. *Break Their Haughty Power: Joe Murphy in the Heyday of the Wobblies.* San Francisco: ISM Press, 1996.

Norwood, Stephen H. *Strikebreaking and Intimidation: Mercenaries and Masculinity in Twentieth-Century America.* Chapel Hill: University of North Carolina Press, 2001.

Oestreicher, Richard Jules. *Solidarity and Fragmentation: Working People and Class Consciousness in Detroit, 1875–1900.* Urbana: University of Illinois Press, 1989.

Ogden, Johanna. *Punjabi Rebels of the Columbia River: The Global Fight for Indian Independence and Citizenship.* Corvallis: Oregon State University Press, 2023.

Okrent, Daniel. *The Guarded Gate: Bigotry, Eugenics, and the Law That Kept Two Generations of Jews, Italians, and Other European Immigrants Out of America.* New York: Scribner, 2019.

Orleck, Annelise. *Common Sense and a Little Fire: Women and Working-Class Politics in the United States, 1900–1965.* Chapel Hill: University of North Carolina Press, 2000.

Ottanelli, Fraser M. *The Communist Party of the United States*. New Brunswick, NJ: Rutgers University Press, 1991.

Painter, Nell Irvin. *The History of White People*. New York: W. W. Norton, 2010.

Palmer, Bryan D. *A Culture in Conflict: Skilled Workers and Industrial Capitalism in Hamilton, Ontario, 1860–1914*. Montreal: McGill-Queen's University Press, 1979.

———. *James P. Cannon and the Origins of the American Revolutionary Left, 1890–1928*. Urbana: University of Illinois Press, 2007.

———. *Revolutionary Teamsters: The Minneapolis Truckers' Strikes of 1934*. Chicago: Haymarket Books, 2014.

Parnaby, Andrew. *Citizen Docker: Making a New Deal on the Vancouver Waterfront, 1919–1939*. Toronto: University of Toronto Press, 2008.

Pearson, Chad E. *Capital's Terrorists: Klansmen, Lawmen, and Employers in the Long Nineteenth Century*. Chapel Hill: University of North Carolina Press, 2022.

———. *Reform or Repression: Organizing America's Anti-Union Movement*. Philadelphia: University of Pennsylvania Press, 2015.

Peck, Gunther. *Reinventing Free Labor: Padrones and Immigrant Workers in the North American West, 1880–1930*. Cambridge, UK: Cambridge University Press, 2000.

Pingree, Elizabeth. "The Footloose Labor System: Work and Migration in the Pacific Northwest, 1850–1940." PhD diss., Boston College, Chestnut Hill, Mass., 2023.

Polishuk, Sandy, ed. *Sticking to the Union: An Oral History of the Life and Times of Julia Ruutila*. New York: Palgrave MacMillan, 2003.

Preston, William, Jr. *Aliens and Dissenters: Federal Suppression of Radicals, 1903–1933*. Cambridge, MA: Harvard University Press, 1963.

———. "Shall This Be All? U.S. Historians Versus William D. Haywood, et al." *Labor History* 12, no. 3 (Summer 1971): 435–53.

Prouty, Andrew M. *"More Deadly Than War!" Pacific Coast Logging, 1827–1981*. Seattle: University of Washington Press, 1985.

Putman, John C. *Class and Gender Politics in Progressive-era Seattle*. Reno: University of Nevada Press, 2008.

Rachleff, Peter J. *Black Labor in Richmond, 1865–1900*. Urbana: University of Illinois Press, 1989.

Rajala, Richard A. "Bill and the Boss: Labor Protest, Technological Change and the Transformation of the West Coast Logging Camp, 1890–1930." *Journal of Forest History* 33 (October 1989): 168–79.

———. *Clearcutting the Rainforest: Production, Science, and Regulation*. Vancouver: University of British Columbia Press, 1998.

———. "A Dandy Bunch of Wobblies: Pacific Northwest Loggers and the Industrial Workers of the World, 1900–1930." *Labor History* 37, no. 2 (Spring 1996): 205–34.

Ramnath, Maia. *Haj to Utopia: How the Ghadar Movement Charted Global Radicalism and Attempted to Overthrow the British Empire*. Berkeley: University of California Press, 2011.

Renshaw, Patrick. *The Wobblies: The Story of Syndicalism in the United States*. New York: Anchor Books, 1967.

Richards, Lawrence. *Union-Free America: Workers and Antiunion Culture*. Urbana: University of Illinois Press, 2010.

Robbins, William. *Hard Times in Paradise: Coos Bay, Oregon, 1850–1986*. Seattle: University of Washington Press, 1988.

Roediger, David R. *Working Toward Whiteness: How America's Immigrants Became White, the Strange Journey from Ellis Island to the Suburbs*. New York: Basic Books, 2005.

Roediger, David. R., and Elizabeth D. Esch. *The Production of Difference: Race and the Management of Labor in U.S. History*. Oxford, UK: Oxford University Press, 2012.

Rosemont, Franklin, ed. *Joe Hill: The IWW and the Making of a Revolutionary Workingclass Counterculture*. Chicago: Charles H. Kerr Publishing Co., 2003.

———. *Juice Is Stranger Than Friction: Selected Writings of T-Bone Slim*. Chicago: Charles H. Kerr Publishing Co., 1992.

Rosenow, Michael K. *Death and Dying in the Working Class, 1865–1920*. Urbana: University of Illinois Press, 2015.

Ross, Carl, and K. Marianne Wargelin Brown, eds. *Women Who Dared: The History of Finnish-American Women*. St. Paul: Immigration History Research Center, University of Minnesota, 1986.

Ruiz, Vicki L. *Cannery Women, Cannery Lives: Mexican Women, Unionization, and the California Food Processing Industry, 1930–1950*. Albuquerque: University of New Mexico Press, 1987.

Salerno, Salvatore, ed. *Direct Action and Sabotage: Three Classic IWW Pamphlets from the IWW*. Chicago: Charles H. Kerr Publishing Co., 1997.

———. *Red November, Black November: Culture and Community in the Industrial Workers of the World*. Albany: State University of New York Press, 1989.

Saramo, Samira. "Capitalism as Death: Loss of Life and the Finnish." *Journal of Social History* 55, no. 3 (2022): 668–94.

Saxton, Alexander. *The Indispensable Enemy: Labor and the Anti-Chinese Movement in California*. Berkeley: University of California Press, 1971.

———. *The Rise and Fall of the White Republic*. London: Verso Press, 1990.

Schwantes, Carlos A. *Radical Heritage: Labor, Socialism, and Reform in Washington and British Columbia, 1885–1917*. 1979. Reprint. Moscow: University of Idaho Press, 1994.

Sellars, Nigel. *Oil, Wheat, and Wobblies: The Industrial Workers of the World in Oklahoma, 1905–1930*. Norman: University of Oklahoma Press, 1998.

Shenk, Gerald R. *"Work or Fight!" Race, Gender, and the Draft in World War One*. New York: Palgrave Macmillan, 2005.

Shor, Francis. "'Virile Syndicalism' in Comparative Perspective: A Gender Analysis of the IWW in the United States and Australia." *International Labor and Working Class History* 56 (1999): 65–77.

Smith, Robert M. *From Blackjacks to Briefcases: A History of Commercialized Strikebreaking and Unionbusting in the United States*. Athens: Ohio University Press, 2003.

Smith, Sharon. *Subterranean Fire: A History of Working-Class Radicalism in the United States*. Chicago: Haymarket Books, 2006.

Storch, Randi. *Red Chicago: American Communism and Its Grassroots, 1928–1935*. Urbana: University of Illinois Press, 2007.

Struthers, David. *The World in a City: Multiethnic Radicalism in Early Twentieth-Century Los Angeles*. Urbana: University of Illinois Press, 2019.

Thompson, E. P. *The Making of the English Working Class*. New York: Vintage Books, 1966.

Thompson, Fred. *The IWW—Its First Fifty Years*. Chicago: Industrial Workers of the World, 1955.

———. "They Didn't Suppress the Wobblies." *Radical America* 1, no. 2 (September-October 1967): 1–5.

Thompson, Fred, and Jon Bekken. *The IWW: Its First 100 Years*. Cincinnati, OH: Industrial Workers of the World, 2006.

Thrush, Coll. *Native Seattle: Histories from the Crossing-Over Place*. Seattle: University of Washington Press, 2007.

Todes, Charlotte. *Lumber and Labor*. New York: International Publishers, 1931.

Tyler, Robert L. *Rebels of the Woods: The IWW in the Pacific Northwest*. Eugene: University of Oregon Books, 1967.

van der Walt, Lucien, and Michael Schmidt. *Black Flame: The Revolutionary Class Politics of Anarchism and Syndicalism*. Oakland, CA: AK Press, 2009.

Watkins, T. H. *The Hungry Years: A Narrative History of the Great Depression*. New York: MacMillan, 2000.

White, Ahmed. *Under the Iron Heel: The Wobblies and the Capitalist War on Radical Workers*. Berkeley: University of California Press, 2022.

Wilkerson, Jessica. *To Live Here, You Have to Fight*. Urbana: University of Illinois Press, 2019.

Winslow, Cal. *Radical Seattle: The General Strike of 1919*. New York: Monthly Review Press, 2020.

Wray, Jacilee, ed. *Native Peoples of the Olympic Peninsula*. Norman: University of Oklahoma Press, 2002.

Zimmer, Kenyon. *Immigrants against the State: Yiddish and Italian Anarchism in America*. Urbana: University of Illinois Press, 2015.

INDEX

RECENT BOOKS FROM THE

EMIL AND KATHLEEN SICK SERIES IN WESTERN HISTORY AND BIOGRAPHY

Red Harbor: Radical Workers and Community Struggle in the Pacific Northwest, by Aaron Goings

Wrecked: Unsettling Histories from the Graveyard of the Pacific, by Coll Thrush

Oregon's Others: Gender, Civil Liberties, and the Surveillance State in the Early Twentieth Century, by Kimberly Jensen

Seattle from the Margins: Exclusion, Erasure, and the Making of a Pacific Coast City, by Megan Asaka

The Forging of a Black Community: Seattle's Central District from 1870 through the Civil Rights Era, second edition, by Quintard Taylor

Pioneering Death: The Violence of Boyhood in Turn-of-the-Century Oregon, by Peter Boag

Reclaiming the Reservation: Histories of Indian Sovereignty Suppressed and Renewed, by Alexandra Harmon

Gold Rush Manliness: Race and Gender on the Pacific Slope, by Christopher Herbert

In Defense of Wyam: Native-White Alliances and the Struggle for Celilo Village, by Katrine Barber

For a complete list of books in the series, visit uwapress.uw.edu